The Cambridge Cultural History of Britain

edited by
BORIS FORD

VOLUME 7

VICTORIAN BRITAIN

CAMBRIDGE
UNIVERSITY PRESS

Published by the Press Syndicate of the University of Cambridge
The Pitt Building, Trumpington Street, Cambridge CB2 1RP
40 West 20th Street, New York, NY 10011–4211, USA
10 Stamford Road, Oakleigh, Victoria 3166, Australia

First published 1989 as *The Cambridge Guide to the Arts in Britain:
The Later Victorian Age*
First paperback edition 1992

Printed and bound in Great Britain by
BPCC Hazells Ltd
Member of BPCC Ltd

A catalogue record for this book is available from the British Library

Library of Congress cataloguing in publication data

Cambridge guide to the arts in Britain.
The Cambridge cultural history/edited by Boris Ford.
     p.   cm.
Previously published as: The Cambridge guide to the arts in Britain. 1988–1991.
Includes bibliographical references and indexes.
Contents: v.1. Early Britain – v.2. Medieval Britain – v.3. Sixteenth-century
Britain – v.4. Seventeenth-century Britain – v.5. Eighteenth-century Britain –
v. 6. The Romantic Age in Britain – v. 7. Victorian Britain – v.8. Early
twentieth-century Britain – v.9. Modern Britain.
ISBN 0-521-42881-5 (pbk.: v.1). – ISBN 0-521-42882-3 (pbk.: v.2). – ISBN
0-521-42883-1 (pbk.: v.3). – ISBN 0-521-42884-X (pbk.: v.4). – ISBN 0-521-42885-8
(pbk.: v.5). – ISBN 0-521-42886-6 (pbk.: v.6). – ISBN 0-521-42887-4 (pbk.: v.7). –
ISBN 0-521-42888-2 (pbk.: v.8). – ISBN 0-521-42889-0 (pbk.: v.9)
1. Arts, British.   I. Ford, Boris.   II. Title.
[NX543.C36   1992]
700'.941–dc20   91–43024
                                                                                         CIP

ISBN 0 521 30980 8 hardback
ISBN 0 521 42887 4 paperback

THE CAMBRIDGE CULTURAL HISTORY OF BRITAIN

VOLUME 7   VICTORIAN BRITAIN

The Cambridge Cultural History

Contents

Notes on Contributors

Roly Bain, an Anglican clergyman since 1978 and a clown since 1983, is now concentrating on clown ministry full-time, specialising in performance and workshops. He remains at the forefront of Holy Fools, a nationwide network committed to the exploration of clowning and the arts in ministry and worship.

Asa Briggs, former Vice-Chancellor of Sussex University, is Provost of Worcester College, Oxford, and Chancellor of the Open University. He is President of the Victorian Society and the Social History Society. He is the author of many books on nineteenth- and twentieth-century history, including *Victorian People* and *Victorian Cities*.

Jacques Carré is Professor of English at the Universities of Besançon and Clermont–Ferrand in France. He has published extensively on British art, architecture and landscape-gardening, and is author of the monograph *Lord Burlington and his Circle*.

Peter Fuller, writer and art critic, is the editor and publisher of the quarterly, *Modern Painters*. He has written numerous books on art, among them *Art and Psychoanalysis, Images of God, The Australian Scapegoat* and *Theoria*.

Andor Gomme holds a personal chair in English Literature and Architectural History at Keele University. In addition to books on literature, he is the author (with David Walker) of *The Architecture of Glasgow*, and (with Michael Jenner and Bryan Little), of *Bristol: an Architectural History*.

John Holloway is Fellow of Queens' College and (until he retired) was Professor of Modern English Literature at Cambridge University. In addition to an autobiography, *A London Childhood*, and volumes of poetry, his critical writings include *The Victorian Sage, The Charted Mirror, Blake: The Lyric Poetry* and *Narrative and Structure*.

Michael Kennedy is staff music critic of *The Daily Telegraph* and was its Northern editor, 1960–86. He has written histories of the Hallé Orchestra and the Royal Manchester College of Music; biographies of Barbirolli and

Boult; and studies of Elgar, Vaughan Williams, Britten, Walton, Mahler and Strauss. He is editor of *The Oxford Dictionary of Music*.

Gillian Naylor is Senior Tutor in Cultural History at the Royal College of Art. She has written two books on the Bauhaus, and a book on the Arts and Crafts movement.

William Price, a Welsh–speaking Welshman, is Senior Lecturer in History at Saint David's University College, Lampeter in the University of Wales and a Canon of St David's Cathedral in Pembrokeshire. He has published widely on religous and educational history in the eighteenth to the twentieth centuries.

George Rowell was formerly Reader in Theatre History at the University of Bristol. He is Chairman of the Society for Theatre Research, and the author of several studies of the Victorian stage and of an edition of the plays of Pinero.

John Summerson, CH, CBE, was Curator of Sir John Soane's Museum, London, 1945–84. He is the author of *John Nash, Georgian London, Heavenly Mansions, Architecture in Britain 1530–1830, Victorian Architecture* and *The Classical Language of Architecture*.

John Nelson Tarn is the Roscoe Professor of Architecture at the University of Liverpool. An architect and architectural historian, his publications include *Working Class Housing in Nineteenth-Century Britain, Five per cent Philanthropy* and *The Peak Park, Its Architecture*.

Norman Vance is a senior lecturer in English at the University of Sussex. He is the author of *The Sinews of the Spirit: the Ideal of Christian Manliness in Victorian Literature and Religious Thought* and *Irish Literature: a Social History*.

General Introduction

BORIS FORD

If all people seem to agree that English literature is pre-eminent in the world, the same would not often be claimed for Britain's arts as a whole. And yet, viewed historically, Britain's achievements in the visual and decorative arts and in architecture and music, as well as in drama and literature, must be the equal, as a whole, of any other country.

The Cambridge Cultural History of Britain is not devoted, volume by volume, to the separate arts, but to all the arts in each successive age. It can then be seen how often they reinforce each other, treating similar themes and speaking in a similar tone of voice. Also it is striking how one age may find its richest cultural expression in music or drama, and the next in architecture or the applied arts; while in a later age there may be an almost total dearth of important composers compared with a proliferation of major novelists. Or an age may provide scope for a great range of anonymous craftsmen and women.

The nine volumes of this *Cambridge Cultural History* have been planned to reveal these changes, and to help readers find their bearings in relation to the arts and culture of an age: identifying major landmarks and lines of strength, analysing changes of taste and fashion and critical assumptions. And these are related to the demands of patrons and the tastes of the public.

These volumes are addressed to readers of all kinds: to general readers as well as to specialists. However, since virtually every reader is bound to be a non-specialist in relation to some of the arts under discussion, the chapters do not presuppose specialist knowledge.

But they do assume a measure of familiarity with the arts, and above all a wish to understand and appreciate the cultural achievements of successive ages in Britain.

The arts of the second half of the nineteenth century in Britain, which are the subject of this seventh volume of the series, have passed out of and then into fashion more dramatically than those of any other age. Between the two World Wars, most of Victorian art was variously felt to be pretentious, sentimental and trite. After the Second World War, its strengths and energy were perceived with a sudden envy and its bric-à-brac with indulgent fascination. In this volume, contributors have set out to discriminate between the distinctive achievements and weaknesses of later Victorian art. The achievements are there to be *read*, for this was surely a great age of the novel. They are there to be *seen* in its Gothic and classical revival buildings, and, if to a somewhat lesser degree, in what might be described as the Victorian High Renaissance in painting and sculpture. They are there in the utterances and work of the great Victorian sages and 'improvers' such as Ruskin, Arnold and Morris. Yet strangely, the Victorian achievement failed to find distinguished expression in music, except in two works by the young Elgar. Lastly, this often solemn-seeming age was a great period for circuses and music halls, and for scintillating domestic comedy.

This volume, with a considerably more detailed bibliography, was originally published in a hardcover edition as *The Later Victorian Age*, under the series title *The Cambridge Guide to the Arts in Britain*.

Part I
The Cultural and Social Setting

Albert Memorial, Kensington Gardens, London (1864–71). George Gilbert Scott.

The Later Victorian Age

ASA BRIGGS

The reign in review

Vantage points

When historians began to reassess the nineteenth century during the 1930s, they started by dividing Queen Victoria's long reign, the longest in English history, into two – early and late. This was the division best represented in the two large volumes of essays called *Early Victorian England*, edited – or rather directed – by G. M. Young and published in 1934. For Young, the break in Victorian England came in 1865. 'The sixties', he wrote, 'are a decade of swift decisive transformation. In front of them lies the world in which we were born. Behind them is a world which has passed out of memory.'

Young was explicit about his vantage point, and the authors of the second of the two volumes, dealing *inter alia* with art, architecture, music and drama, for the most part shared it, including their birthdays, with him. Yet some of them were more prepared to look back in judgement than he was in his brilliant concluding chapter, subsequently printed separately as an essay, 'Portrait of an Age'; and other writers before them had judged their mothers and fathers far more severely than he did, by sometimes attacking indiscriminately everything that was 'Victorian', early or late, behaviour as well as ideas and artefacts, and the 'ism', that went with them. By contrast, Young was already reacting against the reaction to Victoria and Victorianism, a reaction which had begun before Queen Victoria died. For many of those critics of the Victorians who wrote before Young, early-Victorian England was an age of greater self-confidence than late-Victorian England, which they now considered as an 'age of disillusionment'.

Victoria is the only monarch in British history who gave her name to an 'ism' as well as to an adjective. The 'ism', however, does not do justice to her distinctive personal qualities. She sketched and painted, performed and enjoyed music, and wrote letters and diaries in a lively prose style, particularly when she was spontaneous. Albert, who appreciated her talents, had obvious talents of his own, and he was more systematic in his thinking and more directly involved in the arts than she was: he was also keenly interested in the sciences and in their relation to technology, an interest that she did not share.

Albert's first public task in 1841 was advising Peel as head of a commission 'to inquire whether advantage might not be taken of the rebuilding of the Houses of Parliament to promote and encourage the Fine Arts in the United Kingdom'. Queen Victoria's last public task was to lay the foundation stone in 1899 for the Victoria and Albert Museum. In between, and before Albert died and the Queen went into deep mourning, there had been many interesting family and public occasions – among the former their meetings with Mendelssohn and Wagner and among the latter the great Manchester Art Exhibition of 1857, attended, among hundreds of thousands of visitors, by Dickens, Tennyson and Florence Nightingale. One long-term consequence was the Hallé Orchestra.

It is still stimulating to follow the light and shade of Victorian England with G. M. Young as a guide and to copy his attempt, based on the widest reading of what was written at the time, to trace in detail decade by decade, generation by generation, the elements of continuity and discontinuity. Yet it is difficult to remain satisfied with any simple division of Victorian England into two, as Young himself was when he too spoke of an 'illusion' within the reign:

If it had been the Queen and not Prince Albert who died in 1861, the process of English history would have been easier to apprehend. The long life of the sovereign, the long careers of her most famous subjects, created an illusion which the word Victorian enshrines.

In fact, there had been little sense of illusion at the time of the first of the great recognised contemporary Victorian vantage points of the last years of the Queen's reign, the Golden Jubilee of 1887, a time to look back as well as forwards – at economic advance, at political development (including the extension of the suffrage) and at social progress, if with an increasing number of question marks about all three. Even ten years later, at the Diamond Jubilee, when more controversial imperial themes were being emphasised, there was abundant talk in books as well as newspapers and periodicals not only of a 'wonderful reign' but of a 'wonderful century', the title of a revealing book by the biologist A. R. Wallace in 1893. The knowledge that a century was about to end as well as a reign itself stimulated appraisal.

The 1890s was a decade of contrasts and of contradictions, and it is still recalled as a decade complete in itself, interesting largely because, as Richard Le Gallienne, one of its most characteristic writers, put it, 'here was not so much the ending of the century as the beginning of a new one'. Moreover, there had been ever greater breaks in the two immediately preceding decades, the 1870s and 1880s, than there had been during the 1850s and 1860s. Indeed, Winston Churchill was to call the 1880s 'the end of an epoch':

The great victories had been won. All sorts of lumbering loyalties had been toppled over. Authority was everywhere broken. Slaves were free. Conscience was free. Trade was free. But hunger and squalor and cold were also free and the people demanded something more than liberty.

Young himself, more conservative than Churchill, fully appreciated this, just as he fully appreciated how significantly different even the mid-Victorian decades were in tone and texture from the early-Victorian decades, the late-1830s and the 1840s.

The three parts of the reign

In a longer term perspective than that of Young and in the light of further assessment of the Victorian experience, an experience of change and of reaction to it, it seems clear now that there are advantages in dividing the long reign not only into decades, artificial units, or into two parts, but into three – early, middle and late – bearing in mind, too, that if the reaction against Victorianism started before the Queen's death, 'Victorianism' itself can be traced back before her reign began. Dr Bowdler published his family editions of Shakespeare in 1818, the year before Victoria was born.

The mood of each of the three parts of the reign was different. During the period from 1837 to 1851, the year of the Great Exhibition, which was the first landmark in the reign – and explicitly recognised and advertised as such – the main economic, social and political themes of the reign concerned conflict, not without curious cross alliances – conflict between landlords and manufacturers, conflict between workers and their masters, although railways provided a second theme, new and itself controversial. The Victorians of this period were ranged against each other, particularly in the newly industrial provinces, often in bitterness. There was cultural conflict too in the arguments between Evangelicals and Tractarians and in the battle of styles between Greek and Gothic, and there was a sharp contrast in literature between 'silver fork' novels and social novels centred on 'the condition of England'. Disraeli's picture of 'two nations' was not over-fanciful. Indeed, of Liverpool at this time it was written that

two communities dwell side by side within sound of the same bells and under the same chief magistrate . . . practically as wide apart as if they lived in separate quarters of the world.

These were years when talk of 'class' was explicit, when the language of politics was tough and bitter, and when many of the modes of politics were new. Where would it all end? For many of the most sensitive Victorians of this period, it seemed likely to end in fire and blood. So, too, it seemed to Thomas Carlyle (1795–1881), an influential, prophetic voice, who urged his contemporaries to look for 'the signs of the times' before and after the rise of Chartism.

In fact, within three years of the great Chartist demonstrations of 1848 what looked like a united England was pouring into London, many people by rail, to see the wonders of the world assembled in the Crystal Palace. Of all the countries of Europe, England and Russia were the two which did not have a revolution in 1848. In retrospect, it was not the prophet Carlyle nor Marx's friend and co-operator Friedrich Engels who seem closest to a recognition of the truth about the future in the 1840s, but Sir Robert Peel, whose reforms laid the foundations of the Victorian age as we understand it.

Yet Peel, Prime Minister from 1841 to 1846, died in 1850, one year before the Crystal Palace was opened.

The second period in Victorian England from the 1850s to the 1870s has been called by W. L. Burn 'an age of equipoise'. This is a good term, since Victorians who had been arrayed against each other in early-Victorian England now lived relatively quietly side by side – landlords and manufacturers, employers and employed. In politics there was less talk of 'class' than of 'interest' and less demand for large-scale organic reform even when parliamentary reform was the issue. Instead, there was pressure for particular selected pieces of 'improvement'; and although the need for them was often forced on the attention of the public in dramatic terms by the revelation of a particular mid-Victorian scandal, many of the improvements were fashioned behind the scenes as part of the administrative process. Many of the novels of the period – those of Anthony Trollope (1815–82), for example – dealt neither with the big social issues which had fascinated the early Victorians nor with 'silver fork' topics, but with personal and parochial, if often political and ecclesiastical, themes. The favourite political adjective of the period was a hyphenated one – 'liberal-conservative'.

The leading politician of the age, Lord Palmerston (1784–1865), was very different from Peel. His nickname, 'Lord Evergreen', itself suggested that he had been born long before the Victorian age began. In the words of another leading personality of the mid-Victorian age, Walter Bagehot, Palmerston was 'a statesman for the moment. Whatever was not wanted now, whatever was not practicable now, he drove quite out of his mind.' Bagehot (1826–77) himself, brilliant essayist on many subjects, was as representative of this period as Palmerston; indeed, historians have been divided as to whether to call this period 'the age of Palmerston', 'the age of Bagehot', or 'the age of Dickens'. Not being able to agree, they have settled on 'the age of equipoise'.

For those politicians who liked life to be more turbulent and opinions more divisive, a small group, these were not the best Victorian years. Richard Cobden (1804–65), for example, hero of the early-Victorian Anti-Corn Law League, poured scorn on manufacturers who put on 'cocked hats and breeches and ruffles', bought coats of arms and wore swords. Such 'feathers and frippery' were signs that the middle classes lacked confidence. As for the working classes, Thomas Cooper, the ex-Chartist, complained that in Lancashire, where once working men in rags had demonstrated their intelligence and their political thrust,

wherever you went now, you will hear well-dressed working men talking, as they walk with their hands in their pockets, of 'Co-ops' and their shares in them, or building societies. And you will see others, like idiots, leading small greyhound dogs, covered with cloth, on a string! They are about to race, and they are betting money as they go.

It is easy to explain the balances of this period, like the conflicts of the preceding period, in economic terms. During the 1830s and 1840s, the economic fortunes of landlords, employers and workmen diverged, and it was for this reason that there were fierce fights about wages, prices, rents, tariffs and rates. During the 1850s and 1860s – it was a rare phase in history – prices, wages, rents and profits all went up together, though not evenly or uniformly: agriculture and industry both flourished. Yet if economics set the terms of the mid-Victorian balance, the psychology mattered too. The poor, separated from the rich in values as much as in livelihood, were still there, as Henry Mayhew demonstrated dramatically, while drawing on evidence from the early-Victorian years. Many were 'deferential': others seemed to constitute a 'residuum'. Prosperity did not eliminate privation, nor was there a complete absence of economic strife. There could also be 'panic'. Moreover, the highly distinctive creative expression of the period in literature, in poetry as well as in the dominant novel, drew on tension, much of it suppressed.

Two national ideals influenced patterns of mid-Victorian conduct – that of the 'gentleman' and that of the hero of 'self-help'. It was possible, though not always easy, to reconcile them, for the hero of self-help was expected either to behave like a gentleman himself or, when he could not acquire the necessary graces soon enough, to prepare his children through the right kind of private education to behave like gentlemen. Not everyone ceased to be a 'Philistine', however, to use one of Matthew Arnold's (1822–88) three social labels, to which he attached the adjectives 'stiff-necked and perverse'.

Deference helped the social balance. If the mid-Victorians had to choose between two rich men or two clever men, one of whom was a gentleman and the other not, they always preferred the gentleman, G. M. Young has written, and 'the preference operated for the benefit of many gentlemen who were both poor and stupid', Arnold's 'Barbarians'. Palmerston, like many of his contemporaries, found the balance right. Indeed, in his Don Pacifico speech in 1850, he invoked the will of Providence as the final sanction of the social system:

We have shown the example of a nation in which every class of society accepts with cheerfulness that lot which Providence has assigned to it, while at the same time each individual of each class is constantly trying to raise himself in the social scale not by injustice and wrong, not by violence and illegality, but by persevering good conduct and by the steady and energetic exertion of the moral and intellectual facilities with which the Creator has endowed him.

Mr Podsnap agreed.

Even the artist was expected to fit into this pattern; as J. D. Coleridge, later Chief Justice of England, put it in 1854,

the art that has no relevancy to actual life, the passing by God's truth and the facts of man's nature as if they had no existence, the art that does not seek to ennoble and purify and help us in our lifelong struggle with sin and evil, however beautiful, however serene and majestic, is false and poor and contemptible.

Within this context the architect Gilbert Scott was uttering a commonplace when he argued that 'a noble and elevated mind' was necessary in a good designer.

Although there were many arguments about design during the mid-Victorian years, not least in the year of the Great Exhibition – this was a period of vigorous, if in general limited, argument both about the seen and the unseen – there were also many compromises and many versions of the eclectic in buildings and in objects. Behind the varied historical trappings there was often ingenuity, but there was far too much that could be considered 'Philistine' in the visual and musical arts. In music, Mendelssohn, who died in 1847, continued to be praised for his life as well as for his art, and oratorio remained the most acceptable genre. Verdi's *La Traviata* (1857) was attacked for its plot and excused somewhat lamely on the grounds that 'opera houses can never have been devoted to the service and illustration of that which is high, and pure and righteous'.

Much that we think of as characteristically Victorian, including many categories of 'Victoriana', belongs to this relatively brief middle period of the reign, a period not only of balance but of relative security, stability and order. It was then that Samuel Smiles (1812–1904), most Victorian of the Victorians, wrote *Self-Help* (1859), *Character* (1871) and *The Lives of the Engineers* (1862). This last book brought technology into the picture as it must be brought in if any assessment is to be made retrospectively. It was steam technology that controlled the universe of machines, and it could be given the character of a gospel, not unlike free trade. Nonetheless, it was civil, and not mechanical, engineers who, as controllers of 'rude Nature', were for Smiles the real heroes of society. They were the controllers of Nature at a time when not all industry depended on steam. Characteristically, the first editorial of the magazine *Engineering* in 1866 claimed that

No man ever stands as close to Nature as the engineer; none other dare, or can, bid her do this and do that, as the engineer may do and does daily . . . our profession is working out a grand plan of civilization. Fifty years are nothing in the history of mankind – as nothing in relation to time. Yet fifty years have made England a new nation . . . There is tenfold more practical sense, more genuine Christian feeling – tenfold more natural happiness.

Note the easy coexistence of the material and the spiritual in mid-Victorian England, happiness in this world and salvation in the next. Religion must be brought into the picture at almost every point, including the political picture, along with technology. Indeed, it influenced the use of technology in the cities to provide clean water and drains and sewers in the name of 'the sanitary idea'. It also dominated Victorian social and cultural life, not only the life of the dissenters whom Arnold considered to be Philistines, but the life of the 'feudal' village: only in the cities and among sections of the working classes was it less manifest. It was under strain as far as anxious individuals were concerned – they suffered spiritual 'crises' in which they might lose their faith – but its sense of domestic and foreign mission was never stronger.

The seventh Duke of Marlborough was the only member of his family ever to conform to a straight Evangelical way of life, and what could be more Victorian than an account of a visit in November 1858 to his palace at Blenheim, relatively outside the influence of the sanitary idea, by an Oxford visitor? 'Furs and hot water bottles kept us warm and prevented any evil results.' Among the fellow guests were Lord and Lady Shaftesbury – Shaftesbury (1801–85), himself a Seventh Earl, the great Tory philanthropist – and the Dean and Mrs Liddell – of *Alice's Adventures in Wonderland* fame. 'The Duchess', the visitor wrote,

sat evidently racking her brains for some subject of conversation, but was unsuccessful in finding any sufficiently interesting to excite more than a sentence or two from either of her two supporters . . . The Duke also is a 'plain' man in all its meanings, but it is in itself an immense merit to be a religious Duke of Marlborough and this his Grace is.

The age was not an age of nonentities, however, as Shaftesbury proved; and Charles Dickens (1812–70), as well as Trollope, was at his peak during this period, George Eliot (1819–80) was writing some of her best novels and Matthew Arnold some of his best essays, John Ruskin (1819–1900) was questioning many of the fundamentals of Victorian society, and John Stuart Mill (1806–73) was producing eloquent defences of freedom and progress in face of social conformity. His essay on liberty appeared in the same year as *Self-Help*. Alfred Tennyson (1809–92), chosen as Poet Laureate in 1850, a genuinely contemporary poet of his age, asked searching questions too. Moreover, he had some doubts as to where his age was moving, more than the great mid-Victorian historian Thomas Babington Macaulay, who died in 1859: the first two volumes of his *History of England* had appeared in 1848, when there were so many doubts about the future. In 1859, too, there were doubts of a different kind when Charles Darwin's (1809–82) *The Origin of Species by Natural Selection* also appeared in what now stands out as a remarkable year of creative achievement. The young founding editors of the new periodical of the 1950s, *Victorian Studies*, which reflected a growing interest during the decade in all aspects of Victorian England, called their book on the year, published a century later, *1859: Entering an Age of Crisis*.

Life was obviously not quite as simple in 1859 as the most confident of Dickens's and Mill's fellow countrymen believed. It was the year, too, of George Meredith's (1828–1909) ruthlessly honest novel *The Ordeal of Richard Feverel* and of Edward Fitzgerald's (1809–83) deliberately melancholy *Rubaiyat of Omar Khayyam*. There was, in fact, ample room for both optimism and pessimism during the 1850s and 1860s, both for belief and for doubt. Nor was it only 'science' which was responsible for the latter. Matthew Arnold, son of a great headmaster who was one of Lytton Strachey's 'eminent Victorians', spoke of 'this strange disease of modern life with its sick hurry, its divided aims' and in his opening lecture as Professor of Poetry at Oxford in 1857 'described depression and *ennui* as characteristics stamped on . . . many of the representative works of modern times'. He was thinking, of course, of the 'romantic' inheritance in literature and the arts, but at the material level also there could be abundant mid-Victorian uncertainty – fear of 'failing', of losing status. The year 1857 itself was a year of financial 'panic'. Even in the best years, however, it was recognised too, as both Dickens and George Eliot pointed out in very different ways, that there could be ambivalence in success, more cant than principle. Arnold's friend Arthur Hugh Clough (1819–61), author of 'Say Not the Struggle Nought Availeth', published in 1855, took the ten commandments one by one in his famous *The Latest Decalogue* (1862) and suggested how they were being interpreted:

> . . . No graven images may be
> Worshipped, except the currency . . .
> Thou shalt not steal: an empty feat,
> When it's so lucrative to cheat:

> Bear not false witness; let the lie
> Have time on its own wings to fly:
> Thou shalt not covet; but tradition
> Approves all forms of competition.

Mr Pecksniff's 'brazen' doorplate bore the words 'Architect and Land Surveyor', but while he had been a Land Surveyor 'on a pretty large scale', 'he had never [Dickens told his readers] designed or built anything'.

Late-Victorian

Strains and counter-strains, ideals and shams, were the subject of Walter Houghton's indispensable *The Victorian Frame of Mind*, another product of the 1950s, which covered the period from 1830 to 1870, and which stopped short at the break of the mid-1870s. After 1870, Houghton argued, while many of the characteristics of 'Victorianism' persisted,

their dominance and their peculiar coherence was breaking down. Victorianism was dying, and a new frame of mind was emerging, a *late* Victorian frame of mind, which pointed forward to the postwar temper of the 1920s.

The break between the mid-Victorian and the late-Victorian cannot be set precisely. Some saw it in 1867, when the suffrage was extended to include large numbers of workingmen in the towns. For Robert Lowe – and for many others – this was a 'leap in the dark' which changed the terms of politics. 'What an unknown world we are to enter' was another comment, and in the second edition of his *English Constitution* (1872) Bagehot, too, spoke of a complete change of atmosphere. The mood of Trollope was dark in his novel *The Way we Live Now* (1873). Dickens had died in 1870, but there had been darkness too in his last unfinished novel *The Mystery of Edwin Drood*. 'The cramped monotony of my existence grinds me away by the grain', exclaims Jasper, 'I am so weary of it'.

G. M. Young makes as much of deaths as he does of births in his portrayal of generational change, and he goes on to ask of all his characters 'what was happening when he (or she) was 20?', and of all the years in his story 'who was in his 40s then? To the 20s I go for the shaping of ideas not fully disclosed: to the 40s for the handling of things already established.' The approach is useful, though it leaves out childhood experience which in the large Victorian family, in the boarding school and in fiction (that of George Eliot for example) was often more formative than later experience. Within the Young framework deaths to note in relation to the break between mid- and late-Victorian England are those of George Eliot in 1880, of Carlyle (and Disraeli) in 1881 and of Darwin, Trollope, E. B. Pusey (born 1800), the Tractarian leader, and D. G. Rossetti (born 1828), in 1882. Thomas Hardy (1840–1928), novelist and poet, was then forty-two, not so much handling things already established as withdrawing from them, and George Meredith was twelve years older. The only one of Queen Victoria's contemporaries who stayed with her nearly to the end was John Ruskin, born in the same year. He did not die until 1900, but he did not write a line after 1889.

The last years of Queen Victoria's reign from the 1870s to the 1900s certainly had a character of their own. The balance broke down, interests diverged, prosperity was threatened, there was 'a chill in the air', or to choose different metaphors, taking into account what came before as well as what came later, the mid-Victorian years stand out in retrospect as a plateau bounded with precipices on each side.

If we begin not with literature or with politics but with economics, we can chart the end of the great mid-Victorian boom in 1873–4, trace the growing threat of foreign competition, place the end of Britain's privileged position as 'Workshop of the World' in an age not of iron but of steel, consider the sharp, in places even catastrophic, decline of British agriculture under the pressure of imports of foreign cereals; and, not least, find signs of 'a decline of the industrial spirit'. There were new business tycoons, men like W. H. Lever, born in 1851, who 'radiated force and energy', but he was dealing in soap not in steel, and there were new British inventions, like Charles Parson's steam turbine (1880), but heavy industry, including coal mining, on which the economy was increasingly dependent, suffered from ageing buildings and obsolescent equipment.

More seriously, there were many signs of a failure to innovate, conspicuous when the position in Britain was compared, as it often was, with that in the United States, released from civil war, and in newly united Germany. Young was right about 'capital, labour and intelligence flowing away to light industry, distribution, and salesmanship', and when George Kitson Clark, who wrote much of interest on Victorian England, set out to annotate, qualify, and correct him, on this point at least it is he, not Young, who has to be annotated, qualified and corrected today. Young did not, as he suggests, greatly exaggerate the contrast between the last thirty or forty years of the nineteenth century and the period preceding it, although there are continuing differences of opinion among economic historians about the causes of what was happening and the weighting of different elements in the analysis.

Young was right also in his comments on how the social structure was changing. The late-Victorian years saw both the growth of a militant trade unionism, encompassing unskilled workers as well as the skilled 'labour aristocracy' of the mid-Victorian years – the great dock strike of 1889 and the Trades Union Congress of 1890 were landmarks – and the rise of new professional classes, more highly organised and qualified than before but segmented in outlook. Harold Perkin has emphasised how important the later change was; Young put it more generally, with a sense of drama:

We leave behind us the world of historical ironmasters and banker historians, geological diviners and scholar tobacconists, with its genial watchword: to know something of everything and everything of something; and through the gateway of the Competitive Examination we go out into the Waste Land of Experts, each knowing so much about so little that he can neither be contradicted nor is worth contradicting.

This was itself a Victorian comment.

There was, indeed, a very different social structure – and culture – in late-Victorian England from that of early-Victorian England, and while there were echoes of the social protests of the 1840s, for example in the demand for protection and for working-class power in Parliament, there were new notes too. In politics the demand for organic reform, for a basic change in the system, was sufficiently vociferous both during the 1880s and the 1890s, as were the claims of socialism as a 'movement' and a gospel, to alarm the propertied classes, whether as entrepreneurs they drew on profits, as landlords they drew on rents, or as professional people they drew on fees. Moreover, by the end of the period there was growing pressure from a minority of women to secure the vote and other rights that were associated with it. The idea of the sexual double standard was itself challenged. So also was male dominance in the world of work.

Finally, there was a growing preoccupation, moral and statistical, with the facts of poverty, which had been overlooked by many, though not all, of the mid-Victorians, along with a growing uneasiness about Victorian social institutions and conventions, even, sometimes particularly, the most confident and prestigious. Charles Booth's (1840–1916) *Life and Labour of the People of London* (1891–1903) was a massive multi-volume enterprise, and in the distant and ancient cathedral city of York Seebohm Rowntree discovered a similar pattern – along with a cycle of family poverty, as disturbing as the trade cycle which Booth considered healthy as well as inevitable. Socialists of various hues – and there were many – drew different conclusions about policy from either Booth or Rowntree. Which mid-Victorian would have written as Oscar Wilde (1854–1900) did, obviously under the influence of George Bernard Shaw (1856–1950), that 'the virtues of the poor may be readily admitted, and are much to be regretted. The best among the poor are never grateful. They are ungrateful, discontented, disobedient and rebellious. They are quite right to be so'? For such critics the 'respectable' or 'deserving' poor were not the backbone of the nation but an anachronism. Shaw himself suggested further that 'all progress depends upon the unreasonable man': 'the reasonable man adapts himself to the world: the unreasonable one persists in trying to adapt the world to himself'.

Wilde was one of a group of late-Victorian rebels who challenged much in Victorian life that had hitherto been taken for granted. There were two contrasting types of rebel, and both in their way could be 'Bohemian' – the refined aesthete, admiring Walter Pater, savouring every sensation and widening or dreaming of widening the span of experience in the demand for 'madder music and stranger wine', until it might spill over into the forbidden and the bizarre – and the nature-loving 'primitive', fleeing with equal abandon from the world of convention, but seeking enjoyment not in the intricate but in the simple. Oscar Wilde was the classic example of the first; Edward Carpenter (1844–1929) of the second. For Wilde, the flight from the respectable led him not only into aestheticism, but into a kind of socialism, a socialism which would permit, he believed – and he was not alone in this – the emergence of a freer expression of individuality. For Carpenter, also a socialist – and also a homosexual – the 'millennium' to dream of was a millennium 'not of riches, nor of mechanical facilities, nor of intellectual facilities', but of what he called 'freedom and joy'. In both cases 'Victorianism' as we normally understand it was left far behind.

One of the most compelling of the late-Victorian rebels, Samuel Butler (1835–1902), the son of a clergyman and the grandson of a bishop, did not publish his novel *The Way of All Flesh* until 1903, after Queen Victoria's reign had ended. It was after, not before, his mother, Christine, was safely buried and his father, Theobald – the names were cleverly chosen – was financially secure, that Ernest Pontifex remarks to Overton:

There are a lot of things which want attacking and yet no one attacks them. It seems to me that I can say things which not another man in England except myself will venture to say, and yet which are crying out to be said.

What Butler did say was anti-Puritan, anti-conventional, yet often undirected and sometimes shallow; Shaw was able to put it into perspective. So also later in time was the twentieth-century socialist, G.D.H. Cole, born in 1889, who concluded that Butler, whom he admired, was 'a *bourgeois* idol smasher as well as a smasher of bourgeois idols'.

The bourgeois element in the late-Victorian revolt was of basic importance, although via the Fabian Society (founded in 1884) and other bodies there were links between it and the ethos of the rising working-class movement. Shaw, very different in temperament from the other most conspicuous of the Fabians, the Webbs, Sidney (1859–1947) and Beatrice (1858–1943), was a central figure in the socialist revolt inside and outside politics: he poked fun at the Victorian belief in law, extolled the will above the law, questioned mid-Victorian tastes, including tastes in music as well as in literature, and through his eloquent defence of the Norwegian dramatist Henrik Ibsen and his writings on Wagner, brought the late-Victorian revolt into line with a general and more formidable European revolt in which the artist took a prominent place.

The attitudes and activities of this very assorted group of late-Victorian rebels – and there were many others – brought to the forefront new elements in Victorian experience and new ways of expressing it: 'earnestness' itself was now criticised as much as cant, as in Wilde's *The Importance of Being Earnest* (produced 1895). The family was attacked as much as the poor law, by Edmund Gosse (1845–1928) as much as by Butler. Pillars of society were undermined before being pulled down, as in William Archer's translations of Ibsen. The title of Grant Allen's novel *The Women who Did* (1895) seemed to speak for itself. There was a reaction during the later 1890s, particularly after Wilde's trial in 1896, but the 'rebellion' had its origins far earlier during the uneasy 1870s, when the young Liberal, John Morley, for a time a positivist, described the air as being 'full of missiles': 'all is in doubt, hesitation and shivering expectancy'. In 1888, one year after 'riots' in Trafalgar Square, a less well-known writer, Elizabeth Chapman, had written of a 'general revolt against authority in all departments of life which is the note of an unsettled, transitional, above all democratic age'. By then there were many signs of revolt in the streets as well as in the study. The journalist T.H. Escott, perceived on all sides 'old lines of demarcation being obliterated, revered idols being destroyed'.

The intellectual and moral 'revolt', which was very strictly limited with a minority appeal – the appeal of sport was far stronger and was growing, as was the popular appeal of 'empire' – was a revolt not only against recent conventions and institutions but also against those embedded in the more distant past; and it pointed, often equivocally, to the 'modernism' or 'modernity', dubious terms, of the twentieth century. *The Yellow Book*, published between 1894 and 1897, which introduced the androgenous art of Aubrey Beardsley (1872–98), contributed to the sense not so much of revolt as of 'decadence', a word coined abroad and much in use. There might be pessimism about outcomes: 'All honest art is of necessity pessimistic; wrote Grant Allen. 'Fin de siècle', murmured Lord Henry in Wilde's *Picture of Dorian Grey* (1891). 'Fin du globe', answered his hostess. 'I wish it were fin du globe', said Dorian with a sigh. 'Life is a great disappointment'.

One new and characteristically English writer who picked up many of the threads of social revolt without striking poses or turning to 'art for art's sake', was the self-made H. G. Wells, born in 1866: he wrote *The Time Machine* in 1895, *The Invisible Man* in 1897 and *The War of the Worlds* in 1897. For a time a Fabian, Wells, a believer in science – his first book was a *Textbook of Biology* – questioned most of the values and achievements of the whole Victorian age. At best it had been a 'hasty trial experiment': at worst a 'misdirected human endeavour'. He dismissed Victorian art and architecture too, asking who would remember it. Indeed he allowed only the discovery of the potential of science, stressed too by the biologist, A.R. Wallace, as a real Victorian achievement.

Victorian critics of Victorianism

In fact, the most powerful indictment of 'Victorianism' as a social and moral code had always come from a minority of the Victorians themselves in each part of the reign, early, middle and late. The age always provided its own best critics, from Carlyle – and Thomas Hood (1799–1845) – to Wilde and Shaw: indeed, it has been claimed with justice that we know the age through its critics, not through its enthusiasts. The criticism was of two kinds, not always distinct. The first, functioning within a historical framework, compared present with past or constructed projections of the future; and long before Darwin it could be evolutionary in approach, not comparative. The second reflected personal experience, and could be ironical or occasionally satirical in tone.

The historical approach led in one of its lines of descent through Carlyle and the prophets of the 1840s and through the Catholic architect A.W. Pugin (1812–52), whose *Contrasts*, an aesthetic and moral commentary, appeared in 1836, to Ruskin, who disturbed the serenity of the 1850s and 1860s, to William Morris (1834–96), who became a general critic of society and an advocate of revolution in the 1880s and through him to W.R. Lethaby. It constituted, therefore, a kind of tradition of criticism, and with Morris it drew not only on medieval parallels but on Marxist ideas also. Evolutionary thought, through many lines of descent, could be conservative rather than radical. Indeed, for all the noise made by Darwin's opponents in the early 1860s, theories of social evolution provided for many Victorians, J.W. Burrow suggests, an intellectual resting place, a

point of respose, [at which] the tension between the need for certainty and the need to accommodate more diverse social facts, and more subtle ways of interpreting them, than the traditional certainties allowed for, reached a kind of temporary equilibrium.

'Repose' may be too strong a word, but for one writer at least there was ample confidence. Among the social evolutionists Herbert Spencer (1820–1903), buried by coincidence opposite Marx in Highgate Cemetery, stands out, Burrow notes, as

at once one of the most modern and the most dated of the Victorian social theorists. On the one hand he is the most prominent and most rigidly deterministic of evolutionists, whose enormous works form a suitable mausoleum for an antiquated conception of science; on the other hand he is being increasingly hailed as one of the chief precursors of a social theory dominated by the basic concepts of structure and function.

      (Evolution and Society, a Study in Victorian Social Theory (1966), pp. 190–1)

His appeal was greater in the United States than in Britain: so also were most theories of 'Social Darwinism'.

    The second approach to criticism is represented by so many diverse practitioners that it is difficult to generalise about them, although it can be traced back, for example, to the best of the poetry of Thomas Hood, and on through the better parts (and there were undeniably worse parts) of the illustrated journal *Punch*, founded in 1842 – with cross references to Dickens and through Dickens to Carlyle and the mordant comment in *The Saturday Review* (1855), well nicknamed 'the Saturday Reviler'. There were conservative as well as radical elements in such criticism, as there was in historical criticism, but in this case at least such elements added to its power of exposure. Moreover, the questions raised could either shock or disturb. 'What was the good of a train taking them quickly from Islington to Camberwell', asked Matthew Arnold, keen to identify 'the function of criticism', 'if it only took them from a dismal and illiberal life in Islington to a dismal and illiberal life in Camberwell?' What was the good of the trans-Atlantic cable linking up a man in New York with a man in London if neither had anything to say? 'However much I may be attacked', Arnold observed, 'my manner of writing is certainly one that takes hold of people and proves effective.'

    Morris's criticism, like that of Ruskin, whom he called 'the first comer, the inventor', concerned the nature of the true wealth of the nation, and the prospects of making England more just, as well as more beautiful. It has maintained its appeal, perhaps, because Morris actually made things as well as wrote about them or about ideas. He was a poet too, 'dreamer of dreams, born out of my due time'. For these reasons he is a key figure in this volume. He also links the second and third periods of Queen Victoria's reign, for it was when he went to the Great Exhibition in 1851, at the age of seventeen, that he described the plethora of objects on display as 'wonderfully ugly', and it was a year later that he shocked his parents by refusing to go to the funeral of the Duke of Wellington. His conversion to socialism a generation later in 1882–3, 'crossing the river of fire', introduced a new phase in his life, that of 'making socialists', which drew him (and Shaw) into Trafalgar Square on 'Bloody Sunday', 13 November 1887. Yet Morris saw his life as a whole, and in 1894 declared that 'apart from the desire to produce beautiful things, the leading passion of my life has been and is hatred of modern civilisation'.

Changing assessments

Morris survived by four years the next great national funeral after
Wellington's, that of Tennyson in 1892. The Poet Laureate, made a baron in
1883, was given a state funeral and a tomb in Westminster Abbey, whereas
Morris was buried in very different style at Kelmscott. Yet while Morris was
influencing and was to influence a new generation, with its own new critics
like W.R. Lethaby, Tennyson could now seem out of date. The novelist
George Meredith was not alone in calling him a great poet spoiled by 'the
Curate's moral sentiments, the British matron and her daughter's purity of
tone'. From the left, in 1891, Henry Salt, friend of Carpenter and host to
Shaw, a 'gentleman' by origin, who was bitter about the 'tattoo marks of
gentility' and loved 'tramps', called Tennyson's Arthur

a Prince Consort idealized, who has cultivated the domestic virtues till he is a positive
paragon of bourgeois respectability; there is no flaw in him except . . . to be an
insufferable nincompoop and prig.

The later shifts in assessments of Tennyson, culminating in those of W.B.
Yeats and T.S. Eliot, both influential figures in the fixing of reputations,
reflect other shifts in sensibility, with the former, himself born in 1865, the
year of Young's Victorian break, describing the 'revolt' of the poets against
Victorianism' as a

revolt against irrelevant descriptions of nature, the scientific and moral discursiveness
of *In Memoriam* . . . the political eloquence of Swinburne, the psychological curiosity
of Browning, and the poetical diction of everybody.

Yet it is difficult to fix reputations for ever, as recent writing on Tennyson
has demonstrated. Times turn, and it is striking to note how a writer in the
Westminster Review in 1855 could anticipate the subsequent late-twentieth-
century reaction against the earlier twentieth-century and late-nineteenth-
century reactions. Tennyson's name, he claimed, would survive if other
voices ceased to be heard:

he, at least, while belonging emphatically to his own age, while giving a voice to the
struggles and far-reaching thoughts of the nineteenth century, has those supreme
artistic qualities which must make him a poet for all ages.

This assessment should be compared with that of Eliot, an assessment
more of an age than of a poet:

Tennyson lived in a time which was already acutely time-conscious: a great many
things seemed to be happening, railways were being built, discoveries were being
made, the face of the world was changing. That was a time busy in keeping up-to-
date. It had, for the most part, no hold on permanent truths about man and God and
life and death.

A further comparison of these two assessments would point to the fact that
the Victorian critic of 1855, writing in a section of the periodical 'Belles
Lettres', the very title of which would have irritated Eliot, could be very
critical indeed of Tennyson also when he chose: 'even seen in the light of the
most reverential criticism', he stated, 'the effect of *Maud* cannot be
favourable to Tennyson's fame'. Yet the fact that there was a section called

'Belles Lettres' in the *Westminster Review* in 1855 itself represented a shift in preoccupations. Thirty years earlier, a pre-Victorian critic in the same review, then Benthamite to the core, had taken a very different line about literature and society: he would be 'glad to be informed', he wrote, 'how the universal pursuit of literature and poetry, poetry and literature, is to conduce towards cotton spinning'. In a famous sentence written still earlier Bentham had claimed that

prejudice apart, the game of push-pin is of equal value with the arts and sciences of music and poetry. If the game of push-pin furnish more pleasure, it is more valuable than either. Everybody can play at push-pin: poetry and music are relished only by a few.

Fortunately it had become plain by the mid-Victorian years that the legacy of Bentham was far more diverse in relation to the arts, including the pictorial arts, than Bentham anticipated. In this respect, indeed, it had already proved to be as diverse as the Benthamite legacy in government and administration.

Tendencies and trends

The sense of change

Given the necessity – in the name of understanding – to break up the long reign of Queen Victoria into three parts, it is nevertheless possible, as Eliot suggested, to trace continuing tendencies or trends within it. For this reason Walter Houghton, despite his title *The Victorian Frame of Mind*, took many of the quotations in his book from the period after 1870, while Humphrey House, just as knowledgeable about the separate parts of the reign as G.M. Young, always insisted on the unities and the continuities.

For House, the Victorians, whatever period of the reign they were living in, were 'peculiar' and knew that they were peculiar. They might be 'heirs of time' – they made more of this than House did – but they were conscious too 'of belonging to a *parvenu* generation'. 'At one moment', House went on in a broadcast *Are the Victorians Coming Back?*:

they are busy congratulating themselves on their brilliant achievements, at the next they are moaning about their sterility, their lack of spontaneity. In either mood they are all agog at being modern, more modern than anybody has ever been before. And in this they were right. They took the brunt of an utterly unique development of human history: the industrialization and mechanization of life meant a greater change in human capabilities in the practical sphere than ever before had been possible.

(BBC, *Ideas and Beliefs of the Victorians*, 1948)

This is not a full or adequate explanation of Victorianism. Nor did it anticipate what was to be an 'utterly unique development of human history' after 1948. Yet it is fair generalisation, just as House was fair also in warning on the eve of a Victorian revival, when the price of Victorian objects and buildings was to rise dramatically – the Victorian Society was founded in 1958 – that it would be

disastrous if the Victorians' stupidities, vulgarities, failures and unhappinesses [were to be] minimised or explained away, or accepted as something else. For many

Victorians were in many respects stupid, vulgar, unhappy and unsuccessful; and these aspects of the age remain visible in the objects, the buildings, the pictures and the literature that have been left to us.

House did not include the music, but had he done so he would doubtless have said the same of it. For him it was necessary, therefore, to discriminate as well as to understand, and he never wanted to play what W.L. Burn was to call the 'beautiful easy' game of 'selective Victorianism', a game which continues to be played long after Burn's death: 'determine beforehand the "pattern" which you wish to discover or the "trend" you wish to follow and then go on to find the evidence for its existence'.

In looking for unities and continuities, the Victorians themselves, complacent or critical, would have chosen to discuss religion, politics, economics and culture, and by the end of the reign they would have made even more of 'Englishness' and its distinctiveness than they did in the middle years, now looking at it in relation not only to continental Europe or to the United States but to Scotland, Wales and, above all, Ireland. They were trying to see things in perspective, for as Eliot observed, they were 'acutely time-conscious'.

The growth of population and wealth

The first continuing trend, of which they themselves were fully aware, was the rise in population, which had its origins in the eighteenth century, and the second was the rise in industrial wealth, which had its origins then and earlier. These were obvious enough at different points in the reign – for example, to G.R. Porter, author of *The Progress of the Nation*, in 1836, and to Robert Giffen, who in 1887 gave a remarkable address to the British Association for the Advancement of Sciences at Manchester, which he called 'the commercial capital of England', with the title 'The recent rate of material progress in England'. Porter's work went through so many editions that it was reported that it was beginning to 'partake of the nature of a periodical'. Giffen, while recognising that there was much talk of a falling rate of growth, even a malaise amongst businessmen, concluded, nonetheless, that he had no cause 'to doubt that the future will be even more prosperous than the past'. The population, which had increased more rapidly in the ten years from 1875 to 1885 than in the ten years from 1865 to 1875, was more fully employed than ever before. There had been a decline, too, in the number of paupers per hundred of the population – from 4.2 per cent in 1855–9, 3.7 in 1870–4 to 2.7 in 1880–4. Prices were falling, but the fall was in the interests of the working classes.

All statistics were – and are – open to argument. The Victorians liked to argue about their meaning far more than they liked to argue about theory – and in 1900, when prices had fallen still further, Giffen, now Sir Robert Giffen, was to call the nineteenth century 'the statistical century par excellence'. There was always argument not only about specific statistics but about statistics in general during the Victorian years, and there were always doubts both about the consequences of a growing population and the environmental and human implications of industrial expansion. The 'upward trends' seemed plain, however, with short-term and long-term patterns of fluctuation, reflected, for example, in wages and in profits, which contemporaries tried to understand, even to justify.

George Kitson Clark in his book *The Making of Victorian England* (1962) had more doubts about the beneficial effects of the rise of population than about the rise in industrial wealth. Indeed, he argued that the rise of population had brought with it 'an increase in human misery', particularly during the early-Victorian years, when the spectre of Malthus was abroad in the land. By contrast, the rise of industry, even if it liberated forces which industrialists could not control, created a more 'dynamic' community in which 'wealth percolated down through the various middle classes to a section of the working class who would otherwise have been very poor indeed'. There were high social costs, however, in the second trend.

The fact of population growth was the first of the great national facts. Between 1831 and 1901 the numbers of people living in Great Britain increased by more than ten per cent each decade as measured in the annual census returns. There were less than seventeen million people when Queen Victoria came to the throne, over thirty-seven million when she died. The young Disraeli caught the drama in the early returns, Malthus the fear. Yet until 1841, when the General Registry Office became responsible for the census, the returns were manifestly inadequate. They were much discussed every ten years, but their full significance and value to the historian became apparent only after the development of quantitative demographic history in the late-twentieth century.

There is still an argument about the reasons for a decline in family size in late-Victorian England. The changes came after the census of 1871. Before then birth and death rates were steady, while the marriage rate rose slowly. After 1871 all these rates began to fall. So, too, with them did family size, the controlling variable. In 1851 the average size of the Victorian family – and it is necessary, of course, to examine the span which determined the average – was 4.7. During the 1860s the figure rose to 6.2. Only one in eight families had only one or two children, while one in six had ten or more. By the last decade of the nineteenth century, however, the figure had fallen to 4.3 and it was to fall even more sharply between then and the outbreak of the First World War when it was down to 2.3.

Was 'the cause' birth control, a term not yet then in use? There was certainly in 1876 the spectacular trial of Charles Bradlaugh, the secularist, and Annie Besant, the future socialist, then theosophist, for republishing an older tract on contraception, deemed by the Lord Chief Justice 'to outrage public decency'. While recognising the importance of the trial, J.A. Banks, the historian who has studied the issue most deeply and has written two books on the subject, separated by a quarter of a century, has given special prominence to the rising economic cost of education and parents' social aspirations for their children. He has also examined the impact of feminism. His second book, published in 1981, was called *Victorian Values*: that was before the term became topical and controversial.

While some late-Victorians were concerned with the family as an institution, reacted against mid-Victorian attempts to sanctify family life, and even claimed, like Grant Allen, that there had then been 'a joint system of marriage and prostitution in which the second element is a necessary corollary and safeguard of the first', Victorians of every generation and of every persuasion were concerned, whether they were impressed or alarmed, with the rise and transformation of cities. Some of the first new industrial cities seemed to represent in the words of a writer in *Beatley's Magazine* (1840) 'a system of life constructed on a wholly new principle', and for Ruskin the population was being 'thrown back in continually closer crowds upon the city gates'. How in such circumstances could 'order' be maintained. How could 'health'?

The order was achieved not only through the operations of the police, reorganised in 1856, but through the strength of the individual and family disciplines, many of them implanted at Sunday School, codes of conduct rather than laws. It could be precarious, of course, and even in years of prosperity there could be 'sensational' crimes reported at length in a popular press. There could also be what the Victorians themselves thought of as an 'habitual criminal class'. The health was achieved not only through the doctors, but through the engineers. Moreover, it demanded public campaigns to provide a framework for control, and it too remained precarious. It was only after 'the Summer of the Great Stink' in 1858 that the Metropolitan Board of Works, also founded in 1856, was allowed by Parliament, one of the main sufferers from the stink, to put out tenders for the construction of high-level and mid-level sewer lines.

There remained serious problems of dirt and disease – with different social classes exposed to different chances of life and death throughout the whole Victorian period. The infant mortality rate, rightly considered to be a crucial index of social control, remained more or less constant around 150 per 1,000 live births until the new century began.

Such statistics have to be considered in examining Victorian attitudes to death which have been the subject of much recent study. There was a whole Victorian folk art of death, expressed at funerals and in cemeteries, and death always provided a main topic of poetry and the theme of main incidents in fiction. Yet religion – and the decline of it – has to be brought into the picture also. Like music, it could console, yet it could be disturbed by death, whereas music and art were usually inspired by it. Economics came in too: funerals were expensive, yet the fear of the pauper's grave was even more profound than the fear of the workhouse. Throughout the reign, in death, as in life, the distribution of wealth mattered as much as its production. It set styles as well as life chances.

Cities and countryside

The Victorian countryside, in places extremely isolated, in places extremely unhealthy, saw many demographic changes in Queen Victoria's reign, and although as late as the 1880s it would be described by T.H. Escott as 'a picture in miniature not only of the English nation, but of the English constitution', there were, in fact, as many differences between villages as there were between towns and cities. Yet it was the cities which captured most attention in mid-Victorian and late-Victorian Britain until 'rural labourers' were given the vote in 1885 and there was increased talk of 'rural depopulation'. After Lady Bracknell had asked Jack in *The Importance of Being Earnest* whether or not his income derived from land or investments, she had been delighted when he replied 'in investments chiefly' and had gone on to provide one of her devastating punch lines

That is satisfactory. What between the duties expected of one during one's life-time and the duties expected from one after one's death, land has ceased to be a profit or a pleasure. It gives one position, and prevents one from keeping it up. That's all that can be said about land.

It was not all that could be said, of course, then, when land values were 'depressed', earlier, when agriculture flourished, or later, when the great landed estate remained a symbol of social status. Yet it is true to say that it was the demography of the city that captured most public attention. When Queen Victoria came to the throne in 1837 there were only five places in England and Wales with a population of 100,000 or more: by 1891 there were twenty-three. The range of reactions to the growth of cities, many of them expressed in novels and in poems, is explored fully in my *Victorian Cities* (1963). So, too, is the ambivalence. Yet since then historians have examined in detail the statistics of many of the cities. From a study of a sample of the York census of 1851, for example, W.A. Armstrong has been able to identify the number of native-born heads of families with more than four children; how birth-spacings varied by class and area; how age-groups were related to birth-places; and how social class was related to having domestic servants or lodgers or to sharing a house.

A different kind of evidence is provided from photographs. The 'age of the camera' has recorded much that would have been lost in previous centuries. Yet while a photographer like Francis Frith (1822–98) could produce commercially a very wide range of urban scenes, it was only in the late-Victorian years that we have the beginnings of a memorable record of the life of the streets or of work in the factories. Even for Frith, with a touch of hypocrisy, the skilful photographer should never rest 'until' he has acquainted himself with the rules which are applied to Art in its higher walks'. It was not until the late-Victorian years that a book appeared like John Thomson and Adolphe Smith's *Street Life in London* (1877–8), although in Scotland during the earliest years of their calotype collaboration, the painter David Octavius Hill and the photographer Robert Adamson had produced magnificent studies, described as 'photogenic drawing', but not in book form, of ministers of the kirk, fisherfolk and soldiers.

In 'higher art', cities – and industry – did not figure prominently, although another and more famous Frith, W.P. (1819–1909), could produce a picture like *Railway Station* in 1862 which *The Times* described as 'belonging to the time', 'typical of our age of iron and steel', and there are interesting industrial murals by W.B. Scott (1911–90) at Wallington Hall, Northumberland. The family and the home were the most favourite subjects in mid-Victorian genre painting, not only anecdotalised but often sentimentalised; and it was the 'charm' of Victorian England, rural and urban, which came through in much landscape painting. It was this same charm which was recorded too in books, like the amply illustrated and recently reissued travel tours by the Revd Samuel Manning and the Revd S.G. Green. Their illustrations took the form of engravings: pictorial photography came later in books and newspapers, after family albums and Kodak family snaps. The Kodak camera first appeared in 1888, the first 'Brownie' in 1900.

Statistical studies, like those of Armstrong, push attention back from the city and the countryside to the family as an institution, but in this field, in particular, little systematic attempt has been made so far to relate 'qualitative' evidence, visual or verbal, to quantitative evidence. There have been many studies of the Victorian family in literature and of the role of *pater familias*, mother, children and even maiden aunts, but they have tended to use other historical evidence as background rather than to sort out, as *Victorian Cities* attempted to sort out, the relationship between what was common in Victorian urban experience and where there was divergence. Nor is there any collective study of the Victorian family covering the wide variety of themes examined by H.J. Dyos and his fellow authors in the two-volume *The Victorian City* (1973) or by G.E. Mingay and his fellow-authors in the two-volume *The Victorian Countryside* (1981).

The provinces

In both these collective studies there is stress on local and regional variation – not simply on the most familiar of all contrasts in the early- and mid-Victorian years, as in the late-twentieth century, that between 'North' and 'South', a social, environmental and cultural contrast, often over-simplified but which is represented not only in literature but in language, in art and in music. Mrs Gaskell's *North and South* (1855) does not stand alone even in her own writing: it was in her *Life of Charlotte Brontë* (1857) that she wrote

in fact, no thing can be more opposed than the state of society, the modes of thinking, the standard of reference on all points of morality, manners and even politics in such a manufacturing place as Keighley in the north and any stately, sleepy, picturesque cathedral town in the south.

There was, in fact, variety in the North – and internal rivalry – with as many differences between Leeds and Bradford or Manchester and Liverpool as there were between Keighley and Trowbridge. And there were obvious differences, too, between Lancashire, Yorkshire, Durham and Northumberland. Then, as now, there was a 'Midlands' also, itself with great internal differences. It included not only Birmingham, which was so often contrasted with Manchester in its economic and social structure and its culture, but Nottingham, Leicester, Coventry and George Eliot's Nuneaton. *Middlemarch* preceded Thomas Hardy's 'Wessex', and a less well-known 'East Anglia', without a major novelist, had ways of life of its own.

There was a difference between parochialism or localism and provincialism, and during the mid-Victorian years the quality of provincial life was much advertised. It was extolled by the provincial press, which included organs of opinion, as well as of information, like the *Manchester Guardian*, the *Leeds Mercury* and the *Birmingham Post*, and it was sustained by local interests and expressed in a very wide variety of voluntary organisations. The Libraries Act of 1850 empowered town councils to finance public libraries out of the rates. It was followed by a similar act relating to museums and gymnasiums in 1891. By then Birmingham (1867), Liverpool (1877), Leicester (1885), Leeds (1888) and many other cities and towns already had museums and art galleries.

In music the North was not only the land of brass bands but also of choral societies; and there, as in other parts of the country, musical performers, like actors, had clearly defined provincial circuits. Voluntary provincial activities in the arts were strong throughout Queen Victoria's reign and in places were much extended, but there were many signs by 1900 of a growing metropolitan influence. If the year 1859 had been an *annus mirabilis* in creative writing, the year 1896 was in retrospect at least an *annus mirabilis* in the history of the emergence of a new media complex, national in scale. Alfred Harmsworth, later Lord Northcliffe, founded the *Daily Mail*; young Marconi arrived in London to sell his wireless patents to the Post Office; the first cinema show was presented in the West End; and the red flag era of motoring came to an end. Old modes of communication were affected also. 'Whoever saw a book worth having come from anywhere but London?' the novelist George Gissing asked. He himself had been born and educated in the North.

London

The growth of London depended on immigration from outside it, and internal migration, much of it short-distance, and external migration far over the oceans, raised interesting questions for contemporaries, just as interesting as the role of the metropolis in relation both to the provinces and to the periphery of empire. Some counties were losing population to other areas in Victorian England, among them Cumberland and Staffordshire: there was also a regular flow of population from central and west Wales and the Scottish Highlands. The land seemed to be supporting the city. Some counties were regularly gaining population, including all the counties in south-east England. Others changed their position. Durham, which had made the most of its coal, began, for example, to lose population through migration between 1891 and 1901. Dorset, brought into the public eye by Thomas Hardy, seemed to change less than most, although Hardy with his bicycle discerned real agricultural change on the spot. Ireland supplied immigrants throughout the century, although after the Famine the United States was the favoured land of promise overseas. From Great Britain too, as many as two-thirds of the three million people who moved overseas between 1850 and 1880 went to the United States.

Australia, New Zealand and Canada figure prominently, however, in the literature and popular art of emigration, a movement of mixed motivation, problem and promise, 'push' and 'pull'. There were certainly some emigrants of whom it might be said – indeed, they said it themselves:

> Brave men are we,
> And none may doubt our emigration
> Was of great value to the British nation.

Yet there were others like the two young people born into a family of twelve and described by a French observer, Hippolyte Taine, in 1856: 'Impossible to describe their energy, their ardour, their decisiveness: one feels a superabundance of energy and activity, an overflow of animal spirits.' The remark had added force given that there was no shortage of energy and activity in Victorian Britain itself. For almost all the emigrants, however, whether they were dreaming nostalgically of home or glad to be making a new life in socially freer territory, there was no return: Ford Madox Brown (1821–93) chose the right title for his famous painting *The Last of England*.

During the late-Victorian years London came to be thought of increasingly as a 'world city' and not just as a national capital. And there was less talk then of the shock effects of the provincial industrial city, which had characterised early-Victorian writing on Manchester, in particular, or of the bustle and strife of Liverpool. Birmingham had its 'gospel', first formulated in the mid-Victorian years, and Glasgow its creative vitality, but imagination was captured mainly by London, east or west. Much was made both of the contrast between the two and of the 'new' power of the 'plutocracy', linking the City and Park Lane. 'All roads may be said to lead to London,' wrote Escott, 'and all impulses to trading activity, all outgoings of enterprise and energy that build up markets in the most distant parts of the earth, make their effects visible and palpable in the capital.'

Gissing (1857–1903), fascinated by London, tried to find system in the turmoil. So, too, did H.G. Wells (1866–1946). The London that they described, anathema to William Morris, was as different from the London of Dickens, sentimentalised in a way he would never have wished, as was late-Victorian England from mid-Victorian England. Indeed, much of the most interesting fiction of the mid-Victorian years had focused on the small town. The change in London brought with it hyperbole. 'Here in London', wrote an American observer in New York's *Century Magazine* in 1883, 'there ferments the largest and most highly developed humanity which as yet the universal mother has given birth to, and here the whole world's intellect comes to pay homage.' 'The astounding fact is that this modern Babylon is inhabited by nearly twice as many people as the continent from which he comes', wrote the Australian, J.F. Hogan.

The Babylon image was seized upon by those Englishmen who looked to Paris rather than to London as an intellectual and artistic capital. Yet it was London that Le Gallienne described as

> Great city of the midnight sun,
> Whose day begins when day is done.

Much late-Victorian poetry concerned London. So, too, did short stories – and guide books. This was the London of the *Strand* magazine, founded by George Newnes in 1890, and of Conan Doyle's (1859–1930) Sherlock Holmes. It was also the London of the new South African millionaires with luxurious homes in Park Lane.

Perceptions of the same city could vary as much as perceptions of different cities through fog (a metaphor for London), through sunlight, or through gaslight:

> London, London, our delight,
> Great flower that opens but at night.

Henry James (1843–1916) complained of the 'horrible numerosity' of London, but nonetheless concluded that it offered 'on the whole the most possible form of life': Gissing by contrast was one of the writers who tried to sense what London was through its particulars, including its railway stations. Nonetheless, there were parts of London which were outside his ken.

It had become fashionable during the 1880s to try to share as well as to look at 'the dim strange other world of East London' – or so it seemed to the future Archbishop Lang; and the claims of Toynbee Hall, founded in 1884, were strong enough to attract people anxious not only to discover *terra incognita* but to share human experience. Yet Canon Barnett, the founder of the Hall, was not alone in pointing to the difficulties:

What will save East London, asked one of our University visitors of his master. The destruction of West London, was the answer, and insofar as he meant the abolition of the space which divides rich and poor, the answer was right. Not until the habits of the rich are changed, and they are again content to breathe the same air and walk the same streets as the poor will East London be saved.

Charles Booth, collector of statistics about the poor, did not talk of saving them. He too, however, had links with Toynbee Hall.

Communications

Behind all Victorian talk of population statistics or of the 'human aggregate', there were difficulties during each of the three periods of the reign in communication between people both because of subjective perceptions of class and of objective differences in the social indicators of class – housing, health, education, dress and manners. It was always easier to generalise in terms of 'classes' and 'masses' than it was to cross social divides. But there were people who tried. Indeed, it was long before Toynbee Hall that the social historian J.R. Green had deliberately preferred to work in the East End than in the West End and had become Perpetual Curate of St Philip's, Stepney: 'I am elbow-deep in services', he wrote in 1864 – by which he did not mean religious services, but 'sick-visiting, mothers' meetings, poor relief, and the 100,000 etceteras of a new mission district'. Green, whose *Short History of the English People* appeared in 1874 – an illustrated edition followed in 1892 – wanted to communicate. So also, still earlier in 1842, did the remarkable first Mines Inspector, H.S. Tremenheere, who had already served as a School Inspector and an Assistant Poor Law Commissioner. 'I encouraged them [the miners] to speak out their minds', he wrote, 'and I carefully took down the substance of all they said to me . . . I then read it over to them, that they might correct or add to any portion of it.'

There were at least as many difficulties in communicating in late-Victorian England as there had been in early-Victorian England, and this was to be a major theme for Edwardian essayists, like G.K. Chesterton (1874–1936) and Charles Masterman. By then, too, there had been much talk not only of segregation within the heart of industrial cities but of the segregation of 'the suburbs'. Chesterton, for once avoiding paradox, reminded his readers that one obstacle lay in the way of literary 'actuality':

Rich men write stories about poor men, and describe them as speaking with a coarse or heavy or husky enunciation. But if poor men wrote stories about you or me they would describe us as speaking with some absurd, shrill and affected voice such as we only hear from a duchess in a three-act farce. The slum novelist gains his whole effect by the fact that some detail is strange to his reader, but the detail by the nature of the case cannot be strange in itself. It cannot be strange to the soul which it is professing to study.

Because of continuing changes in the communications complex from the time of Tremenheere's reports to the first performance of Shaw's *Pygmalion* (1913), it is necessary in exploring every shorter period within that span to examine carefully the relationship between the language, styles and content of communication (or the lack of it) and the media, modes and costs of provision. The study of the complex is itself necessarily complex. As R.D. Altick wrote in his seminal book *The English Common Reader: A Social History of the Mass Reading Public 1800–1900,*

the mass reading public had its roots deep in the total history of the period. Far from being an isolated phenomenon, it was the resultant of many forces, most of which – political, religious, economic, technological – seem on first glance to have little bearing on the growth of the reading habit.

Similar considerations have to be brought to bear on any analysis of the attractions of the idea of 'music for the million' – and the resistance to it – or of the rise and fall of the demand for Baxter prints, Staffordshire pottery figures, or Stevengraphs.

The relationships between fashion, ephemera, rubbish and revival are themselves complex. So, too, although perhaps less so, are those between formal school education, child and adult experience and the formation of tastes. The sense of change came early. Thus, it was in 1843 that W.M. Thackeray (1811–63), writing under the pen-name Michael Angelo Titmarsh Esq. observed that

there are a thousand men [who] read and think today for one who read on this same day of April 1743. The poet and artist is called upon to appeal to the few no longer. The profit and fame are with the many . . . The pit, it is my firm belief, knows just as much about the matter in question as the boxes know; and now you have made Art one of the wants of the public, you will find the providers of the commodity and its purchasers grow more refined in their tastes alike.

Raymond William has written generally in his book *The Long Revolution* (1961) of 'a cultural revolution' beginning in the late-eighteenth century and continuing through the Victorian years which involved 'the aspiration to extend the active process of learning, with the skills of literacy and other advanced communication, to all people rather than to limited groups'. Yet this was not the only element in a continuing communications revolution, a term not used by the Victorians themselves, which also involved both religion and technology. Nor does Williams deal in detail with the contradictions and ambivalences of interpretation of what was being 'invented' within the communications complex and with how the Victorians responded to it. He has nothing to say either about Victorian 'nonsense' – the still living universes of Lewis Carroll or of Edmund Lear – and very little to say of Victorian music and of Victorian painting, both of which belonged unmistakably to a specific, though changing, social context.

Political change

It is a necessary part of Williams's thesis that alongside the communications revolution there was a continuing 'democratic revolution' from which escape was impossible. It involved not merely the extension of the suffrage, a major, if interrupted, Victorian theme, but the identification of new democratic issues, deriving from the French Revolution. Williams recognises that as far as the unfolding of this theme, as compared with other themes, was concerned 'conflicts were most explicit' and that 'the questions of power involved' made it 'very uneven and confused'.

Concerned as they must be with detail, political historians, including historians of Chartism in the early-Victorian years and of socialism in the late-Victorian years, would point to the changing uses of the word 'democracy' – in early-Victorian England it remained for many a bogey word – and, above all, to developments in the language of 'class'. They would also note the severe numerical limitations to each extension of the franchise in 1832, 1867 and 1884–5, the complexities of electoral geography, the persisting influence of religion on political beliefs and loyalties, the attack on 'corruption', and the continuing restraints on the role of political party, not least in local government. Party, they have shown, was a changing force in Victorian Britain both at the constituency level and in Parliament. Their interpretations vary, but whatever their stance, they would all acknowledge that there was political development, if not necessarily advance, on all fronts in Queen Victoria's reign, and while refusing to draw a Whiggish straight line through the 'great reforms' of 1832, 1867 and 1884–5 as was once fashionable, they would all accept that as a consequence of franchise extension both the political structure and the identification of political issues were very different in 1901 from what they had been in 1837.

The Queen remained on the throne: other institutions changed in function, as indeed did the monarchy itself, even when they retained the same name. Meanwhile, the civil service, described by the sensitive Fabian political scientist, Graham Wallas, as the one great political invention of the nineteenth century, adapted itself without strain both to liberal-conservative government during the mid-Victorian years and to an increase in the power of the state in late-Victorian years. The very term 'state' could not be taken for granted. Indeed, political historians have recently become as much interested in its use by different groups at different times as in landmarks of legislation and in administrative processes. Most Victorians felt that both their 'constitution', a favourite subject for their own historians, not merely Bishop Stubbs, and their processes of government, much admired abroad,

particularly by Liberals, had their origins in a more distant medieval, even
Saxon, past. For most of them, England, to quote Tennyson, stood out
among other countries as

> A land of settled government,
> A land of just and old renown,
> Where Freedom slowly broadens down
> From precedent to precedent.

The feeling was strengthened – and extended to the empire of settlement
overseas – at the two Royal Jubilees. France had its revolutions, the United
States its Civil War, Germany its unification through Bismarck's blood and
iron: Britain, it seemed, knew how to change without force or revolution.

This, indeed, was the secret of British history for the great French
historian Élie Halévy who broke off in the mid-Victorian years his *History of
the English People* and resumed it only for the years after 1895. England, he
believed – and he used this term rather than Britain – was a country of
freedom, 'of voluntary obedience, of an organisation freely initiated and
freely accepted'. And it remained so despite a change of mood and, of style in
English politics by 1895, a change, in Halévy's view, for the worse when
compared with English politics in 1851. For this he blamed the growth of
tropical Empire, where white settlers were at best tiny minorities and where
the law was imposed, not formulated. It grew by a third during the last three
decades of the nineteenth century. The very term 'imperialism', carrying with
it a sense of mission, Rudyard Kipling's (1865–1936) notion of 'the white
man's burden', had not been used in the 1897 or 1895 sense during the 1850s
when Halévy broke off: it referred largely then to the France of Napoleon III.

Political historians continue to debate not only the characteristics of
'imperialism' and the Halévy thesis, and what Halévy said about religion as a
factor influencing stability, but much of the conventionally tidy political
history of Victorian England, particularly that centred on the 'duel' between
Gladstone (1809–98) and Disraeli (1804–81), when, in W.S. Gilbert's
(1836–1911) words

> . . . every boy and every girl
> That's born into the world alive
> Is either a little Liberal
> Or else a little Conservative.

Gilbert's verbal skills were associated with an acute gift of political and social
observation, apparent not only in *Iolanthe* (1882) but in many other of the
Savoy operas in which he co-operated with the composer Sir Arthur Sullivan.
The operas were popular with the Victorians not only because of Sullivan's
tunes, some of which became as well-known as hymn tunes, but because of
Gilbert's lively topical preoccupation.

Cultural change

In passing from political history to cultural history, music and painting can
and must be brought in at every point in the reign when considering the
'long revolution' in communications. So, too, technology can and must be
included. In early-Victorian England it was the advent of new physical

communications, railways, which constituted the great divide: indeed, W.M. Thackeray compared before and after the railway with before and after Noah's Flood. The era of the stage-coach in consequence acquired a kind of golden glow, recaptured in prints more effectively than in words.

Railways did not provide a major theme for novelists or for poets, but early-Victorian novels and poems are shot through with references to them and with railway imagery, and more generally, the imagery of steam. A classic text is Dickens's *Dombey and Son* (1846–8) which should be compared for its railway passages with Trollope's *Dr Thorne* (1858). By 1858 there was also a 'railway literature', a favourite mid-Victorian term, reading deemed suitable and agreeable for railway journeys: *The Times* complained in 1851 that railway library stock was assembled 'on the assumption that persons of the better class who constitute the larger portion of railway readers lose their accustomed taste the moment they enter the station'. W.H. Smith, 'Old Morality', who started his first bookstall in 1848, would not have agreed. Nor would many of the publishers of new 'yellow-books', who, in any case, would have felt that there was more than adequate compensation in the fact that there were increasing numbers of readers among the non-better class.

The printers of railway timetables by contrast prided themselves on their better taste. Thus, Bradshaw and Blacklock, the original publishers of the great railway guide, also produced superb coloured lithographs of railway lines and railway locomotives. There was considerable – and in quality very varied – illustration of railway construction, of railwaymen, and of railway disasters, much of it in the illustrated press, much of it gathered together in the superb twentieth-century collection of the late Sir Arthur Elton.

During the mid-Victorian years railways, like factories and industrial cities, lost some of their shock impact, and began to be considered in terms of a 'system', functioning regularly and capable of being well-mapped. The result was that some, though by no means all, of their first imaginative impact was lost. In communications history it was now the electric telegraph and the Press which captured – and to some extent directed – the artistic and the popular imagination. The power of the two was, of course, interdependent, and the story of each must be related also to the story of the postal system, which had begun a new phase with the much acclaimed introduction of the penny post in 1840.

The pioneering phase of the history of the telegraph ended in early-Victorian England, in the year of the repeal of the Corn Laws, in 1846, but some of the most exciting international achievements, notably the laying of the transatlantic cable in 1858, belong to the mid-Victorian years. 'Since the discovery of Columbus', wrote *The Times* proudly in 1858, 'nothing has been done in any degree comparable to the vast enlargement which has thus been given to the sphere of human activity.' Three years later the rhetoric was equally abundant when the paper duties were repealed. The *Morning Star* wrote:

This day should henceforward be a red letter day in all English calendars. This day the chief obstacle to the dissemination of knowledge among the people is renowned. This day the tax which was imposed with the direct object of putting fetters upon public writers who expose the abuses of government and of the governing classes . . . is swept away for ever.

The Press, hailed by the influential mid-Victorians as a 'fourth estate', was to have a somewhat different historical role in the future. It is possible, indeed, if far too simple, to divide its history, like the reign, into three parts – early years of conflict, when there was an active and aggressively radical 'pauper press', unlicensed and often licentious, and when journalists of the stamped press also were 'thundering' their claims; the mid-Victorian years, when there was assurance and expansion; and the late-Victorian years, when a new popular press emerged with new journalistic values based on a combination of mass circulation and mass advertising. The version of the story told by historians like Stephen Koss and Lucy Brown is more complex, but there is no argument about the increased influence both of the mid-Victorian newspaper press and the increased power of the periodical.

The Daily Telegraph, the price of which had been reduced to a penny in 1856 and which was to build up a readership of 200,000 during the early 1870s, then claimed to be the largest circulation in the world, was, not surprisingly, particularly eloquent about the significance of 1861. It was not only newspapers that would benefit from the repeal of the paper duties, it exclaimed. 'Every class of literature would benefit', Shelley and Scott as much as W.H. Ainsworth, Charles Lever or Mayne Reid.

The periodical press, which devoted a substantial proportion of its pages to reviews of books, fiction and non-fiction, was at its most prestigious during the mid-Victorian years, when the Whig *Edinburgh*, the Tory *Quarterly* and the Utilitarian *Westminster* were joined by the *Fortnightly* (1865), which soon became a monthly, the *Contemporary* (1866) and the *Nineteenth Century* (1877). This for Wilkie Collins (1824–89) was 'the age of periodicals'. They might have small circulations, although the first number of *Cornhill's* (1859–60), launched at the same time as *Macmillan's*, sold 120,000 copies and continued to have a shortlived success. (So, too, did completely forgotten reviews like *The Broadway Magazine*, the first issue of which sold 100,000 copies in 1867.) They certainly had access to 'the best'. *Cornhill's* included in its first year Trollope's *Framley Parsonage*, Thackeray's *Roundabout Papers* and the *Unto This Last* essays by Ruskin which mounted his assault on orthodox political economy, while the *Contemporary Review* drew heavily on the arguments and debates of the prestigious Metaphysical Society.

The Daily Telegraph was right, therefore, to claim that the demand for periodicals and for books were complementary, whether readers bought the books for themselves or borrowed them from libraries, among them Charles Edward Mudie's, based in New Oxford Street from 1852 onwards. Mudie had at least as much influence on tastes as any periodical: he was 'the Librarian who rules the roost'. He had no monopoly of commercial librarianship, but between 1853 and 1862 he added to his stock almost a million volumes almost half of which were novels. History and biography came next, and he had to set aside a special room for the piles of the third and fourth volumes of Macaulay's *History*.

It would be interesting to compare the sales of books either to libraries or to individuals with the sales of prints, pictures, sheet music, or Staffordshire figures, but precise statistics are hard to come by. George Baxter, who showed the way whereby '50,000 facsimiles of a painting may be produced with perfect uniformity and at a moderate expense', had over 100 engraved steel plates in his 1860 Sale Catalogue when financial difficulties forced him out of business and 100,000 items were catalogued in it. Not surprisingly, Lord Brougham, who believed in 'the diffusion of knowledge' through books – a Benthamite aspiration – claimed that his prints had done more than any other modern discovery to 'make the great mass of people fond of good pictures and familiar with them'. Meanwhile, Vincent and Alfred Novello, supported by the *Musical Times*, which they owned, extended the supply of cheaper music and fought as hard as any book publisher for the repeal of the paper duties. Publication of music in parts was as common before then as publication of novels in serial form.

There were contemporary critics of the artistic scope of Baxter, whose laborious methods could not compete with the emerging skills of what was often considered chromolithography, just as there were contemporary critics of photography as a 'foe-to-graphic art'. There were contemporary critics, too, of British musical taste, of British musical education and training and, above all, of the failure to produce great composers. Yet during the mid-Victorian years achievement in the process of extending the public for 'high art' and for 'serious music' provided a source of considerable satisfaction for the promoters of art and music. The cultural statistics, too, were made much of by remarkable men like Henry Cole (1808–82) and Lyon Playfair, who believed that they had the answers to all the questions relating to the arts and the public, even when confronted by determined ministers and by critics as different as Ruskin and Dickens.

Shortly before his retirement from official life in 1873 and more than twenty years after the Great Exhibition of which he had been a main promoter, Cole noted how the South Kensington Museum which he had founded had 'been visited by more than twelve millions of visitors' and had 'circulated objects to one hundred and ninety-five localities holding exhibitions'. The Museum had been open on several evenings a week, and both the curious and the studious had been bought by such means to appreciate 'those common principles of taste, which may be traced in the works of excellence of all ages'.

The same note was struck in 1872 in a report of the Provisional Committee of the Albert Hall, opened by the Queen in 1871. The success of the Penny Subscription concerts held in 1872 'to enable all classes to enjoy music', the Committee stated, had exceeded all expectations: such had been 'the desire of persons, chiefly of the artisan class, to hear the performances . . . that the numbers admitted to the gallery have increased to 2,000 and upwards, and generally many have to be turned away'.

Recent historians, notably C. Ehrlich, have charted the increasing popularity of the household piano during the mid-Victorian and late-Victorian years. The number of home-produced and imported pianos increased dramatically between 1851 and 1901, with imports and, after 1878, imports from Germany leading the way as in the case of many other articles. More interesting, perhaps, were the factors influencing demand. 'We have got more pianos than perambulators', a South Yorkshire Miners' leader told an 1873 Select Committee on Coal, and far away in Hardy's Dorset when

Gabriel Oak woos Bathsheba, he promises her a piano which 'farmers' wives are getting to have now'. Ehrlich collects many such 'random statements', but he concentrates on the economics, including the cheapness both of piano lessons and of sheet music. It was appropriate that *Music in the Home* by the well-known pioneer of choral sight reading and of tonic sol-fa, J.P. Hullah, was published in 1877.

At the beginning of the twentieth century one English person in thirty-six had purchased a piano (as against 1 in 1,000 in Germany and 1 in 260 in the United States). Quite soon, however, the piano was to be supplanted by gramophone and wireless. Indeed, it was in late-Victorian England that 'the culture of time and space', as Stephen Kern has called it, was beginning to be transformed radically as a result of the extension in the uses of electricity and the invention of the automobile, the telephone, the phonograph and wireless. Broadcasting was not to be developed for various reasons, partly technical, partly social, for another generation, yet there were prophets eager to point to the possibilities of 'instantaneous' and 'global' communication of 'messages', including both news and entertainment.

The telegraph had been the first invention to harness electricity for economic and social purposes, but it was not until 1881 that *Punch* could introduce a cartoon showing King Steam and King Coal watching the infant Electricity and asking 'what will he grow to?' The gospel of steam was even more under threat than the gospel according to St Matthew, for electricity carried with it an element of mystery, even of magic, which seems to have attracted the European imagination more than the British. Indeed, the British were slower to retract from the world of steam than several continental countries and the United States. It was not an Englishman, but a distinguished American, Henry Adams, who after visiting the Great Chicago Exhibition of 1893 and the Paris Exhibition of 1900, where there was a whole 'Palace of Electricity', compared the modern cult of the dynamo with the medieval cult of the Virgin.

It is interesting to note, however, that Adams's explorations of time and space, which led him to meditate on the automobile as well as electricity, began, like those of many enterprising Englishmen and women, not with electricity but with the bicycle: when he was over fifty, in his own words he 'solemnly and painfully learned' to ride one. In Britain there was a whole bicycle culture or rather a cluster of cultures, including that of Robert Blatchford (1851–1943) and the socialist Clarion Clubs. There were also feminists who liberated their clothes conventions when they took to the road, not caring that they shocked the readers of *Punch*. Nonetheless, there was a peculiarly English twist to an article in the *Fortnightly Review* in 1891 which conceded that it was possible for an individual to cycle 'without imperilling his or her social status'.

Before Queen Victoria's death the automobile was very much a symbol of social status as the horse-driven carriage had been. Indeed, the first journals devoted to the subject elaborately compared the costs of keeping a horse and keeping a car. The magazine *Autocar*, 'published in the interests of the mechanically propelled carriage', was founded in the *annus mirabilis*, 1896. Railways had collective implications from the start: motor cars began as individual perquisites and a full appreciation of their social significance came later. There were no intimations of the mass production of motor cars: the United States, a continent of large distances, was to lead the way.

The implications of the telephone, were not easy to predict either: at first, it too was thought of as a 'pleasure object'. In time, it was to produce its own culture – particularly, again, in the United States – and if not to reduce the volume of, at least to change, the content and alter the timing of written correspondence. Already in 1892, however, the Post Office acquired the trunk line system, a significant difference from United States practice. The Post Office controlled also the first uses of wireless which was thought of not as a medium of broadcast communication but as a substitute for land and sea communication by telegraph. The 'broadcast' element was considered a liability, not an asset, and when a generation later it was thought of as an asset the Post Office again intervened as it did not intervene in the United States.

Confronted with the same new technology, Britain and the United States were to follow different paths, though they were often to cross and even converge. In the case of the cinema, however, which was to raise related social and cultural questions in the future, the United States – through Hollywood – was to have an exceptional international role, not discernible in 1901. In terms of technology the development of moving pictures followed naturally from the discovery of still photography, but already by 1900 moving pictures were no longer associated with individual peep show cabinets, as Thomas Edison had believed they would be, but with public performance in buildings specially set aside for the purpose. They were not yet picture palaces, however, and the content of the first films, some of which were British, owed as much to the traditions of the magician as to the themes of the music hall or the theatre.

During the 1890s there was much popular writing about science, technology and the shape of things to come. Wells was not alone. Greater disposable incomes, increased leisure and continuing urbanisation were the key factors determining choices in technology and the economic and social outcomes of technology. And advertising increased in volume and began to change in content as the technologies advanced. W.H. Lever could not have sold soap in huge quantities without it, nor could Pears. Gissing had noted the ubiquity of street advertising in London; Morris gave his last public address to the recently founded Society for Checking the Abuses of Public Advertising; Northcliffe, who had doubts about advertising, saw its importance in press finance. There was even talk of introducing advertisements on gramophone records.

The phonograph was not the least important of the late-Victorian cluster of inventions. It emanated like so much else from Edison's American laboratory, although the name given to its improved version – the gramophone – was given it twenty years later by Emile Berliner, the improver, in 1897. An early Edison advertisement had described it as a 'talking machine', and Gladstone, Browning, Tennyson and Cardinal Manning were to sing its praises in their own voices. Yet its potential value for reproducing real singing and other kinds of music was recognised from the start, sometimes provoking alarm rather than eulogy. Sir William Preece, the Engineer-in-Chief of the Post Office and the man who welcomed Marconi to London in 1896, was quick to note that it was the potential, not the performance, of the 'fabulous phonograph' which was being saluted in the late 1870s and early 1880s: 'the instrument has not yet quite reached that perfection when the tones of a Patti can be faithfully repeated: in fact, to some extent it is a burlesque or parody of the human voice'.

The gramophone was used for popular entertainment before it was used seriously for 'serious music', and in this respect its history can be compared with the history of the cinema and with the history of the late-Victorian popular press. All things connected. Before Harmsworth (1865–1922) founded the *Daily Mail*, George Newnes (1851–1910), who was to found the *Strand Magazine*, had established *Tit-Bits* in 1881: it had an immediate circulation of 800,000. Harmsworth followed with *Answers*, which offered competitions with handsome prizes. He was an early motorist too, and in 1902 himself edited a volume called *Motors and Motor Driving*. Everything was being speeded up. As a serious new professional periodical, *The Electrical Engineer*, put it in 1892, 'A few years ago the public were content to send a message to London and get an answer within an hour; now they can get it in a minute or two; but still the cry is for quicker communication.'

Wireless was still not part of the entertainment complex, but *Science Siftings*, another popular periodical of the 1890s, could claim in the year of the Queen's Golden Jubilee that Marconi's invention would 'add a fresh lustre to the year. Further developments of this wonderful discovery will be eagerly awaited'. In the *Strand Magazine* of 1898 Arthur Mee, who was to make his name with a *Children's Encyclopedia*, quoted Bellamy's *Looking Backward* in which a young man 'was amazed to hear charming music in a room in which there was neither musician nor instrument'. He was told not to be surprised. 'Labour saving by co-operation' – and by technology, in this case the telephone – had been carried into the 'musical service as into everything else'.

Education and the Forster Act

Edison had believed, as Marconi believed, that there would be educational uses in the new cluster of inventions. These were slow to come, however, even when the profit motive was not dominant. Nonetheless, the relationship between communications and education, which was to raise important twentieth-century questions – the two forces might even seem hostile – was not without its interest to the Victorians during each of the three 'periods' of the reign. Indeed, before the reign began Carlyle berated the 'Paternoster-row mechanism' with its 'Trade-dinners, its editorial conclaves, and huge subterranean puffing bellows'. During the middle years Arnold, in particular, wrote about the relationship between school education and culture, pleading for a national educational system, and at last in 1870, at the beginning of a decade when education became in John Morley's phrase 'the great national question', the first major national Education Act was passed, its proposer, W.E. Forster (1819–86), Arnold's brother-in-law, gave many reasons for its introduction, but ended with the stirring peroration:

Civilised communities throughout the world are massing themselves together, each mass being measured by its force; and if we are to hold our position among men of our own race or among the nations of the world we must match up the smallness of our own numbers by increasing the intellectual force of the individual.

The term 'intellectual force' was, in fact, strictly limited in application in the first years of implementation of the 1870 Act, which was concerned largely with education in the three Rs, a far narrower education than that deemed necessary by Arnold, and which did not offer much promise either for technical education. Indeed, for a critic very different from Arnold, H.G. Wells,

The Education Act of 1870 was not an Act for common universal education, it was an Act to educate the lower classes for employment on lower class lines, and with specially trained, inferior teachers who had no university quality.

The effects of the Education Act of 1870, which filled in gaps in voluntary, mainly religious, provision, and of compulsory schooling, with a leaving age fixed at ten in 1876, at eleven in 1893 and at twelve in 1899, have been much debated. Thereafter, however, the Board School as an institution had an influence often distinct from that of the family and always distinct from that of the streets. It proved impossible, moreover, to stop education for all at the three Rs point. In practice, the curriculum of Board Schools broadened inevitably to include, for example, music and art, and the question now arose of how these subjects were to be taught. Secondary education also followed almost inevitably. It used to be argued that one effect of the new educational structure was 'to open the floodgates of literacy' and to create a new reading public. Raymond Williams and others have shown why this was unconvincing. 'The basic history of literacy in the century', Williams states, 'seems to be a steady expansion, led by the towns . . . and by men, and this simple expansion was also a steady development of real reading capacity'. In other words, he is referring back to a trend or tendency and not to an event.

The arts

In examining trends, historians sometimes distinguish between 'planned' social changes, initiated through policy, and 'unplanned' social changes, emanating from 'the market'. In the case of the arts and sciences, however – and of education – it is not easy to rest content with this distinction. Educational reforms have a long period of implementation, and in a changing society it is difficult to separate their influences from a host of other influences: 'unplanned changes' often follow more or less as anticipated by far-seeing impresarios seeking profits. Moreover, even when there is no national policy to take account of, a further distinction has to be drawn in the arts between the concept of 'the public' and the concept of 'the market'. The State played such a minor role in supporting the arts during the Victorian years that in seeking to elucidate this further distinction it can almost be left out of the picture, if not of the analysis. It neither controlled 'the heritage' nor determined 'the tradition', by 'invention' or otherwise. The National Trust for Places of Historic and Natural Beauty founded in 1895, was not a

State venture. Nor were the *New English* [later *Oxford*] *Dictionary* (1884–1928) or the *Dictionary of National Biography* (1885–1900).

'It is the policy of a great nation to be liberal and magnificent', Martin Archer Shee, portrait painter and future President of the Royal Academy, had written in 1805 in the preface to his *Rhymes on Art*. 'A drop from the ocean of our expenditure would sufficiently impregnate the powers of taste, to a country naturally prolific in every element of genius.' There was scarcely a drop from the swelling ocean in mid-Victorian or late-Victorian times, for it was the policy of the state, if it had a policy, to be liberal and mean. Thus, the Royal Academy of Music, founded in 1823, was always short of funds and suffered in consequence, and when the government offered a £500 annual grant in 1868 this was thought to be a landmark. The older Royal Academy of Arts, founded in 1768, had greater access to power and influence – and was more criticised in consequence – but it, too, suffered from the kind of official interference that had led the government not to provide funds for the National Gallery to acquire Sir Thomas Lawrence's collection of drawings of the Old Masters. Even Cole at the height of his power failed to persuade Palmerston to let him purchase the Soulages collection of medieval Italian majolica, wood carvings and bronzes for his South Kensington Museum which was eventually to be transformed into the Victoria and Albert Museum. Looking at the majolica, Palmerston is reputed to have asked 'what is the use of such rubbish to our manufacturers?'

When Henry Tate offered his collection of paintings to the National Gallery in 1890, subsequent negotiations between the Treasury, the Gallery, and the South Kensington Museum about how to house it were so awkward and protracted that Tate offered to build a gallery himself. It was a Conservative government on this occasion which was the negotiator. Yet the Corporation of London proved itself no more generous than the government when it set such a high price on a site that once again the scheme fell through. Finally, a Liberal government, Gladstone's last, offered a piece of land at Millbank in exchange for Tate's collection and a benefaction for the building. Appropriately it was on the site of Bentham's model penitentiary.

The idea of a national theatre had been canvassed in 1879, when the Stratford Memorial Theatre was opened: indeed, it had been canvassed more than a century earlier by David Garrick. Yet the State, in Arnold's words, 'left the English theatre to take its chance'. Just as significant, perhaps, was the fact that there was no agreement about what the policy of such a theatre should be. Ought it to 'soften, purify and elevate', to shock or just to entertain? The actor Henry Irving (1838–1905) was to demand an 'exemplary theatre' that would produce plays at 'the highest artistic level'.

This meant that most of the plays would have had to be old since it was not until the last decades of the century that contemporary British drama achieved any high artistic level. Meanwhile, the popular theatre and what have been called 'the theatres of the left' did not seek to follow such a policy, and the very absence of the State left a space for a variety of initiatives, some radical, some 'patriotic', some both. In the theatre, as in music, 'popular entertainment', in particular, had its own conventions. They were not always determined by 'the public', but neither were they always fashioned in the market place. The role of the music hall has recently been studied in depth, as has sheet music (and the pictorial covers that went with it), but questions remain. Why were 500,000 copies of 'The Lost Chord' sold between 1877 and 1902? Public tastes clearly counted. During 'the naughty nineties', when London was Babylon, 50,000 copies of 'The Holy City' were being sold each year.

It was in relation to the novel, the main Victorian art-form, liberated during the late 1880s from its three-decker format, that the question of the impact both of the 'public' and of the 'market' on the artist was most frequently discussed, although William Morris, a good businessman in that he knew how to create tastes for his (and related) products, raised it on many occasions. 'Both my historical studies and my practical conflict with the philistinism of modern society,' he told the socialist Andreas Scheu in 1883, 'have *forced* on me the conviction that art cannot have real life and growth under the present system of commercialism and profit-mongering'. Gissing, who moved completely away from socialism, concentrated in his *New Grub Street* (1891) on the pull of the 'public' – and the market – on the author. Milvain advocated in the name of the 'new generation' the production of 'novels out-trashing the trashiest that ever sold 50,000 copies':

Literature nowadays is a trade . . . our Grub Street of today is quite a different place [from Sam Johnson's]: it is supplied with telegraphic communication, it knows what literary fare is in demand in every part of the world, its inhabitants are men of business.

Another character, Whelpdale, makes a great business success out of *Chat* by brightening the title to *Chit Chat*, reducing the length of the articles in it to two inches, and insisting that 'every inch must be broken up into at least two paragraphs'.

Three years later in his novel *In the Year of the Jubilee* Gissing put into the mouth of another character, Luckworth Crewe, the question 'How could we have been what we are without the modern science and art of advertising?' 'Till advertising sprang up', Crewe went on, 'the world was barbarous. Do you suppose people kept themselves clean before they were reminded at every corner of the benefits of soap?' Exit the sanitary idea, as expounded by Edwin Chadwick, Charles Kingsley, Charles Dickens and George Eliot. Art was something different, and although Walter Allen has said of Gissing's novels that 'from them one might think that the whole purpose of life was that men and women should read', in fact the novels have much to say about the visual arts, and in the posthumously published *Will Warburton*, Gissing refused to condone the painter Norbert Frank's forsaking of painting for fashionable portraiture, a genuine deterioration under the pressure of financial need.

Nonetheless, Gissing, usually perplexed in his attitude towards art and literature, did not object to the fact that Wells, with whom he corresponded, made his living out of journalism and had begun by writing an article for *Tit-Bits*. The argument between Wells and Henry James about the nature of the novel was post-Victorian. Yet Wells and Gissing spent a night with James at Rye in 1901, and two years earlier James and Edmund Gosse had bicycled over from Rye to see Wells at Sandgate when they heard he was ill. Other visitors were Barrie (1860–1937) and Joseph Conrad (1857–1924). These were fascinating very late Victorian links, as fascinating as earlier and often curious links in the London literary and artistic world of the 1850s and 1860s or the less curious inter-generational links between the members of the cluster of Victorian families identified by Noel Annan as 'an intellectual aristocracy'.

Epilogue

Such links certainly attracted G.M. Young; and it is appropriate that an introductory essay on the Victorian period which began with him should also end with him. In 1953, when the Victorian revival, heralded by John Betjeman, was beginning, Young gave a broadcast on 'Coronation Year, 1902' in which he described vividly how he felt as a young man of nineteen when Queen Victoria died. 'The political changes, the social changes, yes, even the scientific achievements of the Victorian age had left the outer fabric of our life very much as it always had been', he claimed. The motor was a toy, and the aeroplane a fairytale. 'We looked forward to leading, with some improvements, the sort of life our fathers had lived.'

It was a conservative judgement, and it applied only to the kind of social groups, not quite an 'intellectual aristocracy', to which Young himself belonged.

England was a very good country for gentlemen. And it all rested on two things – an income tax so moderate that it was hardly felt: and an unlimited supply of cheap, efficient domestic service. Pull those pillars down and that social hierarchy topples. That also we could not foresee.

The majority of the population neither paid income tax nor enjoyed cheap efficient domestic service. For some of them there were many pillars to be pulled down, but for the majority there was less interest in scaling heights or lowering the great than in minor status differences, most conspicuous perhaps in the status hierarchies of domestic servants themselves. Within ten years of the Queen's death the mood was very different. There was also ample publicity. Militant mass movements had been created. So, too, had self-conscious avant-gardes. And in 1914 there was war.

Part II
Studies in the Individual Arts

All Souls Church, Halifax (1855–9). George Gilbert Scott.

1 Architecture

JOHN SUMMERSON

Introduction

Easily the most striking thing about architecture in Britain in the half century
before 1900 is the perpetual concern with *style*: the nature of style, the
classification of styles in history and the moral or aesthetic relevance of historic
style to modern practice, to say nothing of that recurrent *ignis fatuus*, a 'new
style'. These considerations, complicated enough in themselves, were
rendered more so by the vast multiplication of building types from the fifties
onwards, the correspondingly increased complexity of planning and
equipment and the new scale imposed by the needs of an expanding
industrial society.

In 1850, however, the stylistic face of British architecture was still almost
unruffled. There had, indeed, been a flurry of argument over the style of the
new Houses of Parliament but in general a tolerant eclecticism prevailed.
Architects and their clients took pleasure in four styles: Greek and Italian,
Gothic and Tudor. An architect of standing would profess competence in
these without necessarily evaluating one above the other.

The profession of architect was still fairly select: there were probably not
more than 500 in the whole country, nearly all of them trained in the offices
of the previous generation. An élite of 228 constituted the Institute of British
Architects, founded in 1834 to protect the status of the profession and
promote the cause of architectural scholarship. The building trade was highly
efficient, at least in its upper reaches, with the firm of Cubitt setting a
magnificent example. Altogether it was a happy time for architecture: serene
and confident under a gracious queen and her concerned and intelligent
consort.

That, at least, was how it seemed to the average educated Englishman and
the enquiring foreigner. But under the surface things were not quite so
happy. In the heads of some young architects the conviction was growing
that English architecture was altogether too smooth and English architects
too pleased with themselves. These young people looked at the new steam
mills of Manchester and Leeds, the locomotives fuming and clanking from

Euston to Birmingham. They looked at iron bridges and station sheds, at iron passenger-carrying steamships crossing the Atlantic. They began to talk of a New Age, the age of steam and iron, and to ask whether, every age in history having created and displayed a style of architecture of its own, the age of steam and iron should not do likewise.

A building which, for a brief flicker of time, seemed to supply the answer was the Crystal Palace, the building erected in Hyde Park to house the Great Exhibition of the Industry of All Nations, ceremonially opened by the Queen in May 1851 and ceremonially closed by the Prince six months later. It had been a roaring success. Built nearly all of iron and glass with a lively use of colour, entirely uncommitted to any previous architectural style, it combined the daring elegance of Gothic with classical symmetry and a new kind of precision obtainable only by mechanical processes. Here, surely, a new style was being born.

This, however, was not the case. The Crystal Palace, designed by Joseph Paxton (1801–65), a ducal gardener who was also a technologist of uncommon skill, served magnificently as a shelter for an international exhibition, but this conservatory style (for such it was) served for very little else. The iron shed of Paddington Station was among the Palace's few legitimate successors. Nobody wanted to live in transparent houses, still less to keep their money in transparent banks. And apart from all this there was the deep conviction that, fine as it was, the Crystal Palace was not *architecture*.

Already in 1851 loose talk about a new style was being overtaken by a very different type of argument. In 1836 the twenty-four-year-old Augustus Pugin

The Crystal Palace, Hyde Park, London (opened by Queen Victoria in May 1851). Joseph Paxton.

had published *Contrasts*, his graphic satire on contemporary life and architecture, demonstrating in pairs of contrasted pictures the superiority not only of Gothic architecture to modern Classic but of medieval to modern society (see p. 231). His later writings amplified his belief that there was only one true style for a Christian England. It was useless to talk of a new style; the alternative to the modern was already there, ready to hand, and it was the Gothic.

Pugin died in 1852, aged forty, but he had launched a rocket into the Victorian world which was to inflame a whole generation of architects. Gothic imitation had been in vogue since Horace Walpole and was widely practised before Pugin was born. But it was Pugin who put *belief* into it. He was a Catholic and for him Gothic architecture was Catholic architecture. But Anglican architects proved no less able to adopt the Gothic style as an article of religious faith and to feel it in their bones.

Pugin was an architect. Another prophetic voice of 1851 was that of John Ruskin (1819–1900), not an architect but a man of letters whose love of architecture developed by way of a passion for mountain scenery, natural history, the picturesque and the art of J.M.W. Turner. He began with an essay on 'The poetry of architecture' in 1834. *The Seven Lamps of Architecture* came out in 1849 and the first volume of *The Stones of Venice* in 1857. It was this latter which had the profoundest effect. Ostensibly a history and description of the architecture of medieval Venice, it contained much which was neither of these but an expression of the author's own beliefs in the relation of art and society and the ethical implications of that relationship in architecture. Chapter 6 in volume II of *The Stones*, entitled 'The nature of Gothic', was a passionate assault on the inhumanity of an industrial society, the subjection of the craftsman to machine ideals, and the extinction of his creative powers, comparing the situation unfavourably with the rough and even savage vitality seen in ancient work. Towards the end of the chapter are some highly pertinent observations on Gothic architecture and it may be said that the chapter as a whole is one of those epochal documents on which thought, throughout history, has significantly turned.

Pugin and Ruskin both attacked contemporary social conditions and both encouraged a revival of Gothic. But as personalities they were worlds apart. Ruskin said, rather scornfully, that he owed nothing to Pugin's influence. Pugin, though only seven years older than Ruskin, seems not to have noticed him; he was far too busy building. Pugin encouraged by example, building scores of churches, as well as country houses, schools and monasteries and publishing books of designs. Ruskin's encouragement was less direct. He exposed the virtues of Gothic in his writings but only on few occasions did he actively promote Revivalist projects. Much of what the Revival produced he disliked and ignored. There is indeed one building which deliberately set out to realise Ruskin's ideals – the Museum of Physical Sciences at Oxford, designed by Benjamin Woodward (1815–61) with his partner, Thomas Deane, in 1854 and finished about 1860. It is of brick and stone with a touch of Italian Gothic about the windows and a courtyard with iron columns and an iron vault – an equivalent of Gothic in metallic terms. Ruskin had a strong appreciation of Woodward's work and the stone carving and iron

Museum of Physical Sciences, Oxford, view from south-west (1854–60). Benjamin Woodward and Thomas Deane.

ornament are somewhat in the spirit of the *Seven Lamps*. Ruskin was disappointed with the final result but the brick and stone exterior had a considerable effect on later secular Gothic buildings.

But it was mainly in church building that the Gothic Revival expressed itself. Through the fifties, sixties and seventies, hundreds of new churches were built, for reasons partly religious, partly social and partly economic. From the 1830s the Church of England experienced a strong revival of interest in the forms and meaning of the liturgy and this merged readily with a philanthropic desire to bring the consolations of religion to the poor as well as with a rising enthusiasm for the Gothic styles. The expansion of London and the great industrial towns, moreover, rendered churches obligatory as social symbols. No estate development was complete without a church; a site would be reserved for one in the first instance by the ground landlord to attract a good class of resident. The structure would be paid for partly by one of the church-building societies and partly by the new residents themselves. These estate churches are usually of a competent text-book type of 'Decorated' Gothic. It was the churches of pious and philanthropic intent in the twilight areas of the cities which attracted the patronage of wealthy individuals and the employment of the more original and high-minded architects such as William Butterfield and George Edmund Street.

The Gothic Revival was mainly an affair of churches, vicarages and schools. Country houses did not lend themselves well to rigorous imitation of their ancient prototypes; the nobility, with rare and extravagant exceptions, maintained a predilection for Italian Renaissance; the gentry for the relaxed and readily adaptable Tudor.

In public buildings the style question produced endless controversy and several disasters. Barry's Houses of Parliament, approaching completion in 1860, were continuously under fire either for being too Gothic or not Gothic enough; either for being a 'late and debased' version of the style or for being classical at heart and merely veiled with Gothic lace. When, in 1856, a competition was held for new War and Foreign Offices in Whitehall the top awards predictably went to classical designs based on the new Louvre in Paris. They were never built, however, and the government proposed to set the competitions aside and introduce their own official architect. This led to the famous 'battle of the styles' which resulted in the appointment of George Gilbert Scott who had come only third in *one* of the competitions with a Gothic design, but had influential friends. His design would have been carried out but for a change of government which brought in Lord Palmerston as prime minister. He insisted categorically on an Italian building. Scott protested but eventually, sacrificing his Gothic conscience to his obligations as a family man, designed an Italian building (and made a remarkably good job of it). It was the Revival's first great set-back.

Secular Gothic triumphed in Manchester, where a local architect, Alfred Waterhouse, won two competitions in succession; the Assize Courts (1859) and the Town Hall (1867). In both cases the resulting buildings were a success both with the architect's clients and the public and, in the first case, even with Ruskin. The same cannot be said for the building which eventually resulted from a competition held in 1866 for the Royal Courts of Justice in the Strand, London. The adjudication was grossly mishandled and the appointment of George Edmund Street was both unfair to other competitors and injudicious in itself. His design, never entirely suited to its purpose, was re-orientated and distorted at the last moment and soon condemned as a disaster. It was not quite that, and it contains many beautiful strokes of design, but it put paid to any further public buildings in the Gothic style.

In 1870 nearly all the leading architects in England were of the Gothic persuasion but among younger men there was, around that year, a sudden and surprising change of direction. This was no mere inflexion of taste; it was part of an historic change in English society: the supersession of a great wealth-building generation by a generation of spenders. By 1870, the heroic figures of the industrial upsurge of the early-Victorian years were dying off. Their heirs and successors had more leisure, a greater sense of social responsibility and a more delicate feeling for the amenities of life in town and country. They took strongly against the heavy conventionalities and stylistic dogmatism of their fathers' generation; there was a sense of discovery of the intrinsic value of the arts ('art for art's sake') and a feeling for the folk-arts of the countryside. It was this generation – the generation of Walter Pater and Thomas Hardy – which, in architecture, produced the style of architecture which acquired the label 'Queen Anne'.

It must be said at once that the style which issued under this name had next to nothing to do with architecture produced in England within the regnal years of the monarch whose name it took. Warm red brick and tall sash windows were indeed conspicuous components of the style but nearly everything else in 'Queen Anne' was totally alien to Queen Anne. Much of it was picked up from the seventeenth-century English vernacular; some of it was Flemish and some sheer improvisation. A somewhat Pre-Raphaelite kind of sunflower was a favourite ornament.

Who invented the 'Queen Anne' style it is hard to say. There had been hints of nostalgic regression as early as 1862 when Thackeray, the novelist, built himself a 'Queen Anne' style house in Palace Green, Kensington. It was an amateurish affair and nobody took much notice of it. But five years later came the Hon. George Howard, building almost next door to the Thackeray house a residence of a wholly different kind, rather Gothic in outline but with tall eighteenth-century sash windows and sensitively designed moulded brickwork. It was the work of Philip Webb, to whom we shall come later, and it really did set young architects trying to free themselves from the bondage of Gothic prototypes. It is a rather eccentric building but alive with ideas, and one of these ideas was certainly the recovery of early eighteenth-century craftsmanship and design – in short, 'Queen Anne'.

With 'Queen Anne' in the ascendant the seventies saw the beginning of the end of Gothic Revivalism. Refugees from Sir Gilbert Scott's over-productive office like J.J. Stevenson and E.R. Robson took up with the new fashion. Stevenson built for himself a model 'Queen Anne' house in Bayswater Road (owing much to Webb) and E.R. Robson, appointed architect to the London School Board which the Education Act of 1870 had brought into existence, adopted 'Queen Anne' as the style for his new 'Board schools'. Gothic survived mainly in church-building but turned from the hard and spiky style of Scott and Street and the rational influence of Viollet-le-Duc, to the softer, more homely and adaptable English 'Perpendicular'. George Frederick Bodley was the new leader, building churches in pure English style but turning to 'Queen Anne' for vicarages and secular buildings.

The eighties saw a continuous development of 'Queen Anne' in various directions, the most important of which was a move towards more literal interpretation of the original style of 1702–14 and its Georgian sequel. J.M. Brydon, whose roots were in the Scottish classical tradition, developed a Georgian style based on Wren and Gibbs, leading to his new government offices in Whitehall, begun just before his death in 1901. There was an increasing interest in foreign Renaissances, especially those of France, Belgium, Holland and Spain. Ernest George built rows of wonderfully picturesque houses in Harrington Gardens, London, in Flemish Renaissance; Bodley built the headquarters of the London School Board in very plausible Francis I; Norman Shaw mixed French and Dutch Renaissances in his New Scotland Yard and built a series of houses in Queen's Gate ranging from Flemish Renaissance (Nos. 196 and 180) to the real Queen Anne (No. 170); Thomas Collcut celebrated Queen Victoria's Golden Jubilee (1887) by winning the competition for the Imperial Institute with an idiosyncratic version of Spanish Renaissance including a tower (the only part still existing) whose silhouette derives from Segovia.

In addition to all these, there was something called 'modern French' which meant simply a reflection of what was going on in Paris and contained something of the academic 'Beaux-Arts' manner. The former hotels (now offices) in Northumberland Avenue, London, are good examples and the style was adopted for hotels, offices and official buildings in the big commercial cities.

If play with all the Renaissance styles of Europe was the overall characteristic of the eighties, the radical movement against style asserted itself in various ways. The young men in Norman Shaw's office formed the Art Workers' Guild in 1885 to promote the Ruskin gospel and the Arts and Crafts Exhibition Society followed in 1887, with Walter Crane as its first president. The idea was to bridge the gap between architecture and the arts, to take the decorative arts out of the hands of commercial enterprise and to restore the dignity of the artist-craftsman. Few architects followed Webb's rigorous elimination of 'historic' style but it survived as an ideal. W.R. Lethaby, who had worked in Shaw's office, promoted it in his writings and his few but significant buildings.

By the turn of the century, radicalism had come full circle. In 1851, the radical call was for a *new* style. By 1900 it was for *no* style. But in neither case did the radical philosophy prevail. In the fifties it was overwhelmed by the Gothic Revival; in the nineties by a new enthusiasm for the classical and the Baroque.

There was, indeed, one London area where a reconciliation of the styles was attempted, not altogether without success. This was South Kensington. The Great Exhibition of 1851 had brought to the Exhibition Commissioners a very handsome surplus and this, supplemented by government funds, was employed in the acquisition of some twenty acres of ground southward of Kensington Road, the idea being to provide sites for museums and educational buildings which would consolidate and extend the purposes of the Exhibition. Prince Albert was the prime mover, with Henry Cole, secretary of the Department of Science and Art, as his chief agent.

The first use to which any of the property was applied was the formation of a garden for the Royal Horticulture Society. This was formally laid out in 1860–1 with continuous arcades along the east and west sides. These arcades were in an Italian fifteenth-century style, not hitherto imitated in England and having a harmonious relationship as well with the age of Gothic as of the Renaissance. They were designed partly by an architect, Sidney Smirke, and partly by an officer of the Royal Engineers, Francis Fowke (1823–65), who was attached to the Department of Science and Art as its architect and engineer. Fowke brought in an artist, Godfrey Sykes, who helped with the decorative modelling, and the arcades (long since demolished) were the first statement in what we may call the 'South Kensington style'. In a succession of important buildings on the estate, Fowke and Sykes, working with Cole, developed the style with originality and vigour. Fowke designed the temporary buildings for the Exhibition of 1862 and the first permanent buildings of the South Kensington (now the Victoria and Albert) Museum. He went on to design what is now called the Huxley Building in Exhibition Road and, finally, the Albert Hall in 1867–71. He died, however, in 1865 and although the Hall follows his design, the structure, with its great iron roof was the work of another sapper, Henry Scott.

Victoria and Albert Museum, South Kensington, London. Aston Webb's new building, begun in 1899.

  The antecedents of the 'South Kensington style' are German, of the school of Gottfried Semper who had enjoyed the patronage of the Prince Consort. The materials throughout are red brick and terracotta and stress is laid on the sculptural modelling of detail. Iron was also freely used and modelled in the same spirit. The collaboration of Fowke and Sykes is best seen today in the quadrangle of the Victoria and Albert Museum.

  But the South Kensington story does not end with Fowke. Just before he died he was awarded the commission for a huge building on the 1862 Exhibition site to contain a Museum of Natural History and a Museum of Patents. After his death this design was taken over by Alfred Waterhouse, reduced in size and remodelled as a Natural History Museum in a style which takes something from Fowke and fuses it with Waterhouse's version of German Romanesque. Waterhouse, following Fowke, adopted terracotta, using it, however, much more extensively, and between 1877 and 1908 produced the Natural History Museum as we know it today. It is one of the outstanding creations of the period, rational, hard-headed but not without artistic flair in the detail. The next phase of South Kensington architecture was very different. A competition for the completion of the Museum of Art, now the Victoria and Albert Museum, was held in 1891. Alfred Waterhouse

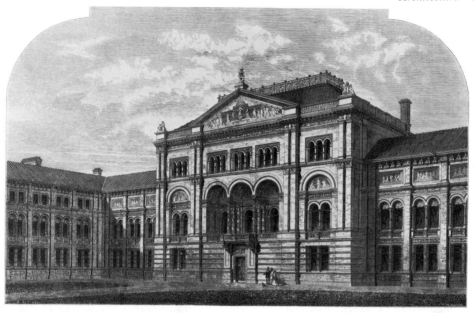

Central portion of the 'South Kensington Museum' (1866); later to become the Victoria and Albert Museum. Francis Fowke, architect, with ornament modelled by Godfrey Sykes.

Central hall, Natural History Museum, South Kensington, London (1873–81). Alfred Waterhouse.

was the assessor but the design by Aston Webb to which he awarded the prize departed from the South Kensington tradition in every respect and inaugurated the reign of Edward VII with a grandiose Renaissance flourish.

Three Gothic architects

Our Gothic Revival was peculiarly English. Other European countries did indeed build modern Gothic buildings and restore their cathedrals with antiquarian zeal, but only in England did a whole generation of architects tear up its classical roots and dedicate itself to the revival and reinterpretation of medieval styles. Why did this happen? It may have had something to do with the strong antiquarian interests, coloured by romantic patriotism, of the late Georgians. It certainly had something to do with the mass of topographical writing and pictorial description characteristic of the age of Sir Walter Scott. More narrowly it owed a strong debt to the two Pugins, father and son: the former the first to publish geometrically exact details of Gothic buildings, the latter a genius who caught the spirit and mastered the techniques of the Middle Ages to the extent that everything from his pencil had the exact and perfect accent of the Gothic.

Pugin's early death in 1852 left his followers standing on their own. Each had to crystallise his own attitude to the Revival's future. No natural leader emerged and between 1852 and 1870 about half a dozen architects made great reputations as builders in Gothic. The only way to understand the Revival is to look at each of these innovating masters separately. I shall here discuss only three, all born before 1820: Scott, Butterfield and Pearson.

We start with George Gilbert Scott, born in 1811. He was the oldest and, from a worldly point of view, the most successful of the three. He conducted a huge practice and built some of the most conspicuous public works of his time. His early arrival on the scene meant, however, that he had one foot in the Georgian world and it was only when he was thirty that the Gothic mania claimed him. He never had quite the same sense of dedication as his younger contemporaries.

Scott built more than 140 churches. He generally adopted what was called the 'Middle Pointed' (or 'English Decorated') style. To this he added a few idiosyncratic touches, notably in the stylised foliage of his capitals and the occasional admission of elements from French Gothic. A Scott church can usually be recognised as such. He had curiously little feeling for plain walling; he thought in terms of enriched openings and was prone to put just a little more carved and moulded work into the design than was necessary to strike the authentic 'Middle Pointed' note. This gives his work a rather artificial and showy look. Nevertheless, Scott's churches, when he had money to spend, are never uninteresting (when he had not, they are sadly dull). His own favourite was All Souls, Haley Hill, Halifax (1855–9) whose steeple is the chief architectural glory of that Yorkshire town. In London, St Matthias, Richmond (1856–8) and St Mary Abbots, Kensington (1872–3; steeple by his son, Oldrid) are his best; Ranmore Church, Wotton, Surrey (1859) with its

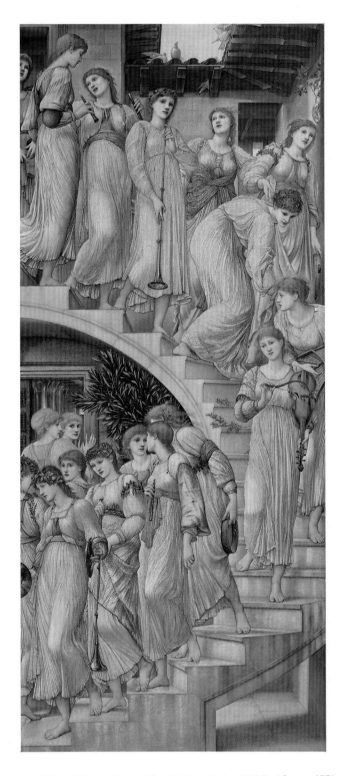

1. Edward Burne-Jones, The Golden Stairs *(1880). (See p .177)*

2. *Hubert von Herkomer*, The Queen on Her Deathbed *(1901). (See p.163)*

3. *John Everett Millais*, Ophelia *(1852). (See p.163)*

4. *George Frederic Watts,* The Sower of the Systems *(1902). (See p.194)*

5. *James McNeill Whistler,* Nocturne in Black and Gold: The Falling Rocket *(1877). (See p.175)*

6. *William Dyce*, Pegwell Bay, Kent *(1859)*. *(See p.189)*

7. *William Holman Hunt*, The Scapegoat *(1856)*. *(See p.182)*

8. *Brooch by C.R. Ashbee (1903). (See p.252)*

9. *Pottery by William De Morgan* (c.1900). *(See p.248)*

10. Sideboard by Philip Webb for Morris, Marshall, Faulkner & Co. (c.1862). (See p.244)

11. E.A.Hornel, Summer *(1891). (See p.221)*

octagonal central tower is an original and spirited creation, this time in 'Early English'.

But Scott is remembered today less for his churches than for his public buildings. For these there was often no obvious medieval precedent, at least in England, and he cast his eyes over the resources of France, Flanders and Italy. The Cloth Hall at Ypres was one useful source and Italy supplied Gothic equivalents for the classical cornice, as well as the triangular gable and the pillar mullion. His competition design for the War Office of 1856, so unkindly blasted by Palmerston, made great play with these things and when he came to design the huge hotel at St Pancras for the Midland Railway Company (1868–74) he brought the mixture to a new pitch of affluence, adding a Flemish town-hall gable over the entrance front at one end and a spired clock-tower on the 'Big Ben' model at the other. As a whole it is a preposterous piece of stylistic showmanship but there are some good passages of design, notably the hotel entrance porch and the gabled front of the hotel staircase in Midland Road. The staircase itself is a tour de force in Gothicised classic.

The other great challenge to Scott's abilities as a public architect was the Albert Memorial in Kensington Gardens (1864–71). Scott's idea was to enlarge a medieval type of jewelled ciborium (in itself a small canopied shrine) to the scale appropriate to the setting of a colossal statue. The result is impressive in scale and silhouette, as well as in the unseen infrastructure which carries the load. The mixture of materials – polished granite, white marble, Portland stone, bronze and mosaic – intended to convey, in large, the jewelled effect of the original source is perhaps less successful. Queen Victoria liked it, however, and Scott was knighted in 1872. He died in 1878 and was buried in Westminster Abbey.

Scott was the great restorer. He restored Westminster Abbey, sixteen cathedrals and over 300 churches. His approach to restoration has been much criticised, often unfairly. Compared with earlier restorers, he was scholarly and conservative. But he was essentially a practical architect and saw his duty to an old church as two-fold: first to secure the structure, second to leave the church as an orderly and consistent whole, appropriate to modern Anglican worship. Ruskin in the *Seven Lamps* had taken a quite contrary view: *all* restoration was *wrong*; ancient buildings should be propped and patched, further decay resisted and that was all. In the light of this ultra-romantic philosophy Scott was a vandal; he scraped shabby old plaster off old walls, replaced weathered masonry with new and removed fittings of later periods which he thought inappropriate. So strong was the feeling against Scott's methods that a society was formed to resist them. When William Morris founded the Society for the Protection of Ancient Buildings in 1877, the main idea was not so much to save them from demolition but to save them from Sir Gilbert Scott. The Society (commonly known as 'anti-scrape') still flourishes and a modified version of the Ruskin philosophies is today the established principle.

Born three years later than Scott was an architect of very different calibre, William Butterfield (1814–1900). His career runs parallel with Scott's and he

The former Midland Grand Hotel, St Pancras Station, London (1868–74). George Gilbert Scott.

was even more deeply absorbed in Gothic church-building. He built rather
fewer, however (about seventy, including collegiate and domestic chapels),
and ran quite a small office. He was a severe and withdrawn personality and,
unlike Scott, had no desire for public acclaim. Scott was a family man,
Butterfield a bachelor. Scott was an evangelical, Butterfield high church.
Scott's churches are conventional, Butterfield's outrageously unconventional.
His style is arresting, often alarmingly so; a streak of sheer ugliness is
indisputably present. He puzzled his contemporaries and he puzzles us today.

His first important church was All Saints, Margaret Street, London, begun
in 1849 on the invitation and largely at the expense of the high church leader,
Alexander Beresford-Hope. But its building-history was chequered and it was
not consecrated till 1859, by which time 'Mr. Hope's church' had become
one of the curiosities of London architecture. If we are to understand
Butterfield we must try to understand All Saints.

Butterfield's work there consists of the Church itself, a clergy-house and a
school, built on a very cramped site round three sides of a tiny court-yard,
the church occupying the whole of the side furthest from the street. Along
the street is a dwarf wall rising to left and right in a gabled archway and
originally supporting a wrought-iron screen (disposed of as 'salvage' during
the war). The group is built almost entirely of red and black brick, stone
being used for window tracery and for one other feature – an enormous
pinnacle mounted on a brick buttress. This is the most arresting feature in
the group. The lower part is carved with a relief of the Annunciation; the
upper part turns into a colonetted spirelet with, at the point, a wrought-iron
cross, bringing the whole some fifty feet from the ground. Filling the south-
west corner of the church is the base of the tower. This rises to a bell-stage
and is then neatly joined to a grey-slated spire, not in the familiar English
'broach' style (where a square-based pyramid penetrates an octagonal one)
but simply by a splayed cube carrying an octagonal pyramid – a most original
and elegant form.

The presence of the tower and spire, not at first apprehended from the
narrow street, may explain the presence of the pinnacle. The one is assisted
by the other, 'conspiring' in a most literal sense to established a dramatic
impression of ascent, strongly reinforced by the sharp, unmodulated edges of
school and clergy-house. But then this rocketing surge is scored across by the
double courses of black bricks built into the red walls and forcing their way
round the whole group, including the tower, and echoed in the slated spire –
everywhere, in fact, except the pale, virginal, pinnacle of the Annunciation.
Even cloaked as it is with London grime, the black brick running against the
rose-red structure creates a wonderful intensity. When it was new it must
have been an astonishing sight.

Entering the Church we find a short three-bay nave, clustered granite
columns with caps of the boldest stiff-leaf and arches so wide and high that
they make the church seem like a telescoped version of something much
larger. The proportions are strange and if you were expecting something on
the model of the typical English parish church you could be forgiven for
thinking them perverse. Yet English it is in its parts if not in the whole; all
the traceries and mouldings are from recognisable homeland sources. What is

not English is the dazzling over-lay of tiles and marble mosaic which is sometimes recognisably Venetian and sometimes quite simply Butterfield enjoying himself with the rather ferocious polychrome pattern-making for which he is mostly remembered. The whole assemblage, inside and out, is an exciting and moving architectural experience with an unmistakable sense of dedication.

No other Butterfield church is quite like All Saints. But many contain similar gestures of disjuncture in style and strange proportions. Reviewing his

All Saints Church, Margaret Street, London, from south-east (1849–59). William Butterfield.

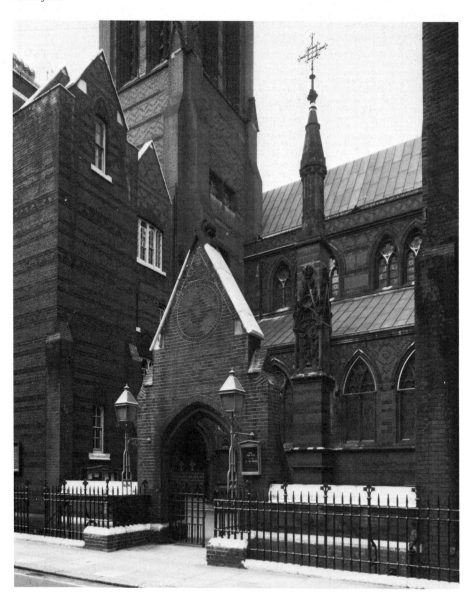

Interior of William Butterfield's All Saints Church.

work one sometimes gets the feeling that there were not one but two
Butterfields, doing the same job but doing it without mutual confidence and
for at least part of the time at loggerheads. One of the Butterfields is a happy
man who enjoys the simple pleasures of geometrical play and bright colours.
The other Butterfield is a severe antiquarian: calling his colleague to order
and quoting medieval precedent. Sometimes the two Butterfields fuse into
passionate unity. They do so in some of his village churches, in the new
buildings at Rugby School, in some smaller works such as fonts and pulpits,
but most of all perhaps in Keble College, Oxford, whose chapel was built at
the height of the architect's career in the seventies. This is a building that
really lifts the heart. Externally, the whole mass is divided, horizontally and
vertically, in almost (but not quite) classical ratios, with rich but disciplined
diapers bringing the sheer brick walls to life. The interior is breathtaking. It
reflects, perhaps, the Upper Church at Assissi, but the handling is wholly
Butterfieldian with the 'happy' Butterfield predominating. All the details are
large and bold. The mixed materials – stone, brick and various marbles – are

Keble College Chapel, Oxford (1868–82). William Butterfield.

combined with powerful effect. The total impression is a blaze of happy invention, a hymn of praise. If All Saints, Margaret Street is Butterfield's *Magnificat*, Keble College is his *Te Deum*.

The case of John Loughborough Pearson (1817–97) is as different from that of Butterfield as his from Scott's. Pearson was modestly industrious, not flagrantly ambitious or deeply enigmatic. His output was considerable but not spectacular (he built seventy-five new churches). He was in no way eccentric either in his life or his art. There is a normality about Pearson reflected in his work, and it is no surprise to learn from his biographer that, whether by intuition or by calculation, his proportions tend to be governed by the 'Golden Section', that ratio of part to part which is found in natural growth and in classical art. None of this necessarily makes Pearson an interesting architect. But with his sense of discipline went power of invention of a high order.

   Like all the Gothic men of his generation, he started where Pugin left off, and his first churches, in Yorkshire, could almost be by Pugin himself. Having seen something of French Gothic he caught the fashion for 'early French', and developed a sense of mass with details vigorously modelled. But this passed and carved and moulded detail was never to be one of Pearson's strong points. He contented himself with the conventional syntax of thirteenth-century England and Normandy. What increasingly absorbed him was *vaulted space*.

It was in 1859 that a specially interesting church commission turned him in this direction. As with so many of the more inspired churches of the time, it was to be built in a slum. A philanthropic clergyman in Lambeth was founding what we should call a 'social centre', to consist of schools for children and apprentices, a master's house, an art school and a soup kitchen. The teaching had a religious base and it was the founder's ambition to consummate the scheme with an impressive, dominating church. Pearson's first design was too costly. In the executed version he stuck to the plan but reduced the superstructure to bare essentials. St Peter's, Vauxhall, as the church is called, still stands. Towards the street the Church shows a 'west' front with a narthex (or full-width vestibule) clipped on to a trio of heavy buttresses, a rose window above and a turret on one corner. The interior moves from this grim overture to something magnificent. A five-bay nave of rather low arches leads to an apsidal chancel; above the arcades is a mass of plain wall and above this a clerestory. But the glory of the Church is the vault, springing from shafts between the clerestory windows. It is of brick with stone ribs, runs the whole length of the nave and radiates gracefully as it turns in the apse. No Victorian church had yet attempted so complete a realisation of the Gothic principle.

After Vauxhall, Pearson thought of brick and stone vaulting almost as the sine qua non of a successful Gothic church. He thought out his plans in terms of vaulted space and where money would not run to a vault his not very original carpentry reads like an apology. But a vault there nearly always is.

Finished in 1864, Vauxhall established Pearson as one of the leading Gothic men but it was not till 1870 that another great London opportunity confirmed his pre-eminence. In the rapidly developing middle-class London suburb of Kilburn, a group of high churchmen seceded from the congregation of the parish church and, led by an ambitious Tractarian curate, formed a new district and erected a temporary iron tabernacle, to be replaced when means became available by a permanent church. This was begun in 1870 and the spire completed just before the architect's death in 1897.

The spire is the highest in London and the tower and west end make altogether a stunning composition; but to understand this church we must start from inside. Entering from the west we are at once aware of a continuous vaulted space, ten bays long and very high. We then notice that there are two arcades, one above the other. The lower arcade supports a gallery. The upper arcade rises from the gallery into the vault. The lower arcade opens into the aisles; the upper arcade opens into compartmented recesses running back to the outer wall of the church. Nearly all the light in the church comes from the wide, deep lancets in these recesses, so that although the church is brilliantly lit it is also indirectly lit. The arrangement, with its sense of serenity and repose, was not Pearson's invention. He found it at Albi in southern France which he knew, at least from photographs. Structurally, it is simply a matter of bringing the buttresses which a vault requires *inside* the church instead of letting them project outside. It is these internal buttresses which separate the bays of the upper arcade and produce the compartments. Pearson's handling of this theme is delicate and precise,

St Augustine's Church, Kilburn, London (1870–80); view from west, and interior. John Loughborough Pearson.

his rather thin, crisp 'Early English' detail defining the various structural elements with sober elegance.

Pearson built four other magnificently vaulted churches in London: St John, Red Lion Square (1874–8; destroyed in the war); St John, Upper Norwood (1878–82); St Michael, Croydon (1880–1); and the Apostolic Church, Maida Avenue (1891–3). In 1878 he was selected to design the Cathedral for the lately recreated diocese of Truro and this was to be by far his biggest work. Bishop Benson had set his heart on a Gothic building which should be the equal in all essentials of the great English cathedrals of the past and set an instant episcopal seal on the modest market town of Truro. This is exactly what Pearson's cathedral does. Seen from the railway its clustering towers at once convey the 'cathedral' message. On close acquaintance it is still 'venerable' in aspect, though its impeccable purity of style, clean as a new pin, induces a slight sense of disappointment. How could the architect of St Augustine's, Kilburn, so completely bottle up his invention and deflate his genius? The answer quite simply is in Pearson's innate modesty and in the depth of his respect for the thirteenth-century masters of England and Normandy.

Pearson died in 1897, by which time the eastern part of the Cathedral was finished and the nave foundations laid. It was only in 1903 that the central tower was raised, the west towers following in 1910. By that date the Revival of Gothic architecture was seen by many as one of the more questionable adventures of their Victorian grandfathers. But Pearson's work never suffered the ridicule and revulsion heaped against Scott and Butterfield. The grace and elegance of his vaults and the almost classical 'normality' of his designs secured him a safe passage through the hurricanes of reaction.

Richard Norman Shaw

Never since Sir Christopher Wren was English architecture so nearly
dominated by one man as it was by Norman Shaw (1831–1912) between 1870
and his death. Robert Adam, to be sure had, in his day, swept all before him
in the decorative arts, but his day was short. After him, Nash's reign was
never absolute: there was always the envious Soane lurking in the wings. In
the next century Gilbert Scott was the most conspicuous of the Gothic
Revivalists but he was never their leader; every Goth paddled his own canoe.
But Shaw rose to a position of authority early and retained it without
argument or challenge for forty years; his influence was irresistible. How did
this come about? That was a question asked by Professor Beresford Pite in a
lecture he gave in 1900 on tendencies in English architecture. Of Shaw he
said,

Why and how does this genius charm? Is it the man rather than the work? The artist-
architect or the architect-builder? Is the spirit of his work modern . . . a living
actuality, typical of our attainment in life and art?.

Even today, these questions are not easy to answer. Personality was
certainly a prime factor in Shaw's success. He brought sunshine into the
architect's office just when it was needed; when young architects were
becoming restless under the heavy seriousness of the High Victorian masters
and when some kind of stylistic break-away had become inevitable. Shaw
enjoyed the practice of architecture and saw to it that the people around him
and the people he served enjoyed it too. 'Life in Shaw's office', said Lethaby,
looking back on the eighties, 'was one long party.' His pupils loved him and
he in turn trusted the best of them by putting some designing in their hands.
His clients became at once his personal friends and, more than that,
colleagues sharing the quest for the right answers to their needs. Shaw was
striking in person, devoid of conceit, a self-confessed non-intellectual who
wrote enchantingly funny letters to his friends. He was a devout churchman
in a private way.

Having said all this, we need to ask: was Norman Shaw a great architect?
Not, I think, in the sense of having achieved buildings of overwhelming
beauty or deep imaginative insight. It would be difficult to name a Shaw
building to rank with Wren for classic serenity, with Vanbrugh for emotional
depth or, one might even say, with Mackintosh for invention. He was not a
spiritual architect; he was too much of the world, worldly, and sometimes
even rather irresponsible in the way he handled the heritage of history. He
was a man of his time and when Pite asks if the spirit of his work was 'a
living actuality, typical of our attainment in life and art', he really answers
his own question. It was.

Shaw was born in Edinburgh in 1831 of mixed Irish and Scottish descent.
He came to London and was articled to the ducally patronised William Burn.
After a period of travel he entered the office of George Edmund Street in
1859, following Philip Webb as Street's head man. He was on his own from
1864. In 1866 he built a church at Bingley, Yorkshire, in the Streetian style
and of the finest quality (it was demolished after a structural failure, in 1974),
but his early works were nearly all country houses and it was in these that his
first style developed.

This style was what he called 'Old English' and this needs explaining. 'Old English' was a way of describing ancient architecture which had picturesque appeal but could not necessarily be assigned to any precise style or period. It was a patchwork. Typically it could be a farmhouse which had started life as a Gothic hall, had been equipped with a massive chimney in Tudor times, re-roofed under the Stuarts and partly tile-hung under the Georgians. Such a building, with all its accidentals, had had an appeal to painters since Gainsborough. To architects of the Pugin school it was mongrel stuff, not for imitation. Shaw however, accepted the artistic totality, as found, and absorbed it into this vocabulary. Hence the stone, brick, timber and tile-hung houses, like Leyswood (demolished) and Glen Andred, built in Sussex in the sixties. Hence also the transformation of Sir William Armstrong's hunting lodge at Cragside, Northumberland, into a fantastical, almost Bavarian vision of towers, gables and chimneys rising and spreading on the crag which gives the house its name. A house like this, built and extended over a period of years (1869–85) necessarily rambles. But few of Shaw's plans are 'compact'. He used space in the leisurely expansive way which his clients expected and enjoyed. And with such planning goes the dramatic counterpoint of his massive tile roofs and soaring chimney stacks.

Shaw was building 'Old English' country houses all through the seventies. In London he had different problems, and at least two different styles. In 1871 an office building was required for the shipping firm of Shaw Savill, in which his brother was a partner, in Leadenhall Street. It was to be called New Zealand Chambers. The company's own offices were to face the street;

Cragside, Northumberland (1869–85). Norman Shaw.

the rest of the deep site was to go for lettable offices. How was the street front of the building to express itself? 'Old English' would hardly do in the mainly Italian Renaissance context of the city. Why not go instead to the *English* Renaissance and the kind of thing which London merchants were building before the Great Fire? This meant reviving a coarse and florid vernacular which had long ago been written off as 'debased'. Shaw did this and did it in style, with tiered windows of a mid-seventeenth century type (mullion and transome, with an arched centre light) between plain brick piers and masses of plaster ornament. It was found extremely shocking, but it was not forgotten. Ten years after it was built, so Blomfield informs us, 'people were not quite sure whether they should regard the building as a freak or a work of genius'. But it was a long time before they stopped imitating it. Unhappily, New Zealand Chambers vanished in the 'blitz'.

New Zealand Chambers, Leadenhall Street, London (1871), now demolished. Norman Shaw.

In 1872 London offered another problem, this time grandly domestic. The rich diplomat MP, William Lowther, wanted a London house. Not however the usual London type in a street or a square; something more like a country house, but dressed for fashionable London life. Here, as in the city, 'Old English' would be altogether too quaint and at this point Shaw turned to 'Queen Anne'. The new style was just coming over the horizon, with J.J. Stevenson's 'Red House' in Bayswater Road (1871) and the first of E.R. Robson's Board Schools. Shaw went a long way ahead of these in sheer inventiveness, building the curious and entertaining building in Kensington Gore which is now the home of the Royal Geographical Society.

At Lowther Lodge, some very odd things happen. The oddest, perhaps, is the way the first-floor windows in the entrance front marry with the dormers in the roof, showing their way through the heavy coved cornice. There are other strange gambits and the ribbed chimney stacks grow to preposterous heights. The ornaments, beautifully executed in cut brick, are what must vaguely be called Renaissance. There is no question that Lowther Lodge is a fascinating composition; after 120 years it still sparkles with fun and teases the eye and nobody quite knows what it is all about.

By 1880, Shaw was becoming as active in town-house building as he had been (and still was) in country work. He built some twenty houses in London and most of them still stand, though converted as flats and the planning consequently spoilt.

One of the first and most interesting was his own house, now numbered 4 in Ellerdale Road, Hampstead, begun in 1874. Built on sloping ground, of narrow red bricks, it rises high and is almost bleak. Two vertical tiers of bay-windows project towards the road and between them is a scatter of variously shaped windows whose irregularity seems to suggest that the inside of the house controls all. The interior confirms this. A broad panelled staircase faces you as you enter and turns right to reach the main floor. To the right of you now is the backdrawing-room, a low-ceiled room with some Queen Anne-ish joinery and an imported eighteenth-century chimney piece. To the left is the dining-room, square and nearly twice the height of the drawing-room, panelled half way up, with tapestry above, then a typical Shaw ceiling of moulded and varnished joists. Over the fire-place in this room is the architect's 'den', approached by a hidden stair. The 'den' projects into the room, the space below making an ingle-nook. A little casement in the 'den' allows its occupant to communicate with people in the dining-room. Opposite this a tiny bay-window looks out towards London. Here Shaw struck out the first designs for many of his later works. In 1885–6 he added a grand new entertaining room at the back, with an ante-room, connecting with the old drawing-room, making an informal, irregularly lit vista of nearly seventy feet. The house has been sadly altered but its loose unselfconscious plan and its happy spatial organisation exactly reflect the personality of its builder.

Shaw's London houses display him as a witty and resourceful planner and a rash and humorous mixer of styles. Tudor, Flemish, Dutch and Queen Anne (to say nothing of 'Queen Anne') play together, sometimes affecting a severe discipline, as in 196 Queen's Gate (1874–6) and Swan House, 17 Chelsea Embankment (1875–7), both early in the series; sometimes wickedly

Norman Shaw's own house, Hampstead, London (begun 1874).

casual, with windows appearing in odd places, like the (demolished) 180 Queen's Gate (1883–5) or Kate Greenaway's tile-hung cottagey house, 39 Frognal, Hampstead (1884–5). At 170 Queen's Gate (1888–90) comes a surprise: a square-cut, dead-pan, sash-windowed classical mass which one might almost date to the reign of Anne herself, with a Wren-style door-case and, inside, a domed hall. This looks like a turning point and so it was.

Between 1886 and 1890 the Shaw style swung round to a full acceptance of the classical. In 1886 Shaw designed the police headquarters on the Victoria Embankment – New Scotland Yard (now government offices, known as 'Norman Shaw North'). Here he is still juggling with styles. The inspiration is from Azay-le-Rideau on the Loire, with its unforgettable *tourelles*, but the fenestration is Wren-like and when the client found the capacity of the first design too restricted Shaw added a high roof with massive Dutch gables, making in all a hazardous agglomerate which nevertheless succeeds by the sheer intuitive magic which so intrigued Beresford Pite. Then comes the almost pure eighteenth-century manner at 170 Queen's Gate and although this was, as it happened, the stylistic choice of the client rather than the architect it seems to have opened the way to all the classicism which followed – Bryanston, Dorset, the very grand house, now a school, for Viscount Portman, based mainly on Pratt's seventeenth-century masterpiece, Coleshill, Warwickshire; another great house in Northumberland, an insurance office in London, a bank in Liverpool and finally the monumental contributions to the London scene leading to the new Quadrant and the Piccadilly Hotel. We call all this 'classicism' and we call it 'Baroque' but it is not quite either. It is simply old Shaw at play with new, extravagant games whose rules he had never learned. It still contains much of the careless rapture of 'Queen Anne' and even (in the gable of the Piccadilly Hotel for example) a tiny trace of Old English.

Shaw died in 1912 leaving behind not only a formidable output of nearly 200 buildings but a school of architects mainly consisting of his pupils and assistants. W.R. Lethaby, Mervyn Macartney, Ernest Newton and E.S. Prior had all been in his office and constituted the Shaw 'family'. Reginald Blomfield (1856–1942) and E.L. Lutyens (1869–1944) were outsiders but no less deeply influenced by the man and his work. Lutyens said of him in 1901: 'I believe Norman Shaw is a really great and capable designer, one of the first water, I put him with Wren.' That, perhaps was going rather far, but not by so very much.

The nineties

The last decade of the nineteenth century was one of the most creative and complex in European architectural history, not least so in Britain, and it may be worth attempting here an elementary analysis of what was going on in those years and to distinguish the main threads in the tangle. The first thread is Ruskin; not the man himself, who by 1890 was sheltering in his melancholy retreat at Brantwood, but his books and, even more than his books, his disciples; and among the latter principally Philip Webb.

Philip Webb's position in English architecture and his long-term influence are curious and must be given a retrospective glance. Born in the same year as Norman Shaw and his predecessor as Street's head man, he was in almost every way the reverse of Shaw. Where Shaw was outgoing and sociable, Webb was private and reclusive. He had a small office in Gray's Inn and prepared all his drawings himself. He never exhibited at the Royal Academy or allowed his works to be illustrated in the professional press. He published no books. His influence radiated through friendships, through conversation and through example. He built four houses in London and eight in the country. His clients had to be acceptable to his way of thinking; and, notwithstanding Webb's strongly socialist views, they also had to be rich.

Ruskin had given architecture a conscience. Not every architect was moved by this fact, but for Webb it was the mainspring of his work. The Gothic Revival he believed was a misguided adventure; the literal antiquarian imitation of Gothic missed the whole essence of the Ruskinian philosophy. Architecture must be an affair of good building practice and good craftsmanship based on tradition and independent of 'style'. After having served as Street's chief assistant, Webb set up on his own in 1859. His first work was to be the 'Red House' at Bexley Heath, Kent, for his friend William Morris. The 'Red House' is a studiously simple red-brick building on an L-shaped plan with a steep tiled roof. Pointed arches, flat-topped windows with sliding sashes, circular, segmental and other types were introduced where they seemed appropriate. No specific 'stylistic' reference can anywhere be detected. Even the drawing-room fireplace was naked red brick and the interiors of the house were to be enriched, not by conventional architectural ornaments, but by the hands of Morris and his fellow artists, Burne-Jones and Rossetti. Webb's later houses do not have the same reticence. Their exteriors are not lacking in architectural ornament but it is of a kind gathered not from acknowledged masterpieces of the past but from the English vernaculars of various periods. The ornaments were made from Webb's drawings and embodied only marginally the initiative of the operative craftsman. The fact is, of course, that the artisan capable of original design no longer existed: he had been bred out of the building trade in the eighteenth century. Webb's ornaments came from his own observations of old work, strongly modified in his imagination. The total results are sometimes picturesquely charming but at others gauche and incoherent. It is easy to sympathise with Norman Shaw's estimate of Webb: 'a very able man indeed but with a strong liking for the ugly'.

Shaw's respect for Webb's work was, nevertheless, genuine and he even sometimes borrowed from him. The pupils and assistants in his office were also drawn to Webb, especially William Richard Lethaby (1857–1931), Shaw's chief assistant from 1879 to 1891. Lethaby's loyalties were divided between Shaw and Webb, with a strong affection for Shaw as a man, but a stronger leaning towards Webb as a philosopher. Lethaby and a small group of Shaw's circle liked to think of themselves as the Shaw 'family' and Pite, in the lecture already quoted, considered them to be the most promising element in English architecture as it entered the new century. The 'family' did not imitate Shaw; they were a group of liberated young men, each of whom chose his own intellectual or emotional directive in the nineties. Lethaby's few buildings sail very close to the Ruskin–Webb ideal which he promoted in his lectures and books. Reginald Blomfield, on the other hand, took off from Shaw's late classicism and developed a line in French classicism of the eighteenth century, while Ernest Newton built country houses in an amiable blend of Tudor, Stuart and Georgian. E.S. Prior stood somewhere between Webb and Lethaby and built a church (St Andrew, Roker, Northumberland) on Gothic principles but omitting nearly all the Gothic ornaments.

Outside the Shaw 'family' was a whole constellation of able architects, mostly born in the fifties and making their own interpretation of the Ruskin–Webb philosophy. Perhaps the most important and certainly the best known today was C.F.A. Voysey (1857–1941). The son of an unorthodox clergyman he was, in his quiet way, a totally unorthodox architect. He created a type of house, immediately recognisable by its long, low disposition, its low-ceiled rooms, its unmoulded mullions and transoms, and its sloping buttresses placed to strengthen the walls at strategic points. Voysey's houses

Architect's drawing for a house at Gartmel Fell, Windermere (1895). C.F.A. Voysey.

have the puritan simplicity of Webb's 'Red House' without the sense of
challenge and with a 'cottagey' appeal which, nevertheless, did not prevent
his plans from embracing very ample accommodation.

Another outsider making his own way in the nineties was C. Harrison
Townsend (1851–1928), whose most significant buildings are the Bishopsgate
Institute, the Whitechapel Art Gallery and the Horniman Museum, all in
London. The interiors of these buildings are nothing much but the exteriors
attempt a new stylistic approach combining local influences with something
of the American, H.H. Richardson. Other exciting departures in the nineties
were Smith and Brewer's Mary Ward Settlement in Woburn Place; Baillie
Scott's early work in the Isle of Man; C.R. Ashbee's houses in Chelsea; and,
most exciting of all, Charles Rennie Mackintosh's Glasgow Art School.
Begun in 1896, this latter was not finished till 1909 (see also Chapter 7).

Meanwhile the Gothic Revival never quite extinguished itself, and the
greatest church of the nineties in England, the Westminster Roman Catholic
Cathedral, is essentially the work of a Gothic revivalist. The fact that
Cardinal Bourne insisted on his architect adopting a style associated with the
earlier Christian centuries made it necessary for John Francis Bentley
(1839–1902) to tour Italy and investigate the Byzantine style from books
(chiefly Lethaby's study of Santa Sophia). But the Cathedral is not, as is often
supposed, Byzantine; its general conception is that of an aisled church, with
low galleries threading through high arches carrying a vault – the principle
which Pearson had adopted at Kilburn, the main difference being that at
Westminster the arches are not pointed but semi-circular and the vault
consists of a series of saucer domes. This grandly simple carcase Bentley
clothed in a stylistic garment which fuses Byzantine and Renaissance with
consummate skill. The modelling of the high, slim tower – an inspiration
from Sienna – is a superlative performance. But Lethaby, while admiring
Bentley's skill, took the radical view that only the unadorned brick structure

Horniman Museum, Forest Hill, London (1902). C. Harrison Townsend.

was true architecture; the Cathedral would have been better without the 'style'. The interior, still today a bare brick-work carcase without the intended marble revetment, makes Lethaby's point with impressive solemnity.

Side by side with the radicals and Gothic revisionists were those who turned to a whole-hearted revival of the classical. A leader of this school was John Belcher (1841–1913) who spent five years study in France and, with his two successive partners, Beresford Pite and J.J. Joass, broke completely free from insular tradition. His revolutionary Chartered Accountants Hall in the City (1893), in which Pite had a hand, is a Baroque fusion of architecture and sculpture of great brilliance. In 1897, with Joass's assistance, he built the dramatically eloquent town-hall at Colchester, inspired by Bérard and Delmar's Palais des Beaux-Arts at Lille and with an exciting, if rather feverishly modelled tower. After buildings such as these there seemed no direction in which an English architect might not venture to try his hand.

By 1900, Victorianism was dead and buried. The Queen herself died in 1901. John Ruskin had died in the previous year and estimation of his

Westminster Roman Catholic Cathedral, London (1895–1903). John Francis Bentley.

writings was soon to go sharply into decline. Nevertheless, the radical element in English architecture was not so easily extinguished. Sustained in England by Lethaby's teaching and writing, its effective future lay within Europe. In the early 1900s, English architecture was discovered in Germany. Hermann Muthesius brought out his book on English church architecture in 1901, to be followed three years later by his three-volume treatise, *The English House*. In Vienna, Adolf Loos's philosophy, though rooted in classicism, came very close to Lethaby's and he was already

Chartered Accountants Hall, City of London (1889–93). John Belcher.

designing interiors in an English style in 1899. In Holland, Van de Velde discovered Voysey. In 1901 British architecture stood at a peak of success; it was the most promising architecture in Europe. But it was not in England that the promise matured.

Architecture, industry and commerce

What, in the architecture of the half-century with which we are concerned, does 'industry and commerce' mean? It must include factories of all kinds, textile mills, foundries, iron-works, potteries; warehouses and granaries; gas-works and water-works; railway works, stations and railway hotels. Passing to commerce it must cover banks, credit houses, the offices of insurance companies and offices for letting. And much else; in short, a whole world of building some of which had roots in the Georgian past but most of which had no roots at all and required an appropriate architectural expression ad hoc.

The early Victorian factory was often no more than a stark aggregate of brick sheds, brought together as the company's business grew. A successful company might, in due course, decide to rebuild and to bring in an architect to provide a comprehensive design. The factories and mills of the 1820s, 30s and 40s which so impressed and disturbed foreigners by their colossal scale and terrifying monotony were rarely architects' work. They were built by contractors with the advice of engineers specialising in that vital consideration, fire-proof construction. The architect came in only when the industrialist began to see himself as an acceptable public figure, a benefactor to society and just possibly a philanthropist. Architecture was a way of claiming prestige for the business and its master.

Opportunities for architectural display asserted themselves less in factories than in warehouses, especially when these were in the commercial areas of cities. The monster textile mills required correspondingly huge warehouses providing accommodation for finishing processes, show-rooms, packaging rooms, counting houses and virtually unlimited storage space. These warehouses commonly went up five or six storeys and required to be lit from close-spaced, remorselessly identical windows. There were no precedents for such buildings and they invited a kind of original thought which did not run in the heads of Royal Academicians nor indeed in those of the average members of the Institute of British Architects. In the fifties the problem was tackled, not without success, by architects who never became household names outside their own localities but who did achieve industrial buildings of considerable nobility.

Manchester led the way. In 1845 Edward Walters, a Londoner who, on Richard Cobden's advice, had set up practice in Manchester, built the Schwabe warehouse in Mosley Street, in an Italian style deriving from the London clubs of Sir Charles Barry. It was succeeded by other warehouses in that style and a school of young Manchester architects was soon following Walters's lead. They succeeded, to a remarkable degree, in re-deploying the elements of *cinquecento* palaces to achieve results which critics were able to acclaim as both good sense and good taste. Through the sixties and seventies 'Italianate' (a useful word for this free handling of the style) warehouse architecture flourished. Stone, brought by rail from Derbyshire, replaced brick as the facing material. The most magnificent warehouse of all was that of S. and J. Watts, designed by Travis and Magnall, 1856–8. Each of its storeys has a different treatment but they add up triumphantly. No longer a warehouse, it has now been successfully converted into an hotel.

In Yorkshire, the worsted mill owners followed Manchester's lead. Bradford's Italianate warehouses, black as soot, are still an impressive spectacle. Here the architects Lockwood and Mawson had a virtual monopoly and it was they who designed Saltaire, the industrial village on the outskirts of Bradford, created by Sir Titus Salt for the weaving of alpaca in 1854. The factory itself, covering five and a half acres, dominated the village. The style is Italianate, with two pretty belvederes on the skyline.

At Nottingham, centre of the lace industry, T.C. Hine was the presiding architect; his chief work, the Adams and Page warehouse in Lace Market, has the mass and outline of a French château. Bristol is a special case, where a city evolved a style of industrial architecture entirely its own. It is often loosely called 'Bristol Byzantine' and seems to have been introduced by Archibald Ponton. It is a massive round-arch style, mostly red brick, with a strong flavour of early Venetian architecture as illustrated in the *Stones of*

Granary, Welsh Back, Bristol (1873). Ponton and Gough.

Venice. The best known example is Ponton and Gough's granary in Welsh Back, built in 1873.

In London, the mid-Victorian warehouse architecture falls far short of what was achieved in the great provincial towns. Where London was pre-eminent was, of course, in the building of banks, insurance offices and office blocks. Between 1835 and 1870 the City ceased to be residential. The wealthier merchants moved to houses in Bayswater and Kensington, the clerks to new dormitory suburbs like Peckham, Fulham and Hornsey. The old houses, many of them dating from the rebuilding after the Great Fire of

1666, came down; warehouses and offices went up. The Italianate prevailed, much of it rather tame but with occasional flashes of pride and glamour.

It was the insurance companies who set the pace by announcing their presence with classical façades rich in allegorical sculpture. Most of these have disappeared but the Atlas office survives in Cheapside with a fine sculpture of Atlas carrying his load above the entrance. The Royal managed to get itself a site in Lombard Street, the privileged street of banking, in 1857 and rebuilt itself there in 1863 in the grandest style (it was the first insurance company to spend lavishly on advertising). It has gone, and so has the Crown Life whose building by Dean and Woodward (of Oxford Museum fame) in New Bridge Street brought a Ruskinian touch into London façade architecture. Its influence was widely felt before it was demolished to make way for the London and South-east coast railway in 1865, less than ten years after it was built.

The architecture of banking was more reserved and more sophisticated. The older banks had been family residences (Hoare's Bank in Fleet Street still is one), but the new joint-stock companies brought in classical monumentality. In the sixties there was an explosion of bank building in Lombard Street but none of the buildings survive. The finest surviving Victorian bank in the City is the National Provincial (now National Westminster) in Bishopsgate, built in 1866–9, saved from demolition by a

National Westminster Bank (formerly National Provincial Bank), Bishopsgate, London (1866–9). John Gibson.

planning compromise permitting the giant 'Nat West' tower to rise on the adjoining site.

Railway architecture produced some remarkable works, but by 1850 the great age of architectural railway design was nearly over. Paddington, finished in 1854, is the most interesting example in our period. The triple shed, jointly designed by Brunel and the architect Matthew Digby Wyatt, represents a conscious attempt to create an architectural style appropriate to the type of structure and the material – iron. Wyatt had been associated with the Crystal Palace as architectural supervisor. He now attempted to develop the potentialities of iron and glass in the new direction in which the Crystal Palace seemed to point, but with a more ornate character. His highly eccentric iron capitals and the not-quite-Gothic ornaments in the spandrels of Brunel's elliptical trusses are not a great success, and the Paddington sheds, in fact, mark the point at which the design of such structures was taken over entirely by engineers. The great shed at St Pancras (1868) was wholly the work of W.H. Barlow and has no stylistic insignia whatever.

Paddington station is screened by its massive hotel, the first hotel to adopt the grand manner and, indeed, the first really grand hotel in London. It has nothing in common with the station and is among the earliest attempts (1850–2) to bring a Parisian silhouette to London. The architect was P.C. Hardwick. It pioneered that major Victorian creation – the railway hotel, and was followed by the Grosvenor at Victoria (1860–1) and by the hotels at Charing Cross (1863–4), Cannon Street (1865–6) and, grandest of all, St Pancras (1868–74). Railway hotels on similar lines followed in all the provincial cities. Their importance as social centres has usually been more striking (with the exception of St Pancras) than their architectural quality.

By 1880, what we may call the 'heroic' period of Victorian industry and commerce was passing to a more stable, less innovative, condition. Factory building became an engineering rather than an architectural enterprise. The railway network was virtually complete. In London the great banks had all settled into their monumental homes and country branch banks were among the attractive building opportunities of the eighties and nineties. Urban rebuilding became largely an affair of investment in 'business premises' – shops below and lettable offices above – following the drift of style through the succession of Renaissance fashions with which the Victorian century ends.

The Parrot Walk, Regent's Park Zoological Gardens, London. Engraving by Gustave Doré (1872).

2 The Public Park

JACQUES CARRÉ

The love of gardens and gardening was one of the few tastes which many Victorians of all social conditions had in common. This unusual consensus must be related to the lingering uneasiness about the urbanisation of Britain. The environment in which the majority of British people lived in the second half of the nineteenth century was solidly architectural, and any glimpse of greenery, even in microscopic suburban gardens, was deeply enjoyed. It took some time, however, before the newly-created local authorities brought themselves to preserve existing open spaces and to create public parks. The blue books of the 1830s and 1840s had exposed the overcrowding, pollution and lack of sanitation of many large towns; but it was not until 1848 that the Public Health Act enabled municipalities to finance what were then called 'public walks'. As a consequence, the next half-century saw the laying out of one or several parks in all towns of some importance. Together with the monumental public buildings then erected, these public parks are the most spectacular manifestation of Victorian civic art.

Like buildings, however, parks have a dual significance: they may be seen as artistic forms – one may study, for example, the connection between the eighteenth-century landscape garden and the Victorian parks; and they may be assessed in social and ethical terms, as an instance of the improvement of the urban conditions under the aegis of the middle classes. I think these two approaches – aesthetic on the one hand, functional on the other – have to be combined if we wish to have a fair appreciation of these new urban spaces reserved for healthy leisure.

Although we now take for granted that public park means municipal park, it was far from being the case at the time, and it is perhaps useful to identify the various types to be found then. In the case of London, first, one has to remember that some of the new public parks such as Victoria Park, in Bethnal Green (opened 1845) and Battersea Park (opened 1857) were in fact Royal Parks. By the end of the nineteenth century, as much as a quarter of the acreage of open spaces in the County of London was Crown property. In addition, one could find among the more popular London parks some which were tended by institutions like the Zoological Society (Regent's Park Zoo), the Royal Botanic Society (Kew Gardens and Regent's Park) and the Royal Horticultural Society, which opened in Kensington in 1861 a superb garden, complete with conservatory, described by a contemporary as 'a very complete amalgamation of the French, Italian, and English schools'!

While the world of fashion flocked to Kensington to inspect this showpiece of Victorian garden-art, the ordinary Londoner would have preferred the vast and somewhat pretentious gardens laid out by Joseph Paxton (1801–65) at Sydenham in 1854, as a setting for the re-erected Crystal Palace. Such 'commercial' gardens (there were others at Walworth and Muswell Hill) were formed by private companies as more edifying versions of the old Georgian pleasure-gardens, which had all closed down, with the exception of Cremorne. At Sydenham, together with an immense terrace decorated with statues, an axial grand avenue and huge symmetrical fountains, Paxton had provided popular attractions such as a menagerie, a panorama, a bandstand and a peripheral 'jungle' featuring prehistoric animals in artificial stone. In the provinces there were no such vast commercial gardens, and to some extent the municipal parks provided the same mixture of formality and entertainment.

Engraving by Charles Daubigny (1867), inspired by Joseph Paxton's Crystal Palace Garden, Sydenham and its prehistoric animals in stone.

Whereas in London the Royal parks had been available to the public for more than two centuries, in the rest of the country public parks were a new urban feature, felt to be a major improvement of living conditions. Such sheer novelty posed a number of problems to the designer, both as regards form and function. The public park was perceived essentially as an empty space, as vacant land in the middle of intensely busy towns where each square foot had a precise role, whether for housing, trade, industry or administration. When the need for such recreation grounds was identified, the question of their significance in the urban context had to be answered; in such a utilitarian-minded society, the layout of the park had to serve an explicitly defined purpose. The following formula coined by the Revd J.E. Clarke in the late 1850s neatly sums up the social function of public parks: 'Recreation is the RE-creation, the creation anew of fresh strength for tomorrow's work.' In an age when most cities were heavily polluted by coal smoke, parks were first of all perceived as 'lungs', thanks to which the residents could at last breathe a purer air and perhaps improve their health.

This alleged healthiness of parkland was in fact more symbolic than real, especially in the smaller and more central parks which suffered from the same pollution as the neighbouring urban areas. This false perception of the park as a clean, natural enclave in the midst of the insanitary city may be connected with the nostalgia cherished by Victorian town-dwellers for the rural environment they or their parents had been born in. Psychologically, the park was identified as a sheltered oasis of nature in which current urban problems could temporarily be forgotten. The provision of a continuous screen of trees or some other visual obstacle on the periphery of most recreation grounds perfectly achieved this sense of isolation.

On the other hand it was often asserted that public parks could be morally regenerating as well as beneficial to health. Local authorities, philanthropists and employers hoped the park's attractions would be stronger than those of the tavern or other disreputable places of entertainment where working-men resorted in their leisure-time. This is probably why the designers always provided space for a number of sports and games such as archery, bowls, croquet, quoits and above all cricket. Football was not often allowed and never encouraged, being considered rough and vulgar. The games which were favoured by the local authorities were clearly of the more sedate sort, and likely to require skill rather than sheer energy. Another attraction provided in public parks was of course the display of horticultural wonders such as exotic shrubs and trees, and new hybrids of native plants. The larger parks often included a 'rosarium', or an 'arboretum', and sometimes a subtropical or alpine garden. And there was almost invariably a winter-garden in the brightly-lit conservatories. To realise the appeal of such features, we must remember the degree of enthusiasm which horticulture could induce in the Victorian public throughout the period.

The most common form of leisure enjoyed in public parks, however, was simply walking, or driving through the park (when the middle classes frequented it). Formal terraces and grand avenues fit for perambulation were always provided, allowing strollers to see and be seen. The mixing of social classes was indeed desired by the promoters of public parks, who believed that the working classes would find there an opportunity of imitating the manners of their social superiors. As early as 1833, the Parliamentary committee which reported on 'Public Walks' mentioned this advantage:

A man walking out with his family among his neighbours of different ranks, will naturally be desirous to be properly clothed, and that his wife and children should be also; but this desire duly directed and controlled is found by experience to be of the most powerful effect in promoting civilisation, and exciting industry.

(*Parliamentary Papers*, 1833 (448), vol. XV, p. 9)

The public park was clearly seen as a testing-ground of the new urban ethos defined by the commercial and professional middle classes. This may be why so many philanthropic industrialists, especially in the north of the country, donated land to the local authorities for the creation of public parks (for example at Sheffield, Halifax, Hull, Southport, Middlesbrough, Saltaire and Glasgow). Within the boundaries of these recreation grounds, the lower orders were expected to imbibe the good behaviour and even possibly the good taste of the classes above them.

Joseph Paxton, the most imaginative of Victorian garden designers, who was himself a text-book case of social ascension, wished not only to allow different sorts of people to meet in parks, but also to provide them with opportunities for educational and cultural improvement. When he was asked to lay out Queen's Park in Glasgow in the late 1850s, he suggested a kind of arts centre should be erected in the middle of the grounds:

I propose the central part of the building to be used for a variety of purposes. Its general use I would recommend to be as a museum for works of art, and it could also be appropriated to periodical exhibitions, musical promenades . . .

(quoted by D. Maclellan, *Glasgow Public Parks*, 1894, p. 72)

The bandstand and upper terrace, People's Park, Halifax.

The intended building was never built, and there were only a handful of museums and galleries within public parks, as at Peel Park, Salford. If the idea of associating parkland and cultural pursuits failed on the whole to materialise, we must note that it was taken up later in the century by the first town-planners such as Ebenezer Howard, who gave museums pride of place in his ideal Garden City. To some extent, the public park was part of an urban utopia which remained in the making until the age of the New Towns. The achievements of the Victorian designers, nevertheless, express remarkably well the confidence of the middle classes in their social and moral values, and more generally their increasing control over the urban civilisation.

While they firmly established the meaning and function of public parks, the High Victorian landscape-gardeners were faced with a stylistic problem. How was the heritage of the eighteenth-century English landscape park to be adapted to the urban scene? A style which had been devised for the pleasure-grounds of aristocratic country estates did not seem obviously appropriate to cater for the leisure pursuits of urban masses. And yet, in most public parks, one can immediately recognise the basic layout devised by 'Capability' Brown (1716–83) and Humphrey Repton (1752–1818) in the late Georgian period. From them the Victorian designers borrowed the habit of using a belt of trees and shrubs to screen unsightly objects in the landscape. But while Brown and Repton had often contrived distant views of the surrounding countryside, when it was attractive, Paxton and his successors generally hid the city from view by planting opaque vegetation on the periphery of their urban parks. In order to maximise the use of available space, a circular alley was opened along that belt of trees, and sometimes within it, also in the Brownian manner. Within the park, a network of winding lanes could be found. However, the Victorians introduced prominent formal features such as terraces ornamented with balustrades, vases and statues, and tree-lined grand avenues along the axis of the principal entrances.

What remained directly inspired by the Georgian landscape-garden were the irregular lakes studded with islands which were obtained by damming brooks or by pumping water into the site. Such lakes were of course used for boating, but they also increased the sense of space in so far as they were centrally situated and prevented any direct crossing of the park. The sinuous paths which bordered them provided opportunities for long circuitous walks. In the disposition of trees, the Victorian gardeners imitated the 'clumping' and 'dotting' of Lancelot Brown, but they did not adhere to his concept of the park as a single visual unit. They liked to raise artificial banks and hillocks to enhance the beauty of individual trees planted on them, and also to divide the internal space of the park into isolated compartments, thus achieving variety, even on a cramped site.

The example of Battersea Park in London, designed in the late 1850s by John Gibson (1790–1866), can illustrate that mixture of tradition and innovation in the layout. The marshy riverside site was dismally bordered, to the east, by gas-works and railway-lines. The designer's first concern was to screen them off by raising artificial rock-work and planting them with opaque shrubs. Two intertwining peripheral lanes were provided: one for carriages

Ornamental balustrade, Stanley Park, Liverpool.

Plan of Battersea Park, London, from 1860.

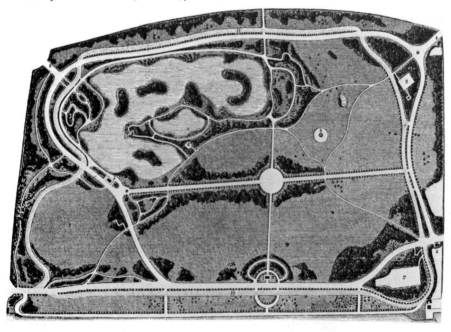

(and, in the 1890s, for cyclists), the other for riders. Smaller footpaths were laid out elsewhere – including a riverside walk. Two straight elm-lined avenues had their intersection towards the centre of the park. One of these was hidden from view by thick plantations on both sides, thus preventing the stroller from discovering the whole of the park at once. In the various glades thus created could be found such special features as a subtropical garden, a cricket ground, lawn tennis courts, a gymnasium and a bandstand.

More than in the structure, it was in the equipment and decoration of their public parks that Victorian designers left their unmistakable stamp. Pavilions, kiosks, bridges, fountains and gates in a variety of styles from the Gothic to the Moorish or Italianate still give a period flavour to those parks where they have survived, as at Southport and Leamington Spa. The arch-Victorian garden-building is, however, the glass and cast-iron conservatory; each public park prided itself on one of those Crystal Palaces in miniature, which secreted luxuriant exotic plants in their sultry depths. Decimus Burton's (1800–81) great Palm House at Kew is a magnificent example. As far as floral decoration was concerned, Victorian municipal gardeners tended to follow, albeit with some delay, the prevailing fashions. The age when landscape-gardeners had ignored flowers had gone by since John Claudius Loudon (1783–1843) had rehabilitated the individual plant and tree with his 'gardenesque' style of the 1830s, best seen in the public park at Derby (significantly called 'Arboretum'). Also the numerous botanic gardens, such as the highly popular gardens at Kew, focused the visitor's attention on rare and exotic plants and shrubs.

The conservatory, Hesketh Park, Southport (1864).

The 1850s saw the triumph of 'bedding out' in the public park — the display in summer of bright-coloured flowers such as calceolarias arranged in regular beds along the terraces or avenues. Towards the end of the century, William Robinson and the devotees of the 'wild garden' criticised this practice for its gaudy and short-lived effects. In the 1870s and 1880s, municipal parks adopted the fashion of carpet-bedding, or 'mosaiculture', with its recourse to dwarf foliage plants of subdued colours arranged in geometric or even figurative patterns. Towards the same time, rock-gardens planted with Alpine species were often formed in private gardens, but were only rarely to be found in public parks. This staggering succession of decorative styles testifies to the imaginativeness and eclecticism of Victorian gardeners. It is a sad reflection of the indifference of our contemporaries to public parks that most of the original flower decoration has disappeared (notable exceptions being Hesketh Park, Southport, and Saltaire Park, Bradford).

A word must finally be said about the men who made a name for themselves as designers of public parks. There was throughout the period, as we have seen, a marked conservatism in the layouts, contrasting with inventiveness in architectural and floral embellishments. This may be due to the origins and training of the Victorian landscape-gardeners, who were almost invariably men of humble station and had often started their career as under-gardeners in some country estate. Being primarily horticulturists, they would naturally tend to concentrate on garden decoration rather than on structure. Joseph Paxton was undoubtedly the guiding spirit of public park designers in the High Victorian period, although he died in 1865. Among his *protégés*, who worked with him at Chatsworth, one finds three of the foremost gardeners of the next generation: John Gibson, the creator of Battersea Park, who ended his career as superintendent of London's Royal Parks; Edward Kemp, who was in charge of Birkenhead Park, then laid out two of the most attractive surviving gardens, Hesketh Park at Southport and Stanley Park at Liverpool; Edward Milner, who collaborated with Paxton in the Sydenham Crystal Palace Gardens and in the 'People's Park' at Halifax, and then designed other parks at Preston and Buxton.

For all these men, the character of a park was obtained by a combination of formal architectural features such as terraces and colourful plantations. For Paxton's contemporary Robert Marnock (1800–99), however, the architectural treatment of the park was to be minimal; what mattered was the selection and arrangement of plants and trees in relation to the natural site. Marnock, who was for a long time Curator of the Royal Botanic Society's garden in Regent's Park, only designed a few public parks (notably at Sheffield), but had a major influence on men like Alexander Mackenzie (*c.*1829–93) who laid out Finsbury and Southwark Parks.

On the whole, one should not exaggerate the differences in style between those two groups of landscape-gardeners. The High Victorian public park has a clear individuality, perhaps more recognisable in the detail than in the overall effect. Unfortunately, its more ephemeral features, notably the flower-beds and exotic plants and trees, now have to be recreated in imagination if one tries to assess the aesthetic quality it once had. Much as in other visual

The terrace, Stanley Park, Liverpool.

arts of the time, notably architecture, certain characteristics stand out clearly, such as a taste for colour, stylistic eclecticism and profuseness of decoration. Crude as these qualities may now seem, they certainly conferred a special attractiveness to urban parks often set in grimy surroundings, and contributed to brighten up the image of the city in its residents' eyes.

'*Little Dorrit's Party*'. *Illustration by Phiz for* Little Dorrit *(1855–7) by Charles Dickens.*

3 Literature

JOHN HOLLOWAY

Introduction

The best synoptic guide to the general quality of life, and also of literature, in England in the 1850s and 1860s, is Hippolyte Taine's *Notes sur l'Angleterre* of 1872; and in Taine's account, there is one particular word which is eye-catchingly recurrent. That is the word 'energy'. 'This need for action and striving . . . will supply the necessary *energy*'; 'an Englishman needs to be doing something . . . he . . . has a surplus of *energy*'; 'that persevering attentiveness and *energy* which I have noticed so often'; 'each speaker trumpeted his own little fanfare in honour of Anglo-Saxon *energy*'. I pass over the many places where Taine identifies the thing, without happening to use the word. But besides this, one need look no further than the simplest statistics of the time: annual output of published books more than quadrupled between 1840 and 1870; civil public expenditure nearly trebled; woollen exports more than quadrupled; coal exports increased ten times over; rail travel, and exports of iron and steel, more than twelve times.

The 1850s and 1860s were years of success, prosperity and expansion (though one should never forget that the prosperity included terrible poverty), and the writing of the time reflects that basic reality. There are the glittering portraits of grandiose financial speculators like Mr Merdle in Dickens's *Little Dorrit* (1855–7) or, somewhat later, Trollope's Mr Melmotte in *The Way we Live Now* (1875), where the very title hints at a newer, brasher, more plutocratic order. That both of those characters crashed in the end was but part of the hectic exuberance of the time. Charlotte Brontë's *Shirley* (1849) depicts this energy-crammed productivity scramble in a northern industrial context, and so does Elizabeth Gaskell's *North and South* (1855); while Dickens's *Hard Times* (1854), set in Preston (which is called Coketown in the novel) shows something of a southerner's reaction to the northern industrial scene, and to the materialism and 'gospel-of-work' ethic as well as, more widely, to the Benthamite 'utilitarianism' that seemed to be its ultimate rationale: the 'greatest good of the greatest number' easily seeming to equate with the greatest volume of goods, and nothing more than that.

In the prose of this period, and indeed before it, this condition of life and society was reflected clearly: as in Carlyle's 'gospel of work' – 'know what thou canst *work* at'. Likewise in the verse. Elizabeth Barrett Browning in her 1861 poem entitled 'The North and the South' (of Europe though, not England) wrote:

> Now give us men from the sunless plain . . .
> By need of work in the snow and the rain,
> Made strong, and brave by familiar pain!
>   Cried the South to the North.

That is to see the matter much as Taine did, on his visits to England of 1859 and (in all probability) 1862: 'cold, rain, bad weather . . . are enemies against which he [the Englishman] is obliged to struggle unceasingly'. In the verse of the period, possibly the clearest evidence of the sense of energy is in the work of Gerard Manley Hopkins. What, after all, was his conception of 'instress' but the intrinsic energy of being of every individual reality, considered by itself as a part of Nature, radiating out into the rest of Nature its own irresistible selfhood? –

> Each mortal thing does one thing and the same:
> Deals out that being indoors each one dwells;
> Selves – goes itself: *myself* it speaks and spells;
> Crying *What I do is me: for that I came.*

At the same time, there is a certain selectivity of response to the 'selving' of the things of the world. (The matter will be resumed below.)

One of the most moving poetic expressions of Victorian energy and indeed exuberance comes in the verse of A.H. Clough:

> Say not the struggle naught availeth,
> The labour and the wounds are vain,
> The enemy faints not, nor faileth,
> And as things have been they remain . . .
>
> For while the tired waves, vainly breaking,
> Seem here no painful inch to gain,
> Far back, through creeks and inlets making,
> Comes silent, flooding in the main.

The poet intimates that victory comes unexpectedly, slowly, even surreptitiously; but with the inevitability of the great natural processes. One thinks also of Browning's 'The Statue and the Bust', with its moving indictment of those who lack the force of character (the 'energy') to fight in the struggle of life; also of Tennyson's poem on the aged Ulysses who, so legend says, set sail again in old age, and went beyond the farthest limits of the known world. Dante (in the *Inferno*) treated that as insensate curiosity, self-assertion and pride, and a great sin; for Tennyson it was a supreme example of energetic and idealistic aspiration:

> I cannot rest from travel: I will drink
> Life to the lees . . .
> I am a part of all that I have met;

THE LADY OF SHALOTT.

PART I.

On either side the river lie
Long fields of barley and of rye,
That clothe the wold and meet the sky;
And thro' the field the road runs by
      To many-tower'd Camelot;

Illustration by W.H. Hunt for 'The Lady of Shalott' (1842 edition) by Tennyson.

> Yet all experience is an arch wherethrough
> Gleams that untravelled world, whose margin fades
> For ever and for ever when I move . . .
> We are not now that strength which in old days
> Moved earth and heaven; that which we are, we are;
> One equal temper of heroic hearts,
> Made weal by time and fate, but strong in will
> To strive, to seek, to find, and not to yield.

W.E. Henley's much later poem 'Invictus' (the unconquered one) expresses much the same attitude, though in a different and darker mood. At a very different level of seriousness, there is Thackeray's stage-Irish ballad on 'The Crystal Palace, 1851', the astonishing mega-greenhouse erected in Hyde Park that housed the Great Exhibition of 1851, symbol and embodiment of Britain's energy and productivity:

> With ganial foire
> Thransfuse me loyre,
> Ye sacred nymphs of Pindus,
> The whoile I sing
> That wondthrous thing,
> The Palace made o'wondows!
>
> . . . 'Tis here that roams,
> As well becomes
> Her dignitee and stations,
> Victoria great,
> And holds in state
> The Congress of the Nations.
>
> . . . Here come likewise
> Her bould allies,
> Both Asian and Europian;
> From East and West
> They send their best
> To fill her Coornucopean.

In Thackeray's rollicking poem there are reminders of an important aspect of mid-Victorian expansionism, and this is how British expansion overseas is reflected in the literary works. Taine records that biographies of Nelson, and of Wellington, were favourite reading of the working class itself, and Tennyson opens his 'Ode on the Death of the Duke of Wellington' with:

> Bury the Great Duke
> With an *Empire's* lamentation . . .
> Let us bury the Great Duke
> To the noise of the mourning of a *mighty nation* . . .

Among innumerable minor examples one may mention the sonnets, somewhat later, of W.S. Blunt, and Richard Trench, to Gibraltar; and more particularly, because less blatant, Arthur O'Shaughnessy's well-known 'Ode'. Often enough, this has been taken ('sitting by desolate streams') as indulgence in post-Romantic melancholy. But the poet does not think only of the 'World-losers and world-forsakers' among his 'music-makers':

Yet we are the movers and shakers
Of the world for ever, it seems . . .

With wonderful deathless ditties
We build up the world's great cities,
    And out of a fabulous story
    We fashion *an empire's glory*.

It is of interest to contrast that poem with another and later one, Kipling's well-known 'Recessional' of 1897. This continues to glory in the 'power', the 'dominion over palm and pine', of the British Empire; but it does so in terms far more sombre, more anxiety-filled even, than the jingoism of which it is sometimes accused. Kipling saw empire as a task and challenge, not a luscious bonanza; and much doubted that his readers and their compatriots were adequate to it. But this more sombre side of his poem, as there was to Henley's poem mentioned just now, serves as reminder that mid-Victorian energy did not operate simply in an environment of buoyancy and optimism. In large part, the more intellectual and humane manifestations of energy were in response to a challenge, deeply and sometimes almost agonisingly felt, that seemed to the more thoughtful writers and thinkers to come from fundamental circumstances of the time, or even of the human situation in general.

One profitable way in which this may be approached is to consider the response of the Victorian poets to Nature. Wordsworth and Coleridge opened for themselves buoyant and joyous relations with Nature. Perhaps Shelley's keenest interest was in the most basic forces and transformations of the biosphere ('O wild west wind . . .'). For Byron 'high mountains were a feeling, but the hum Of human cities torture'. Keats's perhaps most famous ode was to one of the seasons as a whole. In the mid-Victorian poets, there is no absolute contrast, but something different comes to the fore. Their most memorable lines celebrating the natural world prove very often to be intense and brilliant realisations of a brilliant detail. Tennyson's

    Deep tulips, dashed with fiery dew,
    Laburnums, dropping-wells of fire

is an example; another is Arnold's description of the 'nook' that he is 'screen'd' in to compose his 'Scholar-Gipsy':

    Through the thick corn the scarlet poppies peep,
    And round green roots and yellowing stalks I see
      Pale blue convolvulus in tendrils creep:
        And air-swept lindens yield
    Their scent, and rustle down their perfumed showers
      Of bloom on the bent grass . . .

The quality of Arnold's interest is clear; even if, as has often been pointed out, the lime does not flower in August. Browning's verse, over and over, displays the same preoccupation. Similarly there is an interesting contrast between the response of Keats, and of Hopkins, to the Highlands of Scotland. Keats begins his 'Lines Written in the Highlands after a Visit to Burns's Country':

> There is a charm in footing slow across a silent plain . . .

But there is something beyond detail in his landscape, and it soon transforms anything to be called charm into a kind of awed, semi-mystical gloom:

> Runnels may kiss the grass on shelves and shallows clear,
> But their low voices are not heard, though come on travels drear;

Hopkins's 'Inversnaid' of 1881, however, is the polar opposite in its approach to the world of the Highlands. The vast landscape contracts to the small hillside stream, seen in brilliant isolation:

> Degged with dew, dappled with dew
> Are the groins of the braes that the brook treads through,
> Wiry heathpacks, flitches of fern,
> And the beadbonny ash that sits over the burn.

Nature, miniaturised, is vivid and delightful.

On the larger scale, the mid-Victorian poets saw things otherwise. For Tennyson in his *In Memoriam* (1850), Nature in toto was 'red in tooth and claw'; and he asks:

> Are God and Nature then at strife,
>   That Nature lends such evil dreams?
>   So careful of the type she seems,
> So careless of the single life;

– nor is Nature in the last analysis careful even of the type:

> She cries, 'A thousand types are gone:
> I care for nothing, all shall go . . .'

In 1849, Arnold published his sonnet ironically entitled 'In Harmony with Nature'. Nature is 'cruel . . . stubborn . . . Man must begin, know this, where Nature ends';

> 'In harmony with Nature?' Restless fool,

is how the sonnet begins. One of J.S. Mill's *Three Essays on Religion*, published during the 1850s, says plainly of the idea 'to follow Nature', '. . . monstrous'. Late in the century (and unpublished until 1934, in fact), Ernest Dowson wrote his 'Sonnet to Nature' and is even more outspoken:

> Thou unclean harpy, odorous of despair,
> . . . I know thee, evil one, and I am ware
> Of all thy vileness . . .
> Who feedest on the children of thy womb . . .

Dowson could be blatant to the point of banality, because by late in the century his point was a commonplace.

A key to the changed conception of Nature is not far to seek. Meredith's sonnet 'Lucifer in Starlight' is a clear pointer. Satan, tired of Hell, takes wing above the earth; but something happens which makes him soon despair. 'He look'd, and sank'. What daunts him is sight of the stars, and they do so because they are, in Meredith's words:

> The army of unalterable law.

No longer, in Wordsworth's terms, 'exquisitely fitted . . . to the mind of Man', Nature is an ice-cold and terrifying cosmic machine.

It is not appropriate here to trace the earlier stages of how the concept of ubiquitous impersonal law extended from the innocuous region of Newtonian physics to areas where it was not innocuous – a bare reference to Malthus's *Essay on Population* (1798) and what was in effect an extension of it in Ricardo's *Principles of Political Economy* of 1817 must suffice. Shelley in *Prometheus Unbound* (1820) mentioned the age of the earth itself as 600,000 years: the somewhat ironical reference back to the seventeenth-century Archbishop Ussher, who based his calculations on the Bible and thought the earth's age only a hundredth part of that, ought not to be missed. But by 1833, Charles Lyell's *Principles of Geology* saw the earth's age in terms of many millions of years: and argued that once this was allowed for, the whole natural history of the planet could be explained without reference to anything but the impersonal working of natural forces (volcanoes, sedimentation, erosion and so forth) such as the scientist observes at work, in total objectivity, from day to day.

Darwin himself by no means saw his theories as daunting. He thought that species were 'ennobled' by having evolved from primitive life, and wrote:

When we reflect on this struggle, we may console ourselves . . . that the war of nature is not incessant, that no fear is felt, . . . and that the vigorous, the healthy, and the happy survive and multiply.

(*On the Origin of Species*, 1859, chap. 3)

But as we have seen, Tennyson, who was thinking in the 1840s and in pre-Darwinian terms about the extinction of species, took a very different view. T.H. Huxley, writing to Kingsley in 1862, said that from the evolutionary point of view, man is thrown on his own resources in the world 'like a half-trained chess-player combating against a remorseless opponent'.

Most remarkable is what we find in Herbert Spencer's *First Principles* of 1863. Spencer extends Darwin's basic ideas from the evolution of species, to the development of everything in the cosmos; from the galaxy itself to human society and the development of the individual. Everything tends toward fuller integration on the one hand, and more complex differentiation on the other. Then, right at the end of his book, the dreadful if obvious thought strikes him. If the 'dissipation of motion and integration of matter' leads, harmoniously and optimistically, to order and equilibrium, once the order and equilibrium are complete, is that not stagnation? And must not the end-product of stagnation be extinction? It is not without significance that, eleven years earlier, Lord Kelvin had first enunciated the celebrated 'Second Law of Thermodynamics'. In his last chapter, Spencer specifically raises the question of whether the universe is going to die: his answer is the pathetic hope that perhaps there may be forces of rejuvenation in the remotest nebulae.

No wonder George Eliot, as reported by R.H. Hutton, once said 'in the furthest time there is nothing but one great catastrophe'. And in his *Erewhon* (1872) Butler satirises the 'justice' of the Darwinian struggle to survive, depicting how the Erewhonian legal system involves punishments not for successful crime but for human misfortune; and in another section, the 'Book of the Machines' imagines, in what is clearly a skit on Darwin's *Origin of Species* and also his *Descent of Man* (1871), that the machines themselves will be the superior species that will drive homo sapiens into extinction.

More will be said later of how deeply the sense of life as governed by impersonal necessity entered into the mid-Victorian novel; but Tennyson gave clear expression to a widely-felt sense of what the contemporary earth sciences (to use a later phrase) implied for humanity. 'And he, shall he, Man, her last work' he writes in *In Memoriam*,

> Be blown about the desert dust,
> Or sealed within the iron hills?
>
> No more? A monster then, a dream,
> A discord.

Laboriously, tentatively, Tennyson's poem wins through, or claims to win through, to a final modest optimism; but the overall impact of the poem is one of uncertainty, perplexity, difficulty – of the strong man, daunted by the deepest facts of life. Here is the darker counterpart to the world of mid-Victorian energy and assertion.

A sequel to that frame of mind may be traced clearly enough in Tennyson's next poem, *Maud*, published in 1855. This is a Victorian novel in verse, a portrait of mid-Victorian society preoccupied, as so often in the fiction of the time, with wealth and with marriages that related to wealth. But out of that came quite another interest: that of the plight of the speaker of the 'monodrama'-poem. And his plight is in fact to be plunged deeper and deeper into a condition for which the best term is the perhaps too-much used 'social alienation'. At the end of the penultimate part of the poem, this condition is unqualified; the final section resolves it through the desperate expedient of war.

For Matthew Arnold the literary or social critic, the thinker and writer of prose, to turn away from the problems of his own society was the last thing he allowed himself to do; but in his verse, it is precisely such a movement of mind and feeling which, repeatedly, he dramatises. 'The Scholar-Gipsy' (1853), surely his best-known piece, celebrates the elusive, half-ghostly figure of one who, in life, did not succumb to the 'repeated shocks' of the social bustle: 'Free from the sick fatigue, the languid doubt' which assails most men. '. . . fly our paths, our feverish contact fly' are Arnold's concluding words to his protagonist, unsullied by the drag of human society. And when, in 'Dover Beach' (probably written in 1851), Arnold writes:

> Ah, love, let us be true
> To one another! for the world, which seems
> To lie before us like a land of dreams,
> . . . Hath really neither joy, nor love, nor light
> Nor certitude, nor peace, nor help for pain,
> And we are here as on a darkling plain . . .

he is uniting a fairly widespread mid-Victorian sense of alienation to the Victorian ideal of high-minded love between the sexes.

It is to the point also to mention a somewhat unexpected figure in this

THE PALACE OF ART.

I BUILT my soul a lordly pleasure-house,
  Wherein at ease for aye to dwell.
I said, "O Soul, make merry and carouse,
  Dear soul, for all is well."

Q

Illustration by Dante Gabriel Rossetti for 'The Palace of Art' (1842 edition), by Tennyson.

context, Cardinal Newman. In his early 'Chorus of the Elements' he had already diagnosed, along traditional lines (as had of course always been readily available to the Christian), the alienating nature of man's natural environment, and the Christian move away from that:

> Thus God hath will'd
> That Man, when fully skill'd
> Still gropes in twilight dim;
> Encompass'd all his hours
>   By fearfull'st powers
> Inflexible to him:
> That so he may discern
>   His feebleness,
> And e'en for Earth's success
> To Him in wisdom turn . . .

As a poet, Newman leaves something to be desired. He is, however, one of the greatest masters of prose in this period. His depiction, in the *Apologia pro Vita Sua* (1864), of how mankind stands alienated in the natural world, is probably the finest in Victorian literature, and serves to show how easily an older and a newer sense of the matter were both available to the age:

Starting then with the being of a God . . . I look out of myself into the world of men, and there I see a sight which fills me with unspeakable distress. The world seems simply to give the lie to that great truth, of which my whole being is so full . . . I look into this busy world, and see no reflexion of its Creator . . . I am far from denying the real force of the arguments in proof of a God, drawn from the general facts of human society, but these do not warm me or enlighten me; they do not take away the winter of my desolation . . . To consider the world in its length and breadth, the many races of men, their mutual alienation, their conflicts . . . their aimless courses . . . the blind evolution of what turn out to be great powers . . . the progress of things, as if from unreasoning elements, not towards final causes . . . all this is a vision to dizzy and appal.

It was part, one might say, of the intellectual energy of Victorianism, that such profound disquiet could co-exist, and sometimes partly fuse in one and the same mind, with a Dickensian or Browningesque exuberance.

There was another respect in which the mid-Victorian age was an age of paradoxical combinations. The immense productivity and commercial expansion co-existed with appalling poverty, and this was widely registered in the writing of the time. Thomas Hood's 'Song of the Shirt' angrily records how Victorian labour went with poverty:

> 'Work – work – work?
> My labour never flags;
> And what are its wages? A bed of straw,
>   A crust of bread – and rags.

Elizabeth Barrett Browning's 'The Cry of the Children' took up the tale, as did Davidson's 'Thirty Bob a Week' near the turn of the century. There is no need to speak of Dickens in this context, but it should be said that Henry Mayhew's *London Labour and the London Poor* (1851–64), though based on the period before 1850 as regards its facts, is probably the fullest and finest study, in the period before us, of how, in the London street crowds, incredible variety and idiosyncrasy went also with poverty.

One other work should be mentioned, though it appeared somewhat before 1850. It is Engel's grim *Condition of the Working Class in England*, which appeared in 1844, and is one of the earliest indications of a most distinctive feature of Victorian England as of later times: the contrast (even within the matter of poverty) between the industrial north of England, and the commercial or more rural south. Mrs Gaskell's novel of just that name, *North and South* (1855) sharply and sometimes agonisingly juxtaposes the northern world of industrial bustle, productivity and at least incipient strife, with conspicuous mass poverty; and southern England where rural poverty, real enough to be sure, could more easily be ignored, and at least the prosperous and 'respectable' part of the population could preoccupy themselves with entertainment, fashion, family connections, and religion.

The Brontës' novels expand this in other ways: *Wuthering Heights* (1847) through its wild scenery, its isolated family life, and the kind of hypertrophy of personality that can go with that; *Shirley* along lines rather like Mrs Gaskell. That no major poet succeeded Wordsworth in the north is perhaps a reflection of what was indicated earlier on: Nature in the more extended, bleaker, wilder forms that it conspicuously takes there would have left the Victorian poets ill at ease. They were more Keatsian (Arnold, Tennyson particularly), and would have felt more at ease in the varied and colourful ecological patterns of the 'warm south'. Hopkins's 'Inversnaid', discussed briefly above, is one of the very few outstanding poems of the time to take its subject from the north.

Here then is a remarkable combination: energy, self-confidence, achievement on the one hand, and on the other, a widespread sense of how mankind lives in a world that may always, and only too easily, prove indifferent or alien. Given those two conditions of life, a certain response to them is predictable. How is the man or woman of superior energy and resource likely to respond? Exactly as Matthew Arnold expressed the matter in a phrase most redolent of the time, and in continuity with its strong if beleaguered Christian–religious traditions. He or she will 'brace the moral fibre', and aspire to confront and overcome difficulty, perplexity or pessimism.

The idea of the heroic, in one form or another, was in fact one of the key 'moments' of the Victorian mind. Carlyle's *Heroes and Hero-Worship* belongs to the 1830s, but his late essay 'Shooting Niagara: and after?' (1867) returns to the idea. He identifies a triple aristocracy: the 'Titular Aristocracy'; the 'silent Industrial Hero' – depicted by Charlotte Brontë in Robert Moore (*Shirley*), and by Dickens in Doyce (*Little Dorrit*) – and the intellectual or literary 'Aristocracy by Patent from God the Maker'. Needless to say, his confidence in any or all of them is somewhat limited. Along with Carlyle one should recall Ruskin's insistence that all forms of artistic achievement depend upon the moral worth of the artist. In George Eliot's novels, the climax of the story is repeatedly the moment of supreme courage – moral courage with both Dorothea Casaubon and Rosamund Lydgate, physical courage with Maggie Tulliver.

In the poetry, depictions of dauntless heroism are also frequent: Hopkins's 'tall nun' in 'The Wreck of the Deutschland', in the mid-1870s; Browning's 'Childe Roland to the Dark Tower Came' (1855) and Arnold's 'Sohrab and Rustum' (1852–3). Along with that is Arnold's recurrent stress upon the supreme literary quality of what he called the 'grand style', and his emphasis in the lectures 'On translating Homer' that the grand style came from lofty and heroic qualities of mind, not literary ingenuities (one recalls Carlyle's reference to the Iliad and to Homer the 'rough, laborious, wallet-bearing man' in 'Shooting Niagara'). Late in the century, celebration of heroism goes on, sometimes in a military and imperial context as with Newbolt's wonderfully yet also a little poignantly outdated 'He Fell among Thieves', set on the North-West Frontier. Sometimes the context recalls Carlyle's 'silent Industrial Hero': as in 'The Mary Gloster', a poem of 1894 in which a Liverpool shipbuilder's dying words to his son (as it seems) lament how iron determination and toil in the older generation are being dissipated in flashy gentrified idleness ('Harrer and Trinity College! I ought to ha' sent you to sea . . .').

Queen Victoria's reign (1837–1901) was the longest in British history. The likelihood that even a complex diagnosis of 'the Victorian Age' would be adequate to characterise such a span of time from end to end is small; and from about 1870 there were signs that profound if sometimes subtle and gradual changes were on the way. Subtle, some aspects of change at that time certainly were not. The military scale, for example, of the Franco-Prussian War of 1870, and the armed might of the new German Empire after the date, were enough to make it clear that Britain could not now be significant as a major military force within the continent of Europe; and so brought to a close a period stretching over nearly 200 years.

The agricultural depression which set in at about that time in Britain, and which continued until the war of 1939–45, was less sudden and dramatic, but must have had more impact on the daily life of the rural population. The cause was the opening up by rail of the vast wheatlands of the American Middle West: which meant that the arable farming of the south and east of England was inevitably priced out of the market. The perplexed doggedness of Iden, the farmer in Jefferies's *Amaryllis at the Fair* (1887) is one reflection of that change. More profoundly so is the nature of Hardy's fictional protagonists one after another. Hardy must have scorned the breezy optimism of Meredith's 'rapture of the forward view'. What one finds in Hardy's work is the grimmer side of Darwinist evolutionary doctrine, but sunk so deep into the fabric of the fiction as not to be at once obvious. The fact remains, however, that his central characters dramatise the situation of those who, in Darwinian terms, are losing the struggle for survival and being driven to harsher and harsher milieux as they follow, albeit unconsciously, the dreary road to extinction. Marty South (*The Woodlanders*, 1887) is a passive, inarticulate woodland species in a world of sharp agents and flashy doctors; Clym Yeobright (*Return of the Native*, 1878) retreats – though he is far from seeing the matter like this himself – from dealing in diamonds in Paris to cutting furze on the wildest of the Wessex heathlands. Other examples will be mentioned in the section on Hardy below, see pp.138–43. Hardy's well-known poem 'In Time of "The Breaking of Nations"' – it was significantly named – was not written until 1915; it is a classic example of a writer celebrating what is in fact doomed, by claiming that it will be everlasting:

> Only a man harrowing clods
>   In a slow silent walk
> With an old horse that stumbles and nods
>   Half asleep as they stalk.
>
> Only thin smoke without flame
>   From the heaps of couch-grass;
> Yet this will go onward the same
>   Though Dynasties pass.

The gloom of Hardy's poem in fact made a strange kind of wishful thinking.

These great if gradual changes were not confined to the agricultural scene. Already, the facts of economic life were beginning to bring in profound changes in the industrial and financial position of Britain, worldwide. Already in the 1860s British income from investment abroad, earlier, had begun to exceed in volume the new investment being made in capital development overseas: we were beginning to live on our savings in the past. From 1879, tariffs introduced in the new Germany to protect the developing German industrial scene were followed by similar policies in other European countries, and by 1890 in the United States. Coal became a relatively more important export than iron and steel, which is to say that there was more of a market for our raw materials than for our manufactures. Britain was ceasing to seem like 'the workshop of the world'; and in fact Carlyle, in his 'Shooting Niagara' had already written:

'In my young time', said to me one of the wisest and faithfulest German friends I ever had . . . 'when you were going to a shop to purchase, wise people would advise you: "If you can find an English article . . . buy that" . . . And now . . . directly the reverse is the advice given . . .'

In the later years of the century there were no famous novels of northern industrial life such as were written by Dickens, Disraeli, Charlotte Brontë and Mrs Gaskell in the middle years; while Gissing's novels, notably *The Unclassed* (1884), contrast with Dickens's work, and indeed also Mayhew's masterpiece, in depicting the city life of London as not a medley of splendidly assertive vitality, but rather of endless extent and dreary anonymity.

For those in comfortable circumstances of life, things were far from that; the fundamental reality shaping the cultural and intellectual life of the later years being perhaps that, as Britain's material pre-eminence and sublime assurance evanesced, there was, in a variety of ways, less preoccupation with the culturally self-contained, nationally speaking, and more contact with other cultures. One of the earliest landmarks was in fact a foreign one: the discovery in Paris, in 1856, by the French etcher Braquenard, of a number of woodcuts by the Japanese 'Ukiyo-E' artist Hokusai. Their flat, decorative, anti-heroic style made an immediate impression (though they seem to have reached the West almost by accident) and the cult of the Japanese woodcut was taken up in the mid-1860s by Lazenby Liberty, who worked in a shop in Regent Street, and later crossed the road and opened his own business, now 'Liberty's', the famous West End store.

In the field of the visual arts, one may say that the tide was beginning to flow. James Abbott McNeil Whistler lived in Paris in the late 1850s and was there again in 1863, the year of the 'Salon des Refusés'. Four years later he held his house-warming party at 96 Cheyne Walk, the precursor of his 'White House' in Tite Street. Wilde epitomised the new decorative style by saying that Whistler's ideal was 'two white walls with a Whistler [painting] on each'. The elderly Ruskin's ineffective scorn for Whistler's 'Impressionist' work is well-known. In 1877, the year before Whistler moved into the 'White House', he decorated the famous 'Peacock Room' for Leyland, the Liverpool shipping magnate, who was already collecting Japanese blue-and-white china. Also in 1877, the Grosvenor Gallery, centre of the newer ideas about art, was opened by the Prince of Wales: twenty-six years before, what the Prince Consort had opened was the Great Exhibition. The Grosvenor Gallery and the 'aesthetic movement' generally were satirised in the Gilbert and Sullivan opera *Patience* (1881). Five years later the New English Art Club was formed under Sickert, and the full influence of French Impressionism had arrived.

Well before these years, the Pre-Raphaelite Brotherhood, of both painters and poets, had rejected the dominant cultural code of the energetic, the heroic – and also the respectable, one might add. William Morris, their immediate successor, not only produced 'The Defence of Guinevere' (1858), a poem in which he intimated that Queen Guinevere's beauty made the question of her fidelity simply boring and irrelevant; but also, over the years, worked out the whole creed of a medieval social harmony, fragmented with the rise of commercialism; and pointed to a new socialist society as the means to create a worthwhile future for mankind. Morris, though in passing, condemned the 'art for art's sake' doctrine that was beginning to come forward; but it is possible to see that his poetry, if not his social and political writings, left a place for it. The first enunciation of this conception in English appears to have been Swinburne's 1862 article on Baudelaire, whose *Les Fleurs du Mal* Swinburne had discovered while in France with Whistler in 1857. One is not surprised to find that the English poet defended the 'vivid and distinctive background of morality' in Baudelaire; the general trend away from the preconceptions of most mid-Victorian literature is discernible, by this time, all the same.

To inter-relate the poetry and the painting of the later years of the century is unavoidable. Ernest Dowson was the son of a Limehouse dock-owner, one who was a type-figure, one might say, of mid-Victorian commercialism and export-prosperity. His son repudiated that world, and concentrated his attention on the élite-society Chelsea stretches of the river; his verse followed closely the Impressionist influence of Whistler's *Nocturnes*:

> Strange grows the river on the sunless evenings . . .
> The river comforts me, grown spectral vague and dumb

J. Addington Symonds's 'In the Key of Blue' owes much to Gautier, also, more generally, to Impressionism; and Wilde's poem 'The Gold Room – a

Harmony' is another example of the same trend. More significant are the traces of Impressionism and of the 'Decadent' movement in the verse of W.E. Henley.

Henley must in the main be seen as an anti-Decadent. His series of poems entitled *In Hospital*, based on his own experience in an Edinburgh hospital in 1873–5 and much revised until their publication in the *Cornhill* in 1888, are among the very first notable modern free-verse poems in the language, and well show his taste for the plain and manly, product of a convinced realism of mind. (His famous lyric 'Invictus' has already been mentioned, see p.90). His 'Song of the Sword', not notable as verse, is notable as a specimen of what might be termed 'jingoistic Darwinism'. So far, he has no place in this part of the discussion. But his *London Voluntaries* tell a different tale:

> What miracle is happening in the air,
> Changing the very texture of the air
> Into something luminous and rare?

The poem from which the lines come is describing the Thames itself, and the affinity to Whistler's *Nocturnes*, and also to Monet and to Impressionism more generally, is unmistakable. Yeats's lines in his famous 'Lake Isle of Inisfree' (1895) point in the same direction:

> . . . peace comes dropping slow,
> Dropping from the veils of the morning to where the cricket sings;
> There midnight's all a-glimmer, and noon a purple glow . . .

Yeats is probably using 'purple' in its older, Latinate sense of 'radiant, colourful'; the Impressionist quality of his scene is unmistakable.

If one risks an interpretation of these complex developments, one is inclined to say that over the closing years of the century, literature in England was largely the product of an élite minority subordinated in a plutocratic rather than simply a commercial–productive society. Trollope's significantly-named *The Way we Live Now*, with its charlatan plutocrat, idle aristocracy, and degenerate gilded youth, points already in this direction. Conrad's *Nostromo* appeared in 1904, but the substance of this novel is the transition from a commercial enterprise (the silver mine in Central America) threatened by a traditional robber-baron order, to the same enterprise sweeping the old order away, commercialising everything, and in fact corrupting everything to its own sub-commercial values; while the bluff sea-captain Mitchell, epitome of the older British virtues, becomes a rentier and retires to a parsonage in Sussex.

It is in the novels of Henry James in this period that one finds the most detailed studies of plutocratic society. *The Awkward Age* (1899) depicts a society less industrious, more opulent, more 'refined' and exquisite perhaps, than we can find in mid-Victorian fiction; but one also in which standards of virtue are inconspicuously coarsening, a coarsening which is subtly affecting even the phraseology of casual upper-class conversation. *The Spoils of Poynton* (1897) relates these ideas to material possessions. On the surface, the novel relates the struggle of Mrs Gareth to dissuade her son from marrying a beautiful girl with no taste, thereby alienating from his mother the family house and all the treasures of art it contains. Look more closely, however, and James's condemnation of plutocratic vulgarity goes deeper. If the Brigstock family that the girl belongs to are rich nobodies, Mrs Gareth is a rich nobody too; and her splendid house is no traditional family seat, but simply a 'matchless canvas for a picture', that is to say the 'spoils' that she has acquired in a lifetime spent as a 'treasure hunter'. James, in this novel, is suggesting that vulgar plutocrat and exquisite 'aesthete' are fundamentally the same. Both are, in ways more or less subtle, vulgarised and dehumanised: both are, in their different ways, 'empire-builders'.

James's short stories extend this picture. 'The Real Thing' (1893) depicts a penurious colonel and his 'lady' who put themselves forward, as models of traditional upper-class authenticity, to a book-illustrator. By the end of the story, they strike the reader as total frauds. 'The Death of the Lion' (1894) depicts an author of true quality taken up by a ruthless literary-lion-hunting hostess. By the time the pressure has brought him to his death, she is already on with another, this time the sham kind she deserves. 'Broken Wings' of 1903 shows an unsuccessful artist and equally unsuccessful woman writer who realise at last that a life of adulation by the landed gentry and of endless country-house visiting has kept them apart and condemned them to years of emptiness and frustration. James saw deeply how the spacious opulence of his time was in fact only covert barbarism.

Circumstances were to change. Yeats records, somewhat dogmatically and enigmatically, in the Preface to his *Oxford Book of Modern Verse* (1935), that suddenly in 1900 everyone abandoned their subtleties and exquisiteness and became down-to-earth. Pound, not long after that, writes very plainly of how foreign influences and models are important for him, but that he is far indeed from meaning French Impressionism. If *The Picture of Dorian Grey* (1891) had been based upon the exquisite aesthetic-movement *A Rebours* of Huysmans, George Moore's *A Mummer's Wife* (1885), had been set largely in the English Potteries, but was based upon the realism of Zola's *L'Assommoir*. The Nineties poets were a passing phenomenon; though one should not underestimate their delicate and evocative charm. Even to praise them like that, however, shows the distance that late nineteenth-century writing had moved from its mid-Victorian counterpart.

Dickens's later novels

Dickens's novels are richly of his own time, and his later ones even more than the earlier. This means that there is danger in judging them too readily by reference to our own time, and our own experience of it. A recent experience brought this home to me sharply. Walking one day through the spacious shopping arcade in a town I am familiar with, my eye fell on the bench where, often all day, sit a half-dozen middle-aged or elderly men whom a callous tongue would refer to as tramps, drop-outs, people of 'no fixed abode'. Certainly they stood out as different from the busy throng of tidily-dressed, neatly-washed, steadily-preoccupied 'spenders' all round them; and as I looked at their flushed, weathered, unshaven faces, often with signs of past or maybe present illness on them, and their ill-assorted, worn-out garments, broken-down shoes, and miscellaneous bottles of liquor, the thought suddenly came to me that here was a row of thoroughly Dickensian characters, and that what made them so was that they were a relic from the past: they were people who had not known, or had slipped through, the complicated networks of negotiated wages, health services, and education that have sustained, and smoothed out, the rest of us. And when one of them jumped up, seeing I suppose a likely patron, and began an endless, contorted, idiosyncratic, ingratiatory yet a trifle sinister begging patter, I was immediately and forcibly reminded again of Dickensian characters, and I came to see that the notion of Dickens as a caricaturist is largely a product of the smoothly tidy and elaborately sustained society of the later twentieth century.

Most of the later novels of Dickens (1812–70) are set in the London of his own most formative years, the London of the 1820s and 1830s (his earlier novels are discussed by John Beer in volume 6.) Perhaps the greatest literary account of the life of any great city, and certainly one of the greatest of nineteenth-century literary achievements, Henry Mayhew's *London Labour and the London Poor* (1849 onwards), looks back to those years and shortly after them; and it magisterially depicts the immense scale and variety, and also the vividness and intensity, of the street life of London. Hippolyte Taine confirms the picture:

. . . it adds up to twelve cities the size of Marseilles . . . enormous, enormous – that is the word which recurs all the time. And . . . rich and well-cared for . . . Paris is mediocre by comparison . . .

That was only part of Taine's story:

. . . near where I was is Shadwell, one of the poorest quarters. By the depths of its poverty and misery, as by its extent, it is proportional to London's enormous size and wealth.

(*Notes on England*, trans. Edward Hyams, 1957)

In a letter of 1846, Dickens exactly confirms how it was contact with the unique and astonishing reality of Victorian London that provided him with inspiration. Writing from Lausanne to John Forster, he said:

. . . the difficulty of going at what I call a rapid rate, is prodigious . . . I suppose this is partly the effect of the absence of streets . . . I can't express how much I want these . . . The toil and labour of writing, day after day, without that *magic lantern*, is immense.

(*my italics*)

It is worth while to give some space to this point, in order to be quite clear that, in his later novels especially, Dickens shows the strength not of the gifted caricaturist, but of someone whose almost unique achievement (though Mayhew stands to a great extent beside him) was to see the extraordinary range and life of Victorian humanity in London.

So we have, for example, in *Bleak House* (1852–3), Miss Flite, 'a curious little old woman in a squeezed bonnet, and carrying a reticule, came curtseying and smiling up to us'; or Krook, the slum scrap dealer and drunkard:

He was short, cadaverous, and withered; with his head sunk sideways between his shoulders, and the breath issuing in visible smoke from his mouth, as if he were on fire within . . . he looked from his breast upward, like some old root in a fall of snow.

Shelley had already used that comparison, writing in *The Triumph of Life* of Rousseau in the after-life; but Dickens's account loses nothing by that. Again, in *Little Dorrit* (1855–7) there is the crabbed and tyrannical clerk who rejoices in the name of Flintwinch:

his neck was so twisted, that the knotted ends of his cravat usually dangled under one ear . . . his features [had] a swollen and suffused look; and altogether, he had a weird appearance of having hanged himself at one time or another.

Dickens also saw the upper classes of the London world, or their genteel hangers-on, with the same combination of two distinctive qualities: exactly specific detail and sizzling intensity of perception:

. . . In person Mrs General, including her skirts which had much to do with it, was of a dignified and imposing appearance; ample, rustling, gravely voluminous, always upright behind the proprieties . . . If her countenance and hair had a rather floury appearance . . . it was rather because she was a chalky personal creation altogether, than because she mended her complexion with violet powder, or had turned grey.

This was the more-than-governess whom Mr Dorrit found to 'cultivate a surface' on his daughters, once he had come into money.

Dickens's intensity of perception, and of reproduction, in his writing, was not confined to people. There is a similar quality in his dialogue. Examples of this are endless, and at first it seems superfluous to offer examples. If one does so, however, there soon emerges something which is of interest. If one attentively re-reads, for example, chapter 12 of *Our Mutual Friend*, where the down-river ruffian Rogue Riderhood goes to Wrayburn and Lightwood to denounce Hexam, or chapter 16 of *Bleak House*, where Jo the crossing-sweeper boy takes the disguised Lady Dedlock to the grave of her old lover, or chapter 54, where Inspector Bucket begins to expose Mademoiselle Hortense, one finds a similar concentration of effect, a similar intensity, this time through representation of passionate emotion of varying or indeed contrasting kinds, and in part violently expressed or in part tensely released. This discovery leads to a more far-reaching one, about not simply the content of the later novels, but about what one might call the static organisation of that content and, incipiently at least, about its dynamic organisation.

By 'static organisation', I have in mind how Dickens's comprehensive variety of material is far from being mere miscellaneity: an endless sequence of types, say, from the street poor of London, such as doubtless Mayhew (to say nothing of the reality) could have supplied him with. Dickens's variety of material is a variety that will naturally organise itself into polarities. That is true of those later novels which do not set themselves predominantly in London, quite as much as of the others. In *Hard Times* (1854) there are the contrasting worlds of Bounderby's rigid household, Stephen Blackpool's penurious one, and Sleary's circus. In *A Tale of Two Cities* (1859), there are Sydney Carton and Mr Stryver the London lawyers, Cruncher the odd-job man who waits at the door of the bank, and the French aristocrats and the citizen revolutionaries of Paris. In *Great Expectations* (1860), Miss Havisham the 'rich and grim lady', Magwitch the convict and transportee, Joe Gargery the half-literate, golden-hearted blacksmith, and so on. Always, the roll of Dickens's characters offers us such contrasts of personality: but more to the point is what these polarities offer the novelist for development of the narrative, for dynamic organisation.

But before this point is taken further, it seems important to note a third respect in which the later novels manifest Dickens's powers of intensity and vividness. This is what is manifested in his depiction of the scenes themselves in which the varied action of his narrative takes place. It may be the picturesque but poverty-stricken and almost derelict landscape of France:

. . . the corn bright in it, but not abundant. Patches of poor rye where corn should have been, patches of poor peas and beans . . . there remained a broken country, bold and open, a little village at the bottom of the hill, a broad sweep and rise beyond it, a church-tower, a windmill, a forest for the chase, and a crag with a fortress on it used as a prison.

(*A Tale of Two Cities*, II, 8)

Or it may be the grimly drab Essex marshes of *Great Expectations*:

. . . this bleak place overgrown with nettles was the churchyard; and . . . the dark flat wilderness beyond the churchyard, intersected with dykes and mounds and gates, with scattered cattle feeding on it, was the marshes; and . . . the low leaden line beyond was the river; and . . . the distant savage lair from which the wind was rushing, was the sea.

(chap. 1)

Arthur Clennam, going one evening to his mother's 'dismal old house', introduces what is perhaps Dickens's most characteristically vivid scene of all, the somehow sinister gloom of the London streets by night:

. . . as he went along, on a dreary night, the dim streets by which he went seemed all depositories of oppressive secrets. The deserted counting-houses, with their secrets of books and papers locked up in chests and safes; the banking-houses, with their secrets of strongrooms and wells . . . the shadow thickening and thickening as he approached its source; he thought of the secrets of the lonely church-vaults . . . and then of the secrets of the river, as it rolled its turbid tide between the two frowning wildernesses of secrets.

In that passage it is the sinister scene itself which forebodes the sinister developments of the narrative; and there is a similar suggestiveness about the 'distant savage lair' of the sea, in the words quoted just now from *Great Expectations*. But illustration soon becomes superfluous. Dickens's power in this respect is unrivalled. It is known to all, and would be as well illustrated by the threatening down-river scenes of *Our Mutual Friend*, or the sinister – and once again, so often dusk or night-time – scenes of Chesney Wold in *Bleak House*, or (in another dimension, one might say) the immense dream-staircase that Mrs Sparsit, in her vindictive imagination, watches Louisa Gradgrind descend in *Hard Times*. But the staircase with the 'dark pit of shame and ruin at the bottom', and the secret-laden city at night, and the savage lair of the sea, all pointedly illustrate how Dickens's masterly scenic descriptions have, as their underlying purpose, to contribute to the slow but relentless progress and resolution of his narrative.

'Narrative' is in one sense a misnomer. At least in his later novels, Dickens stands in contrast to other Victorian novelists, who tell one story only (like, for the most part, Hardy), or at the most two or three (like George Eliot; though this rather in her more elaborate books, like *Middlemarch*). A work like *Our Mutual Friend* sets before the reader a multiplicity of potentially independent fictions. There is the tale of Bella and John Rokesmith; of Hexham and his daughter; of the latter and Eugene Wrayburn; of Rogue Riderhood; of Bradley Headstone, Lizzie and Charlie; of the Veneerings, of the Lammles, of the Lammles and Fledgeby, of Jenny Wren, of Riah, and perhaps something else besides.

In his later novels, Dickens's fundamental work is to bring his distinct groups of characters, and their separate stories, into relation; until the dramatis personae, numerous, idiosyncratic and varied as they are, come to constitute one integrated whole. In *Great Expectations*, we begin with the ruffianly, transported convict Magwitch, the timorous blacksmith's apprentice Pip, the crazily eccentric wealthy old lady Miss Havisham and her haughty *protégée* Estella. Each character seems to belong to its own separate and contrasting world. By the end, Estella has turned out to be the convict's daughter and the ex-apprentice's bride. Early on, Herbert, the son of the prosperous Pocket family, patronises Pip; before the end, it is Pip who has set him up in business; later, it is he who helps to establish Pip, and it is he who becomes the runaway transport's protector. In *A Tale of Two Cities*, Madame Defarge the ruthless revolutionary proves to have been personally the victim of the tyrannical aristocrats whom she seems at first only to pursue on grounds of principle; the physician Dr Manette, the victim of the aristocratic family whose son, later in the novel, is the one to rescue him and to marry his daughter. So it is throughout these novels: each two groups of characters prove, sooner or later, to come together, sometimes through what might loosely be termed, in Dickens's own phrase, a 'mutual friend'. In the novel of that name in fact, John Rokesmith comes first to be a lodger in the Wilfer family (Book I, chapter 4); five chapters later, Boffin is speaking to the Wilfer family and actually calls Rokesmith 'our mutual friend'. Two chapters later again, Rogue Riderhood makes the acquaintance of Mortimer and Eugene. Dickens consistently utilises in the organisation of his novels the insight that one finds, expressed in abstract terms, in thinkers like Mill or Michelet: society is a single, vast, comprehensively interacting unity.

Needless to say, Dickens himself rarely expresses this insight in abstract terms himself, but in one place in *Bleak House* he comes near to that. He writes that John Jarndyce and Alan Woodcourt are both 'thinking, much, how strangely Fate has entangled this rough outcast [it is Jo the crossing-sweeper] in the web of very different lives'. There is also something rather like that in *Little Dorrit*, II.25, where Dickens writes 'half a grain of reality, like the smallest portion of some other scarce natural productions, will flavour an enormous quantity of diluent'.

More typical of Dickens's manner of expressing such ideas is a phrase that comes at the beginning of *Little Dorrit*, II.24: 'So quietly did the mowing of the old scythe go on, that fully three months had passed unnoticed.' Whether Dickens refers here to the figure of Time, or Death, the phrase reminds one how much of legend, fable and folk-tale there is, not only in Dickens's passing references to such things, but associated with the very structure of his narratives. The proverb-titles to the successive books of *Our Mutual Friend* ('The Cup and the Lip', and so on), point the same way. It looks, in particular, as if Taylor's 1824 translation of Grimm's *Tales* had great influence on Dickens in his thinking and planning of the novels. The death of Blandois in *Little Dorrit* strongly recalls the wicked stepmother's death in Grimm's 'The Juniper Tree' (she is struck on the head by a falling millstone). In *Our Mutual Friend*, the proud but in truth good-hearted Bella may be likened to the proud girl in 'King Grizzlebeard'; and Mr Boffin, often referred to in the novel as a 'brown bear', is like the bear in Grimm's 'The Grateful Beasts'. In *Hard Times*, Bounderby's appearance and behaviour somewhat recall Grimm's 'The Man in the Bear's Skin', while Cissy Jupe is a little like the poor girl adopted into the rich family in 'The Three Spinning Women'. Moreover, Mrs Sparsit in the same novel, constantly at her spinning (or rather, netting), and with one foot constantly in the 'stirrup', recalls the Spinning Women in the same tale in Grimm. Little Dorrit herself is another Cinderella-like figure, and her sister Fanny somewhat reminiscent of Cinderella's sisters, in their pride if not their ugliness.

This train of thought could be taken further. Dickens's characters are far more richly individualised than those in Grimm, or in the folk-tale generally. But the fact remains that they not infrequently conform, at least to some degree, to the fundamental patterns and antitheses of the folk-tale or the fable; and in one respect this is of major significance. The fact emerges as soon as one notices how often folk-tale narrative culminates in total transformation – youngest son of the poor man marries king's daughter, and so on. Regularly, and of course with greater seriousness and fulness of presentation, this is how Dickens resolves his narratives in the later novels.

Thus his characters move through the whole gamut of human fortune. Pip the poor orphan becomes mysteriously rich and dominant, then finally achieves happiness in his original obscurity; and the proud Estella, losing her upper-class connection, finds life's solution with him. In *Little Dorrit*, Arthur moves from being patron of the debtors' prison to becoming one of its inmates, and the heroine goes beyond her period of riches to resolve her life in the same obscurity as Arthur. Her father falls from his spurious wealth into poverty and senility. Merdle passes from fabulous wealth and celebrity, to disgrace and suicide. In *A Tale of Two Cities*, the feckless Sidney Carton quietly becomes the supreme hero, the implacable revolutionary Madame Defarge succumbs to an insignificant English domestic servant. In *Bleak House*, Sir Leicester goes from haughty complacence to half-helpless tenderness; his icily haughty wife ends her life in disgrace, obscurity and truth. The vast wealth that once went with the Jarndyce estate ends in nothing.

Over and over, the pattern is from extreme to extreme, sometimes from grief to contentment, often from pride to expiation and humility. Dickens is able to elicit these myth-like extremes, with immense slowness, fulness and

The Marshalsea becomes an Orphan

Illustration by Phiz for Little Dorrit *(1855–7) by Charles Dickens.*

detail, not just from folk-tale simplicities, but from a detailed, vivid and comprehensively integrated encyclopedia of social panorama. It is here that his command of artistic organisation, and the range and profundity of his vision of society, seem chiefly to reside.

George Eliot and the web of provincial society

There is no doubt that, with Hardy, George Eliot (1819–80) is the greatest novelist of the nineteenth century as chronicler of life in the English provinces. What Dickens was for London, George Eliot was for the Midland market town and for Midland rural life. Beyond question, though, she has further claims on the attention of the serious reader. In the first place, if Dickens represents in fiction the variety and vitality of Victorian life, it is George Eliot who most introduces into fiction its serious searching after knowledge and insight. Moreover it is chiefly in her fiction that we find representations of the Victorian response to the intellectual and other difficulties of life: that is to say, the dedication of its best individuals to high-mindedness, to self-perfection, to the life of self-effacement and aspiration.

George Eliot's willingness also to engage in study and research before she began to write may be seen in a variety of ways. She was not above study of the humblest matters, if that was going to add to the depth of her work. In the first place, that depth and fulness came from a knowledge of the detail of provincial life acquired by her through early experience. That was the source of her splendid familiarity with Midland dialect and with the detail of farming and artisan life, of country wild life, as we see these things in novels like *Adam Bede* (1859) or *The Mill on the Floss* (1860). *Silas Marner* (1861), however, has a solitary ageing handloom weaver as its central character. The handloom weavers, in the early years of the nineteenth century in which the novel is set, were men in a distinctive situation. Their skill and their necessarily solitary life set them apart from most artisans, and they were as likely to work in country districts, where their raw materials came from, as in towns. That solitary life, and the need also for serious application in their work, tended to make them devout Dissenters in religion; and their walk of life was also being steadily taken over by the larger entrepreneurs. They were no longer independent craftsmen, but paid piece-workers, and their work was being taken over more decisively still by the factory weaving, which in the end relegated them to extinction.

The increasing plight of the handloom weavers was the subject of many official reports and the like, and it is clear that before finalising her novel George Eliot studied these with care. One incident must suffice in illustration. In chapter 21, Silas, restored to happiness and vigour through his adopted daughter, goes back to look at the diminutive dissenting chapel, in a nearby town, from which he was ignominiously ejected almost a generation before. It is no longer there: simply swept away by a large new factory. George Eliot has embodied the gradual historical realities of the handloom-weavers' lot, in a moving symbolic sequence.

For *Middlemarch* (1872) her preliminary studies were more extensive; though this has not always been given adequate attention. First, the situation of Ladislaw, grandson of the Polish refugee immigrant to Britain. George Eliot may have been especially conscious of the Polish situation because of the futile Polish insurrection of 1863, only a few years before she wrote the novel. But the chronology of the book is also aptly arranged so that the events of the story themselves are near in time to the earlier insurrection of 1830, and so also that Ladislaw's grandfather might well have quit his native land during one of the partitions of Poland between Russia, Austria and Prussia: the last being in 1793. Ladislaw's presence in this Midland town is no Dickensian accident, but accords with the history of the period.

That is true also of the intellectual position of Mr Casaubon, the learned (or pseudo-learned) clergyman. His ambition to discover the 'key to all mythologies' related to some of the most significant intellectual movements of the time: first, to the appearance in 1864 of Max Müller's *Lectures on Language*, and more fully, to Sir George Cox's *The Mythology of the Aryans*, published the year before *Middlemarch*. Cox's book was a 'key' to all Indo-European mythology; Casaubon's dream was an obvious extension of Cox's book. Similarly, Dr Lydgate's self-dedication, in the 1830s world of the novel, to discovery of the 'primitive tissue' fits with the work of the French medical scholar Marie-François Bichat (mentioned explicitly in chapter 15), with the studies of 'protoplasm' by Dujardin, and also von Mohl, over the 1830s and 1840s, and the achievement in the 1860s of Max Schultze, who showed that, chemically, the basic substances of animal and vegetable organisms were the same. Schultze in fact carried these matters on into the very years when George Eliot was writing the novel; and it is also the case that her treatment of how doctors (not Lydgate alone, but the more conservative doctors) were related to hospitals, hospital committees, fees, and the dispensing of medicine, shows her to have had detailed knowledge of the contemporary situation and contemporary controversies. Finally, in her last major novel, *Daniel Deronda* (1876), she displays thoughtful knowledge of the contemporary Jewish question, and the rise of Zionism.

Such things, however, will count for the reader of today as the outworks of George Eliot's achievement. Central to it is her extraordinary understanding of the interrelated intricacies of the Midland rural scene. In *Adam Bede* (1859), the underlying reality, spreading right across the book, is the pervasive contrast between the rich, placid county of Loamshire (Stafford-shire in fact) and Stonyshire to the north of it, where the land is wilder and life harder (Stonyshire is doubtless Derbyshire). Dinah Morris's Methodism comes from the more industrial north, but it finds a ready soil in the village of Hayslope in Loamshire. The reason is that Hayslope is a microcosm of rural variety – and interrelatedness:

'Why, sir, there's a pretty lot o' workmen round about, sir. There's Mester Burge as owns the timber-yard over there, he underteks a good bit o' building an' repairs. An' there's the stone-pits not far off. There's plenty of employ i' this countryside, sir. An' there's a fine batch o' Methodisses at Treddles'on – that's the market-town about three mile off – . . . though there's only two men of 'em in all Hayslope: that's Will Maskery, the wheelwright, and Seth Bede, a young man as works at the carpentering'.
(chap. 2)

In this novel, George Eliot makes her story out of how the graduations of social life in a village community will be interrelated; partly in kinship, but largely in the doings of their daily life. Adam Bede the skilful carpenter loves the pretty but foolish niece of a local tenant farmer, and she is seduced by the son of the local squire, their landlord, friend of the parish parson who strikes up good relations with the Methodist woman preacher, beloved of Adam's brother: it is she who cares for the mother of the two young men. Innkeeper, village schoolmaster, owner of the local carpentry-shop, land-agent, even to some extent the servants up at the big house, slowly intertwine in their daily lives.

Silas Marner is a shorter, simpler tale, almost like a fable in its simplicity. Its basic narrative is the slow transformation of weaver Silas from being a pillar of his local Methodist chapel in a small manufacturing town, to being a recluse, alienated and isolated from society; and then his equally slow return into the society of Raveloe, his adopted village, as his human contacts, first by chance then by design, are progressively renewed. George Eliot in fact records, in a letter of 1861 to her publisher, that the story 'came to me first of all quite suddenly, as a sort of legendary tale . . . but . . . I became inclined to a more realistic treatment'. In this novel also, we see the comings and goings between lonely weaver's cottage, village housewife, 'big house', and local inn (for which George Eliot writes the male villagers' conversation with amazing 'rightness').

There is, however, a deeper movement of connection, and of feeling. Silas Marner is a story of the slow imprisonment and then the slow liberation of the human individual. Silas the recluse hoards his modest gains until he has a small fortune, stolen from him one night, when he is out of his cottage, by the bad son of the local squire. Needless to say, he becomes more of a recluse, even than before. But later, a small child, an orphan, wanders into his cottage, in the dark also, like when the gold disappeared. A fundamental change begins:

. . . The gold had kept his thoughts in an ever-repeated circle, leading to nothing beyond itself; but Eppie was an object compacted of changes and hopes that forced his thoughts onward, and carried them far away from their old eager pacing towards the same blank limit.

Slowly but steadily, Silas is restored to human society:

By seeking what was needful for Eppie . . . he had himself come to appropriate the forms of custom and belief which were the mould of Raveloe life; and as, with reawakening sensibilities, memory also reawakened . . . he recovered a consciousness of unity between his past and his present.

In *The Mill on the Floss* the reader finds a similar pattern of complex interconnections between miller Tulliver and his family, and the lawyers and businessmen of St Ogg's, the local town; as well as the local farming community, the peasantry (represented by Joe the good-natured pedlar), and even the local gypsies. The pattern is rendered more complex by the fact that it is the miller's three sisters-in-law who have married into the three town business families which figure prominently in the novel, while his own sister has married a poor farmer. Family ties – and dissensions – become intertwined with connections of money or the lack of it, and of social position. At the same time, there are elements in the book which enable us to see it as not wholly fitting into the conception of a straightforward panorama of provincial-life social continuity. Stephen Wakem, the lawyer's son, has yearnings to be a painter, Maggie the miller's daughter has more powerful if less articulate yearnings towards some kind of fuller life than Dorlcote Mill and the town of St Ogg's offer her.

Even so, George Eliot remains conscious of the power of social conditioning over her characters:

You have known Maggie a long time, and need to be told, not her characteristics, but her history. For the tragedy of our lives is not created entirely from within . . . 'character is destiny'. But not the whole of our destiny.

In the end, we see that Maggie has been made, by the limitations of her social environment, into someone who could not be expected to avoid whatever disaster that environment had in store for her; but at the same time, we see that her tragedy is a partial triumph. When she drowns in the great flood (for the coming of which George Eliot has prepared us throughout the novel, by subtle passing touches) it is through a heroic act on her own part which led to final reconciliation with her brother, and so perhaps the deepest possible spiritual reward to herself. More must be said of this side of George Eliot's work; and already, if one casts one's mind back to *Adam Bede*, it is clear that there is heroism and idealism there also.

First, however, attention must be given to the 'web of provincial society' as this appears in *Middlemarch*; here it is not only developed much more elaborately than elsewhere, but the deeper strand of thought which, for George Eliot, underlies it, also becomes clearer. In this novel one finds an elaborate interplay of life between countryside and provincial town, the country houses of Mr Brooke and Sir James Chettam, the prosperous town residents like Vincy or Bulstrode, the world of provincial doctors like Lydgate and his elegant but egotistic wife (Vincy's daughter), clergymen like Farebrother, Rosamund's raffish brother Fred Vincy with his ill-managed country interests, and the widening circles of countryside life in Caleb Garth's sober traditional household; Stone Court, Mr Featherstone's run-down house; and the Reverend Mr Casaubon's arid house of a gentleman-clergyman, Lowick. George Eliot's panorama widens further, in fact, to include characters like the indigent but self-important Mrs Waule, the disreputable rolling-stone Raffles, his hostile stepson Rigg, and the irate country labourer Hiram Ford. No catalogue will suffice to present the elaboration of George Eliot's social and also topographical panorama in this novel.

There is one distinctive and most interesting way in which, in *Middlemarch* (the very name combines the ideas of 'centre' and 'boundary', and hints at her ambition to be exhaustive) the interrelatedness of the dramatis personae is made more real. By the close of the book, unobtrusively, the principal characters are all interrelated in the literal sense. Vincy and Featherstone are connected by their wives' being sisters. But the first Mrs Featherstone was related to the Garth family, and Vincy and the second Mrs Bulstrode were siblings. The relationship of Will Ladislaw, the Jewish-Polish outsider in this provincial society, transpires less readily, but on studying the novel closely one comes to realise that Will Ladislaw's grandfather had in fact married Casaubon's aunt (that was why her family repudiated her), and that his father had married the daughter of the first Mrs Bulstrode by her previous marriage to a Mr Dunkirk.

George Eliot makes these linkages unobtrusive. They are almost Dickensian in their elaboration and completeness, as well, one might say, as in their improbability. But in her case, they manifest much more considered and articulate intellectual interests than in Dickens's case. For George Eliot, the 'stealthy convergence of human lots' (as she calls it in chapter 11 of this novel), the 'long pathways of necessary sequence' (chapter 16), are represented in one way by those covert kinship relationships; but that is only one way out of a number. The 'play of minute causes' (chapter 6), the 'presentiment of endless processes' (chapter 15), or the 'train of causes in which he (Bulstrode) had locked himself' (chapter 61), are three more points where George Eliot makes explicit what is her fundamental and overriding awareness of life. It seems likely that when in *Middlemarch* she linked the main characters together by obscure threads of family relationship, she did so simply in order to give one more dimension to the system of inter-relationships that preoccupied her. When she said, in chapter 11 of the novel, 'Municipal town and rural parish gradually made fresh threads of connection', that was part of this same abiding interest. 'I have so much to do in unravelling certain human lots, and seeing how they were woven and interwoven, that all the light I can command must be concentrated on this particular web', she wrote in chapter 15.

Fundamentally, her conception of this weaving and interweaving was not one of picturesque coincidence and happy accident, but deeply characteristic of the highest intellectual ideas of her time; because it was one of slow-moving, inconspicuous, but for all that all-comprehending causality. As Joseph Jacobs, her contemporary, wrote in an essay on George Eliot's fiction, 'Her works gave the new feeling about life that seemed to be rendered necessary by the triumph of Darwinism in England.' In the last analysis, her 'web of provincial society' is enriched by her own experience and her rich powers of observation and recollection, but is present in her work in the first place because it issues from her deep convictions about causation.

Arnold Bennett, in his Diary, once wrote of Herbert Spencer 'filling me up with the idea of causation'. George Eliot (partly through the influence of the same Herbert Spencer) was also filled with that idea; but clearly, something remains to be said, for to read any one of her novels is enough to establish the presence of something hardly present in Bennett. What is remarkable in George Eliot is that her sense of society as a web of causation goes with a sense of the individual as, at least potentially, a being of high and aspiring moral endeavour and moral excellence. We see this as clearly in a short and simple tale like *Silas Marner*, as in the more complex and ambitious *Middlemarch*. There is Nancy Lammeter's 'spirit of rectitude, and the sense of responsibility for the effect of her conduct on others . . . an unselfish clinging to the right, and a sincerity clear as the flower-born dew, were her main characteristics'; and it is that same clear and unselfish clinging that makes her, with beautiful promptitude, propose instantly that they adopt Eppie, when she learns that Eppie is in fact her husband's daughter by a previous marriage. But George Eliot displays how other and humbler characters can have the higher moral life that introduces its own causal necessities. The instant Godfrey Cass, when he and Nancy pay their momentous visit to Silas in his cottage, has put his proposal to adopt Eppie into words, Silas also rises morally to the occasion: 'Eppie, my child, speak. I won't stand in your way.' Eppie, however, is of a comparable moral stature. She too does not hesitate. 'Thank you, ma'am – thank you, sir. But I can't leave my father, nor own anybody nearer than him'; and when Godfrey Cass tells her the truth about her birth, it does not even begin to disturb her attachment to Silas and the bonds of affection which have formed in her over the years.

In *The Mill on the Floss*, Maggie Tulliver is clearly a person of similar nobility of moral character, despite her failings and imperfections. She constantly seeks a fulness and aspiring quality in life beyond the scope of the narrow St Ogg's world, and rejects dubious invitations to such life even when it is too late to reject them without bringing scandal on herself, at least in terms of the St Ogg's conventionalities. She is, in fact, a half-educated, self-educated, muddled Dorothea Casaubon. In *Adam Bede* the three main characters – Adam himself, Arthur Donnithorne and Dinah Morris – struggle with the difficulties and limitations of life, seek to do what is right even if (in Arthur's case) they are inadequate to the struggle, and confirm, rather than call into question, the aphorism from Novalis that in *The Mill on the Floss* George Eliot cited only to call into question: 'character is destiny'. All three characters instantiate Victorian ideals of the individual's aspiring search for self-perfection, whether as altruisitic (if erring) country squire, virtuous

Illustration by W.J. Allen for The Mill on the Floss *(1860) by George Eliot.*

workman of sterling character, or quietly strong-minded, high-principled and
modest woman. With all three, necessary causation issues in the end not from
social conditioning, from the 'web of provincial society', but from the self-
dependent inner resources of the individual spirit.

No reader of *Middlemarch* will be in doubt that the same must be said about
Dorothea's character and her moral life, difficult as she too sometimes found
its realities. George Eliot's intimation, in the Prelude to the novel, that
Dorothea should be seen as a modern Saint Theresa is a clear indication. But
that is only half of George Eliot's allegiance in this book to the conviction
that individuals can rise above, and exist outside, social conditioning.

With *Middlemarch*, George Eliot's decisive demonstration of this comes in
chapter 81, among the most splendid passages in the whole of English fiction.
Dorothea, the provincial Saint Theresa in embryo, called the previous day on
that embodiment of cool, egocentric composure, Rosamond Lydgate, and
found her in what appeared to be a lovers' scene with Ladislaw – with whom
she is herself, in secret, as good as in love. Despite her inward grief and
despair, she goes back the next day, hoping, with much uncertainty, that she
can say something to Rosamond which may help the precarious state of her
marriage: 'even if we loved someone else better . . . it would be no use . . . I
know, I know, that the feeling may be very dear . . .' And so on. But she
encounters a surprise. For this once, Rosamond also rises to a height of moral
self-effacement. 'You are thinking what is not true . . . He was telling me
how he loved another woman, that I might know he could never love me . . .
now I have told you, and he cannot reproach me any more.' Dorothea replies
in the same words: 'No, he cannot reproach you any more.' In this supreme
moment, the selfish woman has risen as much above herself as the unselfish.
For George Eliot, there is in the end one thing which can override the 'web
of provincial society' and its networks of objective causality: the innermost
self-determination of the individual, in its search, in the supreme moments of
life, for the Good.

Victorian sages and improvers

The term 'improver' is used here in a literary context, not a practical one:
otherwise, Florence Nightingale and General Booth of the Salvation Army,
along with many others, would call for treatment. The literary sages and
improvers of the second half of the century ought not to be seen without
reference to major thinkers of its earlier years. Ruskin (1819–1900) is clearly
one of the 'sages' of the period, and calls for discussion at some length; but a
discussion of Ruskin which made no reference to Carlyle (1795–1881) or to
Coleridge (1772–1834), would be defective. Ruskin's admiration for the
Middle Ages, and conviction that that period of society was superior to his
own time, was prefigured in Carlyle's *Past and Present* of 1843. Ruskin's
sense of the historical process as proceeding with a certain inevitability and
bringing out, in the course of time, fundamental truth, is clear in Carlyle's
French Revolution (1837). His most central conception, which was of reality
as essentially spiritual and a reflection of the Divine principle, is central to

Carlyle's *Sartor Resartus* of 1833. It is here that we find Carlyle's famous assertion that the universe is not a dead thing, but 'Alive, and My Father's!' and that an idea which was already to be seen in Coleridge's *The Friend* (1809–10). Coleridge makes much the same contrast as Ruskin makes later, between surface human pursuits like commerce and economic life, and 'where, on the other hand, the nurture and evolution of humanity is the final aim'. In such fields, 'there will soon be seen a general tendency toward . . . some ground common to the world and to man'; and this ultimate principle or 'rock of strength and refuge' is the unified system of the whole cosmos as a manifestation of the Divine, a spiritual and 'life-ebullient stream which breaks through every embankment'.

Between those words and what Ruskin said in *Modern Painters* (1843–60), part III, especially chapters 3 and 4, on beauty in the external world, there is much in common. Mazzini once described Ruskin as 'the most analytical mind in Europe', and certainly his discussion of natural beauty is more systematic and analytic than what we find in Coleridge. But the essence of it is much the same. Ruskin ingeniously identifies several kinds of beauty in natural objects, but the kind which interests him most is what he calls 'typical beauty': meaning, that various aspects of the sensible world are beautiful because they represent or 'typify' this or that aspect of the nature of God. In seeing created nature, we see Him. One may note instances like Ruskin's saying that symmetry in nature typifies the divine justice, or seeming endlessness, divine infinity; but more important is what Ruskin infers from his doctrine. A right appreciation of natural beauty calls for ability to respond to the manifold attributes of divinity, calls for 'a curiously balanced condition of the powers of the mind'. Only a 'whole man', in his wholeness, responds adequately.

In *The Stones of Venice* (1851–3), Ruskin recognises that that train of thought, applied to the world of human artistic achievement, links art indissolubly to human morality, and thereby constitutes a transforming first principle for critical judgement. Successful artistic achievement is necessarily the issuing forth of the condition of a morally superior society. Ruskin's Carlylean sense of historical necessity transpires in his delineation of how Venetian art rose higher and higher until it reached its climax and then declined, moving all the time in accord with the health of the society from which it came. In one section of *Modern Painters* (IV, 17, 'The moral of landscape'), Ruskin actually identifies two traditions running through English literature: writers who were out-and-out lovers of nature and scenery (he mentions Byron, Shelley, Shenstone), and writers in whom that love was controlled and supplemented by 'hard work or watching of human nature'. Among these, he mentions Johnson. Needless to say, for him the second category is superior to the first. Ruskin's indebtedness to Carlyle may be seen if one turns to the latter's essay on Burns, and notices Carlyle's grounds for admiring that poet; and there is interest also in how Ruskin's two lists, and reasons for the contrast, anticipate the arguments of later critics like Orage or Leavis.

In the later 1850s, Ruskin began to move from art criticism to the theory and criticism of society. '. . . I simply cannot paint, nor read, nor look at minerals, nor do anything else that I like because of the misery that I know of'. Those words come in the first letter of *Fors Clavigera* (1871–84). In Letter 37 he describes how, going one day into the Ashmolean Museum at Oxford to give a lecture on art, he was lacerated by the sight of a destitute child playing outside, and wearing his mother's great shoes. Ruskin turned his attention to, as he saw it, the intolerably complacent findings of the Victorian economists, and his mode of argument was curt and conclusive. He simply denied that the political economists used their key words in the senses normal for those words in the life of man. How is it possible that men of affairs understand the word 'wealth', he asks, when the Tintoretto paintings in the San Rocco Chapel, which represent more genuine 'wealth' than anything else in Europe, are being left to rot in the rain coming through the roof? Wealth is said by the economists to be 'the possession of articles of value'. What of a man wearing a heavy money-belt, but sinking into the sea? The example comes from *Unto This Last* of 1860. Publication of this work was stopped because of the outcry it produced. In 1906, however, British MPs were asked to name the books which had most influenced their development, and *Unto This Last* came next after the Bible.

Ruskin likewise argued that 'utilities' were not those things which would fetch the best price in the market, but what was 'good for life'. What is 'useful' in one man's hands can be the opposite in another's. The articles which became *Munera Pulveris* were also stopped in publication because of the outcry. Whether later economists like Pigou have done enough to take account of Ruskin's arguments, or society, since Ruskin's time, has done enough to preserve its essential as opposed to its market values, the reader will decide for himself. Certainly, Ruskin powerfully exposed the dangers in the Victorian dogmas of *laissez-faire* economics; and the underlying integration in his thought of natural world, human art, and the values of human society whether ideal or contemporary, is remarkable.

John Stuart Mill's (1806–73) greatest achievement may have been the intellectual distance that he travelled, beyond the narrowly Utilitarian and Benthamite modes of thought which (as his *Autobiography* tells us) were so sedulously imposed upon him in youth by his father James. At the age of twenty, Mill underwent some kind of personal crisis, intellectual and emotional. He realised that fulfilment of the Benthamite ideals inculcated in him by his assiduous father would not, in fact, bring him happiness. 'I now saw, or thought I saw; that the habit of analysis has a tendency to wear away the feelings.' It was turning to Wordsworth's *Excursion* (the *Prelude* being still over twenty years from publication) that restored Mill's spiritual balance; and most of his best work thereafter took the form of analysis in fields where strict logic was not enough, or of enlarging analysis through humane and sensitive feeling. During the 1830s, Mill exchanged many letters with Carlyle, who referred to him as 'a new mystic'. Writing to Carlyle in 1832, Mill said that while it was

the artist alone in whose hands truth becomes impressive and a living principle of action . . . yet it is something not inconsiderable . . . if one could address [men] through the understanding . . . yet in a spirit higher than was ever inspired by mere logic.

One finds such an approach repeatedly. It is present in Mill's early articles, over the 1830s, 'The spirit of the age', and even in the *Logic* of 1843, where he distinguishes a special nature for the 'logic of the moral sciences' (that is, the social sciences), and considers that the fundamental concept for those sciences is one of much subtlety: 'it is necessary to consider what is a state of society . . . the simultaneous state of all the greater social facts . . . there exist natural correlations among the different elements'. The matter is beyond logical analysis because of 'the influence exercised by every one of these phenomena on every other'. Mill thus expresses in general terms what George Eliot was at pains to embody in her fiction.

Despite his busy life as a civil servant at the India Office, Mill's writings regularly bring this more humane approach to bear. He made a most praiseworthy attempt (as F.R. Leavis pointed out long ago) to synthesise the thought of Bentham and of Coleridge. In his chief philosophical work *Utilitarianism* (1861), he adheres to the Benthamite idea that moral goodness must be defined through human happiness; but his 'higher spirit . . . than mere logic' quite transforms the Benthamite idea. For Mill, 'Poetry' is better than 'pushpin', it is better to be 'Socrates dissatisfied than pigs satisfied'. Thoughts like that make short work of the crude Benthamite position, but one should not bring to Mill's thought the empty logicality that he rejected himself. *Utilitarianism* offers no final solution to its problem, but one cannot read it without a lasting conviction that moral goodness can never be explained by reference crudely to dogma, or crudely to human gratification.

A sense of Mill as above all a brave and humane explorer of fundamental problems is the best guide to his work. His *On Liberty* (1859) pleads eloquently for freedom of opinion and, more influential even, of expression, in any genuine society; and Mill's desire to achieve 'a spirit higher than ever was achieved by mere logic' could lead him to superb finality of style. 'The peculiar evil of silencing the expression of an opinion is, that it is robbing the human race.' If the opinion is correct, people both present and future are robbed of the chance to exchange error for truth; if wrong, of 'what is almost as great a benefit, the livelier impression of truth, produced by its collision with error'.

In *Representative Government* (1861), Mill again goes to the heart of his subject, with the assertion that the vote in political affairs is not a right but a trust exercised on behalf of society. Hence the secret ballot is wrong, since society should know how any individual exercises that trust; and there is consistency in Mill's saying that although all should have a vote, those best qualified to judge should have more votes than one (of which more below). But Mill's *The Subjection of Women* (1869) best shows his humane clarity of mind. Much of the detail in his essay is chiefly of historical interest; but when in chapter 4 he offers to answer those who ask what, after all, will be the immediate practical gain from changing the situation of women, then at a stroke we find Mill at his best again. He goes instantly to the heart of the matter:

. . . To which let me first answer, the advantage of having the most universal and pervading of all human relations regulated by justice instead of injustice.

After that, there is more to say, but it does not have to be said.

Mill could not have foreseen, though, some of the difficulties his liberalism might have brought in other societies than his own. When he argues eloquently for freedom of expression, the most outrageous opinion that comes to his mind is that of the non-existence of God. In suggesting a system of public examinations for additional votes, he reminds his readers that no difficulty would arise, because everyone recognises the difference between matters of fact, and disputed opinions. Mill had never heard of 'disinformation'. In advocating no secret ballot, he blithely asserted that the days of intimidation in public affairs were over. In these things, Mill was of his own time. That he was among the best of its 'sages' is beyond dispute.

Matthew Arnold (1822–88) was an 'improver' in the practical sense, because of his thirty years as Inspector of Schools. One can tell from his *Letters* how long his days' work were, how much he travelled, how seriously he devoted himself to the position. His impact as a practical improver must be related also to his Reports, of much wider scope, to the Educational Commissioners, and to his special reports on various aspects of the education of the young in Europe. But only at two important points did Arnold's writings bring forward practical proposals for change at the level of national politics. One of these, his call for a system of local government over the whole country, actually came to pass in the year of his death. The other was a repeated call for a system of 'public schools for the middle class'.

That can easily be misunderstood. Mill believed that such schools should be systematically set up by the state; one should also recall that Arnold's general wish to see an increase in state action came at a time when the state took a less active part in society than today. But Arnold called the schools he desired to see 'public' because he wished to see schools offering a higher education (not merely the 'Three Rs'), and comparable to the great schools available to the upper classes, set up for the middle classes; as was the case, he considered, in France.

There, he said, such schools were provided sometimes by the state, sometimes by private bodies, the distinction was not of importance. What was of importance was that in the future the English middle class was going to be dominant, and an adequate higher education for its children was therefore essential not for the convenience of the parents but for the future welfare of the country. Arnold's advocacy bore fruit in the legislation of 1900, which set up a nation-wide system (already in being in some areas) of public 'grammar' and 'county' schools.

In his wider reflections, Arnold took a starting-point like that of Mill in his early 'Spirit of the age' essays (mentioned above). Following Saint-Simon, he thought that society tended to pass through a succession of alternating stages: an 'age of concentration' (when men's attitudes and beliefs would all be related definitely to one all-embracing system) would be succeeded by an 'age of expansion' or 'critical age', in which the dominant mode would be one of enquiry, review, and exploration. Arnold's belief about his own time was that it was, or was just beginning to be, an age of this second kind – a 'critical age'. Hence, the over-riding question was of the spirit, the frame of mind, in which such comprehensive enquiry and review was best conducted.

Thus Arnold's seminal early essay, 'The function of criticism at the present time' (1865) was not about literary criticism at all: he introduced that topic, at a late stage, only to make clear that his main concern was something else. That central concern was for the whole cast of mind in which a 'Critical Age' might best conduct itself. In regard to that, Arnold offers many formulations. In 'The function of criticism' we find, 'to see the object as in itself it really is', and 'to see life steadily and to see it whole'; and he hopes that in twenty years' time

it will be an objection to a proposition that it is absurd . . . I have wished above all to insist on the attitude which criticism should adopt towards things in general; on its right tone and temper of mind.

In 'Literature and science', originally a lecture at Cambridge, later included in the *Discourse in America* (1885), Arnold points to the basic condition of such a clear perspective: it is the balanced development of all sides of the personality. Hence the need for literature as an integral part of higher education. As early as 1852, in his first General Report on schools in England, he had said:

I am sure that the study of portions of the best English authors . . . might be made a part of [the] regular course of instruction . . . Such a training would tend to elevate and humanize.

In his most seminal book, *Culture and Anarchy* (1869), Arnold brings together his conception of the right frame of mind in which men should approach the future, and his belief that the English middle class would predominate, in approaching its problems. What, in his opinion, dominated the middle-class outlook of his own time, was the self-assertiveness and dogma of its Nonconformist religion. 'Strength and fire', and 'Hebraism' were among the terms he used to characterise that. To complement and elevate such a condition of mind stood the 'sweetness and light', the 'Hellenism', of the other great tradition of Europe. Hence Arnold's sustained interest in classical literature, and his faith in literary study as an instrument for educational superiority.

In the end, only such a cast of mind could substitute 'Culture' for the 'Anarchy' Arnold saw in his own time. What he meant by that he made clear in the 'Function of criticism' essay: in one and the same issue of a daily newspaper, he read how a well-known politician had referred to the 'unrivalled happiness' of contemporary Britain, and also how a young unmarried mother had come out of the workhouse at Nottingham, carrying her illegitimate child, had strangled it, and left the body out on a Nottinghamshire hillside. 'Wragg is in custody', Arnold noted that the report laconically but eloquently concluded.

In his later years Arnold turned from general and cultural speculation to consider the position of Christianity in his own time. Here he tried, in works like *Literature and Dogma* (1873), or *God and the Bible* (1875) to intimate to the reader that the dogmas of Christianity, insofar as they claim supernatural reality, were not acceptable to the modern intellect. What is so, is the spirit which Arnold finds in Christ's teaching. There he found a 'sweetness and light' that seemed to him to have immense reserves of moralising and elevating power. In fact, Arnold came near to seeing Christ as the supreme literary figure. His re-interpretation of Christianity did not, as we all know, have an influential future; but there was a logic, a consistency and large-mindedness in how these ideas rounded out and completed his work.

For all their divergence in religious matters, Arnold deeply admired Cardinal Newman (1801–90) as a mind and an individual, and he may well have owed much to Newman's thought. In Newman's 1851 discourses on *The Scope and Nature of University Education*, delivered by him to inaugurate his headship of the new Catholic University in Dublin, the word 'enlargement', by which Newman clearly meant openness and liberality of mind, is the key to the whole. Arnold was like Newman in his wish for a comprehensive, as opposed to a merely scientific, cast to the educational programme; and Newman still held a similar position, specifically about religious faith, in his *Grammar of Assent* of 1870. There, he speaks of an 'illative sense' as a kind of comprehensive, balanced awareness of mind, able to seize, one cannot but say intuitively and in Arnoldian fashion, upon doctrines which are not susceptible of rigorous rational proof.

It may seem strange to include among 'sages' Arnold's niece the novelist Mrs Humphry Ward (1851–1920; daughter of Dr Arnold of Rugby's second son Thomas, and wife of T.H. Ward for whose five-volume anthology Arnold wrote his famous essay 'On the study of poetry'). Mrs Ward, however, was a novelist of a very distinctive kind. Her remarkable imaginative gifts went with a profound awareness of the 'great issues of the day' that George Eliot, for example, may have shared, but that no one explored and dramatised as much as she did in fiction. This gives her an outstanding and highly distinctive place.

Her first novel, *Robert Elsmere* (1888) shows also how many of her novels were distinctive and illuminating in another way. Its hero Catherine's family belonged to a remote part of Westmorland; the landscape and weather conditions are often brilliantly described, the life rhythms of the family and its neighbours are often distinctive, and we see that in Mrs Ward we have one of the few outstanding authors who have shown us the rural far north of England. That is in itself a major achievement; but the main weight of the book lies in the battle it dramatises among its ideas. Catherine, a simple, intense, Low Church Christian supernaturalism; Rose her sister, the musician, interested only in the life of the arts; and Catherine's eventual husband Robert, a clergyman open to the wider influences of Oxford, at first more a churchman than quite suits his wife, later a devout apostate who equates Christianity with goodness (much, in fact, in Matthew Arnold's own terms in his later religious works), and gives himself to humanising the London working class. Such are the clashes – between faith and morals, art and religion, social service and inner piety – which animate the characters and move the action forward.

The History of David Grieve (1892) is set at first in the Peak District; and here Mrs Ward shows, incidentally, a mastery of dialect which in this respect sets her quite on a par with George Eliot or Thomas Hardy, and which shows again in *Helbeck of Bannisdale* (1898), another Westmorland novel. Here also, in David's impossible sister Louie, and his odious dissenting aunt,

Hannah, Mrs Ward shows her gift for depicting loathsome people – as indeed with Mrs Denton in *Helbeck*, the agent Henslowe in *Elsmere*, or the 'smoothie' political careerist Wharton in *Marcella* (1894). At first, with David Grieve, one is inclined to think that Mrs Ward's preoccupations have receded, that now she is concerned with personalities and with narrative. But it becomes clear that Low Church and High Church, faith and loss of faith, the world of industrious 'making one's way' and the world of art, are the cardinal points, as it were, of the novel. In *Marcella* the issues are different. Marcella herself, though in a rural squirearchy setting, is a young enthusiast for sweeping Socialistic reform and self-effacing social service; later she moves to London and toils as a nurse in the service of the poor. Her engagement to a local landed magnate is broken off because she cannot tolerate his improving-landlord status-quo mentality, and in the end is renewed because she becomes disillusioned with doctrinaire nostrums, and in seeing through Wharton's charlatanry she senses the unreality of much of the political scene. (Parliamentary affairs are not central to the novel, but Mrs Ward displays a mature insight and a sureness of touch that, set beside for example Trollope's political novels, bring out what one can only call their endless fertility and entertaining triviality.)

Helbeck of Bannisdale is perhaps Mrs Ward's best novel. Its evocation of the Cumbrian scene is again superb, its indications of how both Helbeck's deep other-worldly Catholicism, and his Laura Fountain's militant if erratic scepticism, are in part (though only in part) a product of family and ancestry, are superb also. The tragic clash between those two world-views is what generates and resolves the narrative, and a narrow, self-righteous kind of Dissent figures vividly in it also. The ever-renewed tension and agony of Helbeck's and Laura's impasse are powerful and moving. Mrs Ward had an imaginative realisation of the force, and the destructiveness, of her 'great issues', as did no other writer. If there is something to add, less in her favour, it is that the task of integrating great ideas with intense personalities and great events was rather beyond even her. Her powers of realisation in matters of the detail of human appearance, behaviour and dialogue are not quite on a par with her gift for ideas – nor for scenery, in fact – and perhaps this is why, if one stops to think, one hesitates to feel at ease that Helbeck and Laura would have fallen, as it were, in love twice over, or that David and Elise would have done so; and one has a sense that Catherine's long-drawn-out taciturn agonies over the sceptical Robert are left for the reader, rather than the author, to make real. The other difficulty with Mrs Ward is that the expositions and analyses of her 'great issues', as indeed sometimes her writing more generally, can be slow-moving and diffuse, even prolix; and that the prominence of such issues can sometimes remind one that her novels 'date' in a way that truly memorable imaginative representation does not. All the same, she remains one of the most remarkable authors of her time.

In both fiction and discursive prose, William Morris (1834–96) also ranged most of his work about the 'great issues' of politics and of art in society. He acknowledged Carlyle, Ruskin and Newman as the chief influences upon him, and of these Ruskin was the most substantial. But Morris notably extended

Ruskin's work in three ways. First, he took the practical side of Ruskin further. In the fields of painting, architecture (beginning with his own 'Red House' at Upton in Kent), weaving, tapestry, wallpapers, stained glass, typography, and production of fine books – as well as in other fields – Morris was the most outstanding as well as prolific producer and improver of the century. Here, the generally medieval cast of his work links him with Carlyle and Newman, as well as with Ruskin.

Second, he went beyond all of these in that in his later years (when he was a prolific lecturer all over Great Britain) he repeatedly stressed how the society of his own time was damaging and destroying the natural environment in which it lived and its descendants would live. He was the first to see the importance of environmental conservation to the whole of the future (for him, it simply followed as a wider aspect of his criticism of reckless, ignorant, so-called 'restoration' of medieval buildings); and it could well be argued that in the long term this was his most important contribution.

Thirdly, Morris was the only one of the 'sages' of the century to take his speculations on into the politics of the day. This development came very shortly after he took up lecturing on problems of design, in the late 1870s. He began a long period of studying the writings of Karl Marx; and in 1883 he joined the Socialist Democratic Federation and became active in left-wing politics. But he encountered difficulties. He underestimated the powers of self-defence and resistance of Victorian middle-class society and its economic system, and indulged in ill-founded optimism for the almost immediate success of the Socialist cause. Besides that, he found difficulty in working with the self-assured and autocratic Hyndman. In 1884 he, and in fact a majority of the leading members, left the Democratic Federation and founded the Socialist League. But it was not long before Morris found the anarchist presence in the League as unacceptable as Hyndman had been; and by 1890 he and his closest associates withdrew into themselves, confining their activities to the Hammersmith Socialist Society, which they now formed. In the same year, Morris extended the practical side of his artistic work by founding the Kelmscott Press and turning to the production of new type-founts and fine editions. 1890 was also the year of his most extended expression of what he believed: the moving, medievalist Utopian romance-cum-prophetic manifesto, *News From Nowhere*. But the last word of that title expresses something of Morris's disappointments in his last years.

Walter Pater (1839–94) is not often thought of among the sages of the Victorian period; but he deserves a word in conclusion. A comparatively early essay like 'Sebastian van Storck' is ostensibly set in the past, but beneath the surface it seems to be a meditation on the full significance of the recently-discovered Second Law of Thermodynamics, and so the ultimate running down of the whole universe. *Marius the Epicurean*, about a Roman youth who is an early convert to Christianity, is at the same time a curious allegorical presentation of the life of the intellect in the nineteenth century: the Utilitarian philosophy, John Stuart Mill's humanisation of this, Arnold, and something like the Oxford Movement, can probably all be identified. Finally, his last works: *Gaston de Latour* (1895) is set in the period of the French Wars of Religion, and *Emerald Uthwart* (1892), apparently in the time of the Waterloo campaign. But in the former of these there are not only, once again, suggestions of the great questions of Pater's own time (the 'Lower Pantheism' of the book being much reminiscent of the 'cosmic emotion' conception of the 1870s and 1880s); but also, if one thinks of what was to happen in Europe twenty years later but could already be seen on the horizon, a remarkable brooding awareness of the nature of modern war from the standpoint of the common people. 'The unquiet temper of war was still abroad everywhere'; the great cannon 'took the householders by surprise . . . a fanatical war of forty years'. The same is true of the shorter piece of 1892. The newly commissioned Uthwart goes to Flanders; they 'come in sight of the army in motion, like machines moving'. Uthwart ends, like a displaced person of the twentieth century: '. . . a roundabout and really aimless journey . . . lingering for food at some shattered farmstead . . . a part of the ruin into which he creeps as darkness comes on'. Such strange, haunting, prophetic words take the reader out of Pater's period, and into our own later time.

Browning, Hopkins, and the individualising imagination

Dickens affords the most conspicuous example of the Victorian quality of energy in the writing of the period; but it is natural enough that apart from him, the most striking examples should be found in the verse of the time. The greater compression and therefore intensity of effect in verse, as against prose, naturally throws such a quality as energy, of apprehension as of presentation, into relief; and it is also natural, if one begins by thinking in this context of Dickens, that the first name to come to mind among the poets of the time should be that of Browning.

It is not however as a portrayer, like Dickens, of human personality that Robert Browning (1812–89) will first catch the reader's attention. Rather, it is in the way he presents the single item of sensuous detail, and imprints it, almost with violence, yet almost in passing, upon the reader's mind. One may offer as examples the 'faint half-flush that dies along her throat' that the painter sees in the youthful bride of the elderly Duke ('My Last Duchess'); or the 'little waves that leap / In fiery ringlets from their sleep' ('Meeting at Night'); or the beautifully precise and specific, yet also almost in passing, 'Runnels, which rillets swell', of 'A Lover's Quarrel'. Such examples, terse yet sharp, are innumerable; one need only open Browning's poems at random.

   What is less obvious is that this vividness of perception and sharp aptness of presentation is characterised, almost always, by two interesting restrictions. In the first place, Browning's vividness is seldom at the service of perceiving what is gradual, inconspicuous, or subtle. The 'faint half-flush' of the first example is almost exceptional in its approach to this range of perceiving. What Browning characteristically catches is the event that is small but sharp. There is a striking example of this in a comparatively early poem 'The Flight of the Duchess', of 1845:

> . . . early in autumn; at first winter-warning,
> When the stag had to break with his foot, of a morning,
> A drinking-hole out of the fresh winter ice
> That covered the pond; till the sun, in a trice,
> Loosening it, let out a ripple of gold,
> And another and another, and faster and faster,
> Till, dimpling to blindness, the wide water rolled:

One can even detect, sometimes, how Browning falls into a kind of sharp miniaturisation of the sensuous details that engage his attention; as in 'Cleon' (1855): If Cleon the painter could speak to Zeus, the poem says, what he would say is that in the natural world there is only one point of weakness; which is that created nature, apart from mankind, has no self-consciousness. This aside:

> All's perfect else: the shell sucks fast the rock,
> The fish strikes through the sea, the snake both swims
> And slides, forth range the beasts, the birds take flight,
> Till life's mechanics can no further go –
> And all this joy in natural life is put
> Like fire from off thy finger into each,
> So exquisitely perfect is the same.

It is perhaps of interest that while what Browning claims for his natural world is perfection, what he describes here is in fact different; simply the intense, vivid, self-assertive activity of every detail of the natural environment.

Browning was a great admirer of Shelley (1792–1822), whose powers of natural description are often misunderstood and underrated; but the two poets responded to Nature in significantly different ways. Occasionally, one finds touches of exact and vivid description of particulars in Shelley, as in his 'yellow bees in the ivy-bloom'; but in the main, his attention was turned in two directions in which Browning did not follow him. He was drawn to depict not the small vivid effects of Nature, but its largest panoramas. We see that clearly in such a poem as the 'Ode to the West Wind' with its 'tangled boughs of air and ocean', or in the extraordinary description of the planet Earth in cross-section in Act IV of *Prometheus Unbound*. Both of these examples, however, emphasise just that other aspect of Shelley's descriptive interests which Browning did not share. 'Air and ocean' make a tangle of boughs for Shelley because he makes his poem out of an unravelling and untangling of the boughs so as to re-construct the system of nature, the functioning of natural forces in the biosphere – an interaction of climate and weather. Browning seems at pains, in his choice of metaphor, to avoid any such entanglement. 'Like fire from off thy finger': it is what is individualising and singularising in the natural world that catches his imagination and guides his choice of metaphor.

Exceptions to this view of Browning can doubtless be found – there must be such in so voluminous a poet – but the trend is remarkably steady. A handful of further examples may clinch the point, in the context of his treatment of one of the broadest of natural phenomena, the change from one season to another. In 'By the Fireside' he writes:

> . . . the drop of the woodland fruit's begun,
> These early November hours,

– but at once, his vivid particularity asserts itself: they are hours –

> That crimson the creeper's leaf across
>   Like a splash of blood, intense, abrupt,
> O'er a shield else gold from rim to boss,
>   And lay it for show on the fairy-cupped
> Elf-needled mat of moss,
>
> By the rose-flesh mushrooms . . .

In a moment, the great seasonal change has been transmuted to the other end of the spectrum of response. Aptly enough, two other poems show exactly the same tendency about the coming of the other seasons. In the famous 'Home-Thoughts, from Abroad', Browning thinks of the coming of an English spring. Again, the transition is evident:

> And after April, when May follows,
> And the whitethroat buildings, and all the swallows!
> Hark, where my blossomed pear-tree in the hedge
> Leans to the field and scatters on the clover
> Blossoms and dewdrops . . .

In 'Up at a Villa – Down in the City', set in Italy, May brings in another season:

> Is it better in May, I ask you? You've summer all at once;
> In a day he leaps complete with a few strong April suns.
> 'Mid the short sharp emerald wheat, scarce risen three fingers well,
> The wild tulip, at end of its tube, blows out its great red bell . . .

Whatever season it is, 'life's mechanics can no further go' in transforming the pervasive and panoramic into vivid particularity.

What has been said so far, however, is an adequate account only of the subordinate part of Browning's oeuvre. It is not, after all, as a poet describing nature that he is important in our literature, so much as on account of his studies of individual character and personality. Certainly, the poems which depict the enigmatic characters in which Browning took delight, are also full of vivid touches of description of *things*. 'How it Strikes a Contemporary' is the portrait of a poet such as Browning perhaps aspired to be himself. The detail floods in upon the reader, with this poet's 'very serviceable suit of black', his 'scrutinizing hat', how he 'walked and tapped the pavement with his cane', sat quietly in the evening in his modest house

> Playing a decent cribbage with his maid
> (Jacinth, you're sure her name was) o'er the cheese
> And fruit, three red halves of starved winter-pears, . . .

Likewise in 'Fra Lippo Lippi': '. . . a titter / Like the skipping of rabbits by moonlight'. In 'The Bishop Orders his Tomb at Saint Praxted's Church', there is the precious piece of lapis lazuli that the cupidinous bishop has hidden away to grace his tombstone:

Bedded in store of rotten fig-leaves soft,
and corded up in a tight olive-frail.   [*basket*]

Likewise in 'Andrea del Sarto' the coming of 'settled dusk' at once turns into
'the watch-lights show the wall, / The cue-owls speak the name we call them by'.

But between this subordinate self, and Browning's central self as portrayer
of human individuals, there is a contrast summed up in two lines from his
own poem 'Parting at Morning':

And straight was a path of gold for *him*,
And the need of a world of men for *me*.

Browning's major poetic achievement is as creator of a 'world of men'.

Moreover, in this regard he works in a way almost opposite to what has
been discussed above. His guiding interest is by no means simply the
presentation of vivid detail. In these more important poems that is nothing
more than an incidental habit. His guiding concern is presenting character
and personality; and more simply, revealing how a complex and enigmatical
character can be an integrated whole. The Valladolid poet of 'How it Strikes
a Contemporary' is the prim, trim, old-fashioned 'character' of his surface
description, but in the final, fundamental analysis he is the shrewd,
searching, all-seeing, all-comprehending recorder of humanity and its ways,
one worthy of reporting to God himself. Fra Lippo Lippi is an amalgam of
harmless minor peccadilloes and sensuous penchant for pleasures, and at the
same time, a deeply religious man whose love of the sensuous world is based
on intuition that its sensuousness is a divine creation. The 'Bishop' who
orders his tomb is worldly, greedy, and even spiteful, but his love for his son
as we see it, momentarily, here and there in the poem, for their mother
(covertly their mother, of course), for his church, and also his deep if
primitive religious sense, are all genuine parts of his complex nature, and in
the end the reader sees that complexity as a single whole.

In 'Andrea del Sarto' we find faultless, if disablingly academic painter,
affectionate if despairing husband, and kindly, modest, well-meaning man,
brought together into a picture of a single integrated personality. 'Bishop
Blougram's Apology' takes the movement from vivid detail to study of
human type a stage further. Here, there is in fact almost no vivid detail at all;
only the remorseless unfolding of how layer after layer of worldliness in this
prince of the Church appears in the end only as the outward aspect of
genuine religious belief latent below it; until in the last section Browning sets
the whole poem so far, at a discount. He intimates that all we have read so far
was no more than an ad hominem rehearsal of tactical thinking by the
bishop, about whom the truly religious side of experience remains to be
revealed. If mid-Victorian intellectuals generally were preoccupied with how
experience was a systematic whole, it was Browning, certainly more than any
other poet and perhaps more than any other contemporary writer, who
successfully explored how the human personality, over and over, may be a
baffling complexity, but is at the same time a strange and profound unity.

Alongside Browning, if we think about Victorian vividness and particularity,
the name of Gerard Manley Hopkins (1844–89) necessarily suggests itself.

Hopkins was aware of this side of Browning's work: in a letter to Canon Dixon he speaks of Browning's 'skill in which he displayed the facts from different points of view: this is masterly'. He also makes reference to Browning's 'collection of particulars . . . photographs of still life . . . minute upholstery description'. Hopkins, however, does not admire these aspects. His comments include words of judgement like 'pointless' and 'impotent', which I have omitted in the quotations above. Browning 'has all the gifts but the one needful and the pearls without the string'.

It was natural that Hopkins should not be in sympathy with Browning. He did not share the latter's interest in the presentation of what is enigmatical in human character, and his most conspicuous interest as a poet was in the natural world rather than human nature. Also, conspicuously, that interest embodied what Browning's interest did not. Hopkins's concern was with the broad, panoramic effects of the natural world as much as with its vivid localised detail:

It was a leaden sky, braided or roped with cloud, and the earth in dead colours, grave but distinct . . . All the length of the valley the skyline of hills was flowingly written all along the sky . . . All the landscape had a beautiful cast of blue. Many lime-coloured smokes in the valley . . .

(Journal, 23 and 24 September 1874)

But intensity of particularity is frequent, and striking, in Hopkins's poems. In 'Spring' we find:

> Thrush's eggs look little low heavens, and thrush
> Through the echoing timber does so rinse and wring
> The ear, it strikes like lightnings to hear him sing . . .

To follow Hopkins here, one needs to know the sky-blue colour of the thrush's egg, and the loud liquid clarity of the bird's song. Again, in 'Pied Beauty':

> rose-moles all in stipple upon trout that swim . . .

In 'Harry Ploughman' we find a comparable sharpness of vision over the human individual:

> Hard as hurdle arms, with a breath of goldish flue
> Breathed round; the rack of ribs; the scooped flank; lank
> Rope-over thigh . . .

Hopkins, however, was a more self-consciously, thoughtfully, even laboriously philosophical poet than Browning; and for him there was philosophical reasoning as to why it was right to concern oneself with the vivid particular detail. To do so was the beginning of a movement towards the innermost nature of whatever object concerned one for the moment. Hopkins called this innermost, unique nature of the individual object its 'inscape'; he developed this term before he found much the same idea embodied in the *haeccitas* of the medieval philospher Duns Scotus. For Hopkins, 'inscape' was this innermost uniqueness of every individual created thing, and 'instress', a term he used less often, seems to have meant a kind of inner energy, a force which generated and projected 'inscape'.

What, Hopkins asked himself, actually was the 'inscape' of this or that
created object? The word 'created' is key to the answer he gave. Since
everything in Nature is not only created, but also sustained in existence by
the Creator, inscape which is the innermost being is at the same time God-
given being. Two of his most celebrated short poems, 'Pied Beauty' and
'God's Grandeur' make this clear. 'Glory be to God for Dappled Things', the
first beings: but that response is no idle generality, because it is just that
vivid variety, that 'dapple' quality, which indicates God's presence in the
world and creativity of it:

> Whatever is fickle, freckled (who knows how?)
> with swift, slow; sweet, sour; adazzle, dim;
> He fathers-forth whose beauty is past change:
> Praise him.

'God's Grandeur' opens:

> The world is charged with the grandeur of God.
> It will flame out, like shining from shook foil;

– much like what Browning once referred to as the 'flash' of the vividly
present individual. But Hopkins's poem continues by lamenting how men
have blurred and blotched the work of the Creator. Even so, he continues:

> There lives the dearest freshness deep down things;

and the reason for that takes one back to the continuing presence of the
Creator in the created world:

> Because the Holy Ghost over the bent
> World broods with warm breast and with ah! bright wings.

(The poem of course envisages the Third Person of the Trinity as a dove.)
The profound religious intensity and integrity of Hopkins, the poet who
put his priesthood before his poetry, explains the most characteristic
movement of many of his poems. In 'God's Grandeur' the natural world is
impaired by mankind; but even so, the impairing is superficial: the divine
presence is present all the same. In 'That Nature is a Heraclitean Fire . . .',
the moment of sensing how the created world is chaotic is also the moment of
finding

> In a flash, at a trumpet crash,
> I am all at once what Christ is . . .

In the 'The Wreck of the Deutschland', at the height of the storm, the 'tall
nun' who in effect takes charge of the doomed ship 'christens her wild-worst
best' as she cries 'O Christ, Christ come quickly'; and in perhaps the neatest
of all Hopkin's presentations of the idea, in 'The Windhover', the ash that
sparks because it has fallen through the air, the ploughshare that gleams
because it has been burnished by the hard ploughland, and the little hawk of
which the beauty shows through, exactly when it ceases to brace itself,
hanging motionless in the wind, and instead lets the wind swing it swiftly
away – all of these reveal their 'inscapes', in the very moment of yielding to
created Nature, and therefore to the creating and sustaining Power behind

Nature. Inscape, as innermost being, is necessarily God-given being; and to celebrate it (despite Hopkins's repeated unwillingness to compose verse during his priesthood) is in the last analysis an act of worship.

It remained for Hopkins to ask what form of words made sense for uttering the 'Glory be to God' the 'Praise Him', that he saw as the essence of a poem. Clearly a poem must have its own inscape; but also it is the poem's inscape, its unique individuality as another created thing, that is essential to its functioning. Hopkins enunciated his main conception of what makes a poem a poem in an undergraduate essay which he wrote while studying at Balliol: 'The structure of poetry is that of continuous parallelism.' Hopkins's meaning was that in poetry there is more patterning than in prose: though this additional patterning may take any of a number of forms – sequences of rhythm, of rhyme, alliteration or assonance, and then in correspondence with those things, parallelism between the words and in the thought. In these things would lie the 'inscape' of the poem, and thus its adequacy as an expression of the God-given individuality and uniqueness of the created things it dealt with.

Hopkins was thus to concern himself with a second inscape, that of the poem itself, revealing the first inscapes, those in the primary created world. It was a train of thought not without its difficulties for him.

No doubt my poetry errs on the side of oddness . . . But as air, melody is what strikes me most of all in music, and design in painting, so design, pattern, of what I am in the habit of calling 'inscape' is what I above all aim at in poetry. Now it is the virtue of design, pattern or inscape to be distinctive, and it is the vice of distinctiveness to become queer. This vice I cannot have escaped.

(Letter to Bridges, 15 February 1879)

Readers are not likely to agree over the boundary, in Hopkins's case, between the distinctive and the 'queer'. For myself, it indeed seems that he overstepped that boundary in the opening lines of, say, 'That Nature is a Heraclitean Fire . . .' or 'The Leaden Echo'. The energy of impulse so characteristic of Hopkins seems, here, to have about it something of the merely repetitive. 'Spelt from Sybil's Leaves' opens in a not dissimilar way:

Earnest, earthless, equal, attuneable, vaulty, voluminous . . . stupendous
Evening strains to be time's vast, womb-of-all, home-of-all, hearse-of-all night.
Her fond yellow hornlight wound to the west, her wild hollow hoarlight hung to
  the height
Waste; her earliest stars, earl-stars, stars principal, overbend to
Fire-featuring heaven.

This seems to be Hopkins's own highly remarkable kind of 'Parnassian': the term he invented for the style of a true poet, when however he is writing without his own characteristic inspiration.

Perhaps, however, it was this very development in his writing (the three examples just now mentioned are all from his later work) which brought it about that there is a late stage in his writing (often referred to as the 'terrible sonnets'), where Hopkins gives expression to deep self-distrust and unhappiness. The crucial point is that in these poems he does so with a blunt directness very different from the verse just now quoted.

I wake and fell feel the fell of dark, not day

or

To seem the stranger lies my lot, my life
Among strangers.

or

My own heart let me more have pity on; let
Me live to my sad self hereafter kind . . .

are the opening lines of sonnets which, for the laying bare of a great poet's troubled but defiant loneliness of spirit, have no equals in the language; and it is part of the complexity of Hopkins's case that, had he been alive to see the great reception of his verse when at last (in 1918) it was published, that would have yielded him not even the crumb of 'comfort', a craving for which is the recurrent motif of his last poems.

Trollope and James: invention . . . insight

Trollope (1815–82) and James (1843–1916) particularly lend themselves to being considered together; though to say this is far from suggesting that they are alike.

If one were to ask which Victorian novelist gives the broadest and richest panorama of the life and society of his time, the answer must be, Trollope himself. Dickens offers but little by way of portraiture of the life of the British aristocracy. Trollope has, recurring in one novel after another, not only the Duke of Omnium and all his cronies, followers and rivals, but also a substantial range of characters from low life like Abel Handy and Greg Moody, the illiterate almsmen in *The Warden*, or Bunce the rough and Radical lodging-house husband in *Phineas Finn*. In *The Way we Live Now*, the extremes are from Melmotte and the Emperor of China, to Squercum, the shifty, insidious lawyer, and Ruby the orphaned peasant girl. Besides this Trollope offers his readers the most comprehensive overview of the interpenetration of London, metropolitan life (both high life and low life) and rural England, and his pen runs to the intricacies of the legal world (*Orley Farm*, 1862; *The Way We Live Now*, 1875) both ultra-respectable and shady, through the if anything greater intricacies of the ecclesiastical world, the cathedral close and the country parsonage. There is also his gifted irony in regard to the high-sounding fatuities and altruistic careerism of the world of the Press – Tom Towers, Mr Supplehouse, the 'Jupiter', Mr Alf, the 'Evening Pulpit'. Finally, it is right to mention the vivid American scenes in a work like *Dr Wortle's School* (1881) the American characters, at least, in *The Way we Live Now*, and how, most notably in *Phineas Finn* and *Phineas Redux* (1873), Trollope supplements his pictures of English life by dealing with the society of rural Ireland – a society which, for all its difference and remoteness, had substantial bearing upon both private and public life in England.

To recall this unrivalled range of subject, however, is no more than a

'*Lady Mason after her confession*'. *Illustration by John Everett Millais for* Orley Farm *(1862) by Anthony Trollope.*

beginning in praise of Trollope, and a novelist of little real merit might
conceivably spread his canvas comparably wide. In the first place, Trollope's
people are not only drawn from over the whole social diapason; they are
remarkably vivid and varied.

> . . . it was in London, not in the country, that Mr Sowerby indulged, if he did
> indulge, in his bachelor mal-practices . . . Mr Sowerby was one of those men who are
> known to be very poor – as poor as debt can make a man – but who, nevertheless,
> enjoy all the luxuries which money can give . . . it seemed that there was no end to
> his horses and carriages, his servants and retinue.
>
> (*Framley Parsonage*, ii, iv)

– space prevents quotation of Sowerby's masterstrokes of dialogue, his
endless adroit oscillations between wheedling compliment, and bullying his
victims over money. But in contrast to him, Trollope has equal facility in his
presentation of the traditional, high-minded, narrow and yet ultimately
generous Lady Lufton and the humorous, resourceful, quick-witted,
straightforward heiress Miss Dunstable. His inventiveness is altogether
remarkable. A crippled Italian seductress, an oily careerist parson, a strict,
generous, high-minded, outspoken country doctor, a wealthy, upper-class,
shy Scottish landowner and domestic bully – and of course Mrs Proudie, the
bishop's wife, about whom everybody knows – these are the mere beginnings
of an almost endless catalogue, easily drawn up, of Trollope's seemingly
inexhaustible fertility in characterisation. That is also of Trollope's powers of
invention in respect of incident. Henry James, the reader may sometimes feel,
is by no means the same. The incidents that take his narratives on to their
conclusions are sometimes rather few and far between. The novelist seems to
be husbanding his resources. Trollope's narratives take the reader onward
almost too easily. He reminds one of Johnson's praise of Shakespeare: 'he . . .
constrains him who reads his work to *read him through*'.

There is, however, more to say. If one's first response to Trollope is to be
absorbed, to read on and to read him through, when one begins to reflect on
his books, the consequences are different and are less in his favour. One
begins, little by little, to doubt whether character and incident really come to
integration in his novels as fully and closely as, in a truly serious novel, we
look to them to do. Would Marie Melmotte in *Framley Parsonage* really have
fallen so deeply in love with the contemptible and indeed ridiculous Felix?
And would a clergyman like Mark Robarts really have fallen so completely
into the clutches of a Sowerby? Would Phineas Finn really have fallen deeply
in love with the serious or even slightly solemn Lady Laura Standish, then
with bright, pretty Violet Effingham, and then finally returned to a love for
the sweetly innocent, rural West-of-Ireland Mary Flood Jones true enough
and deep enough to make an adequate resolution of the whole book? If he
could change and change like that, would Lady Laura have loved him, and
gone on loving him, though in all innocence, throughout years of her married
life? Or would Laura not have seen through Mr Kennedy, if he was going to
turn from the gentle, shy man into a canting religiose bully, and a tight-
lipped domestic tyrant?

To raise such questions is not to settle anything in Trollope's disfavour.
Anything, no doubt, can happen in life; and James's treatment of his

characters is enough to remind one of that. But to put the matter thus is to move a step nearer to what is a fundamental weakness in Trollope. The point is, if the transformations and tergiversations which are so much what equip him to hold the reader's attention are to satisfy, as it were, on second thoughts, they call for a more searching, more insistent delineation of character than Trollope seems even to seek to achieve. His plots turn many of his characters into tricksy half-puppets, or into profoundly interesting human enigmas: but over and over, he does not solve the riddles that he poses. Rather it is his immense fertility, fluency and facility that enable him, or at least cause him, to sail smoothly past fascinating difficulties of his own making. In other words, there is a good case for saying that Trollope is the first, and probably the best, of our popular novelists. Thoughtful students of the human scene may in the last analysis set him regretfully aside: 'readers of fiction', in a certain sense, will be slow indeed to tire of his entertainments.

The book which perhaps does most to escape this severity of judgement, of relegation, is a short, early, comparatively simple work: *The Warden*, of 1855. Even here, Trollope's easy, fluent shortcomings can be traced. It is a *donnée*, at the opening of the narrative, that Mr Harding's devoted and clear-headed daughter is in love with the man who is attacking her father's whole position in life – and remains in love; and it is also a *donnée* that the devoted and outstandingly clear-headed Dr Bold should have put himself into that position. Perhaps, the reader is even more disquieted, on reflection, by the scene in which John Bold suddenly abandons his high-minded and public-spirited efforts, though without in any way coming to believe that it was objectively ill-judged. Leaving those matters aside, however, Trollope undoubtedly achieves, in this work, something that seems beyond him in his more ambitious novels.

Mr Harding, warden of the cathedral almshouses at Barchester, is a gentle and retiring man whose main qualities are personal kindliness, especially to inmates of his almshouse, and love of music. There is a strong case for arguing that, in the self-contained, secluded and comfortable society of this west-of-England cathedral close, his own income has over the course of time been grossly enlarged at the expense of those whom it is his duty to care for. That is the situation which John Bold has launched an attack upon, an attack soon to be reinforced by the verbosities of the egregious 'Jupiter', the cupidity of most of the inmates, and the greed of Bold's lawyers. On the other side is Mr Harding's overbearing son-in-law, Archdeacon Grantley, and the distinguished but morally purblind barrister, Sir Abraham Haphazard. In portraying all these characters, Trollope's genius for vivid and lively portrayal and sharply idiosyncratic dialogue is as good as it is anywhere. But with Mr Harding himself, he achieves something deeper. His growing awareness that the position he holds is morally precarious, and his resolution, supported convincingly by his daughter, to free himself from that by abandoning the wardenship, transpire in a way that convinces us of how here, at least, Trollope has achieved that deeper and more humane insight into character, and control of it, which often escape him. Mr Harding experiences the conscious and self-chosen disastrous lot of one kind of truly and convincingly tragic character; and Trollope, with a fine sense of life's realities and of the culminating movement of the tragedy, convincingly recounts how Mr Harding's personal disaster brings tragedy for the credulous old men whose lives depended, somewhat intangibly, upon his kindliness. The success of *The Warden* is something most unusual with this novelist; I believe that he owed it to the very brevity and simplicity of the book, a brevity and simplicity which necessarily excluded the fluency, facility and boundless inventiveness which elsewhere gave him so high a place in something less than the highest category.

It is both difficult, and in a sense embarrassing, to turn from discussing Trollope oneself, to Henry James's essay (of 1883) on Trollope in his collection, *The House of Fiction*; but a temerarious transition like this is beneficial at least because it reminds one that James the great novelist was also the author of the finest array of essays on novelists and the novel which we have in our language, and that one of his principal merits, in his prose as well as his fiction, is a truly astonishing precision and delicacy of style. He speaks of Trollope, illuminatingly, as 'strong, genial and abundant': but his own geniality of distinction, word by word as a writer, is the most conspicuous if not the greatest of his gifts, as opening almost any page of his writings will confirm. He understands Trollope superbly: 'with his extraordinary gift, there was always in him a certain infusion of the common'; 'his inestimable merit was a complete appreciation of the usual'. Nor has he any difficulty in intimating something that limits Trollope's achievement even while it perhaps adds to his 'readability':

His observation of the common behaviour of men and women was not reasoned nor acquired, not even particularly studied . . . it was enough for him that he felt their feelings and struck the right note, as it were, because he had the right ear.

Such kindly but penetrating observations are typical of James as critic.

In defining Trollope's merit, James as good as defined his own by contrast. James's own inestimable merit was a complete appreciation – one achieved not by ear, and not particularly studied but exactly the converse – not of the 'usual' but of what, in the end, silences the reader with a sense of its incomparable distinctiveness, its unique depth and fulness. A depth and fulness, however, not to be understood in any simple terms. 'The air of reality (solidity of specification) seems to me to be the supreme virtue of a novel': but that itself is not so easily explained.

It goes without saying that you will not write a good novel unless you possess the sense of reality . . . it is equally excellent and inconclusive to say that one must write from experience . . . Where does it begin and end? Experience is never limited and it is never complete; it is an immense sensibility, a kind of huge spider-web, of the finest silken threads, suspended in the chamber of consciousness and catching every air-borne particle in its tissue.

Such words, from James's magisterial 'Art of fiction' essay of 1884, recall the very similar words that Virginia Woolf used in her essay 'Modern fiction' of the early 1920s; and emphasise how much James was a part of modernist literature and the twentieth century, as well as of an earlier time also.

Another way of approaching the difficulty as well as the fascination of

James, and of recalling his distinction as a writer of the short story, is to recall his 'The Figure in the Carpet' (1896): not one of his greatest tales, but peculiarly indicative of his deeper fictional interests. A gifted young critic learns, in conversation with a distinguished novelist, that in the latter's work there is a continuing and underlying covert significance which, once identified, will be the key to all.

In the tale, that secret never reveals itself; but there is profound guidance here over what to be ready to respond to in James's own longer works: to see there, whether in a nouvelle like *Daisy Miller* or in the long novels, some 'finest, fullest intention of the lot . . . a triumph of patience, of ingenuity'; and for the reader, 'My whole lucid effort gives him the clue – every page and line and letter.' Those are the phrases that James uses himself in the story.

Daisy Miller of 1878 – originally sub-titled 'A Study', in contrast to Trollope's 'not . . . particularly studied' fiction – relates the tragic history of a young American girl staying in Geneva and then in Rome, and the young American man who finds her a delectable enigma:

Certainly she was very charming, but how extraordinarily communicative and how tremendously easy! Was she simply a pretty girl from New York state . . . or was she also a designing, an audacious, in short an expert young person? Yes, his instinct for such a question had ceased to serve him, and his reason could but mislead . . .

Again and again, the riddle of Daisy reappears in one form or another. '"Common" she might be, as Mrs. Costello had pronounced her; yet what provision was made by that epithet for her queer little native grace?'; or again, 'by his own experience, when young persons were so ingenuous they were less articulate and when they were so confident were more sophisticated'. In Rome, where the young American rejoins Daisy once more, there is the same sustained uncertainty; '. . . Daisy, on this occasion, continued to present herself as an inscrutable combination of audacity and innocence'. Just as, in all innocence, she was unconventionally informal with Eugenio the Genevan guide, so she seems to have neither prudence nor propriety in how she allows the obsequious, insidious Giovanelli to take her about in Rome, culminating in a near-midnight visit to the Colosseum. James permits himself one clear revelation only, and that by no means over-clear, of her complex mixture of muddle, innocence, open-heartedness, self-assertion – and true love, in fact for Winterbourne himself. It comes when, his tolerance at last exhausted, he says to her,

'I believe that it makes very little difference whether you are engaged or not.'. . . He felt the young girl's pretty eyes fixed upon him through the thick gloom . . . . 'I don't care,' said Daisy, in a strange little voice, 'whether I have Roman fever or not!'

The 'figure in the carpet' (to quote the title of one of James's short stories) is at last complete for her; and when Giovanelli, asked (after her funeral) by Winterbourne why he took Daisy to 'that fatal place', deadly with malaria, says simply 'For myself I had no fear; and she wanted to go', and goes on to reveal that he had become certain there was no possibility that the charming heiress would accept him, the brutality of character that underlay his polite exterior is at last revealed, and the figure in the carpet is completed for him also.

For James, the encounter between innocence and depravity proved to be of perennial interest; not in any simple form, but with all the subtlety his elaborate mind could give it. He superimposed this preoccupation upon that which he had with the situation – or fate – of the American in Europe. In *The Awkward Age* (1899), however, the innocent heroine is not American: James is interested here in the 'epoch of transition' between an older London high-society world of personal integrity, perfectly straightforward and almost – though not quite – naïvely simple, and a newer one in which, as with his heroine Nanda Brookenham here, that integrity can go with insight into the London society world, and its miscellany of character, that is wonderfully exact and incisive. Moreover, in this longer work, James displays his preoccupation with the gradual but rich development of what he calls his 'idée-mère', his 'scant but quite ponderable germ'. Slowly, the full potentialities of his major characters, and their potentiality for almost self-contradictory qualities, transpire to the reader in what James himself, in his Preface to the novel, half-apologetically describes as 'appreciable, or more exactly perhaps . . . almost preposterously appreciative, over-treatment . . . what "over-treatment" may, in the detail of its desperate ingenuity, consist of'.

The Portrait of a Lady (1880–81), unquestionably the finest of James's nineteenth-century novels, conforms to a similar pattern; but to finer effect. James's Preface here too, as its speaks of the 'germ' of the book, its 'growth', the 'lurking forces of expansion', the 'evolution of the fable', displays the same kind of preoccupation with what in his central essay 'The art of fiction', he calls 'solidity of specification . . . the supreme virtue of the novel' – 'I conceive the needful accretion as having started, the right complications as having started.' Isabel Archer is a young American woman, 'seeing the world' in Italy, who marries Gilbert Osmond, an American expatriate living in Italy, and a connoisseur. The novel is an instance of one fundamental shift of interest in later nineteenth-century fiction, from the period of courtship to that of later married life, when the enlarging illusions of courtship wear thin. Little by little the reader sees that Isabel's intelligence and even a touch wary high-mindedness have not saved her from marrying a man who is nothing short of fiendishly self-centred, mean-minded, mercenary, and even Philistine. At the same time we see how Madame Merle, who seems at first the generous-minded and distinguished friend of them both, is a marginally coarser version of Osmond, and also, for that matter, his discarded mistress.

At his best, James excels all other novelists in English for his 'solidity of specification' in respect of individual character and its gradual but encyclopedic revelation as the novel proceeds. His subject-matter is not a matter of actual development and change of character. Rather, it concerns itself with the progressive revelation of what has been in a character from the start. The action of his best novels is to create for the reader a succession of scenes, dialogues, transient crises, which have as their function to release this fullest potential. James often succeeds – certainly he does in *The Portrait of a Lady* – in rounding off his presentation of character by displaying how total fulness of characterisation can touch the edge even of inconsistency of character. Chapter 45 of *The Portrait of a Lady* shows one example. As we progress through the dialogue between Isabel and her old friend Ralph Touchett, and they speak of Lord Warburton, her erstwhile and unsuccessful suitor, and his attitudes to Isabel's charming step-daughter, we at first have an uncomfortable feeling that both Warburton and Isabel are hovering on the verge of inconsistency; and then, almost with awe, sense what one might perhaps term the multi-valent integrity of James's consistency and logic. Trollope's doubtful consistencies are clearly of another order, and a much less distinguished one.

In so short a discussion as this, one confined as it must be in this volume to the novels which James published before 1900, it is not possible to write fully either of his merits, or his development. Nor, indeed, can one quite justly evaluate the element of excess which his work occasionally displays. The fact remains that, as novelist, as writer of short stories, and as theorist and critic of fiction, James is unquestionably one of the most major figures in our whole literature.

Hardy and the rural tradition

There is a sense in which Hardy (1840–1928) embodies rural tradition more substantially than George Eliot. Over much of Hardy's work, his chief concern is the daily life and the annual round of Wessex village people. The middle-class characters stand more on the periphery of the novel, and in general they are treated with rather less sympathy. That is clear from the earliest of Hardy's 'Wessex' novels, with Farmer Shiner and Parson Maybold in *Under the Greenwood Tree* (1872); to say nothing of the daintily flirtatious schoolmistress Fancy Day. For Hardy, it is the villagers, in all their finely shaded variety, who are the abiding centre of interest. He is easily familiar with the Dorset dialect of his time, and uses it to achieve a slow building-up of rustic character, and the leisurely though occasionally sharp turn of the relaxed country humour in dialect, of which he was a master.

For the individuality of the countryman, his eye could also be sharp. Michael Henchard, the hay-trusser in *The Mayor of Casterbridge* (1886):

At his back he carried by a looped strap a rush basket, from which protruded at one end the crutch of a hay-knife, a wimble for hay-binds being also visible . . .

Giles Winterbourne in *The Woodlanders* (1887) at Sherton Abbas market:

. . . standing, as he always did, at this season of the year, with his specimen apple-tree in the midst, the boughs rose above the heads of the farmers, and brought a delightful suggestion of orchards into the heart of the town.

In an earlier novel, *Far from the Madding Crowd* (1874), in his portrait of the 'reddleman' Diggory Venn, Hardy draws on his knowledge even of the out-of-the-way rustic figure:

The traveller with the cart was a reddleman – a person whose vocation it was to supply farmers with reddle for their sheep . . . like his van, he was completely red. One dye of that tincture covered his clothes, the cap upon his head, his boots, his face, and his hands. He was not temporarily overlaid with the colour; it permeated him.

Hardy's knowledge is just as varied and detailed in respect of the rural round of the year, and its seasonal celebrations. After describing Venn's journey over Egdon Heath, he depicts the Guy Fawkes Night bonfires that spring up in the darkness:

. . . Some were distant . . . bundles of pale strawlike beams radiated round them in the shape of a fan. Some were large and near, glowing scarlet-red from the shade, like wounds in a black hide.

One sees Hardy's searching sense of metaphorical life kindling a poetry in the scene. His picture of the village-women's May-Day dance in *Tess of the D'Urbervilles* (1891) acquires the same intense poetic life:

The banded ones were all dressed in white gowns – a gay survival from Old Style days, when cheerfulness and May-time were synonyms . . . the sun lit up their figures against the green hedges and creeper-laced house-fronts . . . in addition to the . . . white frock, every woman and girl carried in her right hand a peeled willow wand, and in her left a bunch of white flowers . . . There were a few middle-aged and even elderly women in the train, their silver-wiry hair and wrinkled faces, scourged by time and trouble . . . almost grotesque.

With that scene one may compare the village girls who go out in darkness in *The Woodlanders*, so as to sow hempseed as part of the pre-Christian ritual for dreaming of their future husbands; or the village choir's Christmas round in *Under the Greenwood Tree*. Whether it is a matter of individual character, or scenery and scene-setting, or colourful incident, Hardy creates interest by drawing on an encyclopedically intimate acquaintance with country life. Casterbridge the country town (the Dorchester of the real world) is one end of the spectrum; the other is the wild heath lands, Giles's lonely forest-cottage, or the scenes of many of the poems ('Near Lanivet, 1872'; 'At Middle-Field Gate in February'; 'Winter in Durnover Field').

Those who are still countrymen – or even gardeners – will know that in one profound respect rural life differs significantly from town life. This is in respect of the element of chance. In seeing how Hardy organises his novels, one must make substantial allowance for this; or else his own remarks in, for example, the 1888 essay 'On the profitable reading of fiction' will be disquieting. He says there, 'Among the qualities which appertain to life construed . . . by the light of imagination . . . is that of self-proof or obviousness'; speaking also of a 'story which . . . has the merit of being well and articulately constructed'. The profound respect of difference between town and country life of which I spoke, consists in the different part played by chance in the two. If this is overlooked, Hardy's 'articulate construction' can seem like rollicking Dickensian fortuitousness. But for rural life, chance is another thing. This applies not only to the vagaries of the weather, which play so great a part in the articulate construction of, say, *The Woodlanders* (the disastrous rain in chapter 4) or *The Mayor of Casterbridge* (the fluctuating weather and in the end disastrous harvest, chapter 37), or (in the storm in chapters 36 and 37) *Far from the Madding Crowd*. In a thinly populated traditional countryside, chance governs also the personal affairs of people more than in a town. Gabriel's sheep are lost (chapter 5) because no-one is at hand to arrest the long-drawn-out disaster; and in *Under the Greenwood Tree*, it is mere chance that Dick tells Maybold of his engagement to Fancy ('Autumn', chapter 7), before Maybold posts off his letter to a friend with the same news about himself, or sees the outrageous little Fancy for a second time.

Here, however, so far as Hardy's major, 'Wessex' novels are concerned, one needs to record a significant development. That decisive chance event in *Under the Greenwood Tree* was a fortunate chance. Much the same may even be said of how Bathsheba is in Boldwood's house (*Far from the Madding Crowd*, chapter 53), when the odious Troy reappears and reclaims her. But from then onward, chance begins to play another role. If, in *The Return of the Native*, Mrs Yeobright had not turned away from her son's house so promptly, and had then not been bitten by an adder, disaster would not have occurred. If Henchard had not suddenly been prompted to lie to Newson that his daughter had died, if the weather had been clement when the fugitive Grace Fitzpiers met Giles Winterbourne in the woods by night, if Tess's letter for Clare had not slipped under the carpet, tragedy would again have been averted. Hardy, echoing George Eliot in part, wrote 'Character is Fate, said Novalis' (*Mayor of Casterbridge*, chapter 17). He undoubtedly subscribed to that belief. Clym's high-minded but susceptible doggedness, Grace's susceptibility, Henchard's old-fashioned ways, obstinacy and bad temper, Tess's curious mixture of drive and diffidence, Angel Clare's doctrinaire feebleness, all work into what Hardy, in the essay quoted from already, called 'the inevitableness of character and environment in working out destiny'.

'She stood up in the window-opening, facing the men'. Illustration by Helen Paterson Allingham for Far From the Madding Crowd *(1874) by Thomas Hardy, in* The Cornhill Magazine, *May 1874.*

But it is the environment Hardy depicts which in large part makes possible the prominence of chance in the resolution of his narratives; and, little by little, chance comes to seem like the instrument of a destiny which, if not malevolent, at least displays a kind of giant indifference, unknowingness even, towards the affairs of mankind. Hardy expresses the idea in 'Nature's Questioning':

> Has some vast Imbecility,
>   Mighty to build and blend,
>   But impotent to tend
> Framed us in jest, and left us now to hazardry?

Hardy's language as a poet, its curiously uncouth and seemingly unworked, yet repeatedly telling aptness, blends with his thought, and sharpens it, again and again. (Hardy's poems are discussed by Jacques Berthoud in volume 8.)

Hardy tried to give expression to the view that to speak of 'Chance' in human affairs too much anthropomorphised what lay beyond the human. In his dramatic epic of the saga of Napoleon, *The Dynasts* (1904–7), he wrote of human events:

> Emerging with blind gropes from Impercipience
> By listless sequence – luckless, tragic Chance
>   In your more human tongue.

In one of the minor novels, *A Pair of Blue Eyes* (1873), there is an incident which for Hardy is highly significant. The hero is in danger of his life, having half-fallen down a cliff-edge. As he hangs there (chapter 22), he finds himself staring at a fossil in the face of the cliff. It is of an extinct trilobite, 'Separated in their lives by millions of years, Knight and this underling seemed to have met in their place of death.' The sequence well illustrates Hardy's abiding consciousness of the world, including the world of mankind, as an evolutionary spectacle; all the more so perhaps for being so little pondered as such, at least at the human level.

With this in mind, one can see that, increasingly as he went on, Hardy's narratives seem to plot out an evolutionary course for his most treasured human protagonists; rather as if his deepest level of vision was to see evolution, on the human plane, as a process of discontinuous but inescapable extinction. In *The Mayor of Casterbridge*, Henchard is slowly driven from being the chief and pivot of his local society to being a hopeless outcast, devoid of both friends and possessions. In *The Woodlanders*, Giles descends from being established 'in the apple and cider trade' to his 'unadorned stone' in a secluded corner of the churchyard; and Marty, the woman who loved him, ends as a 'solitary and silent girl . . . clothed in a plaitless gown, the contours of womanhood so undeveloped as to be scarcely perceptible in her'. The 'marks of poverty and toil' on her are plainly present, however; save in the last scene of the book, where in the half light she tends Giles's neglected grave.

The history of Tess (*Tess of the D'Urbervilles*) is a prolonged parable of unsuccessful struggle for survival. From the placid obscurity of her youthful life in the village of Marlott she is driven out by misfortune; in the 'Phase' of the book appropriately called 'The Rally' she re-establishes herself in the favourable terrain of the 'rich dairies', and nearly succeeds in reproducing, that decisive biological test of successful survival. But the Rally fails. She is driven away to less favourable territory, she fails to resist the intrusion of a predator (Alec the twice-over seducer), and her final situation is that of a pet animal in a cage (in the Budmouth lodgings with him). *Jude the Obscure* (1896) may be well seen as the parable of an organism that sought to establish itself in a new territory, and failed to do so.

To leave the matter there, however, would be a mistake in respect both of Hardy and of his time. 'Victorian England' was not a homogeneity; and in the 1880s and still more the 1890s there were social changes other than the modernisation of agriculture and rural life, and the depopulation of rural areas, as reflected in *The Mayor of Casterbridge*, or *Tess*. Such matters as those, Hardy could in large part accommodate to his sense of Darwinian struggle for survival. But the widely-publicised divorce cases of the last years of the century, the movement for women's suffrage, and the feminist movement more generally in the period, were other matters. Farfrae in *The Mayor of Casterbridge* is a cool, astute, calculating representative of modernity; but Hardy does not find him antipathetic, and his picture of how Farfrae displaced Henchard is more or less detached and objective.

Dr Fitzpiers, and Lucetta, in *The Woodlanders*, show Hardy's fiction moving, though hardly conspicuously, into another mode. The old allegiances to rural life and customs, and also to a Darwinian sense of life, are still strong, but there is a new sense that education and modernity bring emancipation in large part as some kind of self-centred and predatory amorality. 'Those strange studies that used to distract you so much', Grace says to Fitzpiers towards the close of the book, about his philosophical and similar interests; and Hardy is sensible also of how the philandering Fitzpiers exerts pressure on Grace, because their marriage somehow constrains her as it does not him. Hardy seems to be turning his attention from biological to social pressures that act upon his characters and his narrative; those pressures being class, or economic – and also legal.

In *Tess*, the change goes further. Alec D'Urberville is an upstart, nouveau-riche, commerce-based reprobate doing violence, throughout the book in one way or another, to virtuous rural traditionalism. Angel Clare, under his mere surface gloss of forward-looking secularism, speaks for the purblind, self-righteous traditionalistic religion of his family, fettered to repressive and punitive dogmas that, once again, victimise the female sex. The novel seems written more out of Hardy's sense of society's moralising injustices, than out of any preoccupation with Darwinism. There is a topical, a 'tract-for-the-times' quality about this book that sets it rather apart from its predecessors.

Jude the Obscure takes this further. Its two most prominent preoccupations are the denial by contemporary society of educational opportunities to those born outside the social classes which were conventionally allowed them; and the inextinguishable, long-drawn-out torments that come from the power of sexual love when it becomes entangled with the traditional 'sanctity' of the marriage 'bond'. Those who most suffer the torments are Jude and Sue – developed, rounded, more or less humane characters. Those who suffer less are Phillotson, relatively arid and conventionalised, and Arabella, all casual animality. Hardy makes his interest clear in the Preface to the first edition:

A novel addressed . . . to men and women of full age; which attempts to deal unaffectedly with the fret and fever, derision and disaster, that may press in the wake of the strongest passion known to humanity; to tell, without a mincing of words, of a deadly war waged between flesh and spirit; and to point the tragedy of unfulfilled aims.

In the Postscript of 1912, Hardy added:

The marriage laws being used in great part as the tragic machinery of the tale, and its general drift on the domestic side tending to show that the civil law should only be the enunciation of the law of nature.

(A view, incidentally, that Samuel Butler had caricatured in his novel *Erewhon* in 1872.) The furore of adverse criticism (or abuse) with which Hardy's novel was received by many reviewers is today an interesting historical detail.

These aspects of Hardy's last major novels have a particular interest in the present context. They remind one that by the closing years of the century the 'Victorian Age' had, in any conventional sense, gone. A new society, with new values and new modes of living and of writing, was coming in. Hardy, living on until he died in 1928 at age eighty-eight, is the figure in English writing who most clearly and prominently bridges the old and the new.

'*At the Play*', *from* The World, *12 December 1878.*

4 The Drama of Wilde and Pinero

GEORGE ROWELL

The paradox of the Victorian theatre lies in its enormous popularity – more people attended more performances than in any age before or since – coupled with its exclusion from recognition as one of the arts. Among those who rejected the theatre were the aristocracy, who transferred their patronage of the performing arts to opera and ballet; the educated and religious, who shunned the theatre and took to reading; and the government, which recognised merit in writers, painters and musicians, but ignored it in playwrights and players. The only knighthoods conferred on theatre practitioners before Henry Irving's in 1895 were for composers (Henry Bishop, Julius Benedict, George Macfarren). When Sullivan was knighted in 1885, apologists claimed the honour was in recognition of his 'serious' music, though it was conferred during the run of *Iolanthe*. Gilbert had to wait another twenty-five years.

The history of the nineteenth-century British theatre is fittingly divided by the retirement of William Charles Macready in 1851. He and his predecessors, John Philip and Charles Kemble, Edmund Kean, the younger Mathews and Madame Vestris, were actors first and managers (if at all) second. Their efforts to sustain and improve the standard of performance proved fitful and often met with financial failure. Even in Shakespeare productions they were frequently defeated by the limitations of their stage and audience. The century's most famous piece of dramatic criticism – Coleridge's 'To see him [Kean] act is like reading Shakespeare by flashes of lightning' – is at the same time its most damning: so much was lost, so little illumination provided. If Charles Lamb lauded the comedian Munden in ephemeral farce and deplored Kemble in Shakespearean tragedy, it was the treatment of the text, not the acting, that shaped his judgement. Acting might redeem a worthless piece; it could only distort and might destroy literature.

The actor-managers who succeeded Macready's generation were managers first and actors second. None had the all-consuming fire of Edmund Kean or the authority of Macready, but two at least, Charles Kean and Samuel Phelps, brought truth and taste to a distracted discipline. It is significant that they achieved this in outposts of theatrical London: at Sadler's Wells, a former pleasure-garden in Islington, and the Princess's, a converted bazaar in Oxford Street. At Drury Lane or the Haymarket, Phelps could never have sustained his twenty years' success at Sadler's Wells. Even the Bancrofts, leading managers of the 1860s, achieved delicacy and distinction in drawing-room drama and kitchen comedy at the Prince of Wales's, off the Tottenham Court Road, a house whose earlier nickname of the 'Dusthole' suggests its reputation.

In the 1870s, siege was laid to the theatrical citadel: the Strand. The Lyceum had had a chequered history reaching back into the previous century, but its fortunes were restored by the personal success of Henry Irving, leading actor from 1871 and lessee from 1878. Three years later the building of the Savoy Theatre celebrated the triumph of 'new and original' comic opera. But neither the Lyceum under Irving nor the Savoy under D'Oyly Carte essayed 'new and original' English drama. Like Charles Kean at the Princess's, Irving made the foundations of his house Shakespeare and romantic (usually French) drama. Even the smartly situated St James's, poised between Piccadilly and Pall Mall, depended, when managed by the impressive team of John Hare and the Kendals in the 1880s, on adaptation and revival.

By now the British public and the British playwright were growing insistent. The managers of the 1880s had fostered a discriminating cross-sectional audience whose tastes were sharpened by the catering, if not the actual bill of fare. By the last decade of the century the London theatre public included for the first time since Sheridan's day a substantial element able to judge the stage's mirror of English society by their own environment. A tribunal could be assembled able and anxious to pronounce sentence on society drama and Comedy of Manners.

The theatre could also recruit writers qualified to provide such a hearing. If earlier Victorian playwrights had mostly been artisans, apprenticed to a trade they then practised for a bare subsistence, the law as much as the manager was to blame. Copyright in a dramatic text effectively ceased when the play was published, and the dramatist had to choose between selling his work to a manager or to a publisher. All this changed with the achievement of dramatic copyright by the Berne Convention of 1887 and the American Copyright Act of 1891.

The new theatrical opportunities for a writer can be illustrated from the switch in direction of Oscar Wilde's (1854–1900) career. After his arrival in London in 1878 he set about achieving literary fame by publishing poetry and criticism. Although intensely theatrical by temperament and taste, he could find no outlet in the British theatre. His early plays, *Vera; or The Nihilists* (1880) and *The Duchess of Padua* (1883), were exotica whose unsuccessful performances in America were engendered by the author's controversial appearances on the lecture-platform. *Salome* (1893), written in French and on a theme inviting the Lord Chamberlain's ban, completed this phase. The London stage was still alien country to Wilde when in 1890 he conceived *The Picture of Dorian Gray*, in substance a society melodrama, as a novel.

But the appearance of more sophisticated audiences and more discriminating managers to satisfy them gave Wilde new inspiration. In particular, George Alexander, a young actor of distinguished manner and fastidious taste, was making the St James's a court for the well-bred and expensively educated. Wilde could expect from him and his audience a sympathetic hearing for his 'New and original play of modern life', as he significantly labelled *Lady Windermere's Fan* (1892), thus distinguishing it from both the translations of other practitioners and his own essays in costume drama. The play's production effectively marked Wilde's debut as a practising dramatist. His first night speech:

Ladies and Gentlemen, I have enjoyed this evening immensely. The actors have given us a charming rendering of a delightful play, and your appreciation has been most intelligent. I congratulate you on the great success of your performance, which persuades me that you think almost as highly of the play as I do myself . . .

demonstrated not only his confidence in himself, but his confidence in the sophistication of his audience.

Fifteen months later, on 27 May 1893, Alexander staged *The Second Mrs Tanqueray*, a play which in the view of the leading young critic of the day, William Archer, 'opened a new period in our dramatic history'. Certainly it opened a new period in Victorian drama, and in the career of its author, Arthur Wing Pinero (1855–1934).

The two architects of Victorian society drama had strongly contrasted preparation for their task. Wilde, the intellectual and aesthete, turned to the theatre when he judged it mature enough to listen to him. Pinero apprenticed himself to the stage from adolescence; for ten years mainly as an actor, supporting first Irving and then the Bancrofts, and for another ten as a Jack of all plays. He provided most of the leading London managers with curtain-raisers, afterpieces, adaptations, sentimental comedies, and, with increasing skill and success, farces (a genre only just fully grown in the Victorian theatre, which had previously kept its farces short and mostly from the French). Pinero's precisely engineered models for the Court Theatre engagingly blended humour and humanity, to such effect that *The Magistrate* (1885) at least has since kept a firm grip on the stage.

But he aspired further. In 1891 the *New York Herald* questioned a number of prominent London theatre figures on the likely impact of Ibsen (three of whose plays, including the notorious *Ghosts*, had received their British première in the preceding months). Some reactions were predictable: Clement Scott, doyen of dramatic critics, prophesied that Ibsen would never influence English drama until there was 'a general taste for inhaling sewage instead of smelling dew-coloured roses'. Pinero's answer was more considered: he looked forward to 'a drama based wholly upon observation and experience, which lays aside the worn-out puppets and proverbs of the theatre, and illustrates faithfully modern social life'. The shared viewpoint with Wilde's 'new and original play of modern life' is evident.

In fact Pinero had already offered an essay in this vein: *The Profligate* (1889), a somewhat cautionary tale of male promiscuity among the privileged classes, had been the opening play at the Garrick Theatre, but Pinero had yielded to the demand of the manager, John Hare, for the profligate's reclamation. This experience, rather than the impact of Ibsen, fired Pinero to undertake a companion-piece in which the victim of male profligacy met a tragic end. The result, originally designed by the calculating George Alexander as a matinée offering, became a full-scale triumph as *The Second Mrs Tanqueray*.

The 'modern social life' which Pinero and Wilde aimed to depict was essentially modern society life. One factor influencing their choice of setting was clearly the chance to reflect their audience: the St James's stalls

A scene from Act IV, The Second Mrs Tanqueray *(1893) by Arthur Wing Pinero.*

presented them with a group portrait such as had faced no playwright earlier in the century. But there were other motives than that of letting their public see themselves. Pinero felt strongly that only the well-bred were articulate enough to provide literate drama. As he told William Archer:

I think you would find, if you tried to write drama, not only that wealth and leisure are more productive of dramatic complications than poverty and hard work, but that if you want to get a certain order of ideas expressed or questions discussed, you must go pretty well up the social scale.

(William Archer, *Real Conversations*, 1904, p. 21)

Wilde also looked to 'people well up the social scale' to give voice to the paradox and epigram which were his characteristic vein. Both dramatists also accepted the familiar framework of the French well-made play, as practised by contemporaries such as Victorien Sardou: the leading character's involvement in political scandal; the mysterious charmer struggling to establish herself in society but confronted by living evidence of her past; the threat from compromising letters; the misconstrued midnight assignation.

But Pinero and Wilde saw in this common ground contrasted opportunities. To Pinero it offered a platform for human characterisation and humane comment. In particular the plight of a woman without fortune in a society which denied her honourable ways of earning independence claimed his attention. Before becoming the second Mrs Tanqueray Paula keeps house for a series of 'protectors'. Agnes in *The Notorious Mrs Ebbsmith* (1895) seeks a political career but finds a married politician. Theophila Fraser in *The Benefit of the Doubt* (1895) looks for solace from the coldness of her husband in the warmth of another man.

Wilde, on the other hand, while basing his serious plays on serious situations, found it impossible to keep a serious face. The emotional core of *Lady Windermere's Fan* is the courage of Mrs Erlynne in saving the daughter she dare not recognise from ruin at Lord Darlington's suggestion; but an audience prefers the lady's ripostes to her detractors and her conquest of Lord Augustus Lorton. *A Woman of No Importance* (1894) centres on Mrs Arbuthnot's determination to keep her illegitimate son for herself. Wilde described its opening as 'the perfect act' because 'there is absolutely no action at all'. The playgoer might attribute its superiority to the absence of the sententious Mrs Arbuthnot and the stimulus of Lady Hunstanton's hospitality. *An Ideal Husband* (1895) tells how Lady Chiltern comes to love her husband when she forgives him his far from idealistic behaviour in the past; but the characters who earn the audience's gratitude are the reptilian Mrs Cheveley who 'looks rather like an orchid and makes great demands on one's curiosity', and Lord Goring who 'is clever but would not like to be thought so'.

Between 1892 and 1895 Wilde and Pinero established a drama which was adult, original, and restored the English play to the level of literature. But it did not amount to a drama which 'illustrates faithfully modern social life', as Pinero had hoped, for both playwrights took too limited a view of their task. If Wilde's work has survived more strongly, it is because he was less committed to a theatrical crusade. Later audiences were to welcome *Lady*

Windermere's Fan and *An Ideal Husband*, grateful that Wilde could not suppress his characteristic ironic tone. *A Woman of No Importance*, on the other hand, is neglected because its one perfect act is followed by three increasingly imperfect. Pinero's path in *The Second Mrs Tanqueray* and more particularly *The Notorious Mrs Ebbsmith* is paved with good intentions.

Perhaps both writers sensed a need for something lighter. In the next decade Pinero was to return to the tragic vein of *Mrs Tanqueray* in *Iris* (1901) and *Mid-Channel* (1909), as his career reached its high point with his knighthood in 1909 (and then fell gradually and rather sadly away until his death in 1934). But his next play for Alexander and the St James's was an elegant piece of over-elaborate fantasy, *The Princess and the Butterfly* (1897), and his most successful society drama, *The Gay Lord Quex* (1899), proved closer in form and spirit to *risqué* French farce. He was happiest in contrasting West End drawing-rooms with backstage dressing-rooms as in *Trelawny of the 'Wells'* (1898), which he modestly called 'a comedietta', but which proved an abiding achievement.

Wilde's reaction was more immediate. Even while struggling to finish *An Ideal Husband*, he wrote quickly and easily the satyr play to complete his dramatic cycle. The title of *The Importance of Being Earnest* (1895) contains a double quip: not only a pun on the name 'Ernest' but a demonstration of the importance to Wilde of not being earnest. For the connoisseur the play's inversions of the values of society drama are delectable: the significant object which provides suspense is not a compromising letter, a tell-tale fan, or a dual purpose brooch-bracelet, but a hand-bag, 'a somewhat large black leather hand-bag, with handles to it'. The concealed relationships and

A scene from Act III, Lady Windermere's Fan *(1892) by Oscar Wilde.*

A scene from Act II, Trelawny of the 'Wells' *(1898) by Arthur Wing Pinero.*

assumed identities are summed up in the term 'Bunburying'. The fatal female is transmogrified into a governess, and her past consists of writing 'a three-volume novel of more than usually revolting sentimentality'. But for the playgoer seeking entertainment, it is provided by the intoxication of Wilde's dialogue, undiluted here by sententiousness. The play's original collapse amongst the ruins of Wilde's personal disaster has been reversed by the approval of succeeding generations. With *Twelfth Night* and *She Stoops To Conquer*, it ranks amongst the perennial favourites in British comedy.

It was also Wilde's last word on the English stage. Scholarship attributes this to the decline in his mental and physical powers after imprisonment, but it may also have been a conscious exercise of taste and judgement on Wilde's part. For him there was no way back or forward from *The Importance of Being Earnest*. It could not be improved upon. This may account for his tame surrender to Frank Harris of the scenario which Harris worked up as *Mr and Mrs Daventry* (1900), and which was playing successfully as Wilde lay dying.

The brilliance of Wilde's reputation has largely eclipsed that of Pinero, though it was Pinero who sustained the drama's claim to artistic parity with the novel in the last decade of the nineteenth century. The hare's speed has since been measured by the tortoise's plod, but it was the tortoise's challenge which provided the race. The next generation, taking their tone from Shaw, dismissed Wilde as a playboy and Pinero as a playwright, using both the 'boy' and the 'wright' with contempt. But between them they restored the British theatre to the academy of British arts.

Staircase at Endcliffe Hall, Sheffield (1860). Flockton and Abbott.

5 New Homes for Barons and Artisans

JOHN NELSON TARN

The second half of the nineteenth century was extraordinarily rich in the quality of domestic architecture and perhaps more diverse in its range and quantity than during the previous fifty years. Taste changed considerably between 1850 and 1900, the newest fashion in the fifties was for Ruskinian villas and by 1900 the up-to-date house was modelled on vernacular cottage styles; in between came houses both large and small in almost every style previously conceived. The houses of the rich, as always, attracted the attention of architects, but so, too, did housing for the artisan; and while the battles raged about public health, the supply of water and the removal of drainage, considerable attention was also given to housing design and layout in the wider concept, which led to the development of the concept of town planning by the end of the century. The organisation and planning of the house itself reached a pitch of sophistication which, in its attention to every nuance of comfort and technical innovation, outstripped the efforts of earlier generations. Life in the country house was lived according to an elaborate ritual in an increasingly complex sequence of rooms, each designed for its proper purpose and furnished accordingly. So sophisticated did the English house become that it was the envy of Europe. Hermann Muthesius, who was appointed technical attaché to the German Embassy in London in 1896, wrote the following year:

There is nothing as unique and outstanding in English architecture as the development of the house . . . Indeed, no nation is more committed to its development, because no nation has identified itself more with the house.

The other characteristic, and it is part of the reason for this rich and innovative period, is that the driving force behind the obsession with the home were the newly rich of all classes. The neat suburban terraced house of the artisan and his lower-middle-class neighbour, finished in Ruabon red brick and terracotta, with its stuffy little parlour used once a week, was no less an icon than the ornate small villa of the Oxford don, or the minor Sheffield cutler and Mancunian cotton merchant. These might, in the first place, be set in the same rigid rows as became typical in the by law streets which comprised so much of the nineteenth-century town. But, as the century passed and the middle class became richer, so their villas sprang up in suburban settings more Arcadian than had been known before and more destructive of the essence of urbanism. By then the town was no longer a place of beauty: the effect of the Industrial Revolution had been to render it unwholesome and ugly, so that those who could sought an alternative place in which to live. Those who had really succeeded and made their mark in society built mansions, sometimes in the suburbs of the town where the source of their wealth actually lay, sometimes they decamped to play the role of a real gentleman in the country. Their homes were dynastic gestures, although surprisingly the dynasties were brittle and short-lived, often they did not survive more than two or three generations. What had seemed solid achievement and permanent wealth in a stable society was often destroyed by the First World War.

The English interest – and it was not shared in the same way by the Scots – in the house, a home on the ground usually of two or three storeys in height, was unique amongst Europeans. It gave the house a much more substantial role in society as a whole. The industrial affluence of the British and their imperialism induced a feeling of ascendancy which caused so much of the creative zeal which lay behind the domestic richness of these decades. That curious English social characteristic which seeks the middle way rather than extremes, and so avoided bloody revolution during the nineteenth century, also invoked the movement for intervention in the problems of poverty and instigated slum clearance. Lord Shaftesbury, Angela Burdett-Coutts, Octavia Hill, all of whom worked to improve the lot of the poor by model tenement building and personal housing management, might have been influenced by that best of Victorian virtues, Evangelical guilt, whose effect was interventionist and positive. British too was the predicament in which William Morris – 'this earthly paradox' as he was once described – found himself. He was a creative artist who believed in the nobility of labour, but who failed to see how to give to the working man the joy of craft-made goods in an age which cried out for the machine to be harnessed to good design and turned from being a human treadmill to a source of growing wealth for everyone.

During the nineteenth century the British never came to see the machine as a source of good domestic design, but they did heed Morris's advice, and there was a powerful movement to reform taste. The clutter of the Victorian home with its over-designed and often crude furnishings gave way to the airy interiors of the Queen Anne revival and the search for a new domestic language in the vernacular styles of the Arts and Crafts movement.

The fascinating thing is that the link between rich and poor can be found at both ends of the period. Two examples will suffice. First, Titus Salt, who was a successful mill owner in Bradford. In 1850 he decided to move his works out of the city because he could not expand adequately there on the existing site. He went up the Aire valley and founded a new mill and built a self-contained village for his work force. In terms of housing standards it was modest; rows of houses carefully graded according to the rank and station of the worker, arranged on the hillside. But the same architects, Lockwood and

Almshouses (above) *and mill-workers' houses* (below) *at Saltaire, Yorkshire (1853–63).*
Lockwood and Mawson.

Mawson, designed the houses, the church, the mill and the various social facilities which Salt considered necessary. They would have built Salt a house, too, a site was earmarked but he never built it. The point was that the village was complete and possessed a unity. Secondly, in 1889, William Lever embarked upon a similar new industrial venture when he set up his soap works at Bromborough on the Wirral and began to create a model village where a better and healthier workforce could reside. The outcome was Port Sunlight, very different architecturally but, socially, another example of that same benign paternalism.

Saltaire reflected the acceptance of a traditional urban pattern and sought to rectify the problems of bad building and the lack of water, sanitation and fresh air. Port Sunlight, forty years later, looked to a new environment, with spacious open frontages, allotment gardens at the rear and a rich variety of architectural design which gave each group an identity of its own. The size of individual rooms in Saltaire and Port Sunlight were similar, although the houses at Port Sunlight usually had more rooms. The essential difference was that at Saltaire the houses were diminutive versions of the traditional Georgian terraced house, while at Port Sunlight they were romantic essays inspired by cottages with lattice windows and roses round the door.

For the ingle-nooks and the rest of the picturesque trappings of the vernacular revival, it is necessary to turn to the homes of the younger middle and professional classes, the more discriminating of whom employed architects like Voysey and Philip Webb. But, already, a younger generation of architects, men such as Raymond Unwin and Barry Parker, were preparing to bring this style down to the working class in the Garden City concepts of the early twentieth century. These concepts were, however, rooted in the writings of Ebenezer Howard, whose 'Tomorrow: a peaceful path to real reform' was published in 1898.

Where does one look for the epitome of the period if not to the suburbs of the great industrial cities and the homes of the self-made barons of commerce and industry? To Halifax, for example, where the Crossleys – who made carpets – filled the town with benefactions and built their own homes; to the suburbs of affluence, the Park at Nottingham, Victoria Park at Manchester, Sefton Park at Liverpool. But these were cities whose greatness did not belong exclusively to the second half of the nineteenth century in any special way.

In Sheffield, where the steel industry came into its own at this time, the expansion of the city westwards up the valleys that lead to Derbyshire had been going on apace since the 1830s. Now, after 1859, the rich steelmen began to develop the south-facing slopes along the Fulwood Road and beyond the road to Manchester. Topographically, Broomhill, Endcliffe and Ranmoor, deserve John Betjeman's description of them as the most beautiful suburb in England. The roads curve gently down to the valley bottom and today the planting is rich and mature and the views at times are still breathtakingly beautiful. Many of the houses and their well-kept grounds have gone and the landscape has filled up with modern villas. But enough does remain to recall the flavour of the heyday of steel. In the early 1860s, two of the greatest of the steelmen both bought sites in Endcliffe: John

Port Sunlight, Wirral (begun 1889), a housing block not completed until 1934. Lomax-Simpson.

Brown chose land off Endcliffe Vale Road and Mark Firth a site nearby, off Fulwood Road. Here, each set down for posterity the worldly physical symbol of his success. Brown was a local lad, apprenticed to an iron master, and with £500 of capital scraped together rapidly developed in business on his own, first as an iron master – his firm led the way in the design of armour plated ships – and then he took out a patent to make steel by the Bessemer process and his business expanded considerably. Mark Firth and his brother grew up in the iron trade and, together with their father in 1842, they set up in business on their own at the beginning of a period of great development in the industry and they, too, prospered.

By 1860, Mark, like John Brown, was ready to build. Both chose the Italian-ate style: no Gothic for them, both houses remind one of Osborne House or a gentlemen's club rather than an Elizabethan mansion or a muscular Christian retreat. Today, it requires an effort of will to capture their essence for, since 1916, Endcliffe Hall has been the home of the Territorial Army and, only a year or two later, Mark Firth's home, Oakbrook, became a convent. But the fabric of both houses is still in good order, although the furnishings have gone and the decoration strays far from the original. Oakbrook is still set amidst sweeping lawns, discreetly hidden behind its high wall, so that to drive off the Fulwood Road, past the lodge and down the shrub-lined drive until the front of the house appears with the great porte-cochère, must be very like the vista the Prince and Princess of Wales enjoyed when they came to stay for the opening of Firth Park in 1875. Indeed, the porte-cochère was added especially for their visit when Firth re-arranged the entrance to the house and it is the only piece of bombastic design. Endcliffe Hall, by contrast, apart from the terraces has lost all its garden, and between the lodge in Endcliffe Vale Road and the house a housing estate has grown up.

Brown's house is the grandest of the two, designed by the local firm of T.J. Flockton and Abbott in what was described at the time as 'Italian treated in the French manner'. The tower has lost its mansard roof and so looks less French than it once did, but the rest has the appearance of relaxed opulence created by the generous proportions of the design and the extensive external ornament. It is built entirely of ashlared sandstone, in essence a formal composition, but never quite perfectly balanced so that the effect is picturesque. The great tower rises out of one elevation, another has a projecting canted bay in the centre and a three-bay conservatory at one end joined to the entrance porch and the ballroom around the corner. The skyline is punctuated by more specifically French chimney-stacks rising out of the low-hipped roofs set behind parapets. In the tower is a great prospect room with a balcony and floor-length windows giving panoramic views in three directions.

Internally, the house is designed around a formal show-piece: the top-lit staircase hall with its wide and shallow stairs, branching and returning at the half landing, and surrounded by balconies. There is a wealth of florid cast-iron balustrading topped with wreathed mahogany handrails; the ceiling is deeply coffered and there is plenty of moulded plasterwork so that the effect today, devoid of pictures and ornaments, is still sumptuous. So, too, must

Endcliffe Hall, Sheffield (1860). Flockton and Abbott.

have been the suite of reception rooms, entered through polished mahogany doors, each with its individual decorative scheme and elaborate plasterwork which survives nearly everywhere. Some rooms still have some of the stencilled decoration, again French and surprisingly elegant, and many of the fireplaces in cast iron with delicate painted and enamelled decoration and mirrored overmantels are still in position. Here, to sharpen the image is the contemporary account:

The house contains, among its most noble apartments, a grand saloon for the pictures and statuary, in which there is an organ. Sir John has many valuable works of art, with which the walls of his various rooms are enriched, and abundant evidence of his sound judgement and cultured taste are seen on every hand. The buildings, furniture and decorations were all designed in Sheffield, and almost entirely executed by Sheffield workmen.

The saloon remains, only the organ has gone although its place can clearly be seen. The glazed dome in the centre of the room is darkened but otherwise it is recognisable. When is was furnished and decorated originally, it must have been one of the grandest saloons in Sheffield. The lasting impression is of external restraint and traditionally safe design, but of formidable grandeur and studied opulence internally; a show house for the great occasion.

By contrast Oakbrook remains a house for living in and for family parties rather than great entertainments. For one thing, it is smaller and less ambitious in concept. But more than that, the attitude to detail is more refined and delicate. Externally, the house is also of stone, an oblong block with a low campanile at one corner and, of course, the royal porte-cochère. The design is again Italianate, and it is generally considered that William Flockton was the architect. Two storeys, of generous proportion, face south across the valley and west towards the moors. One can still see the splendour of the site despite the developments since the 1860s and the lawns still sweep down and set off the house as Firth intended. But the setting is hemmed in by subsequent suburbs and expansion and it is a far cry from the days when the house was built when, apart from his neighbour, Sir John Brown, Firth was 'the pioneer of Ranmoor'.

You enter the house beneath the great canopy, through glazed doors into a porch with delicately stained glass detailing; to your right is the stair, more chaste than Brown's, and to your left a wide passage leads to the old front door. On either side are the main rooms — dining-room, drawing-room, ball-room, morning-room, library. There is fine woodwork in oak, mahogany and walnut, an array of delightful marble fireplaces, French in inspiration, and delicate in execution. The plasterwork on the ceilings and cornices has survived in excellent condition, but here it is not heavy for the rooms are all more domestic in scale. There is a considerable range in the design of the plasterwork and in the ballroom the whole of the centre panel was originally painted and, if the surviving panel over the door is anything to go by, it must have been a charming classical scene, giving the room an eighteenth-century French character to which the plaster detail responds. There are some charming touches, the 'Venetian' lamps in the hall, decorated with the Prince

Oak Brook, Sheffield (1860s). William Flockton.

of Wales feathers, the elegant decorative arches on the staircase and the fine
cast-iron work on the stair which rises in two flights, generous but by no
means opulent.

Mary Walton, in *Sheffield, its Story and its Achievements*, describes Mark
Firth as '"manly and massive", eating in the workshop the meat pie lunch which
the wife of a workman cooked for him daily'. Oakbrook is a far cry from
those early beginnings but it is a home, unlike Endcliffe Hall which is a
palace. Paradoxically, it was to the home and not the palace that the royal
visitors made their way and it was the man from the most humble beginnings
who reached for the social skies!

Dante Gabriel Rossetti, Astarte Syriaca *(1877)*.

6 Fine Arts

PETER FULLER

Introduction: high and low art in the Victorian era

The death of Victoriana

On 25 January 1896, Lord Leighton of Stretton (1830–96), President of the Royal Academy, and the most eminent of English nineteenth-century classical painters, died. The previous day he had become the only artist ever to receive a barony. 'Leighton's death', according to his biographers, 'was a national event.' It was as if 'some seemingly impregnable bulwark had collapsed'. Leighton's body lay in state in the Octagon Room at the Royal Academy; on his coffin were his palette, brushes and mahlstick. His foreign honours were displayed on a cushion at his feet. Leighton was buried in St Paul's in a ceremony which would not have discredited a great statesman.

But the torch of the Victorian Olympians was soon to falter. Five years later, Hubert von Herkomer (1849–1914), sometime social realist turned successful portraitist, was summoned to Osborne House on the Isle of Wight to paint Queen Victoria herself on her death bed. His picture, colour plate 2, which still hangs in the Queen's dressing-room at Osborne, is like a cobwebbed version of John Millais's (1829–96) famous drowned *Ophelia* (colour pl. 3), painted almost half a century before; but the brilliance of Pre-Raphaelite colour and detail has been replaced by a ghostly silver pallor. A whole sensibility, which had always been obsessed with the imagery of death and dissolution, itself seemed to die, or at least to become cocooned, with the passing of the century and its Queen.

In 1904, G.K. Chesterton wrote a remarkable little book about one of the greatest of Victorian painters, G.F. Watts; Chesterton described how an era had 'suddenly become unintelligible'. It had all happened very 'sharply':

A whisper runs through the salons, Mr. Max Beerbohm waves a wand and a whole generation of great men and great achievement suddenly looks mildewed and unmeaning.

For Chesterton, the Victorian world already seemed like 'a primal Babylonian empire of which only a few columns are left crumbling in the desert'.

Among those crumbling columns was Edward Poynter (1836–1919), another Victorian Olympian painter to whom, in Jeremy Maas's apt phrase, honours had once attached themselves 'like burrs'. In 1897, this former Slade Professor, Director of the National Gallery and President of the Royal Academy, had presided over the opening of the Tate Gallery – which he no doubt hoped would stand as a living monument to the late-Victorian achievement. Poynter himself had painted works like *Faithful unto Death*, a picture which showed a young Roman centurion remaining at his post as Vesuvius erupted around him. But Poynter outlived his contemporaries: indeed, he survived the Vorticist movement and the First World War. By the time he died in 1919, he was lonely, embittered, dyspeptic, and uncomprehending of an age which was smothering even the lower slopes of the Victorian Olympus with the larva of modernity.

But Poynter's reputation, and that of his contemporaries, still had a long way to fall. The protagonists of the modern movement increasingly came to argue that art had effectively ceased in England with the death of Joseph Mallord William Turner (1775–1851). (And even Turner was not good enough for Roger Fry, who accused him of not probing further 'than that first gasp of wonder'.) The best that Britain was supposed to have been able to offer in the second half of the nineteenth century was a handful of second-rank imitators of the French. 'English form is normally a stone below French', wrote Clive Bell, Fry's closest critical associate.

Whistler was never a match for Renoir, Degas, Seurat, and Manet; but Whistler, Steer, and Sickert may profitably be compared with Bodin, Jongkind, and Berthe Morisot.

No one else really seemed to him worth mentioning: the Pre-Raphaelites, were, according to Bell, 'of utter insignificance in the history of European culture'.

During the last twenty years, attitudes towards Victorian painting have changed. Of course, even today, few would deny the superiority of French over British art in the nineteenth century; but that no longer seems to be the point, or at least not the *sole* point. Study of late-Victorian art has become intellectually respectable once again; indeed, a century on, the late Victorians appear to be confronting our 'post-modern' culture with an awkward critical challenge.

Art and Prince Albert

For many twentieth-century art historians, 1851 has seemed in retrospect like a watershed for British art. That December, Turner died under an assumed name in an obscure Chiswick boarding house. In our period, Turner's late works – which have recently been so admired because they have seemed to prefigure contemporary abstraction – were little known, and less esteemed. With Turner's death, the fire of English high romantic art appeared to have been extinguished.

That same year, the Crystal Palace was built in Hyde Park; historians of modern architecture have tended to look upon Joseph Paxton's glittering steel and glass 'greenhouse' as a prototype of all they were to advocate in the following century. Writers like William Morris (1834–96) and John Ruskin (1819–1900) have been called 'negative and reactionary' (in Nikolaus Pevsner's phrase) for their reservations concerning the building. And, inevitably, the organisers of the Great Exhibition have been much criticised for allowing the Palace to become cluttered with such anachronisms as the Medieval Court of the Gothic Revivalist, by Augustus Welby Pugin (1812–52). Such things have been seen as signs of the incipient decadence of the art of the Victorians, of their inability to identify an aesthetic appropriate to their own secular and industrial age.

Needless to say, it did not seem like that to the Victorians themselves. Obsessed as they were with the relationship between 'art' and 'manufacture', it never for one moment occurred to them that the problem ought to be 'solved' by the dissolution of art *into* manufacture. On the contrary, as George Hedberg has written,

From the time of Prince Albert onwards, many Victorians firmly believed that English art was undergoing a revival or rebirth, which they themselves called a renaissance.

And so there were many calls for the application of art to industry; but the demand for a 'machine aesthetic' was to belong to another age. Even so, by the mid-century, many might also have admitted that the Victorian Renaissance was having more than a few difficulties in getting off the ground.

Soon after Albert's marriage to the youthful Queen Victoria, in 1840, he was appointed president of the Select Committee for 'the promotion of the fine arts of this Country in connexion with the rebuilding of the Houses of Parliament'. Turner, of course, had painted the burning of the old buildings; Albert was determined that a splendid phoenix should rise from their ashes.

A competition was organised, and the exhibition of huge cartoons depicting scenes from British history, in 1843, excited great public fervour. Benjamin Haydon, a pupil of Reynolds, had looked impatiently to the Committee for the revival of English history painting, in the Grand Manner. But prizes were awarded to young and relatively unknown men like G.F. Watts and John Horsley. Embittered, and deranged, Haydon took his own life.

The secretary to the committee, Charles Lock Eastlake (1793–1865), was a history painter in his own right; but Eastlake, who became President of the Royal Academy and Director of the National Gallery, was to be remembered rather as the most influential artist–administrator of the early-Victorian era. His great knowledge of contemporary European art influenced the appointment of those who shared his taste, like the Irish painter, Daniel Maclise (1806–70), and William Dyce (1806–64). Dyce was Director of the new Government Schools of Design and one of the most prominent admirers of the Nazarenes, a school of German, Catholic painters, who worked in Rome, producing austere, idealised religious scenes.

Work on the decorations at Westminster dragged on for almost twenty years; but long before that, it became clear that the techniques employed were simply incompatible with the dampness and mists that rose from the Thames. Those who believed that the efforts of Albert and Eastlake would lead to a revival of British history painting found that their hopes faded as quickly as the frescoes themselves. Some of the paintings disappeared even before they were finished; with Albert's death in 1861, all enthusiasm for the project, and, indeed, English history painting itself, evaporated too.

Even so, it would be wrong to underestimate the indirect influence the Prince Consort exercised over British art. It has been said that the marriage of Albert and Victoria

finally ended the old Whig sophistication, based on the Grand Tour and Latin culture, and replaced it with a Protestant ethos founded on domestic and public virtue.

The remainder of the nineteenth century was stamped by the desire to find a high art which could be seen as moving and meaningful in this increasingly secular, industrial and democratic age. Indeed, to a far greater degree than most contemporary commentators have admitted, the pursuit of beauty, in the later nineteenth century, was bound up with the vicissitudes of religious beliefs which themselves had become, at best, problematic.

All this is reflected in the tastes and the writings of the greatest critic of the era: John Ruskin. At first, Ruskin looked for solutions in the doctrine of 'truth to nature', but he was no empiricist – at least not in the modern, secular sense. He was contemptuous of the idea of *aesthesis*, or the merely sensuous response to beauty. He elevated the idea of *theoria*, or the response to beauty with one's whole moral and spiritual being. Therein, for Ruskin, lay the secret of Turner's great strength. Turner, at least until his last years, had attended closely to nature, but not merely to record his impressions of it. Rather he had sought, through his vision, to reveal to lesser mortals the activity and presence of God within the world he had created. It was in this sense that, after Turner's death, Ruskin came to regard him as 'the first Pre-Raphaelite', although, predictably, even he drew back in the face of the vaporous abstractions of Turner's later works. Perhaps only Watts glimpsed their true import.

The Victorian Renaissance and high art

Undoubtedly, the vice of the age was a crass and creeping commercial Philistinism, and a tendency, particularly early in this period, for art to descend into cloying anecdote or mawkish sentiment. But, from the middle of the century until its close, there was no time when the greatest among Victorians artists had lost sight of the high ground altogether.

It was not, of course, the case that romantic landscape of the old school withered away entirely upon the death of Turner. Indeed, during this period, John Linnell (1792–1882) consolidated his considerable fortune from pastoral landscapes; but, today, these seem to us like skilful, yet empty, nostalgic pastiches. Linnell was the father-in-law of Samuel Palmer, whose visionary Shoreham days were over by 1837. Palmer's later, Arcadian scenes are by no means as lifeless as is sometimes suggested; but it is as if the classical references have had to be re-inserted after the golden light of divine transfiguration has disappeared. In the later years of the century, James Hook was perhaps a more authentic heir to the romantic tradition. At least, as

Baudelaire put it, Hook had 'the secret of filling his dreams of Venice with a magic light'.

Many gave up the struggle to find spiritual values in the landscape, and settled for the magical instead – they escaped into 'Faerie Land'. Richard Dadd's claustrophobic *The Fairy Feller's Master-Stroke* (*c*.1855–64) is certainly filled with all the frozen terror of his own parricidal insanity.

Richard Dadd, The Fairy Feller's Master-Stroke *(c.1855–64)*.

Ruskin himself came to believe that Joseph Noel Paton's fairy pictures, like *The Reconciliation of Oberon and Titania* (1847), were 'all we possess in which the accomplished skill of painting has been devoted to fairy-subject'. But today we tend to feel that even Paton's sophisticated means have been marshalled for ends more frail and tenuous than any dew-laden cobweb, especially when compared with such a robust fairy-teller as Lewis Carroll.

But Sir Edwin Landseer (1802–73), animal artist, a favourite of Queen Victoria's, and the most prominent painter of the mid-nineteenth century, is less easily dismissed. Until his recent 'rehabilitation' as a lost romantic, Landseer was pilloried as the embodiment of all the faults of the Victorian world. Yet Ruskin praised Landseer's picture, *The Old Shepherd's Chief-Mourner* – which shows a sheepdog beside its master's coffin – as 'a work of high art' which stamped its author 'not as the neat imitator of the texture of a skin, or the fold of a drapery, but as the Man of Mind'. In 1851, Landseer earned much praise for the picture which he sent to the Royal Academy, *The Monarch of the Glen*. This work had been originally intended for the refreshment room of the House of Lords; but the commission was cancelled. The noble Lords seem to have thought that the subject – a magnificent stag set against sublime, Scottish mountain scenery – was not appropriate. But this picture, too, was not intended to provide merely the likeness of a wild animal – although it does so with striking intensity. Landseer also seems to want to portray the stag as the Lord of its domain, a conquering son who must yet be sacrificed, a Christ in Glory.

Ruskin did not comment on this picture; by this time, his enthusiasm for Landseer had distinctly cooled. He was to accuse him of 'realism at the expense of ideality', 'treatment essentially unimaginative', and of being 'much more a natural historian than a painter'. And, in any event, there were paintings at this 1851 exhibition which, he felt, came closer to the high spiritual art he was looking for. Holman Hunt, John Millais and Charles Collins all exhibited Pre-Raphaelite works at the Royal Academy that year. Not for the first time, they were attacked. Ruskin was prevailed upon to speak out in their defence; he told the readers of *The Times* that 'as they gain experience the Pre-Raphaelites might lay in our England the foundations of a school of art nobler than the world has seen for three hundred years'.

Landseer was not the only mid-century painter with a deep respect for meticulous fidelity to the appearances of natural form; William 'Bird's-Nest' Hunt (1790–1864) – no relation to the pioneer Pre-Raphaelite – anticipated his namesake's obsession with the depiction of detail. Even the celebrated Pre-Raphaelite technique involving a bright palette and a white ground was anticipated in the exceptional genre pictures of William Mulready (1786–1863). Furthermore, the Pre-Raphaelite taste for the achievements of the painters of the early quattrocento in Italy was shared by both Prince Albert and Charles Eastlake. Indeed, the Gothic Revival of the 1840s had led to a revaluation of the heritage of specifically Christian art.

Nonetheless, the widely accepted view was that the craftsmen painters of the early Renaissance were, quite literally, 'primitives'. William Powell Frith (1819–1909) was not alone in believing that Maclise was the greatest painter who had ever lived. It was assumed that painting had 'progressed' since the

Edwin Henry Landseer, The Monarch of the Glen *(1851)*.

time of the 'primitives'. As Quentin Bell has pointed out, most Victorians would have regarded it as merely silly to suggest that Benozzo Gozzoli was a better painter than Sir Edwin Landseer. Although the Pre-Raphaelites had only seen engravings of Gozzoli's work – and, indeed, had seen very little of *any* Italian painting from before the time of Raphael – they did so suggest. In the beginning, at least, they retained their aspirations for an elevated Christian art which appealed to the mind and the soul, as well as to the eye and the heart; but they rejected both classical composition and German idealisations as the means of getting there.

The study of natural, rather than classical, forms was not encouraged at the Royal Academy Schools; indeed, drawing from the figure had only been introduced the year before the Pre-Raphaelite Brotherhood was founded in 1848. The Pre-Raphaelites were therefore being exceedingly bold when they decided to root their aesthetic in truth to nature rather than to the classical proportions and classical canons of composition. But they were no more naturalists than was John Ruskin. When he was not beset by unbelief, Holman Hunt, the most theoretically-minded member of the Brotherhood, believed that nature was the handiwork of God. Indeed, as we shall see, the destiny of Pre-Raphaelitism was inextricably intertwined with the changes that swept through English Protestant thought in the 1850s.

During that decade, Pre-Raphaelitism found many disciples and recruits. Dyce was an early 'convert'; like Arthur Hughes, he developed an increasingly sharp-focused interest in the detail of natural forms. John Brett, John Inchbold and Thomas Seddon were among those who applied the Pre-Raphaelite style in relation to pure, unpeopled landscape. Many who were hostile to Pre-Raphaelitism, like Frith, were nonetheless influenced by aspects of it. Pre-Raphaelitism was a major influence on English painting and letters for the next half-century. And yet when Ruskin spoke out in defence of the Brotherhood, in 1851, it was already disintegrating. After 1860, Pre-Raphaelitism, as an aesthetic, suffered a sea-change into something if not rich, then certainly new, and strange.

As I argue below, one reason why the original Pre-Raphaelite beliefs became untenable was that modern science, and more especially modern theology, were progressively eroding the idea that the natural world could reasonably be seen, or depicted, as expressive of the aesthetic handiwork of God, or as a revelation of divine activity. But, to coin a phrase, the tradition of 'classical' Pre-Raphaelitism did not die out altogether; a form of landscape painting relating to the great Pre-Raphaelite pictures of the 1850s persisted throughout the latter part of the century. Inchbold and that still under-estimated painter, Henry Moore (1831–95), saw that the accretion of detail could not spill over into revelation; they moved towards a more 'painterly', or expressionist, vision of landscape. Of greater interest is the emergence in the latter part of our period of a more ambitious 'post-Raphaelite' landscape painting, offering not so much a paradise garden, as a god-forsaken; or twilight world: Atkinson Grimshaw, was perhaps the most prolific painter of this genre; though Millais's *Chill October* (1870) is its masterpiece, and Benjamin Leader's *February Fill-Dyke* (1881) its popular pot-boiler.

Of the original Pre-Raphaelites, only Hunt was to remain faithful to the Brotherhood's founding aesthetic: and even he was to find it increasingly difficult to do so. Dante Gabriel Rossetti (1828–82) and Millais set off in search of different gods. Millais was early absorbed into the ambience of the Royal Academy; the virtuosity and facility he had once applied to the pursuit of Pre-Raphaelitism, he now put in the service of more mundane ends, including *Cherry Ripe* (1879), *Bubbles* (1885–6), an income of £30–40,000 a year, a baronetcy, and the Presidency of the Royal Academy – which he held briefly in the months before his death.

Rossetti, put out by the early criticisms of the Brotherhood, became, if anything, even *less* interested in sceptical, Protestant, Christian realism than Millais. But in life, he was motivated more by sex than by regard for money or position; he always declined to exhibit at the Royal Academy. In art he determined that if truth could no longer lead to high sentiment, he would, at least, have beauty. Rossetti gathered around him a new generation – including Morris, Edward Burne-Jones, (1833–98) and the poet, Algernon Swinburne (1837–1909) – whose interests had little in common with the biblical and natural historical emphases of the early days of the movement.

John Everett Millais, Chill October *(1870)*.

In Oxford, in 1857, Rossetti and his pupils painted murals in the library of the Oxford Union, which demonstrated little more than that they had learned nothing from the technical failure of the frescoes in the Palace of Westminster. For Rossetti, as the years went by, beauty came increasingly in the form of 'stunners' – women, at once hopelessly mythologised and all too real. The expressionless faces of *La Ghirlandata* (1873; Alexa Wilding) and *Astarte Syriaca* (1877; Jaynie Morris) stare out at us with a dreamy languor, at once sensual and passionless. As A.E. Benson wrote of the latter,

The strange sights that she has seen in grove and shrine seem to have fed her beauty with lurid and terrible royalty, where she reigns in a dark serenity which nothing can appal.

These changes in Rossetti's works at once anticipate and epitomise the changes that swept through Victorian painting as a whole in the later decades of the century. Art historians, who enjoy the creation of new categories, like to speak of 'Post-Pre-Raphaelitism' or, alternatively, of a Victorian High Renaissance, which followed upon the heels of the Pre-Raphaelite or 'early Renaissance' phase. The leaders of this High Renaissance were Watts, and Leighton, 'artists whose predilections tended toward the sixteenth century', and towards a more generalised, and monumental, conception of pictorial form. This shift involved a diminution in the importance given to the depiction of detail, and an ever greater emphasis on pictorial unity, in terms of colour and composition. Leighton's drawing, *A Lemon Tree* (1859) was a virtuoso example of 'truth to nature', according to Ruskinian perspectives.

But the harmonious blandness and idealisation of his mature works seems almost the antithesis to those deliberate, Gothic discordances of form and colour which are so much the hallmark of, say, Holman Hunt. As Leighton himself wrote:

I can only speak of what is not a change but virtually a growth – the passage from Gothicism to Classicism (for want of better words) i.e. a growth from multiplicity to simplicity.

These stylistic transformations sprang out of a deeper shift in sensibility, brought about by changes in underlying beliefs and intentions. For, unlike

Frederic Leighton, A Lemon Tree *(pencil; 1859).*

Hunt and the early Ruskin, the leaders of the Victorian High Renaissance
had no particular brief for Christian art. Even those who, like Watts, believed
in some ultimate divine reality, accepted that this was not rendered visible
through contemplation of natural form. Indeed, in pictures like *Chaos*
(*c*.1882) Watts showed himself to be the only painter in this period who
comprehended why Turner had been driven to the brink of abstraction,
and beyond.

The religion of beauty

For many artists, the only religion available to high art seemed to be the
religion of beauty itself. At first this shift was associated with a revival of
classical, rather than Christian, iconography. But the classicism of the
Victorian High Renaissance was very different, in kind, from that of the early
nineteenth-century history painters. There was something resolutely new,
even *modern*, about it. For the most significant tendencies in 'Post-Pre-
Raphaelitism' had something in common with the new psychologies of men
like Herbert Spencer, Alexander Bain, and James Sully; some of the new
painters, at least, wished to root their aesthetics not so much in God as in the
subjective experiences of the human individual and his fleeting sensations,
perceptions and impressions.

In 1873, this sensibility received its most coherent literary and critical
expression in Walter Pater's (1839–94) *The Renaissance*. Pater's ornate prose
was dominated by a 'sense of the splendour of our experience and its awful
brevity'. He complained that experience was but a swarm of impressions,
ringed around by a 'thick wall of personality'. Each human mind was, for
him, 'a solitary prisoner of its own dream of a world'. We are all, Pater
Argued, *condamnés*: we have an interval and then we cease to be. He saw our
one chance 'in getting as many pulsations as possible into the given time'.
Art, Pater wrote, 'comes to you professing frankly to give nothing but the
highest quality to your moments as they pass, and simply for those moments
sake'. His rueful hedonism came clothed in his love of Greece and Platonic
philosophy; Pater was the first – but by no means the last – of those who
hoped that art would be capable of filling the space vacated by religion, that
aesthetic experience might expand to embrace the numinous.

No painter seems closer to Pater's theories than Albert Moore (1841–93)
who entered the Royal Academy Schools in 1858; at first Moore was deeply
influenced by Pre-Raphaelite ideas, but in the mid-1860s he began to study
the Elgin marbles. He responded strongly to the decorative and timeless
qualities of the draped, classical carvings – especially those of women. The
pictures he produced on such themes, with their carefully balanced colour
harmonies, caused W.M. Rossetti to lament that Moore 'presupposes once and
for all that the innermost artistic problem of how to reconcile realization with
abstraction deserves to be given up'. In other words, Rossetti was
complaining that Moore's painting had neither subject nor incident – that
Moore, in the words of the contemporary critic, Cosmo Monkhouse, 'seeks
only after beauty'. Moore liked to re-work a narrow range of themes, often
drawn from photographs, or fragments of casts, of classical statuary; he gave

many of his pictures the unrevealing title of flowers, like *Forget-me-nots* or *Yellow Marguerites*.

These days, Moore's classical flower maidens are frequently recast as fore-runners of those 'variations-on-a-theme' espoused by modern abstractionists. But, even after he had become President of the Royal Academy in 1878, Leighton himself held to an aesthetic similar to Moore's. Leighton, however, was distracted from the full development of his own work by the high seriousness, efficiency, and even-handed generosity, with which he fulfilled his public functions. 'And he paints, too . . .' quipped Whistler.

Perhaps Leighton came closest to showing what he could do in his last painting, *Flaming June* (1895), a 'subjectless', or ornamental, picture of a sleeping woman, in a diaphanous, orange, classical gown. In his second discourse to the students, in 1881, Leighton stressed that the language of art was 'not the appointed vehicle of ethic truths'. Rather, he stressed the individual's capacity for the experience of aesthetic emotions, 'to which Art, and Art alone amongst human forms of expression, has a key'. The only obligations of the artist were towards 'form, colour, and the contrasts of light and shade', through which such aesthetic emotions could be aroused. 'Art's duty', according to Leighton, was

to awaken those sensations directly emotional and indirectly intellectual, which can be communicated only through the sense of sight, to the delight of which she has primarily to minister.

Of course such thorough-going aestheticism has tended in retrospect to be seen as the particular province of James McNeill Whistler (1834–1903), an American-born painter who was a former pupil of Rossetti's – and a close friend of Moore's. Indeed, for a time Moore and Whistler worked together so closely that Whistler became concerned that their work was becoming indistinguishable. But Whistler dispensed with classical references and turned rather to the arts of Japan for influence and inspiration. In pictures like *Symphony in White No. 3* (1867) or *Arrangement in Grey and Black No. 1* (1872), a portrait of his mother, he came to rely more and more on the orchestration of painterly effects and formal devices.

Despite his characteristically provocative presentation, Whistler's 'Ten o'clock lecture' of 1885, was really Leightonism, stripped of the classical references, lofty idealism and public-spiritedness. Like Leighton, Whistler declared himself the enemy of incident and ethics in art. He complained that people had acquired the habit of

looking . . . not *at* a picture, but *through* it, at some human fact, that shall, or shall not, from a social point of view, better their mental or moral state.

But Whistler denigrated such 'literary' aesthetics and insisted that 'all that matters' was 'the amazing invention that shall have put form and colour into such perfect harmony':

Art should be independent of all clap-trap, should stand alone, and appeal to the artistic sense of eye or ear, without confounding this with emotions entirely foreign to it, as devotion, pity, love, patriotism, and the like.

He explained that this was why he called his own paintings 'harmonies' or 'arrangements'.

James McNeill Whistler, Arrangement in Grey and Black No. 1: The Artist's Mother
(1872).

Whistler's attempt to rid art of what he saw as the constraints of ethical,
social, and spiritual life was at the centre of his quarrel with Ruskin, who was
exceedingly rude about Whistler's painting, *Nocturne in Black and Gold: The
Falling Rocket* (colour pl. 5), exhibited at the Grosvenor Gallery in 1877.
Ruskin called Whistler a 'coxcomb' and accused him of 'flinging a pot of
paint in the public's face'. Whistler sued, and was awarded a farthing's
damages. The trial focused the attention of the public on the rising creed of
'Art for Art's Sake'.

Despite the proximity between Whistler, the father of the radical Aesthetic
movement in art and design, and Leighton, the President of the Royal
Academy, by the late 1880s, George Moore, the novelist and art critic, could
write, 'That nearly all artists dislike and despise the Royal Academy is a
matter of common knowledge.' Moore claimed, 'From Glasgow to Cornwall
there hangs a gathering and a darkening sky of hate.'

The roots of this hate were not only the resentment of a younger
generation against the institutional and economic power of their elders: the
Royal Academy still maintained a virtual stranglehold over the London
picture market. Many artists also objected to what they perceived as the
insularity of English taste – especially its indifference to the new painting that
was going on in France. They also resented the Academy's continued
opposition to painting from nature, and its refusal of *plein air*-ism. Colonies

of artists sprang up, similar to those to be found in France; the most significant was in the Cornish fishing port of Newlyn. Stanhope Forbes joined this community in 1884, and quickly became its 'centre and rallying point'. Like many of the Newlyn artists, Forbes admired Bastien Lepage, a French painter of peasant and rural scenes. Forbes adopted Lepage's large, square brush and created a trellis of rectangular strokes across his pictures. His *Fish Sale on a Cornish Beach* made much of the effects of sunlight playing over slippery fish and mirror-like wet sand: it created a stir at the Academy in 1885, where, as Forbes himself put it, it came 'as a breath of fresh air in the tired atmosphere of the studios'.

Forbes thus joined forces with 'progressive' Academicians – like George Clausen, John Singer Sargent, and Edward Stott – all of whom had trained in Paris; and the so-called 'Glasgow Boys', a loose group of Scottish artists who shared similar ideals. These included W.Y. MacGregor, John Lavery, and the precociously talented colourist, George Henry. Together they formed the New English Art Club.

But no sooner had the *plein air*-ists grouped themselves than they were upstaged by a more metropolitan tendency, led by Walter Sickert (1860–1942), a pupil and former studio assistant of Whistler's and friend of Degas. Aided by Philip Wilson Steer (1860–1942), a former numismatist who had fallen under the spell of Manet, Sickert routed the Newlynists; there were rifts with the Scottish contingent, too. And the London Impressionists were left in control of the society. Reviewing the Club's ninth annual exhibition, George Moore wrote, 'Art has fallen in France, and the New

Stanhope Alexander Forbes, A Fish Sale on a Cornish Beach, *exhibited at the Royal Academy in 1855.*

English seems to me like a seed blown over-sea from a ruined garden.'

At first, both Sickert and Steer liked to emphasise that Impressionism should reach beyond appearances, or what Sickert called 'the sordid or superficial details of the subject'. Although both men pursued intensely personal visions, the 'poetry' for which they yearned proved hard to have, and harder still to hold. Sickert resigned from the New English for the first, but not the last, time in 1897, and despairing of the British, went to live in Dieppe, where he remained until after the turn of the century.

The early modernist critics, like Fry and Bell, tended to regard as 'good' and 'progressive' those painters who looked towards France. But the French themselves did not see British art in that way. The admiration of Delacroix for Constable, and of Gericault for Landseer is well enough known; what, however, is less well understood is the favour with which leading French critics regarded English painting of the *late* nineteenth century – often praising it for its vigorous insularity, and the qualities by which it could so easily be distinguished from the painting of the French.

Baudelaire bitterly regretted the absence of a long list of British artists from the Salon of 1859, describing them as 'enthusiastic representatives of the imagination and of the most precious faculties of the soul'. A quarter of a century later, Ernest Chesneau wrote of the 'startling and unexpected' effect British art had had in France throughout the intervening years. He wrote of the 'exclusiveness' of English art, but claimed that thereby the English school 'has become a truly national art'. In the following decade Robert de la Sizeranne thought the same: 'There are German, Hungarian, Belgian, Spanish, Scandinavian painters', he wrote, 'but there is an English School of painting.' And the greatness of English art was to be found not in imitations of the Impressionists – but rather in what were seen as the more substantial achievements of Rossetti, Leighton, Watts, and, especially perhaps, Burne-Jones. We last glimpsed Burne-Jones embroiled in the fiasco of the Oxford Union murals, under the influence of his teacher, Rossetti. In fact, Burne-Jones had an exceptional feel for two-dimensional decoration, and produced fine designs for glass and tapestries, often working with William Morris's firm. His paintings were marked by a strong mythic sense; and his linear arabesques owed something to the revival of interest in Botticelli, ardently promoted by both Pater and Ruskin.

But Burne-Jones was a nervous and retiring man; he was wounded, in 1871, when his work was linked by a virulent reviewer with Swinburne's torrid flagellometrics and the decadence of 'The Fleshly School of Poetry'. For six years he worked away from the public gaze. When he re-emerged, his painting seemed to have acquired a new cohesion and confidence. Burne-Jones had a great impact at the 1878 International exhibition where he was heralded as a pioneer of the French Symbolist movement. His masterpiece was, perhaps, *The Golden Stairs*, of 1880 (colour pl. 1), which, like Albert Moore's paintings, possessed no identifiable anecdotal content. For Burne-Jones, the minor Impressionism of the New English Art Club was just the painting of 'landscape and whores'. In contrast, Burne-Jones said,

I mean by a picture a beautiful romantic dream of something that never was, never will be – in a light better than any light that ever shone – in a land no one can define or remember, only desire – and the forms divinely beautiful.

At home, Burne-Jones encouraged Aubrey Beardsley (1872–98), whose precocious line drawings imbued the languid arabesques of Pre-Raphaelite design with a new and fetid eroticism. For many, his drawings were like icons of *fin de siècle* decadence; but his great popularity received a sharp setback in 1895, after the disgrace of Oscar Wilde, whose play, *Salome*, he had illustrated.

Watts was another painter who, in the late nineteenth century, aspired to see beyond the dull world of appearances; but Watts's style was far removed from the lucid linearity of Burne-Jones, and his sensibility could hardly have been further from that of Beardsley's precocious aestheticism. Watts wanted to grapple with universal themes of life, death, and the origins of the cosmos.

Aubrey Beardsley, The Woman in the Moon *(1893), from Oscar Wilde's* Salome.

Art and the social scene

Others, deliberately, set their sights much lower. One of the most foolish assumptions about Victorian art is that it was essentially 'escapist'. Rather, as Jeremy Maas has written,

Poverty, prostitution, illicit love, illness, death, bereavement and sudden destitution were all favourite themes, and received similarity of treatment by genre painters from one end of the Victorian age to the other.

The painting of genre, in the wake of David Wilkie (1785–1841), merged into the 'truthful' painting of modern life, even before Pre-Raphaelitism; we find suggestions of this process among some of the members of The Clique – a loose group including Dadd, Augustus Egg, Frith, and John 'Spanish' Phillip – who, as young men in the late 1830s, opposed the Royal Academy. Richard Redgrave also made several studies of the plight of poverty-stricken, if attractive, young women. But, even though he always denied it, Pre-Raphaelitism emboldened Frith to produce his epic, anecdotal compositions *Life at the Seaside (Ramsgate Sands)* (1854), *Derby Day* (1858), and *The Railway Station* (1862).

Egg was more open about his indebtedness to the younger generation, though, like Frith, he also looked back to Hogarth. George Elgar Hicks shared with Frith a penchant for modern life paintings with a cast of thousands – though his preferred subjects, like *Dividend Day at the Bank of England* (1859), seemed to allow for little more than a laboured, documentary interest. The turgid social realism of Frank Holl, Hubert von Herkomer, and Luke Fildes, which flourished in the 1870s, is now more highly regarded – perhaps because it can still serve the additional function of salving the consciences of middle-class voyeurs.

'Society' had its modern life painters, too: James Tissot (1836–1902) was a French painter, a friend of Degas and Whistler, who spent much of his life in London. Ruskin dismissed his elegant pictures of balls, salon life, and beautiful women as 'mere coloured photographs of vulgar society' (see p.282). But both Tissot, and the Scottish genre painter, Sir William Quiller Orchardson (1832–1910) in fact showed a strong sense of abstract design; Orchardson's *The First Cloud* (1887), with its symbolic and compositional intimations of a coming marital catastrophe, anticipates David Hockney's popular twentieth-century picture on a similar theme, *Mr and Mrs Clark and Percy*.

The vulgar sophistication of those whom Tissot and Orchardson depicted was well served by a breed of Victorian Olympian entirely lacking in the lofty ideals of Leighton, or the rarified aestheticism of Moore. For example, Edwin Long's *The Babylonian Marriage Market*, of 1875, was sold, at auction, in 1882 for an astronomical £6,615. Ruskin described this venal painting, with his usual accuracy, as 'a piece of anthropology . . . the natural and very wonderful product of a century occupied in carnal and mechanical science'. He was even less kind about the work of Alma Tadema (1836–1912), a Dutch painter who lived in England, and who made reconstructions of Roman scenes. Despite a necrophiliac obsession with archaeological accuracy and marble surfaces, Alma Tadema's paintings rarely convince us that we are looking at anything other than a very Victorian world, peopled by members of the Healthy and Artistic Dress Union, in, or often out of, their togas. But it is quite wrong to judge the late Victorian era – as Roger Fry once did – by such confections. It wasn't only Ruskin who was aware of Alma Tadema's vacuity. 'The general lack of attraction of his figures', wrote a correspondent in the *Art Journal*, 'is due to their complete denial of spirituality.'

The dealers and the public

The extent, and variety, of such low art in the later nineteenth century is explicable if we remember that painting had to cater for a much larger audience, with much more diverse tastes, than ever before. If, once, these arts had been the province of a relatively tight circle of refined, aristocratic connoisseurs, they were now thrown open to the spectrum of the middle classes, and, on occasion, yet lower orders of men. The horizons of this public were widening, too. Travel, imperial sentiments, and the Great Exhibition all fanned an interest in cultural and scenic exotica, which was met, directly, by innumerable travelling water-colourists, one of the best of whom was the nonsense poet, Edward Lear (1812–88), and specialist painters like David Roberts and John Lewis – much admired by Ruskin.

Already, by the mid-century, a new kind of 'self-made' collector had come to replace the country house patron, and to dominate the burgeoning market in contemporary art; for example, by the time Robert Vernon died in 1850, he had amassed a vast collection of English paintings from the profits he had made from horse-trading during the Napoleonic wars; and the money for John Sheepshanks's array of contemporary British pictures came from industry. Henry Tate amassed a fortune from sugar refining, and an appropriately saccharine collection of late-Victorian pictures to go with it.

Inevitably, dealers emerged to meet the needs of this changing market. In the 1850s and 1860s, Louis Flatow and Ernest Gambart vied for dominance of the Art trade; but later the mantle passed to William Agnew. These developments did not, as has sometimes been suggested, lead to the 'privatisation' of painting. Vernon and Sheepshanks set precedents by leaving their collections to the National Gallery and the newly founded South Kensington Museum, respectively. Tate also gave his collection to the nation, together with the resources for the Gallery which still bears his name. The most important selling exhibition, the Royal Academy's annual show, also came regularly to attract more than 250,000 people, many of whom had no intention to purchase. An army of critics mediated between the pictures and the public. (By the end of the century, 300 journalists were attending the Press Day for the exhibition.)

The Press was involved with the arts in another way too; for if the early-Victorian era saw the collapse of the sadistic political caricature, the mid-century saw the rise of magazines which specialised in wood-cuts and wood-engravings. *Punch*, founded in 1841, became the focus for the decorous, yet subtle caricatures of John Leech (1817–64) who established himself by parodying the cartoons for the Palace of Westminster; the elaborate, illustrated homilies of John Tenniel (1820–1914); and the brilliantly observed line drawings of Charles Keene (1823–91). Not all such work was humorous:

Van Gogh greatly admired the social realist wood-engravings by Fildes, von Herkomer, and the crazy Arthur Boyd Houghton in news magazines of the 1870s, like *The Graphic*.

Art dealers focused their interest in prints of a more immediately commercial kind: they, and sometimes the painters themselves, mounted commercial exhibitions of particular pictures, the purpose of which was to stimulate sales of the engravings; the rewards for success in this market could be astronomical. Such operations have been cited as indications of the banality and commercialism of the Victorian studios; but such works were really sophisticated popular entertainments, comparable to twentieth-century movies. John Martin's coarse apocalyptic scenes were the nearest that the Victorians got to *The Towering Inferno*; and it is just as easy to think of cinematic equivalents for Frith's panoramas of everyday life, or Hunt's pictures, like *The Finding of the Saviour in the Temple*, based on lavish reconstructions of bible stories. Such paintings involved exhaustive research, huge cast lists of models, quantities of costumes and props, and massive investment of time and money. For example, Flatow gave £4,500 for Frith's *The Railway Station*, and the copyright, in 1862; 21,150 people paid to see the picture in seven weeks, during its exhibition at the Haymarket Gallery the following year. Flatow then resold the painting, and copyright, for £16,300. Indeed, it hardly comes as a surprise to learn that Alma Tadema's pictures had a direct influence on the early epic films of D.W. Griffith and Cecil B. de Mille.

The late nineteenth century was a great era of public art patronage too. The establishment and growth of the national museums in the early part of the century, was complemented by the spread of the provincial museums from the 1870s onwards. Manchester, Birmingham, and Leeds are particularly rich in their holdings of Victorian painting. Art education developed more slowly: until 1871, when the Slade School opened, the Royal Academy provided the only serious centre for the study of Fine Art in London. (The Government Schools were restricted to ornamental design for industry.)

But if the Victorians did not expect their artists to become pedagogues, they asked many of them to shoulder more than their share of public duties. The late nineteenth century saw the emergence of a new sort of creature: the artist–administrator. Dyce, Eastlake, Leighton, and Poynter were among those whose creative work suffered as a result of the burden of their other duties.

However, it must be said that the efforts of such men did little, or nothing, to reconcile serious artists to the age in which they lived: Leighton expressed a very widely held view when he said that the whole current of modern life was flowing in a direction resolutely opposed to artistic production. He complained that there was

no love of beauty, no sense of the outward dignity and comeliness of things, calling on the part of the public for expression at the artist's hands; and . . . no dignity, no comeliness for the most part, in their outward aspect.

He bemoaned the fact that everywhere there was 'a narrow utilitarianism which does not include the gratification of the artistic sense amongst things useful'. Leighton agreed that the works of artists were

sought for indeed, but too often as a profitable merchandise, or a vehicle of speculation, too often on grounds wholly foreign to their intrinsic worth as productions of a distinctive form of human genius, with laws and conditions of its own.

Nonetheless, he hints at one of the consolations of being an artist in the late-Victorian era. For never before, or since, had the material rewards been so great, or the social prestige so high. The most successful artists of this era lived on a scale unknown by those who preceded, or followed, them; nor were these rich pickings confined simply to those who, like Leighton himself, pursued orthodox careers within the Royal Academy.

Pre-Raphaelitism and the Pre-Raphaelites

In 1854, Holman Hunt (1827–1910) made a journey to the Holy Land. At Oosdoom, on the shores of the Dead Sea, he painted one of his best-known works: *The Scapegoat* (colour pl. 7). The picture shows a goat standing among skulls, skeletons and discarded horns, in a harsh and desolate landscape. The red fillet around the animal's head reminds us that this is a sacrificial creature, driven out into the wilderness on the Day of Atonement, bearing all the inquities of the Jews, 'unto a land not inhabited'. Lest the point escapes us, Hunt inscribed the appropriate texts from Isaiah and Leviticus on the frame. Of course, he also intended the unhappy beast to stand as both type and symbol of The Saviour.

The painting was first exhibited at the Royal Academy in 1856, and it immediately evoked controversy. For the critic of *The Athenaeum*, Hunt had depicted 'a mere goat' which had 'no more interest for us than the sheep which furnished our yesterday's dinner'; whereas, for Ruskin, 'in his earnest desire to paint the Scapegoat', Hunt had 'forgotten to ask himself first, whether he could paint a goat at all'. Informed opinion is still divided concerning the picture, today. In his book on the Pre-Raphaelites, Timothy Hilton called the painting 'inhuman', and dismissed it as an instance of 'the hard nastiness of Hunt's art'. But for Alan Bowness and, I must admit, for me, *The Scapegoat* is 'one of the most memorable images in the history of art'. Without doubt, the painting offers a key to understanding the success and failure of Pre-Raphaelitism.

The Pre-Raphaelite Brotherhood was founded in the autumn of 1848; the most influential members were Hunt himself; his best friend, John Everett Millais (1829–96), and Dante Gabriel Rossetti (1828–82) who is thought to have been responsible for the idea of a secret society. The other founding members were Rossetti's brother, William, a bureaucrat and scribe; his next-door neighbour, Thomas Woolner (1825–92) a sculptor; James Collinson (1825–81), a minor High Church painter; and Frederic Stephens (1828–1907), who soon abandoned painting for criticism.

The aims of the Brothers were more coherent than is sometimes suggested:

they wanted to create an art of a high and elevating spiritual content, and they believed, in Holman Hunt's words, that the academic tradition tended to 'stifle the breath of design'. The major Pre-Raphaelites were as uncertain in their faith as most thinking Victorians; but they were convinced that aesthetic renewal involved the rejection of 'pagan' or Hellenic canons, and the revival of a specifically Christian art.

But what forms was this new art to take? There were some possibilities 'in the air'. We have already seen how William Dyce tried to introduce into Britain something of the ideals of the German Nazarene School. Ford Madox Brown (1821–93) had also taken part, but without success, in the competitions for the Westminster Palace decorations; he too went to Rome where he came under the heady influence of the Nazarenes. Back in England, Rossetti had sought Brown out, and had indeed become his pupil. Brown was to remain close to the PRB; but he was never invited to become a Pre-Raphaelite, because Hunt objected to his 'Germanic' style, though this is not easy to discern, today.

Hunt, at least, was clear about what he did not want Pre-Raphaelitism to be. He wanted a high spiritual art which was English and not German, Protestant and not Catholic: Pre-Raphaelite and not Nazarene. Hunt had a passing acquaintance with the first volume of John Ruskin's *Modern Painters*, and some knowledge of the second, first published in 1846. It was in the former that Ruskin elaborated his view that Turner, of all artists, had been the most truthful to nature; and that since nature was the handiwork of God, Turner had thereby revealed His glory to the world. In the second volume, Ruskin elaborated his distinction between '*aesthesis*', or the merely sensuous response to beauty, and '*theoria*', or the response to beauty with one's whole moral being. He had much to say about the way in which, in, say, Tintoretto, the depiction of an apparently everyday scene might be redolent with 'typical' symbols of divine reality.

In the beginning, at least, all the Pre-Raphaelites seem to have believed something along these lines. The core of the Pre-Raphaelite aesthetic is usually discussed in terms of 'truth to nature'; in fact, it should rather be described as truth to God's revelation of himself, in nature and the scriptures. In a 'Dialogue on art', published in the last issue of the Pre-Raphaelite magazine, *The Germ*, in 1850, John Orchard makes his principal character, Christian, argue that natural phenomena, like the rainbow, are only beautiful because they 'have a spiritual as well as a physical voice'. Christian continues,

Lovely as it is, it is not the arch of colours that glows in the heavens of our hearts; what does, is the inner and invisible sense for which it was set up of old by God, and of which its many-hued form is only the outward and visible sign.

At first, the paintings of these ambitious young men were well-enough received; but, by 1850, the meaning of the letters, PRB, with which the brothers inscribed their paintings, had become known. Fears of Papist plots were seemingly confirmed when the Italian, Dante Gabriel Rossetti, exhibited his *Ecce Ancilla Domini!*, showing a terrified Virgin Mary cowering on a bed; and Millais sent to the Royal Academy *Christ in the Carpenter's Shop*, a

painting which may, in fact, have been partially inspired by a Tractarian
sermon. But most critics objected violently to what they took to be Millais's
'naturalism'; Dickens, notoriously, slated the work, objecting to Millais's
depiction of Jesus as 'a hideous, wry-necked, blubbering, red-haired boy in a
night-gown'. At this stage, Ruskin still shared the general prejudice, but
Dyce, with whom he was friendly, persuaded him to study Millais's picture
more closely.

The following year, the Brotherhood's paintings showed a shift away from
biblical pictures towards works which derived their strength from the
depiction of natural forms. Increasingly, they came to rely on a technique of
painting directly into a wet, white ground: it is this which accounts for the
brilliance of Pre-Raphaelite colours which have faded very little since they
were first laid down. The Pre-Raphaelites also believed that the picture
should not be illuminated by a focused source of theatrical studio lighting,
but should rather, as Ruskin was later to put it, be lit in the same
indiscriminate way in which the sun lights the world. But these effects are
strangely ambivalent: on the one hand they look back to the flat and stylised
brilliance of medieval stained glass painting; on the other, they seem to
anticipate the 'all-over' literalness of a modern colour photograph.

The harsh criticism continued; but the poet, Coventry Patmore, prevailed
upon Ruskin to write to *The Times* in defence of the Brotherhood. Ruskin
admitted to a 'very uncertain sympathy'; he still feared that the Brotherhood
had High Church leanings. One of the works in the 1851 Royal Academy
exhibition was, in fact, *Convent Thoughts* – a picture of Charles Collins
(1828–73), a close associate of the Pre-Raphaelites. This shows a nun, in an
enclosed garden of lilies, standing in front of a goldfish pool, contemplating a
passion-flower – which reminds her of the crucifixion. The frame is inscribed
with a Latin biblical text, which, being translated, means 'As the lily among
thorns'. The painting is redolent with Catholic symbolism, and apparently
refers to the revival of the convent movement. Ruskin just dismissed all this,
but elaborately praised the one element of the picture which cannot be
incorporated in its symbolic order: the depiction of the leaf of the water
plantain, *Alisma Plantago*, growing in the pond. 'I never saw it so thoroughly
or so well drawn', he wrote. Elsewhere, Ruskin had repeatedly explained his
belief that the shape and structure of the *Alisma Plantago* leaf and plant were
examples almost of the divine prototypes from which God had fabricated the
natural world. Within two years, William Rossetti could write, 'We have
emerged from reckless abuse to a position of general and high recognition.'

Nonetheless, by this time, the Pre-Raphaelite Brotherhood had already
disintegrated: there were, of course, many reasons for this. James Collinson
resigned after his reconversion to Roman Catholicism; Thomas Woolner went
to Australia in search of gold; Ruskin's plan to make Millais into a 'second
Turner' was, unfortunately, disrupted when Millais fell in love with Ruskin's
wife, Effie, whom he married in 1856. Ruskin himself was not sorry to see
Effie go, and felt that these events ought not to affect his relationship with
Millais; but Millais, a simpler, saner and more superficial individual, thought
otherwise. As for Rossetti, he was deeply wounded by the antagonistic
reception of Pre-Raphaelitism; he proved unable to finish his only large oil-

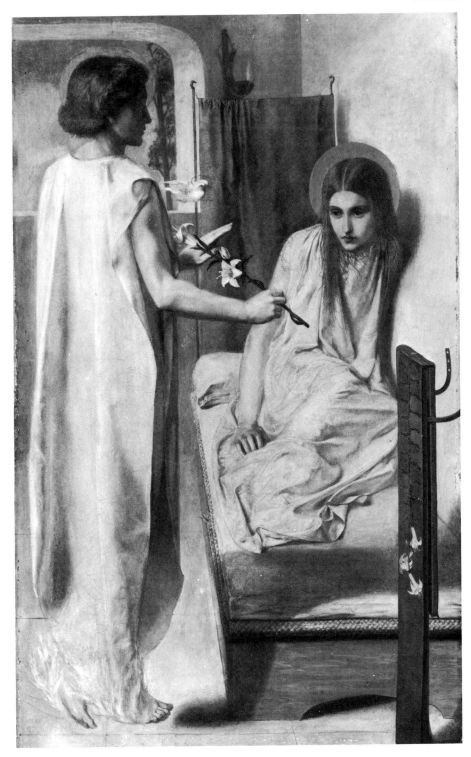

Dante Gabriel Rossetti, Ecce Ancilla Domini! (The Annunciation) *(1850)*.

painting of this period, *Found*, and, for a time, painted only water-colours of medieval, literary scenes.

Hunt's trip to the Holy Land in 1854 was, among other things, a desperate attempt to salvage the aesthetic principles which had informed the movement from the beginning. Surely he would find God in the Holy Land? One of the main differences between Hunt's study for *The Scapegoat* and the finished version was the removal of the rainbow: it was as if, for Hunt, signs of God's covenant were disappearing altogether. He found not his Redeemer, but a mangy goat which dropped dead on him. But if a goat really had 'no more interest for us than the sheep which furnished our yesterday's dinner', then, of course, Pre-Raphaelitism, as he understood it, had become impossible.

Pre-Raphaelite aesthetic depended, in large part, upon the peculiar conditions of spiritual life and religious thought in the late 1840s; as the 1850s progressed, those conditions were subject to violent change. The new biblical criticism from Germany had made very little impact among any of the warring religious parties – Evangelical, Tractarian, main-stream Anglican, Catholic, or Non-Conformist.

Pre-Raphaelitism was not simply 'literary'; it was permeated by *biblical* thinking, that is by the belief that the Bible, as the Word of God, provides knowledge of God's revelation of himself. (This revelatory quality was extended to include the 'touchstones' of worldly literature, like the works of Shakespeare and, for the Pre-Raphaelites, the rediscovered Keats.) Most Christians believed that if the inerrancy of the Bible were successfully impugned, 'the whole Christian faith would collapse'.

But how was Scripture to be interpreted? Both Tractarians and Evangelicals elaborated complicated systems of symbolic typology – by which they interpreted elements of the Old Testament as prefigurements, or prophecies, of the Coming of Christ and the redemptive process in the New. In such literature 'The Scapegoat' of the ceremonies described in Leviticus was interpreted as a presentiment of Christ, the Vicarious Sacrifice. This sort of thinking spilled out into the understanding of nature itself.

But there were, of course, vital differences between the various groupings. The Tractarians and Catholics placed all the emphasis on the authority of tradition; the Evangelicals relied on a more immediate and personal encounter with the the Word of God in the Scriptures. Ruskin had been brought up as a strict Evangelical: it has sometimes been suggested that he simply transferred Evangelical typology to the understanding of art. But this is not so . . . Indeed, it was because he distrusted this sort of painting that he ignored the symbolism in *Convent Thoughts*, and made his remarkable criticism of Hunt's *Scapegoat*.

Ruskin was nothing if not an authoritarian personality; and though he was ardent in his Evangelical rejection of the authority of the clergy and the ecclesiastical tradition, he was always seeking a replacement for them. (We know, for example, that he was greatly tempted by the allurements of Rome.) While he was at Oxford, he found the substitute he was looking for – in a theory of nature. This he was already disposed to do as, since childhood, he had always loved nature with an inordinate, some might say an unnatural, passion.

At Oxford, Ruskin came deeply under the influence of William Buckland, an Anglican Divine and geologist, and a prominent member of the English School of Geology. Buckland taught that modern science was creating a new synthesis of biblical and natural revelation; this was a threat to the traditional typologies of the Tractarians and the Evangelicals alike. He thereby incurred the considerable wrath of both these parties; Ruskin's mother, a good Evangelical if ever there was one, became concerned about Buckland's influence over her son.

As Nicholas Rupke has recently shown us, Buckland was a much better geologist than he is usually given credit for: he was *not* concerned with 'reconciling' the Bible and nature. (Such a project would have had little meaning for him, since he naturally assumed that both were sources of revelation.) Rather, he argued that the more we knew about nature, the more we would come to know about God – whose handiwork he believed nature to be.

Until very recently, Buckland has suffered from tendentious reporting; Ruskin's biographers have tried to dismiss him as a buffoon, and to down-play his influence. But, Mrs Ruskin notwithstanding, Ruskin was personally and intellectually close to Buckland; he even prepared the illustrations for his geological lectures. The English School of Geology was not just a challenge to the Evangelical ideas with which Ruskin had been brought up; it also provided him with much of the theoretical framework for a new, scientific, and genuinely Protestant aesthetics. All this poured out in the first two volumes of *Modern Painters*, which Hunt had read before the founding of Pre-Raphaelitism; hence Ruskin's relentless attacks on what he perceived as Pre-Raphaelite Tractarian tendencies, and his praise of their 'truth to nature'.

All this seems very arcane to us; it would have appeared much less so to Ruskin's readers. Natural theology, (albeit of a less theoretically sophisticated kind) was something of a mania among the English middle classes; many women gathered wild flowers, which they later painted or pressed; many men, like Ruskin himself, collected minerals. The keeping of enclosed, glass containers of ferns, known as 'Wardian cases', peaked, and the craze for keeping aquaria began, in 1850 – the year that Pre-Raphaelitism erupted into notoriety. Few doubted that the ultimate value of such activities was moral and religious. In 1853, Philip Gosse set up the Aquarium at the London Zoo and, the following year, published a book on aquarium-keeping in the home, in which he tried to show how every organism an enthusiast might keep was revelatory of God's 'mighty plan'.

In the late 1850s, however, the lynch-pins of natural theology and, by extension, of Pre-Raphaelite aesthetics began to crumble. On the one hand, it became harder and harder for intelligent, informed men and women simply to shut out the new European critical methodologies, which were beginning to cast such grave doubt on the inerrancy of the scriptures. On the other hand, the urgency with which the naturalists asserted that every organism in nature revealed God could be correlated with the dawning realisation – even among those who held fast to belief in God – that it did not.

Indeed, I would argue that Pre-Raphaelitism was the aesthetic of precisely

John Ruskin, In the Pass of Killiecrankie *(1857).*

this moment in Engish cultural life: Hunt and Ruskin were so dogmatic because their doubts were so grave. As early as 1851, Ruskin admitted publicly that the man who went 'hammer in hand, over the surface of a romantic country' tended to find that his first sense of 'sublimity or mystery' was destroyed rather than deepened. Those like John Brett who applied Ruskin's aesthetic theories most uncompromisingly did indeed find that their paintings came closer and closer to geological illustration.

If a stone is a stone is a stone, a leaf is a leaf is a leaf, or a goat is a goat is a goat, then, of course, there can be no Pre-Raphaelite aesthetic. By the time Buckland died in 1856, his geology, and his natural theology, were hopelessly outmoded; it was becoming harder and harder simply to assume that study of natural form led naturally to spiritual truths. In 1857, Philip Gosse, a Non-Conformist, argued desperately that God had created strata and fossils too. And that he had done so precisely in order to test man's faith. But few went along with this sort of special pleading.

The following year, William Dyce painted the last, and perhaps the greatest, of the classical Pre-Raphaelite landscapes, *Pegwell Bay* (colour pl. 6). It shows us what a long way we have come from, say, Hunt's Edenic landscapes of the early 1850s, like *The Hireling Shepherd*. Dyce was a High churchman and a geologist. He was drawn to Pegwell Bay with its chalk cliffs and its abundance of fossils. He shows us a group of women and children looking for specimens on the shore; there are no biblical texts inscribed on the frame. The painting is filled with menace and foreboding. The lowering sky is a sultry grey. Overhead a comet, a symbol of impending doom and calamity, passes by unnoticed.

From our perspectives today, the watershed looks like the publication of Darwin's *Origin of Species* in 1858, which occurred while Dyce was still working on this painting. For the mid-Victorians and their contemporaries, the appearance of *Essays and Reviews*, edited by Benjamin Jowett, in 1860 was more immediately momentous. C.W. Goodwin's contribution, 'On the mosaic cosmogony', destroyed for ever Buckland's assumption of a synthesis between the scriptures and natural revelation; and Jowett's text, 'On the interpretation of scripture', though it reads innocuously enough today, seemed to undermine the Scriptures themselves as a source of divine revelation. The doors seemed to blow open to continental criticism and continental scepticism. One thing is certain: Jowett's conception of 'progressive revelation' was incompatible with Pre-Raphaelite aesthetics as Ruskin had elaborated them, and Hunt had practised them.

Ruskin, at least, acknowledged this: by this time, he had already undergone his 'unconversion' in Turin and, for the time being, had come to advocate a sensuous (rather than a spiritual) aesthetic and to believe that a 'good, stout, self-commanding animality is the make for poets and artists'. Of the painters themselves, only Hunt forged on as if nothing had changed. Even those of us who, like myself, admire Hunt's stubborn refusal of modernity cannot deny that the terrible, frozen energy manifest in *The Scapegoat* simply disappears as he comes to accept the naked shingles of the world.

George Frederic Watts: beyond Pre-Raphaelitism

One day in 1873, George Frederic Watts and John Ruskin met outside Burlington House during a winter exhibition of Old Masters. Not for the first time, they began to argue about art. Ruskin claimed that the great Italian masters of the High Renaissance were all wrong, because they did not paint what they saw; thus, they violated truth. Then, pointing at a 'scavenger's heap of mud lying at the foot of a grimy lamp-post', Ruskin shouted at Watts, 'Paint that as it is . . . that is truth'.

When Ruskin got back to the Bull Hotel, in Piccadilly, he wrote an angry letter to Watts, whom he accused of being 'paralyzed' by his love of the

Greek style and of never having made 'an entirely honest, completely unaffected study of anything'. Ruskin told him,

You fancy you see more than I do in Nature – you still see less, for I, long ago, learned how impossible it was to draw what I saw – you still struggle to do so; that is to say, to draw what you like in what you see without caring about what others like – or what God likes.

We don't know how Watts replied; but he probably was not unduly perturbed. Watts had always been a thorn in the side of Ruskin's theories, if not his flesh. In 1848, the year in which the Pre-Raphaelite Brotherhood was founded, Ruskin described Watts as (to my mind the only real painter of history or thought we have in England'. Ruskin even borrowed *Time and Oblivion*, the first of Watts's enormous allegories, painted that year, to hang in his home. But soon after Ruskin characteristically wrote to tell the painter that his flora were all wrong – and quoted the Bible to prove it:

I was thinking, after I left you yesterday, that you were mistaken in the botany of one of your pictures. Forget-me-nots do not grow on graves: *anywhere* but on a grave. Neither do they grow among thorns, but by sweet, quiet streams and in fair pastures (Psalm XXII 2–3).

Watts tried to explain to Ruskin that he shared his belief that art must needs be *true*, but that he did not agree with Ruskin's 'near-sighted' view of what truth was. 'My own views', Watts wrote to his truculent friend, 'are too visionary, and the qualities I aim at are too abstract, to be attained, or perhaps to produce any effect if attained.' Privately, he complained that Ruskin 'had no apprehension of "abstract form"'.

But Watts was not impervious to Ruskin's criticisms. After a visit to Venice, in 1853, Watts wrote to Ruskin, 'I can better understand why I fail.' The 'glowing and gorgeous' painters of the Venetian School had 'rendered Nature as I feel her – as I too would render her – but my imagination is not vivid, nor my memory powerful'. In the late 1850s, as Ruskin's faith failed, he became more enamoured than ever of the worldly splendours of the Venetians, and he never missed an opportunity to urge them upon Watts. No painter could have admired Titian more than Watts, who even affected the Italian master's appearance; but his sensibility was always remote from Titian's robust, full-blooded, sensuousness.

In later life, Ruskin himself was haunted by a sense of 'The Failure of Nature'; that which once had seemed to reveal God was now obscured by a diabolic storm cloud and a pestilential plague wind. Ruskin now felt better able to acknowledge Watts as a painter of 'the spiritual truth of myths'. But, for better or for worse, Watts's craving for truths that nature could not reveal took him beyond myths and brought him to the very brink of abstraction, at least a decade before Kandinsky reached the same point.

Watts had a precocious early success with his painting *A Wounded Heron* shown at the Royal Academy in 1837; and he met the first of the many patrons who were to shield his career. Six years later, he won a first prize of £300 with his cartoon *Caractacus* in the first Houses of Parliament Competition. Watts used the money to take himself off to Italy, where he studied fresco techniques and the Ancients. When he returned to England, four years later, he brought with him *Alfred Inciting the Saxons*, which won him £500 in the 1847 Houses of Parliament Competition. (The picture still hangs in Committee Room Ten at the House of Commons.)

But Watts was already moving away from the idea of conventional, classical, history painting. Even before he met Ruskin, he had read the first volume of *Modern Painters* and, in response, painted a remarkable series of 'higher landscapes'; but they seemed to him too remote from human values. He admired Turner greatly; but he put him on 'a lower level' than Michelangelo, Raphael and Titian. Watts experimented with social realism and visited Ireland, producing four large, but theatrical, pictures of the poor, starving and oppressed.

But gradually Watts was conceiving in his mind of the idea which Mary, his second wife, was to describe as 'the ambition of one half of his life and the regret of the other half'. In Italy, he had seen and admired the Sistine Chapel. He wanted to do 'for modern thought what Michel Angelo did for theological thought'. Watts's beliefs can best be described as a kind of deistic humanism. He retained some remote belief in God as the ultimate cause of the universe; but he had scant respect for Christianity, and less for the modern church. Thus he conceived of 'The House of Life'; at first, he envisaged an actual building, the ceiling of which would 'be covered with the uniform blue of space'. Giant wall frescoes, beginning with *Time and Oblivion*, would illustrate the history of the 'progress of man's spirit' from 'the hunter stage' to 'the preaching of Peter the Hermit', and beyond.

But Watts soon came to realise the House would never be built; as Mary wrote, 'in his mind the scheme became more abstract, and less realistic and historic'. The vast allegoric paintings into which he poured so much of his time in his later years were the nearest he got to the realisation of this scheme.

There was not a ready-made market for such work, and Watts was not prepared to set about making one. Unlike many of his contemporaries, Watts found the association between art and money profoundly distasteful. He kept as aloof from the picture trade as he could. He survived by cultivating friends and patrons – and through portraiture. For example, Watts installed himself as a house guest of Sarah and Thoby Prinsep, who lived in Little Holland House, on Lord Holland's estate. As Mrs Prinsep later put it, 'He came to stay three days; he stayed thirty years'. In fact, it was twenty-four; and through them all she cossetted and cared for him.

As for portraiture, Watts found the whole business pure 'torture'; but later in life, he managed to assimilate even this into his lofty ambitions. He invited eminent Victorians to sit for him – without any money changing hands; most did, with the notable exception of Ruskin. Later, Watts admitted, he would have 'felt paralysed in Ruskin's presence'. The loss is ours: Watts's portraits of Tennyson and Cardinal Manning confirm that he really did possess the power to paint 'the shape and colour of a mind and life'.

But Watts's craving to be of public service on a grander scale never left him. In 1852, his offer to decorate Euston Station, at his own expense, with a series of frescoes was refused. But the lawyers of Lincoln's Inn accepted a similar offer to decorate their new Hall with a forty-five feet by forty feet

George Frederic Watts, Cardinal Manning *(1882)*.

fresco called *Justice: A Hemicycle of Lawgivers*. The execution proved harder than the conception: the mural was not completed until 1859; and Watts received only the cost of his materials.

Watts's lack of realism was not confined to his professional life, nor to his pictures themselves; in 1864, aged forty-six, he married Ellen Terry, aged sixteen. Little is known about Watts's sexuality; there was, perhaps, little to know. Bernard Shaw once described him as 'luke-warm'. Naturally, Watts rationalised his motives into a public duty; he wanted to save Ellen Terry from 'the temptations and abominations of the stage'. The marriage broke down within a matter of months; Watts destroyed most of his paintings of Ellen Terry, though *Choosing*, 1864, survives. Watts painted his golden-haired, child-bride surrounded by flowers. At no time in his life did Watts come closer to the post-Pre-Raphaelite sensualism of Rossetti and Burne-Jones. But an unconvincing aroma of ethical intention hangs around even this picture: as Chris Mullen has pointed out, the blooms Ellen Terry is trying to sniff are scentless camellias. Did Watts want to symbolise 'the empty vanity of the actress's profession'?

Once free of Watts, Ellen Terry went on to pursue fame and fortune; Watts himself became increasingly melancholic and monastic; haunted by migraine, and a sense of his own personal and professional failure, he lost himself in 'The House of Life'. The year after Ellen Terry left him, he also turned seriously to sculpture for the first time; her lingering influence has often been seen in the drama and sensuousness of his *Clytie*, which he first exhibited at the Royal Academy in 1868. Watts was, of course, well known among artists and writers; indeed, he was close to Leighton, the President of the Royal Academy. But his reclusive life, and his lofty art, set him apart. The large frescoes were forgotten; to the public at large, he was Watts the portrait painter. Things began to change in 1881, when Watts had his first one-man London show at the Grosvenor Gallery; he exhibited portraits and landscape, as well as large allegories. Watts was proclaimed as a neglected Master; he was heralded as one of the few painters of the day whose work touched upon the highest spiritual themes. In 1884, a vast exhibition of his work opened at the Metropolitan Museum in New York, and was seen by 500,000 visitors. Watts was offered a baronetcy – which he refused; but he did manage to find himself another young wife, Mary Fraser-Tytler, aged thirty-six, whom he married in 1886, when he was sixty-nine.

All this spurred Watts on: indeed, many of his best-known images, like *Mammon*, 1885, and of course *Hope*, 1886 – belong to this period. Hope sits, in Watts's words, 'on a globe with bandaged eyes, playing on a lyre which has all the strings broken but one'. During the last twenty years of his life, Watts also made his most important sculptures – *Physical Energy*, as a dramatic, mounted horseman, a cast of which still rears in Kensington Gardens; and his statue of his friend, Alfred Tennyson, which stands, head bowed, outside Lincoln Cathedral.

How then are we to estimate Watts's improbable achievement? At the end of the last century, few among Watts's contemporaries doubted his stature; though, in one sense, he stood outside the art of his time, he came to be regarded as its greatest exponent. It is true that George Moore dismissed Watts as 'a sort of modern Veronese in treacle and gingerbread'; but Moore's judgement was hardly reliable. Roger Fry – a sounder aestheticist – compared Watts favourably with Whistler, and expressed the belief that, in the future, Watts would be accorded 'a place by the side of Rubens and Titian . . . little short of the summit of human achievement in the arts'.

So far, this has not happened. Much, I believe too much, continues to be made of his self-evident flaws – especially his tendencies to rhetoric and vacuousness. How these attributes can still offend anyone conditioned by the cultural mores of the late twentieth century remains something of a mystery. But Watts has certainly benefited less than lesser contemporaries from the Victorian revival of recent years; for Watts's reputation crumbled on his death, and it has not yet been pieced together again. Watts may yet re-emerge as a scandal to haunt the accepted accounts of what matters and what does not matter in the recent history of painting.

In his brilliant little book about Watts, G.K. Chesterton argued convincingly that, despite the commonplace criticism, Watts was in fact the antithesis of the literary painter. He pointed out that a picture like *Hope* just was not exhausted by reference to the word 'hope'; in front of such paintings, Chesterton claimed, the viewer could discern something

for which there is neither speech nor language, which has been too vast for any eye to see and too secret for any religion to utter, even as an esoteric doctrine.

Chesterton says that this 'something' is made manifest through Watts's forms, and his technique, which 'does almost startlingly correspond to the structure of his spiritual sense'.

Long before I read Chesterton on Watts, I was fumbling towards similar conclusions; when I first saw Watts's work in any quantity, at the 1974 Whitechapel Gallery exhibition of his work, I noted how he was 'floundering towards a universally comprehensible sublimity in paint'. In this respect, I was constantly reminded of Mark Rothko, the American Abstract Expressionist. And, indeed, Watts had drawn tantalisingly close to abstraction.

For example, in 1902, Watts painted *The Sower of the Systems* (colour pl. 4); the subject was suggested to him by the play upon the ceiling of the reflections of his night-light; it is yet another attempt to convey in paint his vision of the moment of creation of the cosmos, or, if you will, 'ultimate reality'. But the allegorical figures have disappeared. Mary Watts described the picture as 'an attempt to paint an unpaintable subject'. The colour is deep blue; the figure seems impelled forward while 'stars, suns, and planets fly from hands that scatter them as seeds are scattered'.

Watts himself once likened his attempts at giving utterance and form to his ideas to the drawing of a child who,

being asked by his little sister to draw God, made a great number of circular scribbles, and putting his paper on a soft surface, struck his pencil through the centre, making a great void.

Watts added that the result was 'utterly absurd as a picture', but said, 'there was a greater idea in it than in Michael Angelo's old man with a long beard'. To his contemporaries – and, in a sense, to Watts himself, as a great classicist – the idea of 'a great void' as the pictorial means to divine revelation was not only infantile, but almost incomprehensible. But Turner, of course, had already comprehended it. And Kandinsky, Malevich, Mondrian, and especially, perhaps, Mark Rothko, would have known exactly what Watts meant; they spent much of their lives in the same spiritual and pictorial pursuit.

Watts's sculpture raises similar problems; R.E. Gutch has pointed out that

George Frederic Watts and his sculpture, Physical Energy, *in the garden of New Little Holland House, Kensington (c.1890).*

in his feeling for form, his sense of texture, materials, and movement, Watts might well be considered as a model of 'progressiveness and originality'.

The similarity between the imaginations of Watts and of Henry Moore has in fact been hinted at by Watts's most recent biographer, Wilfrid Blunt, who drew attention to the remarkable correspondence between one of Watts's last (and one of his finest) paintings, *Mother and Child* (1903–4), and some of

Moore's drawings. Many other such comparisons can be made. For example, Watts continued to experiment with the formal possibilities of his early 'House of Life' designs; one of the most remarkable of these experiments is a small painting of *The Titans*, a version of his idea for 'a number of gigantic figures stretched out at full length' to represent 'a range of mountains typifying the rocky structure or skeleton' of the earth. Moore, of course, was to explore just such concepts in sculpture – but without Watts's lingering attachment to explicit mythic content. Although Watts had no direct

George Frederic Watts, Mother and Child *(1903–4)*.

influence on Moore, the continuity between these two artists may run much deeper than simple resemblances.

But Gutch may be wrong to try and recast Watts as a pioneer, or precursor, of modernity: in his traditionalism, his commitment to humanist spirituality, and his unswerving pursuit of universal values, Moore was as much set apart from the twentieth century as Watts was from the nineteenth. What we can say, however, is that, in the few sculptures which Watts brought to completion, he began to intuit how textures and forms themselves could replace allegoric or mythic content as the means towards the expression of spiritual truths. And this was something which Henry Moore was to develop much more fully in the twentieth century.

Alfred Gilbert and the revival of Victorian sculpture

In the early years of the twentieth century, the 'pioneers' of modern sculpture, and their critical protagonists, liked to dismiss the Victorian contribution to sculpture as if it consisted of nothing more than endless corridors of dusty, and best-forgotten, 'silk-hat' statuary. But Rodin himself did not see things like this. When the critic, M.H. Spielmann, told him that the English thought of Alfred Gilbert as highly as Benvenuto Cellini, Rodin said, 'better than that, better than that'.

Alfred Gilbert's exceptional talents did not spring out of nothing. If Watts worked apart from the Victorian mainstream, Gilbert was deeply embedded in its complex cross-currents. But, like Watts, he was forgotten in the twentieth century at least in part as a result of those shifts in sculptural tastes and expectations which he had done so much to bring about.

By the mid-nineteenth century, the sculptor was more like a minor industrialist than what we conceive of as an artist. Busts and funerary sculptures provided most studios with their bread-and-butter income; the rich pickings came from public memorials and statues. Occasionally, if he found an accommodating patron, the sculptor might have the opportunity to make an 'ideal' piece – an Aphrodite, a Hermes, or perhaps some more elaborate flight of classical fancy. Even so, the Fine Art sculptor jealously distinguished himself, as a man of ideas, from the journeyman craftsman or mason; and so, despite the continuing Gothic Revival, architectural and ecclesiastical sculptures were rarely better than workmanlike.

The profession was given a great impetus by the death of Robert Peel in 1850; but the sculptors' studios were rendered even busier by the death of the Duke of Wellington in 1852, and, of course, of Prince Albert in 1861. This rash of public statuary was accompanied by stylistic dilemmas. For example, the leading sculptor of the day was John Gibson (1790–1866), who ranked below only Canova, and Thorwaldsen in the neo-Classicist Pantheon. Gibson differed from many English sculptors in that he rarely resorted to the common practice of getting studio assistants to 'point-up' from small maquettes but rather, as Boase puts it, 'had constantly his chisel in his hand'. Gibson's most notorious work was *The Tinted Venus*, which he began in 1851, and which became a *cause célèbre* when shown at the International

Exhibition, eleven years later. The Venus celebrated not only the nudity of
Greek sculptures but the fact that they were coloured. Gibson was adamant
that the body 'concealed under a frock coat and trousers' was 'not a fit
subject for sculpture'. But Gibson's *Monument to Sir Robert Peel*, in
Westminster Abbey, is neither nude, nor pink; rather Peel is depicted in the
robes of a classical orator.

There was, of course, a reaction against this sort of thing. We have already
encountered Thomas Woolner as one of the seven founding members of the
Pre-Raphaelite Brotherhood. It has sometimes been suggested that his work
really had little to do with Pre-Raphaelitism; but a glance at the 'naturalism'
of the features or the detail in the flowers of his *Wordsworth Memorial*, 1851,
at Grasmere, reveals that this is not the case. Woolner continued to combine
an ethical and social earnestness with an interest in modern life subjects, like
The Housemaid, 1893; all of which justifies Read's view that he may have
been 'as true and as life-long an adherent' to Pre-Raphaelite principles as the
intractable Holman Hunt.

Even so, the greatest Victorian sculpture of the mid-century was a product
of the Victorian High Renaissance, and especially of Alfred Stevens
(1817–75). Stevens worked for the Sheffield firm of H.E. Hoole, producing
metalwork designs for fireplaces, which won prizes at the 1851 Great
Exhibition. He was also a superb interior decorator – most famously of the
fittings at Dorchester House; but his sights were set on grander things. Much
of the last part of his unhappy life was consumed by the vaunting monument

Thomas Woolner, The Housemaid *(1893).*

to Wellington, in St Paul's Cathedral. The project was dogged by squabbles, controversies and procrastinations and was not completed until long after Stevens's death. The equestrian sculpture was cast from Stevens's mould by John Tweed in 1912; indeed, it was only thanks to the good offices of Lord Leighton that, in 1892, the monument was placed in its present site, for which Stevens had designed and intended it.

Alfred Stevens, the Wellington Monument in St Paul's Cathedral (1911).

Among Stevens's problems was the fact that the public, perhaps conditioned by the churches of the Gothic Revival, the writings of Ruskin, and the popular memorial to Walter Scott erected in Edinburgh in the 1840s, greatly preferred the Gothic as the style for memorials to great men. When the decision was taken to erect a memorial to Prince Albert in Hyde Park, the *Art Journal* commented, 'This will be the most glorious opportunity for British sculptors to show what they can really do.' Gilbert Scott's elaborately ornamented design is everywhere encrusted with works by leading sculptors of the day, illustrating the arts, enterprises and sciences in which the Prince was involved. Albert himself is depicted with stooped head, clutching the catalogue to the Great Exhibition, in a large figure by John Foley (1818–74). Foley was also responsible for *Asia*, one of the groups representing the four continents which guard the extremities of the steps leading up to the monument.

Much mirth has been directed at the Albert Memorial in our own century, when it has seemed to epitomise the excesses and vulgarities of High Victorian Gothic. Though such criticisms are certainly informed by bigotry and the vicissitudes of changing taste, it must be admitted that few of those represented produced of their best; the stiff and lifeless sculptures contrast unhappily with the unrestrained ornamental encrustation of the structure which frames them.

The death of Stevens in 1875, and the completion of the Albert Memorial, drew to an end two opposed traditions in mid-Victorian sculpture. The stage seemed set for some radical transformation, and it was not long in coming. The teaching of sculpture at the Royal Academy had, for some time, been deeply affected by the bracing and cosmopolitan influence of Leighton; and then in 1877, he exhibited his *Athlete Wrestling with a Python*. Remembering this moment many years later, Edmund Gosse recalled the 'vital and nervous' qualities of the sculpture, and its richly 'varied and appropriate' surfaces, studied, or so he claimed, from nature, and therefore abhorrent to the neo-Classical tradition. 'This', he wrote,

. . . was something wholly new, propounded by a painter to the professional sculptors, and displaying a juster and livelier sense of what their art should be than they themselves had ever dreamed of.

Among those who felt the immediate impact of Leighton's work were a group of younger sculptors – including Thomas Brock, Hamo Thornycroft and Alfred Gilbert. They, together with Alfred Drury, Harry Bates and George Frampton, were to forge the New Sculpture movement which brought about what Susan Beattie has called, 'the most turbulent redefinition of sculpture's role ever to take place in Britain'. Easily the most talented of the New Sculptors was Alfred Gilbert.

Born in 1854 into a family of musicians, Gilbert was conspicuously less loved than his adored, sickly, and musically precocious younger brother, Gordon. In 1878, the year after Gilbert had seen Leighton's *Athlete*, Gordon died, and Gilbert went to Rome to continue his studies. Richard Dorment's recent biography of Gilbert argues, convincingly, that sculptures like the finely carved *The Kiss of Victory* may have referred more to his deceased brother than to its overt subject matter: certainly, even in these early days, the life and vigour of Gilbert's sculpture seems to spring as much as anything from the tension between its public and conventional face and his growing need to give expression to the demands of his inner world.

Gilbert soon mastered the secrets of the 'lost-wax' techniques of bronze-casting, which allowed him to produce a finish of even greater intricacy and detail than Leighton's. His fine bronze, *Icarus*, was a sensational success at the Royal Academy exhibition of 1884 and Gilbert confirmed his position as the leader of the emerging new movement in sculpture with the exotic work, *The Enchanted Chair*, made in 1886, but since destroyed. Gilbert was also showered with commissions: his life at once became an impossible contradiction in which he struggled to maintain his creative and imaginative integrity, and to handle the incessant demands and pressures placed upon him by patrons, clients and committees. One of Gilbert's problems was that he was determined to retain aesthetic control over all his own means and materials; no one was ever going to be able to take over his commissions as he had Joseph Edgar Boehm's (1834–90), on the latter's sudden death.

Among his contemporaries, Gilbert had a special admiration for G.F. Watts and his elevated idea of the role of art and its place in society, and for Burne-Jones: he was, in short, a man of the Victorian High Renaissance. Surprisingly, perhaps, of the two he was most immediately influenced by Burne-Jones. In 1888, Gilbert joined the Art Workers' Guild; his work as a goldsmith, and metal worker, was an extension of his sculpture; the flowing, sinuous forms, and his intricate elaboration of details, lent themselves immediately to the decorative arts. There is a creative continuity between the *épergne*, or table-centre, which Gilbert produced for the Royal table, and, later on, his elaborate masterpiece – the tomb of the Duke of Clarence.

Gilbert's mature style has sometimes been seen as a late flowering of the Gothic Revival; if so, it was a very particular Victorian *courtly* Gothic, which amalgamated the concern of the craftsman for his craft and materials with the grand ambitions of the High Renaissance artist, the man of mind and imagination.

In 1887, Queen Victoria's Jubilee led to another rash of public statuary, the length and breadth of the land; Gilbert's statue of the Queen for the Great Hall of the Castle at Winchester, with its swathes of swirling drapery, was the most vigorous and original. Characteristically, he topped the figure with an exotic, detached crown – which eventually collapsed. Gilbert's new design was more ornate than ever; it still hangs precariously above the bronze Queen. Gilbert's Victoria contrasts with the rather stiff and wooden statue of King Alfred, in the city centre, by Hamo Thornycroft, who was developing a more pedestrian, earnest and Morrisian version of 'New Sculpture'.

While working on his Victoria, Gilbert received a commission to create a memorial for Lord Shaftesbury, the Victorian philanthropist. The fountain, topped by the statue of Eros (or Anteros, as Gilbert preferred to call it) remains, today, one of the most celebrated of London's landmarks – and it shows just how intertwined Gilbert's activities as goldsmith and sculptor were. But the elaborate symbolism of the work, involving jets and arrows of an abundant and selfless love, and the nudity of the crowning figure, were

Alfred Gilbert, Icarus *(1884)*.

deemed unfortunate, given the nature of the locale and the professions plied there. Gilbert experienced his first taste of public disapproval.

But he had already received an invitation from the Prince and Princess of Wales to produce a memorial for Eddy, the Duke of Clarence, who had recently died of influenza. Today this extraordinary work in richly ornamented and intricately worked bronze and aluminium almost seems to subsume the Albert Memorial Chapel at Windsor Castle. The Duke's head, and his hands, are in white marble; an aluminium angel watches over him as he floats, in uniform, on his aluminium cloak. The group is encased in an extravagant bronze grille, punctuated with twelve figures of saints. But the making of this chef d'oeuvre almost ruined Gilbert's life.

Even before Gilbert began the Clarence tomb, professional procrastination, domestic extravagance, aesthetic perfectionism, and marital unhappiness had conspired to reduce his affairs to chaos. Inevitably, the tomb only served to increase the pressure on him, and reduced his capacity to execute (but not to accept) more immediately lucrative commissions. In 1901, Gilbert declared himself bankrupt, and departed for Bruges. To make matters worse, it became known that replicas of the figures of the saints from the Clarence tomb were circulating in the London art market. Whether or not Gilbert had acted improperly is still a matter of contention, but he was certainly disgraced. And his failure to fulfil other commissions led to his forced resignation from the Royal Academy.

It was not until 1926, when Eros was temporarily removed from Piccadilly Circus, that Gilbert began to be missed. Gilbert returned to England; though he never received Royal forgiveness, he was, at least, allowed to complete the tomb. Eventually re-admitted to the Royal Academy, he was awarded a knighthood. He died in 1934, and was buried with due ceremony in St Paul's Cathedral; whereupon he was promptly forgotten for half a century. It seemed to many that Gilbert's work was simply irrelevant in the twentieth century; his last major commission – the Memorial to Queen Alexandra, in Marlborough Gate, appeared to confirm how out of touch he had become. It has often, and rightly, been said of this exotic representation of the Virgin and child, in a Byzantine setting, that it evokes the era of *fin de siècle* sensuousness and symbolism, rather than that of the early 1930s, when it was finally unveiled. Even so, in its originality and expressive handling of the swirling bronze forms of the Virgin's drapery – an instance of 'truth to materials' if ever there was one – the sculpture strongly indicates what was rarely later admitted; and that is that the 'pioneers' of the modern movement in the early decades of this century owed rather more to the achievements of the New Sculptors of the 1880s and 1890s than they cared to admit.

Indeed, the sculptural tradition in England may not have been anything like as fractured and incomplete as the historians of modern sculpture once argued. Susan Beattie has described the way in which Gilbert and his colleagues advanced together upon ground prepared for them by Alfred Stevens – and, we might add, George Watts:

In their passion to express, through the solid, material medium of stone or clay, the intangible, secret forces of human imagination, [the New Sculptors] justified [Stevens's] agonised struggle for self-determination and the cause of art without boundaries.

Alfred Gilbert, tomb of the Duke of Clarence. Although most of the sculpture was in place by 1898, it was not completed until 1927.

Epstein looked long and hard at George Frampton's Lloyd's Registry figures, of 1899–1901, before carving the figures for the British Medical Association building in the Strand, which opened his controversial public career. And it was, of course, this self-same struggle which Henry Moore inherited from Epstein, and pursued for much of our own century.

Revaluations: the nineteenth century in the twentieth

When Roger Fry and his associates dismissed 'the horrors of Victorian picture-making' in such an uncompromising way, they were expressing their supreme confidence in the emerging modernist movement. Fry did not doubt that art was 'one of the essential modes of our spiritual life'; but he believed that the pursuit of 'Significant Form' and pure aesthetic emotion was a better way of giving expression to such values than 'truth to nature', or mythic painting – like Watts's. But, today, modernism itself has disintegrated and is beginning to look like 'a primal Babylonian empire'. As our own century draws towards its close, even the giants of modernity seem destined to become 'a few columns . . . left crumbling in the desert' of incomprehension and philistinism.

In these circumstances, the way in which the art of the Victorian era is seen has inevitably changed. Quentin Bell, son of Clive, recently recalled how the gilded youths of Bloomsbury 'laughed at the Pre-Raphaelites'. To them, it seemed that 'everything of importance in the second half of the 19th century had happened in France' and that England had 'turned away from the mainstream of European art and gone whoring after strange gods'.

Even in the 1920s and 1930s, there were those who looked back on nineteenth-century art in a more sympathetic way – Harold Acton, John Betjeman, and Evelyn Waugh among them. But they were regarded as eccentrics, self-consciously planing against the ineluctable grain of modernity. For the 'mainstream' historians of modern art, a 'good' or an 'interesting' nineteenth-century artist was one who somehow prophesied an aspect of modernism. As Robert Rosenblum puts it in his comprehensive revaluation of the art of the last century, 'an ardent faith in every aspect of the Modern Movement warped the 19th century into an odd position as a precusor of more momentous things to come'. And so Constable, an English painter of natural theology, became for Fry the harbinger of French Impressionism; and William Morris, who was uncompromisingly reactionary in his aesthetic, was contorted by Nikolaus Pevsner into a 'pioneer of modern design'.

Signs of a change in the perception of nineteenth-century art came after the Second World War, when the BBC broadcast an influential series of radio talks on Victorian art and culture; and, in 1948 – Pre-Raphaelitism's centenary year – Robin Ironside and John Gere published the first major study of the movement since before the First World War. Ironside was involved as a painter, critic and curator, in the neo-Romantic revival. He challenged the narrowness of Bloomsbury's francophilia, and their conception of 'Significant Form'. He was among the first to voice the heresy that perhaps, after all, the paintings Burne-Jones produced in the 1880s were of more enduring significance than those of minor members of the New English Art Club.

This first revaluation of the 1940s immediately preceded the decay of modernism; in the 1950s, British art again found itself under the thrall of a foreign aesthetic. 'Advanced', or 'avant-garde' opinion in the arts once again repudiated the 'insularity', 'provincialism' and 'literary' qualities of the Victorian painters. As late as 1965, Quentin Bell discovered how difficult it was to explain his interest in the Pre-Raphaelites to his students and colleagues. Even so, some historians, like T.R. Boase and Graham Reynolds, were showing an unprecedented willingness to take the wider field of Victorian art seriously.

There were also signs of another kind of Victorian revival: rising affluence, and a transatlantic, commercial culture stimulated an interest in the schmaltzier and more perverse aspects of Victorianism. The market in Victorian pictures began to stir. By the late 1960s, Victorian art had become fashionable; extensive collections were formed. Prices soared. But a more serious interest in the Victorians was also underway. The burgeoning resources of the art history industry came to be focused upon the major and minor figures of Victorian painting by writers in America and England and doors and windows were thrown open on the dusty and forgotten world of Victorian sculpture.

The attitude of these new art historians was quite different from that of the Bloomsbury critics. They sought neither to plunder the late nineteenth century as a quarry of prophetic types anticipating the New Testament of Modernism, nor to condemn it according to the doctrines of 'Significant Form' – or more recent aesthetic theory. Rather they attempted imaginatively to view Victorian art in its original historical context; they handed the nineteenth century back to itself.

One motive for all this is to be found in what Robert Rosenblum has called the 'internationalization of the history of 19th century art'. The term is, however, misleading; Rosenblum could, with greater accuracy, have described the process as the 're-nationalisation' of nineteenth-century art; for he is referring to the dawning recognition that perhaps French painting was not, after all, the only painting of the last century worthy of consideration. Few questioned that the French School had been the strongest in the world; but it no longer seemed to make sense to regard all other national traditions only for those respects in which they reflected, or failed to reflect, the radiant sun of France.

All this has led to a much more accurate and sympathetic understanding of the development of Victorian painting and sculpture. As I have tried to demonstrate in this chapter, it is now possible to trace the outlines in the latter part of the century of a 'primitive', or Pre-Raphaelite, phase of Victorian art followed by a once forgotten Victorian High Renaissance; and finally by a period of decadence and disintegration. This century's neglect of, in particular, the Victorian Renaissance may tell us more about our own tastes and priorities than about the achievements and failures of nineteenth-century culture.

And yet I believe that confidence in the insights of the new art history can itself be taken too far. For today's art historians are as much of our time as Fry, and the Bloomsbury critics, were of theirs. And one of the weaknesses of cultural life, in the present, is undoubtedly the widespread refusal of evaluative response, and the shrivelling of aesthetic life in a dead sea of relativism and eclecticism. We need not only to give back the nineteenth century to itself, but to make a fresh *critical* sense of it, for ourselves, in the 'post-modern' era we now inhabit.

Harry Bates, figure of Victory, on the pedestal of the monument to Lord Roberts, Glasgow (begun 1894).

7   The City of Glasgow

ANDOR GOMME

Glasgow's loveliest building is its superlative thirteenth-century Cathedral –
reminder of a long history. Yet Glasgow is quintessentially Victorian – in
growth, resourcefulness, individuality. By 1811 it was the second largest city
in Britain; in 1851 its population was 359,000, in 1901 a million; a fiercely
independent place and in the arts largely self-determining. It has the world's
richest concentration of Victorian architecture, unrivalled in its range of
forms and the virtuosity of its adaptation to ever-changing needs, largely
disregarding contemporary artistic fashions and in particular the
conventionalities of routine Gothic. In addition, Glasgow in the late
nineteenth century took a major part in the movement known as the New
Sculpture, founded a highly original school of interior decorators and was the
heart of the most individual group of painters in Britain.

Like Edinburgh, Glasgow grew by 'new towns' laid out with mathematical
precision over the hilly site. Its street architecture has less magisterial
grandeur than Edinburgh's, but the Georgian domestic formula was forced
more deliberately into early Victorian Mannerism. Terraces from the 1820s
onwards show prominent architraves, cornices and parapets; by 1839 Royal
Crescent had overthrown the formula with windows in pairs and trios and an
attic whose miniature pediments repeatedly fracture the upper cornice. The
master architect of early nineteenth-century Glasgow was David Hamilton
(1768–1843), whose Western Club (1841), brilliantly redeploying Renaissance
elements in an anti-classical resolution of vertical and horizontal accents, is
tense with controlled energy: the break with Georgian calm is complete.

Hamilton's pupil Charles Wilson (1810–63), who on Garnethill in the
1840s made use of bold modelling in pioneering the re-ordering of the terrace
formula for tenement planning, is the type of mid-century Glasgow architect
– locally born and trained, energetic, prolific, reliable: in churches and
country houses an eclectic, in city-centre buildings a self-conscious stylist,
most notably in the hall of the Faculty of Procurators (1854), a lush
miniature of the Venice library – yet able to turn Renaissance features to
Glasgow ends, as in the Royal Bank (1850) where the need for large areas of
window inverts Roman palazzo proportions (expansive stonework, small

openings) imported by Charles Barry. In domestic architecture Wilson was the master-mind in developments which hugely influenced the later growth of Glasgow and himself created its finest piece of romantic townscape. Kirklee Terrace (1845) – a long palace-fronted range, magisterially weighty with raised centre and pavilions, massive balconies and cornices – set a pattern for middle-class suburban housing and for the townscape of terraces along Great Western Road: its immediate successors did not aim for such authority and swagger, but post-Georgian manners had gone beyond recall. (To the south, Dowanhill and Partickhill contrastingly mix villas, terraces and tenements among big trees in public and private gardens.) Then Wilson dramatically transformed Woodlands Hill, an outcrop high above the romantically picturesque Kelvingrove Park which he laid out with Joseph Paxton in 1854. On its eastern slopes crescents had relaxed the rectangularity of early Victorian Glasgow; Wilson crested the hill with Park Circus, in which Wood's Bath Circus layout gains new grandeur by being drawn out into an oval, whose north side is a palace range on an unprecedented scale, with doubly projecting flat centre between wings which sweep forward like those of a colossal Palladian mansion. Detail is bold – heavy cornices, emphatic carving on string-courses and frieze, alternating rustication, cast-iron railings, and plate glass – features reinforced in the convex Park Terrace which follows the outer rim of the hill: canted bays now articulate the façade, crowned by mansard roofs with prominent dormers. But the real crown is the Free Church College (1856), a tour de force fusing elements from Wren in

The Park Area, Glasgow, seen across Kelvingrove Park, with Park Terrace in the foreground, Park Circus and Park Towers (c.1855).

Park Circus (1855). Charles Wilson.

England and von Klenze in Bavaria with three Lombardic campaniles whose height and asymmetrical placing offer constantly changing perspectives around the hill.

Also in the 1850s Glasgow pioneered the iron-framed warehouse with glass walls. Within five years the perfect form for a smallish building had been found, thanks to the use of framed girders with wrought-iron reinforcements: the architect was John Baird (1798–1859) who experimented with exposed cast-iron frames as early as 1827; the building is Gardner's, Jamaica Street (1855), simple, spare and elegant, with the minimum of fuss and obstruction. Later iron-framed warehouses gained size at the expense of refinement and usually have masonry substructures; one stands apart – Alexander Thomson's Buck's Head (1863), where, though the first-floor piers are of (reinforced) masonry, the attic is carried partly by wooden-clad iron stanchions, partly by iron columns outside and free of the glass walls. Lattice girders for the horizontal beams enable a light structure throughout, requiring few uprights.

'Greek' Thomson's (1817–75) shortish career was continuously experimental. His nickname should point less to application of detail than to a permanent conceptual framework to his architecture. He used pilasters and square pillars extensively; but only on two churches is there a recognisable temple front, and though there are pediments on the ends of Moray Place (1857–9), they, like the entablature between, stand on square piers virtually without capitals, to which glazing is applied direct: what the eye registers is a row of square posts carrying a very long beam; even though the Athenian stoa may lie behind it, one has only to compare Moray Place with Playfair's Royal Institution in Edinburgh to see how far Thomson has travelled from his model. In Walmer Crescent, a proto-brutalist design (1857) whose façade

Gardner's Warehouse, Jamaica Street (1855–6). John Baird.

Moray Place (1857–9). Alexander Thomson.

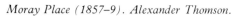

alternates straights and shallow curves, vestigial capitals remain, entirely subservient to a geometrical logic emphasised by recessing the wall-plane part way up the windows so that their frames rise clear of it. Great Western Terrace (1867) has Ionic porches but an uninterrupted flat wall-surface in which windows are just unframed openings – standing away from Thomson's practice of treating masonry not as cladding but as providing or formally expressing its structural members.

Especially in warehouse façades he sought to reduce the solid wall to a minimum: an unexecuted design of 1851 shows as much glass as Gardner's. His assault on the tyranny of the wall reaches a climax in Egyptian Halls (1871–3), where each floor is treated as a glazed colonnade whose entablature acts as the base for the one above; the topmost has continuous glazing set behind free-standing columns. Merchants were cautious about accepting the structural daring of such designs, though Thomson had used the same glazing principles in villas built fifteen years before, whose overall form, built up from interpenetrating small units, anticipates Frank Lloyd Wright by half a century. Here and in churches (Caledonia Road 1856, St Vincent Street 1858), whose interiors are articulated by very slender iron columns – indeed almost everywhere – Thomson's mathematics is lightened by incised chip-carving – Greek frets, acanthus, akroteria.

None of Thomson's contemporaries had the intellectual mastery to reinterpret classical principles in a genuinely personal idiom. James Sellars was both stricter and freer in his use of Greek: Kelvinside Academy (1877) has windows as straightforward as Thomson's, but – echoing earlier schools – the hall is an Ionic temple saddling the centre; a free-standing colonnade ran across the City of Glasgow Bank (1878), though the rest was Italianate. A mightier colonnade, with caryatid-supported attic pavilions dominates the immensely powerful façade of St Andrew's Halls (1873), whose neo-Greek severity is otherwise closely indebted to Thomson. But Sellars's classicism always had room for Renaissance variation, and he later leaned towards the free Glasgow style of the nineties.

The disastrous collapse of the City of Glasgow Bank in 1878 made a cultural watershed. Glasgow's recovery was symbolised in civic and architectural terms by William Young's flamboyant City Chambers (1883–6), whose baroque opulence, anticipating the heroic Edwardian years, set a mark for the ambitious and a style into which Glasgow's surviving classicism was immediately channelled. The presiding genius of the transformation of central Glasgow in the late nineteenth century was John James Burnet (1857–1938) (whose highly talented father had moved from strict classicism into free Italianate – see his brilliant rethinking of Grand Canal façades at Lanarkshire House, 1876). Burnet trained at the École des Beaux-Arts, and his return signalled a Paris-inspired Renaissance: the 'classicism' of the Fine Arts Institute (1879) was strongly French, particularly in its use of figurative sculpture. The smaller Athenaeum (1886) is an exceptionally elegant essay in quiet Mannerism, whose unobtrusively ambiguous accents challenge impeccable Renaissance detail. For larger buildings the canted multi-storey oriel was an indicator of wealth, which Burnet at first found difficult to discipline: see the relentlessly muscular Charing Cross Mansions (1891),

(Above and opposite). *The development of Alexander Thomson's warehouse style in Glasgow (1849–73). Drawings by David Walker.*

whose fantastic roofline owes more to Park Terrace than to direct suggestion from France.

Leases of small house-plots fell in frequently but irregularly. Sites were redeveloped singly, and commercial pressures led to high narrow elevations. The Athenaeum Theatre (1891), designed with J.A. Campbell, is one of the most remarkable – an elevation split into two overlapping sections, one insistently vertical with window and masonry strips, one spreading under an arch into a generous oriel; sources of detail are legion, but the verticals pull all together. Higher and bigger buildings, steel-framed but with load-bearing masonry façades, followed Burnet's first visit to America – Atlantic Chambers (1899), in which sculpture draws the eye up into three-storey oriels balanced about a vertical strip soaring through the eaves-gallery into a richly moulded chimney breast – a superb marriage of utility and elegance. The smaller-scale Glasgow Savings Bank (1896) is fastidiously sculpturesque, enriched indeed with sculpture by George Frampton – the baroque elaboration of banded walls reminding one of C.R. Cockerell.

The 'free style' gave central Glasgow a richly undulating streetscape of three-dimensional surfaces: the eye is constantly caught by recessions and projections of oriels, parapets, cornices, reveals, drawn up by verticals, arrested by features which articulate the huge façades and give them scale. Amassing detail can lead to incoherence; but surprisingly many of these buildings have the panache to carry it off. A few are wonders, like Campbell's

Athenaeum Theatre, Buchanan Street
(1891). J.J. Burnet.

The Hatrack (left), *St Vincent Street*
(1899). James Salmon, junior.

romantic fortress in Hope Street (1902), amazingly sturdy and self-confident, yet nostalgically evocative of an understated Scottish and European past. None are more dazzling than James Salmon's (1874–1924) – the marvellously daring 'Hatrack' (1899), ten convoluted storeys, nearly all glass but full of pert detail on the edge of *art nouveau*, worked out in collaboration with the sculptor Derwent Wood; Lion Chambers (1905), structurally even more resourceful – using a reinforced concrete frame which allowed the rippling glass north front and very thin walls without which, on the narrow site, rooms would have been too small for use.

157–167 Hope Street (1902). J.A. Campbell.

All these architects were native; and except for Burnet, who moved to London on his appointment as architect of the Edward VII Gallery of the British Museum, all confined themselves to the City and its environs. English contemporaries hardly got a toehold; though the vast length of Gilbert Scott's baronial-cum-French-Gothic University (1866–70) dominates the west end, Victorian Glasgow looked after itself. But one architect gained an international reputation, though hardly a national one: Charles Rennie Mackintosh (1868–1928), architect of a mere half-dozen buildings, but a master of modernism. Yet again – despite affinities with Charles Holden – he was one of the world's isolated geniuses and profoundly Scottish.

Mackintosh won the competition for the Glasgow School of Art in 1896; initially only half could be built, but this settled the design of the long, seemingly random south elevation, towering above the hill like a vast medieval castle; of the east end which, for all its vertical accenting, is in line with contemporary London work by Harrison Townsend and Smith and Brewer; above all, of the north front, whose wall of studio windows clasps, just off-centre, the idiosyncratic entrance bay of bulky ashlar and small windows – both heroic and intimate. The façade, dominated by the windows – a straightforward response to the demand for maximum north light – has a distinctive personality marked by sculptural shapes about the door, the balancing of sheer masonry and sheer glass, the uncanny transparent volumes created by window brackets. The western section was entirely redesigned in 1907. On the west front three oriels rise sixty-five feet, incorporating delicately immense library windows, reinterpreting a familiar Glasgow form in a new relationship of projections to wall; again a stark contrast, between a huge sheet of ashlar and myriads of tiny panes, is set off by the boldly modelled doorcase.

Mackintosh's other surviving buildings include two schools, two newspaper offices, Queen's Cross Church, and one of Miss Cranston's tea-rooms – a reminder that he was a through-and-through designer responsible for interior decoration, textiles, furniture, light fittings, even cutlery – an aspect of his work intimately linked with the approach to design now known as the Glasgow style.

A Mackintosh room is as much interior architecture as the inside of a Thomson church. Not only the fixed elements – slatted openwork screens, revolutionary chimneypieces linked to shelves or settles, focuses for the room's style – but chairs and tables too are conceived as sculpture, the whole room, or sequence of spaces, a single complex experience. Not always a practical ideal; but Miss Cranston, an unconscious catalyst of the Glasgow style by employing Mackintosh and George Walton simultaneously, persevered; Walton's Gimson-like furniture stood oddly below a huge frieze in which Beardsleyesque line is flooded with flat washes of colour inspired by David Gauld. On his own Mackintosh reverted to a purely architectural approach with strong tonal contrasts and a rectangularity set off by wiry decoration on screens, doors, lamp-fittings and furniture designed as much for its symbolic value as its utility.

The Art School – whose library is the best-preserved of these intricate experiments in relating interconnecting spaces with fixed and movable

The north front of the Glasgow Art School (east portion 1897; west 1907). Charles Rennie Mackintosh.

furniture – was the nursery of the Glasgow style. The director, Fra Newbery, brought together Mackintosh, Herbert McNair and the Macdonald sisters, whose work showed how easily linear drawing and flowing brushwork translated into chasing and repoussé in metal; with associates working in textiles, book-design and jewellery, 'the Four' created a style with *art nouveau* affinities kept in check by Mackintosh's architectural hand. The Glasgow style in fact bypassed *art nouveau* and did much to create that of the Vienna Sezession. In the City itself the work of the Art School group was paralleled by the house-furnishers Wylie and Lochhead, whose designers made the firm as enlightened as any in Europe and in turn infiltrated Liberty's and Henry's in London, where Walton had preceded them. For a decade Glasgow led the world in the ideal integration of architecture and interior decoration.

Glasgow had long had a creditable tradition in public statuary. Victorian monuments started with Handyside Ritchie's stolid *Scott* (1838) high above George Square, and three interchangeable equestrian bronzes from the swanky but coarse-grained Marochetti (*Wellington* 1844, *Victoria* and *Albert* 1849), copies really of Chantrey's *George IV*. John Mossman, the first native Glasgow sculptor of standing, began a long series with his *Peel* (1859) – in the manner of Foley, decently observed, adequately modelled, but, like so much Victorian portraiture, complacently predictable in stance, dress, gesture and expression.

Mossman is more interesting for his architectural sculpture – in which Glasgow has much to offer, though it began merely with classically draped friezes and pediments filled with figures hierarchically balanced about some presiding allegory. As late as 1886 Birnie Rhind paraphrased Westmacott's British Museum pediment for St George's-in-the-East (it took a wayward genius like M.L. Watson to realise – at the Victoria Rooms, Bristol – that pedimentrary sculpture need not be symmetrical). Mossman's theme of the progress of civilisation, in the frieze on Wilson's Queen's Rooms (1858), is only notionally classical, yet the low-relief figures remain imitations of the Elgin marbles rather than of life. And though in 1857 Ritchie and David Rhind showed on the Commercial Bank how sculpture could be individual and witty but fully incorporated into a façade, allegorical brackets and finials were the rule till, in 1877 at St Andrew's Halls, Sellars got Mossman and his brother to make sculpture literally architectural with massive entablatures supported by atlantes and caryatids. Soon the Burnets, still with Mossman, created fully integrated Beaux-Arts façades – Lanarkshire House, the Fine Arts Institute, where a high-relief frieze *behind* the upper zone of the columns seemed to be the inevitably right climax of the wall, and the Athenaeum, where independent groups and figures so precisely confirm elements defining the Mannerist balance that the façade would be indeterminate without them.

Mossman's glowering *Livingstone* (1877, George Square) rejected the patriotic clichés of Victorian portraiture (the African reliefs on the pedestal are especially characterful); but only in 1894, with Onslow Ford's *William Pearce* at Govan Cross, did New Sculpture reach Glasgow. Also in 1894 Harry Bates started on *Lord Roberts* (Park Terrace), which Watts called 'without exception the finest equestrian statue of modern times' – in its astonishingly vigorous modelling and bold interpretation of the subject rivalling the great Rysbrack of *William III* at Bristol. But Bates's horse and rider are the climax of a complex of architectural sculpture; the vast columned pedestal has a frieze whose cascade of horses is only classical in the fidelity of its portraiture and the power of its brilliant and expressive modelling; and at the ends are figures, of which the Victory achieves a concentration of expressive energy out of the quietest movement, which even

St Andrew's Halls (1873). James Sellars. Since the fire of 1962 the side elevations have been reduced.

Gilbert did not better. Glasgow also owns the only known set of Bates's *Aeneid* reliefs. In 1899 the City anticipated London in commissioning Hamo Thornycroft for its Gladstone memorial. This lacks the ideal groups which support the Strand statue, but the main figure is even more impressively gaunt, in iron-like rectorial robes, the face harrowed by a lifetime of care which has not brought peace; in the pedestal reliefs the very bronze seems alive with nervous energy, creating through the subtlest gradations of modelling astonishing depths within an almost flat surface.

The triumph of the New Sculpture in Glasgow came in 1897, when Frampton undertook the overall scheme for the Art Gallery. His own principal contribution – the colossal group of St Mungo as patron of the arts – set a major challenge to Frampton's hitherto restricted physical range, and the miniature delicacy of the robes has the fineness of his highly personal ideal busts; but so expertly is the group poised and so hauntingly beautiful and insightful are the figures that one is never conscious of overweening size. For the secondary work Frampton selected Derwent Wood, whose tenderly graceful parapet figures hardly prepare one for his violent Expressionism a year or two later on the British Linen Bank in Govan.

Though Horatio McCulloch, who fathered the tradition of Victorian landscape painting in Scotland, was a Glaswegian, one would hardly divine it from his subjects; it was the less well-known John Knox, who died in 1845, whose firm drawing first explored the brilliantly lit Glasgow·streets; his landscapes are noteworthy for a strong sense of geological structure. Knox's pupil, Daniel Macnee was a capable portraitist (once described as Raeburn's understudy). It was in the late 1870s that Glasgow moved to the forefront of British painting, when, some years ahead of Sickert's revolt against the English academy, a group of young men, resentful of establishment rejection, formed a loose association linked by admiration for recent French work, especially the common-life Naturalism of Bastien-Lepage. James Guthrie (1859–1930), Joseph Crawhall, John Lavery and E.A. Walton all fell under his influence and quickly passed beyond, maintaining however his realism, his *plein-air* habit, and the square-brush technique, which in the hands of Guthrie and Crawhall, and later and more emphatically of E.A. Hornel (1864–1933), dislocated the gradation of tones and detail used by Bastien-Lepage to give depth of perspective, and turned the dissolving landscape into psychological space shaping the inner world of the human subject or the artist's relation to it. In Hornel's *Resting* for example (1885), the hinted-at forest background is not a setting in the conventional sense, but a way of spotlighting the self-absorbed girl's isolation. Walton's *Gamekeeper's Daughter* (1886) is superficially more conventional, but the roughed-in blouse and unspecific background allow delicate delineation and tonal moulding of face and hair to reveal how abstracted from any physical environment is the girl's self-concentration. Detachment of subject from observer distinguishes Guthrie's *Hind's Daughter* (1883), where the chunky square-brush surface vividly characterises a whole rural way of life: the technique itself defines the picture's realism – far more tellingly than quasi-photographic accuracy of surface detail.

Impressionism had little direct impact on the 'Glasgow Boys', except perhaps on Lavery, whose landscapes sometimes rely on varied intensities of light to determine distance. Walton's by contrast, started rather by picking up the freehand English tradition of Constable and de Wint. Later, his *Berwickshire Fieldworker* (1884), which has formally a Lepage-like layout, moves the main figure emphatically *into* the landscape to which she belongs – a burnt russet landscape anticipating the glowing colours and dissolution of perspective soon found in Hornel and George Henry, where common elements such as trees and streams assume a demonic distortion which looks forward to the Expressionism of Soutine. Or, as in Hornel's *Summer* (1891) (colour plate 11), the landscape disintegrates into patterns of colour and light, features within it overlapping and interpenetrating one another.

By the mid-1890s the fire was out, and only Crawhall and Arthur Melville (almost unique in understanding Turner's sponge-and-wet-paper technique) kept to an individual path with the vibrant innovative watercolours which had been their special strength. The rest were gradually neutralised by being absorbed. Nothing resembling the Glasgow Boys had happened in British painting before; yet once again their influence was felt more on the continent than in Britain, and they are little-known outside Scotland, where most of their pictures have remained. Curiously the Boys hardly touched Glasgow itself; so the last word must go to John Quinton Pringle, a man not given to crowds or associations, who developed on his own a quasi-pointilliste technique using very small brush-strokes with repeated overworking in dilute paint to produce the most evocative images ever made of the City and its inhabitants.

Sportsman's knife, containing 80 blades and other instruments, with gold inlaying, etching and engraving, including views of the Exhibition Building and Windsor Castle. Made for the Great Exhibition (1851).

8 Design, Craft and Industry

GILLIAN NAYLOR

The spirit of improvement and the use of the machine

I conceive it to be the duty of every educated person closely to study and watch the time in which he lives; and as far as in him lies, to add his mite of individual exertion to further the accomplishment of what he believes Providence to have ordained. Nobody, however, who has paid any attention to the particular features of our particular era, will doubt for a moment that we are living at a period of most wonderful transition which tends rapidly to the accomplishment of that great end to which, indeed all history points – the realisation of the unity of mankind . . . the great principle of the division of labour which may be called the moving power of civilisation, is being extended to all branches of science, industry and art . . . the products of all the quarters of the globe are placed at our disposal, and we have only to choose what is the best and cheapest for our purposes, and the powers of production are intrusted to the stimulus of competition and capital. So man is approaching a more complete fulfilment of that great and sacred mission which he has to perfect in this world . . . Science discovers these laws of power, motion and transformation; industry applies them to raw matter which the earth yields us in abundance; but which becomes valuable only by knowledge; art teaches us the immutable laws of beauty and symmetry, and gives to our productions forms in accordance with them. Gentlemen, the Exhibition of 1851 is to give us a true test and a living picture of the point of development at which the whole of mankind have arrived in this great task, and a new starting point from which all nations will be able to direct their further exertions.

(Prince Albert's address to the Lord Mayor's Banquet, *Illustrated London News*, 11 October 1849)

This extract from Prince Albert's speech introducing his expectations for the Great Exhibition is worth quoting at length, for its optimism and idealism, as well as for its assumptions. At a time when many of Europe's capitals were shaken by social and political unrest, Prince Albert was confident that an age of universal peace and harmony was at hand – a world united by trade and commerce, and redeemed by work. To many of his contemporaries, and, of course, to the Arts and Crafts generation of the 1880s and 1890s, such optimism seemed ill-founded, unjustified, even immoral. Mechanisation and industrialisation were seen as vile and uncontrollable forces, destroying human as well as natural resources. Commerce, far from creating the universalising and progressive commodity culture that Prince Albert envisaged, trivialised both producer and product, substituting quantity for quality, international markets swallowing up and spewing out cheap and trashy merchandise, so debasing the concept of value. And the 'great principle of the division of labour', or so it seemed, lay at the root of all this degradation, destroying traditional skills and the humanism associated with those skills, threatening the very basis of English culture and civilisation.

The power and persuasion of these arguments have tended to obscure or denigrate the pro-industrial enthusiasms which Prince Albert was, of course, not alone in promoting, and which were based on at least a century of economic and social change, and speculation about the nature and implications of such change. In the eighteenth century there were many commentators, realists as well as idealists, who saw industrialisation, or proto-industrialisation, as a progressive, beneficial and creative force:

> These are the glories of the mine!
> Creative commerce, these are thine!

This, for example, is the burden of the Revd John Dalton's *Descriptive Poem*, addressed to *Two Ladies, at their Return from Viewing the Mines near Whitehaven* in 1755. Two years later John Dyer, dedicating his poem 'The Fleece' to transformations in the woollen industries, provided this detailed description of a multiple spinning machine and its operative:

Decorative scissors shown at the Great Exhibition (1851).

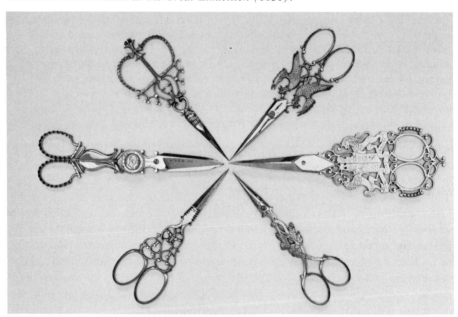

A circular machine, of new design,
In conic shape: it draws and spins a thread
Without the tedious toil of needless hands.
A wheel, invisible beneath the floor,
To ev'ry member of th'harmonious frame
Gives necessary motion. One, intent,
O'erlooks the work: the carded wool, he says,
Is smoothly lapp'd around those cylinders,
Which, gently turning, yield to yon cirque
Of upright spindles, which, with rapid whirl
Spin out, in long extent, an even twine.
    (Quoted from F.D. Klingender, *Art and the Industrial Revolution*, 1968, p. 24)

Arthur Young, in his account of *A Six Months Tour through the North of England* (published in 1770), sums up this idealism and optimism:

When agriculture, manufactures and commerce flourish, a nation grows rich and great, and riches cannot abound without exciting that general industry, and spirit of improvement, which at last leads to performing works, which, in poorer times, would be thought wonders.

Such comments came from what might be described as dilettante observers – philosopher–poets and men of letters. Their optimism, nevertheless, was shared by more objective and 'scientific' analysts of the 'machinery question', the political economists, a new breed of men whose interpretations of the implications of machine-based production were to be so forcefully rejected by the Arts and Crafts generation. Adam Smith's *The Wealth of Nations* (1776), for example, celebrated the division of labour as one of the prime movers of industrial, and therefore economic growth, and his analyses of the implications of factory-based production identified issues that were to become causes a century later:

The greatest improvement in the productive powers of labour, and the greater part of the skill, dexterity, and judgement with which it is anywhere directed, or applied, seem to have been the effects of the division of labour.

Adam Smith's treatise challenged traditional concepts of craftsmanship or making – concepts which are revived (and transformed) in the nineteenth century and which survived well into the twentieth century. 'Skill, dexterity and judgement' – qualities once associated with the age old (and seemingly instinctive) conjunction of head and hand – were now related to the *processes* rather than the products of labour. Even that 'very trifling manufacture' – pin-making – had been transformed by the division of labour. Whereas in the past one skilled workman 'could scarce, perhaps with his utmost industry, make one pin a day', now, with the division of labour speeding up the various processes involved, ten men (even if 'indifferently accommodated with the necessary machinery') could produce 48,000 pins a day:

It is the great multiplication of the productions of all the arts, in consequence of the division of labour, which occasions, in a well-governed society, that universal opulence which extends itself to the lowest ranks of the people.

Adam Smith, the pioneer of political economy, was commenting on the early stages of industrialisation. Within the next fifty years, however, the ideal and the reality of the factory system was to be analysed by a new generation of commentators who had practical experience of commerce and manufacturing processes. Among the most significant of these, at least as far as this survey is concerned, were the mathematician Charles Babbage (whose contributions to the philosophy of manufacture have been largely ignored in surveys of design) and, unfortunately, Andrew Ure.

Charles Babbage (1791–1871), who described political economists as 'closet philosophers . . . too little acquainted with the admirable arrangements of the factory', had visited factories in France, Germany, Austria and Italy, as well as Britain in the 1820s and 1830s. He was aiming to assess potential markets and uses for his 'calculating engines' – forerunners of today's computers – and at the same time he analysed what he described as 'the domestic economy of the factory' with the objectivity, logic and precision of a systems analyst. His *On the Economy of Machinery and Manufactures* (1832, revised and reprinted many times) is a remarkable book, which introduces, as well as descriptions of the organisation and potential of the factory system, concepts of time and motion studies, the grading of skills, profit-sharing and collective decision-making. The book is a panegyric to 'the science of calculation . . . which must ultimately govern the whole of the application of science to the arts of life', and at the same time it is a plea for a scientific, and therefore rational approach to the theory as well as the practicalities of factory production.

The efforts for the improvement of its manufactures which any country can make with the greatest probability of success, must arise from the combined exertions of all those skilled in the theory, as well as in the practice of the arts; each labouring in that department for which his natural capacity and acquired habits have rendered him fit.

(1836 edn, p. 379)

One of the several aims of the book is to trace 'both the causes and consequences of applying machinery to supersede the skill and the power of the human arm . . .' As well as the obvious economic benefits of machine production, Babbage also stressed the perfection of machine-made products, which, according to Babbage, lay in the precision and uniformity of machine manufacture:

Nothing is more remarkable, and yet less unexpected than the perfect identity of things manufactured by the same tool . . . The first object of every person who attempts to make an object of consumption is, or ought to be, to produce it in a perfect form.

Babbage, however, wrote *On the Economy* to convert, as well as to inform. Two years earlier he had published his *Reflections on the Decline of Science and some of its Causes* (1830). The greater part of the book is an attack on the complacency and inefficiency of the Royal Society; at the same time Babbage saw in the decline of this once progressive institution a symptom of what we now call 'the British disease' or the 'anti-industrial spirit'. He deplored the fact that a 'country, eminently distinguished for its mechanical and manufacturing ingenuity' seemed incapable of sustaining or advancing the research and enterprise on which its new found prosperity was based.

Babbage also deplored the 'neglect of science' and the concentration on classics in Oxford and Cambridge and suggested a reform of the curriculum that might have had a remarkable impact on the state and status of 'design' in Britain, for he recommended not only a degree in Political Economy, but suggested that it might be combined with the study of the 'Application of Science to Arts and Manufacture'. The Government School of Design was established four years later, but it was to be more than a century before its activities were elevated to university status: Babbage a prophet of the practical and philosophical rationalism that we now associate with modernism in design and architecture, had few supporters in his own time, and very few indeed among the anti-industrial proselytisers of the next generation.

Andrew Ure (1778–1857) a self-proclaimed 'philosopher of manufacture', believed that the factory system was a benign and beneficial force, relieving countless workers from the relentless toil of hand-labour, enabling them to work in airy and commodious premises, and keeping their children both happy and gainfully employed in the many little tasks that were within their capabilities. Ure, in his now notorious book *The Philosophy of Manufactures*, first published in 1835, offered to provide 'a systematic account of . . . the principles and processes of manufacture' and to 'diffuse a steady light to conduct the masters, managers, and operatives in the straight paths of improvement'.

'Improvement', in Ure's terms, however, could only be achieved through a complete and disciplined identification with the system, men and machines acting in total harmony:

I conceive that this title [the factory system], in its strictest sense, involves the idea of a vast automaton, composed of various mechanical and intellectual organs, acting in uninterrupted concert for the production of a common object, all of them being subjected to a common moving force.

(1861 edn, p. 13)

Ure's ideal, which involved 'the marshalling of human beings in systematic order for the execution of any technical enterprise', anticipated the nightmare factory of Fritz Lang's *Metropolis*, filmed a century later. His vision of the automated factory reduced human beings to automata – any form of individualism on the part of the 'operatives' being identified with waywardness and insubordination. The consequences of the division of labour – 'so fruitful', according to Ure 'of jealousies and strikes among the workmen' – were also overcome by the new system, since machine minders needed no special skills.

By the uniformity of human nature it happens that the more skilfull the workman, the more self-willed and intractable he is apt to become, and, of course, the less fit a component of a mechanical system, in which, by occasional irregularities, he may do great damage to the whole. The grand object, therefore, of the modern manufacture is, through the union of capital and science, to reduce the task of his work people to the exercise of vigilance and dexterity – faculties, when concentrated to one process, speedily brought to perfection in the young.

(pp. 20–1)

Ure's panegyric of the factory system provides one of the most devastating demonstrations of the dehumanising implications of the 'union of science and capital'. He placed the control of production firmly in the hands of the manufacturer, and saw the machine ('the *Iron Man* or modern Prometheus' as he called it) as a 'creation destined to restore order among the industrious classes'.

Evocations of the past

Reactions to these 'models' of the potential of the factory system and the role of machinery were, of course, complex. Remnants of the positivism that inspired Babbage survive in Prince Albert's confidence in the inevitability of progress. 'Progress', however, also implied change, and to many, Prince Albert's vision of a world transformed by the 'power of production' and the 'stimulus of competition and capital' was a threat rather than a promise. For industrialisation, however enlightened, implied more than social and economic revolution; it involved a rejection of the past, and of seemingly age-old traditions that many thinkers, both conservative and radical, were not prepared to accept.

> And all the Arts of Life they changed into the Arts of Death in Albion:
> The hour-glass contemn'd because its simple workmanship
> Was like the workmanship of the plow-man, and the water-wheel
> That raises water into cisterns, broken and burned with fire
> Because its workmanship was like the workmanship of the shepherd;
> And in their stead, intricate wheels invented, wheel without wheel,
> To perplex youth in their outgoings and to bind to labours in Albion . . .
> Kept ignorant of its use: that they may spend the days of wisdom
> In sorrowful drudgery to obtain a scanty pittance and bread,
> In ignorance to view a small portion and think that All
> And call it Demonstration, blind to all the simple rules of life.
>
> (William Blake, *Jerusalem*, c.1814–18)

Thus as early as 1818, William Blake, the mystic radical, was lamenting the loss of an ancient and time-honoured order. For him mechanisation, and all that it implied, on both practical and philosophic levels, was an instrument of negation, pitting the life-denying powers of reason against the creative powers of the imagination.

This rejection of reason and science was consolidated in the 1820s and 1830s, when attacks on the mechanistic dimensions of industrial society were coupled with appeals to tradition, and to the virtues and morality of a pre-industrial and largely mythic past.

Here, for example, is Thomas Carlyle bemoaning the fact that he is living in a Mechanical Age when 'Philosophy, Science, Art, Literature, all depend on machinery':

Our old modes of exertion are all discredited and thrown aside. On every hand, the living artisan is driven from his workshop, to make room for a speedier, inanimate one. The shuttle drops from the fingers of the weaver, and fall into iron fingers that ply it faster . . . Men are grown mechanical in head and heart, as well as in hand. They have lost faith in individual endeavour, and in natural force of any kind.

(*Signs of the Times*, 1829, quoted from *The Victorian Prophets*, ed. Peter Keating, 1981, pp. 47 and 50)

And here is John Ruskin just over twenty years later in *On the Nature of Gothic* (1853):

We have much studied and much perfected, of late, the great civilised invention of the division of labour; only we give it a false name. It is not, truly speaking, the labour that is divided; but the men: – divided into mere segments of men – broken into small fragments and crumbs of life; so that all the little piece of intelligence that is left in a man is not enough to make a pin, or a nail, but exhausts itself in making the point of a pin, or the head of a nail . . . And the great cry that rises from all our manufacturing cities, louder than their furnace blast, is all in very deed for this, – that we manufacture everything there except men; we blanch cotton, and strengthen steel and refine sugar, and shape pottery; but to brighten, to strengthen, to refine, or to form a single living spirit never enters into our estimate of advantages.

Blake, Carlyle and Ruskin belong to that 'Great Tradition' of British dissenters and interventionists who rejected both the ideals and the reality of industrialisation. Their tone is evangelical, and they assume the mantle of sage and prophet in their castigations of the time in which they lived. Fundamental to their theory (and their morality) is a questioning of the nature of progress and the meaning of value which totally undermines the assumptions of political economy (Ruskin's references to pin-making deliberately evoking the founder of the discipline). 'Value' and 'progress' are related to individual rather than collective achievements, so there is no question of a factory aesthetic, as formulated by Babbage. Nor could the factory ever be the focus of a just society – philosophies as well as practicalities of manufacture leading to Ure's anti-humanism. An ideal society, therefore, could only be achieved within the context of tradition:

In our wildest periods of reform . . . you notice always the invincible instinct to hold fast to the Old; to admit the *minimum* of the New; to expand, if it be possible, some old habit or method, already found fruitful, into new growth for the new need . . . The Future hereby is not dissevered from the Past, but based continuously on it; grows with all the vitalities of the Past, and is rooted deep down in the beginnings of us.

(Thomas Carlyle, *Past and Present*, 1843, OUP edn, p. 275)

Here, then, we have an ideal of 'Englishness' which is rooted in an idealisation of tradition and a rejection of change – an ideal that was shared by both Tory and radical lobbies. It is this half-legendary past, with its feudal relationships, that Thomas Carlyle celebrated in his seminal *Past and Present*, and it is a vision and ideal that preoccupied designers and architects as well as writers and social reformers throughout the nineteenth century.

In the late-eighteenth and early-nineteenth centuries, evocations of the past had produced an eclectic and romantic architecture that aspired to the pastoral, as in John Nash's Blaize Hamlets; to the romanticised Gothick, as in Horace Walpole's Strawberry Hill or William Beckford's Fonthill Abbey; or to pastiche Oriental as in Nash's Brighton Pavilion.

Pugin and 'True Principles'

The first architect–designer to reject this nostalgic romanticising of the past and to attempt to reclaim its authenticity was Augustus Welby Northmore

Pugin (1812–52). Pugin was trained as a draughtsman and designer by his architect father (who had left France for England in the 1790s). When he was fifteen, Pugin the younger designed furniture for Windsor Castle, as well as a range of silverware for a leading manufacturer. His career and his subsequent status as an architect, designer and polemicist were established in 1835, however, when he was converted to Roman Catholicism, published his first book *Gothic Furniture in the Style of the 15th Century*, and worked with the architect Charles Barry on the winning design for the Houses of Parliament competition. From then until his death he was designing churches and colleges in England, Scotland and Ireland; he designed furniture and furnishings for the Houses of Parliament; he produced tiles for Minton, metalwork for John Hardman & Co., and established his own enterprise for the design of stained glass, silverware, furniture, and other goods, in Ramsgate, where he built himself a house and the adjacent church (St Augustine's). His last major project was the design of the Medieval Court at the Great Exhibition, which was also furnished with his own designs.

So prolific and extensive an output would have ensured Pugin an honourable place in the history of design and architecture, especially since his genius was acknowledged by his contemporaries, as well as by his successors in the Arts and Crafts generation. Charles Eastlake, for example, one of the first historians of the Gothic Revival, wrote in 1872 that 'There can be no doubt that the revival of Medieval design received its chief impulse in our own day from the energy and talents of A.W.N. Pugin.' Pugin's personal assessment of his achievement, however, was that it was his 'writings, much more than anything I have been able to do, [that] have revolutionised the taste of England'.

Pugin's 'writings' consist of several books on design – his *Gothic Furniture*, for example, and *Design for Gold and Silversmiths* (1836) – which are of specialist interest to historians of the Gothic Revival. Here his concern is with information rather than confrontation. Pugin's preoccupation with the past led him, like so many of his contemporaries and successors, to reject the present. His analyses of what he describes as 'the present decay of taste' were based on the assumption that 'style' reflects the values of the society that creates it; and his invective was not directed at mechanisation or at the implications of Political Economy, but at what he felt were the 'evidences of a lamentable departure from true Catholic principles and feelings'. Pugin's conversion to Roman Catholicism led him to reject all architecture and design that had been produced in England since the Reformation and to denounce the Classical architecture of Greece and Rome. Pugin examined these ideas in several seminal books, of which *Contrasts* (1836) is the most well known – not, in fact, for its text (for the most part a diatribe against the Reformation and subsequent Protestant iconoclasms), but for its illustrations. His 'contrasts' between a town of the fifteenth century and its nineteenth-century equivalent, and his depiction of medieval versus modern attitudes towards the poor, established him as a social critic of architecture and design – a worthy precursor of Ruskin and Morris. Pugin's fervour was religious rather than revolutionary, however, and his theory, when detached from his Catholicism, is mainstream rather than critical:

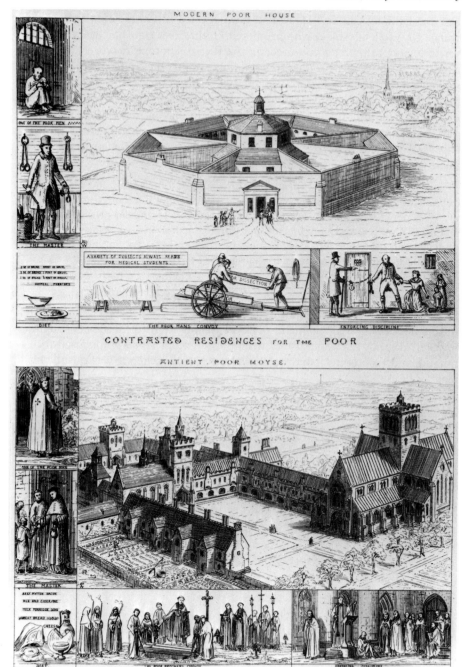

'*Contrasted residences for the poor*', *from* Contrasts *by Augustus Pugin (revised edition, 1841).*

The two great rules for design are these: 1st, that there should be no features about a building which are not necessary for convenience, construction or propriety; 2nd, that all ornament should consist of the essential construction of the building.

(*The True Principles of Pointed or Christian Architecture*, 1841, p. 1)

These essentially classical ideals had been applied to Gothic architecture in France by Viollet-le-Duc, who promoted Gothic as a *rational* rather than romantic style. Pugin's importance in the British context, however, lies in his extension of these ideas to design as well as architecture, and his promotion of what might be described as a functionalist aesthetic. In *True Principles* (1841), for example, he castigates 'the inconsistencies of modern grates, which are not infrequently made to represent diminutive fronts of castellated or ecclesiastical buildings with turrets, loopholes, windows and doorways, all in a space of forty inches'. Household furniture also suffers from these inconsistencies:

... all the ordinary articles of furniture, which require to be simple and convenient, are made not only very expensive but very uneasy. We find diminutive flying buttresses about an armchair; everything is crocketted with angular projections, innumerable mitres, sharp ornaments, and turretted extremities. A man who remains for any length of time in a modern Gothic room, and escapes without being wounded by some of its minutiae, may consider himself very fortunate.

(*True Principles*, p. 40)

Pugin's written invective, therefore, can be as potent as his illustrations, and his practice – his determination to achieve what he believed was 'authenticity' in design – anticipated the ideals of several generations of designers. Pugin, however, did not reject the use of machinery (except when it was used to imitate hand techniques), and he also saw occasions when it was positively beneficial:

... in matters purely mechanical, the Christian architect should gladly avail himself of those improvements and increased facilities that are suggested from time to time. The steam engine is a most valuable power for sawing, raising and cleansing stone, timber and other materials . . . We do not want to arrest the course of inventions, but to confine these inventions to their legitimate uses.

(*An Apology for the Present Revival of Christian Architecture in England*, 1843)

In 1851, in spite of the fact that he was desperately ill, Pugin undertook the design of Medieval Court at the Great Exhibition. One observer described this as 'looking dark and solemn for the display of the taste and art of dead men'. The Great Exhibition, however, was primarily concerned with the taste and art of the living, and as such its messages were contradictory and confusing.

The Great Exhibition and the Schools of Design

The conception and construction of the 'Crystal Palace', as the building in Hyde Park came to be called, was undeniably a triumph of organisation as well as of invention. To Matthew Wyatt, writing the *Official Descriptive and Illustrated Catalogue*, 'such a result could alone have been effected by the natives of a country in which a knowledge of the principles and practice of mechanics and machinery had been long and deeply studied and widely diffused.'

As far as the construction and organisation of this great project was concerned, therefore, the fears of Babbage seemed unfounded: the spirit of science and manufacture had triumphed. The exhibits, on the other hand, told a different story. Demonstrations of 'the wealth of nations' were there for all to see, the industrialised nations displaying machinery, as well as the products of machines, while the work of more ancient cultures was also on show.

This was the first international exhibition ever to be held, and its primary aim, of course, was to stimulate trade. At the same time it had a didactic purpose, for as well as giving artisans an opportunity to see the fruits of their labours, it was also intended to stimulate the *art* of manufacture, and an understanding of taste and style. The problem of 'taste' in manufacture had preoccupied the British as various industries became mechanised, and the problem had become more urgent when trade rallied after the Napoleonic wars. The French, the Belgians and the Germans, or so it seemed to British

Construction of the Crystal Palace around an elm tree in the south-west portion of the building.

observers, were more efficient in the 'arts' of design, and their textiles, ceramics and metalwork demonstrated qualities that seemed to elude the British. In 1835, therefore, a Select Committee was set up (the first of many) in order 'to inquire into the best means of extending a knowledge of the arts and principles of design among the people (especially the manufacturing population) of the country'. As a result of this investigation, a School of Design was established in London in 1837 in order to promote 'the direct practical application of the Arts to Manufacture'; and so began the long (and frequently futile) quest to establish a credible and practical methodology for design training – the problem, at its most basic, focusing on how to train who to do what.

In its early years the School of Design was essentially a teacher training school for young boys, who attended (at first in distressing small numbers) from the age of twelve. They came to learn how to draw – in this case an informational rather than inspirational activity – drawing and draughts-manship being a universal language of communication. When they qualified, the students were intended to teach the same techniques in elementary schools in order to produce a potentially employable workforce, with the more proficient providing further generations of pupils for the network of Schools of Design that were to be established in the manufacturing towns and cities.

Design, then, as far as the Schools were concerned, was a science, not an art; creativity, artistry and the skills associated with handcraft were not involved. In the years leading up to the Great Exhibition the ideologies behind the drawing systems taught became more sophisticated. The students had to progress from drawing simple linear and geometric elements to delineating forms abstracted from nature, so that botanical studies became integral to the system. But any 'progress' made in the Schools of Design prior to 1851 was not apparent in the Great Exhibition, so that despite the general euphoria, the design reform lobby was stringent in its criticisms: 'The absence of any fixed principles in ornamental design is apparent in the Exhibition', thundered *The Times* '. . . it seems to us that the art manufacturers of the whole of Europe are thoroughly demoralised'. Owen Jones, the architect who had devised the colour schemes for the Exhibition, and who was to become involved with the teaching at the Schools, was equally scathing:

We have no principles, no unity; the architect, the upholsterer, the paper-stainer, the weaver, the calico-printer, and the potter, run each their independent course; each struggles fruitlessly, each produces in art novelty without beauty, or beauty without intelligence.

The mid-century campaigns in the Schools, therefore, were directed at the elimination of 'novelty' in favour of 'intelligence', and the formulation of principles or rules to guide the potential designer.

The master-mind behind these activities was Henry Cole (1808–82), who had established himself as a professional organiser. He had helped to sort out the Public Records Office, campaigned for Penny Postage, published children's books, established a firm of 'art manufacturers', introduced a

Raising the ribs of the transept roof of the Crystal Palace.

Journal of Design and Manufacture (in 1847), and he was also one of the principal organisers of the 1851 Exhibition. In 1852 he was appointed Secretary to the newly formed Department of Practical Art (later the Department of Science and Art) which administered the national network of Schools of Design.

One of Cole's first activities was to form the nucleus of a museum collection – mostly of objects bought from the Great Exhibition. Pieces were acquired primarily for teaching purposes, including 'Examples of False Principles of Decoration', as well as work which met his standards. The collection (and the School of Design) moved to South Kensington in 1857 (to a site bought from the profits of the Exhibition), and eventually became the Royal College of Art, and what is now known as the National Museum of Art and Design (more familiarly the V&A).

Following Cole's appointment, the South Kensington School (now the parent body of the national system) was refunded, also from the profits of the Exhibition, and its curriculum and teaching methods were re-examined. At this stage, however, there was no departure from the belief in systems and certainties, Henry Cole (satirised as the utilitarian, 'facts, facts, facts' Mr Gradgrind in Dickens's *Hard Times*, 1854) having no time for inspiration and imagination. The teachers, therefore, were still involved in the establishment of rules and principles of design, and like their predecessors in the early years, they were primarily preoccupied with ornament. These preoccupations produced design methodologies that were to form the basis of subsequent design systems – persistent alternatives to the individualism and 'design as craft' approach of the Ruskinian lobbies.

The School's attempts to regain and sustain credibility resulted in some significant publications, the most important in the 1850s being Owen Jones's *Grammar of Ornament* (1856). Owen Jones had trained as an architect and had travelled widely, including visits to Egypt, Turkey and Spain, and his fascination with the Alhambra had inspired his first major publication *Plans, Details and Sections of the Alhambra*, 1836–45. Jones's interest in architectural polychromy was extended to ideals for 'ornamental art' which he demonstrated in the *Grammar of Ornament* – colour theory predominating in the thirty-seven 'General Principles' he enumerated in the text. The *Grammar* was widely used as a source and text-book throughout the nineteenth century (an American edition was published in 1880).

The illustrations in the *Grammar* document the ornamental systems of a wide range of countries and cultures, and they were selected, according to Jones, in order to demonstrate 'certain general laws' in the 'language' of form – laws which all related, as he put it, to 'the distribution of form in nature'. The ornamental systems, therefore, were classified into certain hierarchies. Egyptian ornament was highly recommended: it was 'a pure original style', drawing its 'inspiration direct from nature . . . the types are few and natural types'. Greek ornament 'carried the perfection of pure form to a point which has never since been reached', while Moresque (from the Alhambra) was 'the very summit of perfection of Moorish art', with 'every ornament a grammar in itself'. The artists of Pompeii, on the other hand 'invented as they drew', an approach which was certainly not recommended – this was ornament 'carried to the very limit of caprice', and 'it oft times approaches vulgarity'.

The decadence of Pompeii, however, paled before the confusions of contemporary European manufacture, as exemplified in the Great Exhibition: 'In the works contributed by the various nations of Europe there was everywhere to be observed an entire absence of any common principle in the application of Art to manufactures'; there was a 'fruitless struggle for novelty', senseless copying, with the 'carver in stone, the worker in metal, the weaver and the painter' all borrowing from each other irrespective of logic or fitness. The answer, therefore, was to study and absorb the experience of the past in order to design for the future, always bearing in mind that natural form demonstrated the inner laws of structure and growth.

One can see the application and implication of these theories in Jones's designs for fabrics and wallpapers – flower and plant forms stylised into flat patterns – any attempt to achieve the 'realism' of three-dimensional form being anathema to this generation of design reformers. The relevance of Jones's and similar theories to pattern-making is obvious; it is more difficult, however, to relate them to three-dimensional work – glass, ceramics and metal, for example. It is clear that at this stage in the development of the Schools of Design, the designer's role was to produce patterns or drawings, and certainly not to be involved with the various processes of making. This is made clear in several of the *Analyses, Manuals* and *Principles* of ornament which were produced at this time. Ralph Wornum, for example, in his *Analysis of Ornament* (1856) – based on lectures that he had given in the Schools of Design – wrote: 'The great art of the designer is in the selection and arrangement of his materials, not in their execution.'

Gottfried Semper: design as an evolutionary process

The one designer associated with the Schools of Design at this period to put forward a viable alternative was Gottfried Semper (1803–79), who had arrived in England, penniless, in 1850. He had trained as an architect in Hamburg and Paris, and had been appointed Professor of Architecture in Dresden in 1834. He designed the Opera House and several other buildings in Dresden, and had also designed ceramics for Meissen. Semper, however, was a republican; he was involved in the 1849 uprising, and like his colleague Richard Wagner, he had to flee Germany. He tried unsuccessfully to find work in Paris, where he had contacts, and he came to London hoping to make more.

He eventually met Henry Cole, and was put in charge of the arrangement of the Canadian, Turkish, Swedish and Danish displays at the Exhibition. The commission, and the experience he had of the Exhibition prompted him to re-examine ideas he had been formulating since his early days in Paris, and which he had expanded in his lectures at Dresden.

The paper he wrote in connection with the Exhibition – 'Wissenschaft, Industrie und Kunst' (1852); ('Science, Industry and Art') obviously refers to the enabling triumvirate evoked by Prince Albert in his hopes for the Exhibition. Unlike his British contemporaries, Semper did not condemn the exhibits on show for their lack of 'style' or 'taste', nor, like Ruskin or Morris, did he reject the ideologies that had produced them on moral and social grounds. For although this 'babel of the arts', as he called it, 'is nothing but a clear expression of certain anomalies in the existing state of society', the 'apparent confusion' could serve a positive purpose: 'While our art industry will muddle on without direction, it will unwittingly perform a noble deed by slowly destroying traditional prototypes with ornamental treatment.' As a result new forms would evolve, which were in keeping with contemporary needs and production processes.

The relevance of evolutionary theory to social developments was to be re-examined following the publication of Darwin's *Origin of Species* in 1859. Semper, however, was inspired by an earlier evolutionary model. In Paris he had frequently visited the Jardin des Plantes, where the French biologist, Georges Cuvier, had assembled his large collection of animals, fish, skeletons and fossils:

In this magnificent collection . . . we perceive the types for all the most complicated forms of the animal empire; we see progressing nature, with all its variety and immense richness, most sparing and economical in all its forms and motives . . . A method, analogous to that Cuvier followed, applied to art, and especially to architecture, would at least contribute to getting a clear insight over its whole province, and perhaps also form the basis of a doctrine of *style*, and a sort of *topic*, or method, of how to Invent.'
(*Kleine Schriften*, 1884; quoted from P. Steadman, *The Evolution of Designs*, 1979, p.67)

While he was in London, therefore, Semper extended these evolutionary theories to design as well as architecture, using the exhibition and its critical aftermath to test his ideas. Like so many observers, he felt that what he (somewhat indiscriminately) described as 'primitive peoples' – Persians, Indians, Arabs, Chinese and Canadian Indians – demonstrated a natural *Stilsicherheit* (stylistic confidence or certainty) that industrialised societies lacked, except in the design of 'functional' objects – weapons, machinery, carriages, etc. This certainty, he felt, could not be re-imposed: 'Hence no proposals for a jury of artists and institutions to act as the guardian of public taste, no dualism of high art and industrial art, no aesthetic police' – a reference, no doubt, to Henry Cole's 'False Principles'. Reform, he hoped, would develop through the natural evolution of design, and through teaching. Teaching in academies and industrial schools, however, was a waste of time; *practical* art had to be taught in workshops, where equivalents to the apprenticeship system could be established: 'A brotherly relationship between a master and his journeymen and his apprentices will signal the end of the academies and industrial schools, at least as we know them today.'

Fortunately for Semper, Henry Cole was unaware of the wider implications of his theories, and in 1852 he was asked to 'establish a class in order to afford instruction in the principles and practice of Ornamental Art applied to Metal Manufacture'. Semper began by giving the students practical experience of the materials they were working with. 'Many a good talent has been spoiled by having been too long engaged in copying and studying from models, even from nature', was his heretical dictat. The class flourished – the numbers grew – and in 1853 Semper was asked to establish a class in

'Practical Construction, Architecture and Plastic Decorations.' By this time, however, his fortunes were improving, and in 1855 he was appointed Professor of Architecture at the Polytechnic in Zurich, a prestigious institution which was to train influential architects from Holland and France as well as Switzerland.

Christopher Dresser and commercial design

The South Kensington School produced one outstanding commercial designer who successfully demonstrated the practical application of Design School theory in a number of industries. Christopher Dresser (1834–1904) joined the School when he was thirteen, and began teaching botany there in the 1850s. His first published work was his contribution to the series of plates depicting 'plant forms from nature' in Owen Jones's *Grammar of Ornament* ('See how various the forms, and how unvarying the principles', Jones had written). Dresser maintained this preoccupation with the 'fitness' of forms based on natural sources and structures throughout his career. 'The principle of adaptation, or fitness, is of paramount importance in its relation to decorated objects' he wrote in *The Art of Decorative Design* (1862).

For Dresser, design was an objective discipline rather than an inspirational art – 'in ornament, as in science, it is necessary to have recourse to an analytical method'. These attitudes, as we have seen, had a long-pre-history in Design School theory. As far as pattern-making was concerned, however, Dresser extended its application to produce work of remarkable originality. His patterns abstracted from skeletal forms, for example, and his diagrammatic interpretation of ice-crystal patterns had no equivalent in nineteenth-century pattern-making.

Dresser's extension of these ideas to three-dimensional design resulted in work that was equally original. In the 1870s and early 1880s he produced metal-work for a number of firms, the undecorated geometric shapes of his coffee-pots, tea-services and wine-coolers, for example, anticipating Modern Movement designs in Austria and Germany (the conceptual as well as stylistic links are perhaps inevitable, Dresser being a 'pioneer of modern design' in that he promoted a science- rather than craft-based aesthetic.)

Dresser's designs for glass and ceramics, however, are very different. His 'Clutha' glass evokes experimental work by Gallé and Tiffany (who also claimed to draw their inspiration from nature), while his ceramics for Linthorpe and other 'art' potteries relates to Pre-Columbian as well as Chinese and Japanese work – a reflection of Dresser's travels, as well as the growing collections at the South Kensington Museum. Dresser visited Japan in the 1870s and was one of the first designers to have first-hand experience of Japanese design and architecture. His book *Japan: its Architecture and Art Manufactures* (1882) is one of the most detailed and perceptive accounts produced in Britain in the nineteenth century.

Throughout his long career Dresser always insisted that he was a 'commercial' designer, and that the 'Principles' he outlined in his many books and articles were eminently applicable to commercial design. Dresser

Silver egg steamer (1884–5) and glass and silver claret jug (1879) by Christopher Dresser.

*Electroplated and ebony soup tureen, cover and ladle (*left 1880) and 'grotesque' earthenware vase (*right 1892–6); by Christopher Dresser.*

campaigned for an educated design profession capable of working on a practical level with manufacturers, and for a conception of the designer that went beyond pattern-making. Moreover, his experience gave him a realistic conception of the capabilities of what he called 'art industries', as well as the markets they served. For the mass-production techniques described by Babbage and Ure were only applicable to certain areas of industry, and many manufacturing processes were semi-mechanised, or still carried out by hand.

In all the industries Dresser designed for – ceramics, glass, metal-work, and even textiles, production methods encouraged specialisations in 'art manufacture', the products of these industries appealing to the increasingly wealthy middle classes who could afford and appreciate them.

In 1899 an article in *Studio* magazine described Dresser as 'perhaps the greatest of commercial designers, imposing his fantasy and invention upon the ordinary output of British industry'. By the 1890s many of the more prestigious consumer goods industries were working with designers. The majority of them, however, would have shrunk from describing their activities as 'commercial' – commercialism and trade being associated with the trivialisation of both the product and the producer.

Ruskin and 'the true function of the workman'

There was, of course, no association of trade with vulgarity in Prince Albert's panegyric to the spirit of the Great Exhibition. For him trade was a herald of peace, progress and prosperity. To the 'official' design reformers of the 1850s – the men associated with the Royal Society of Arts and the Schools of Design – the 'taste' of many of the exhibits was deplorable, but this could be remedied by an understanding of the nature of 'style', and its links, in all cultures, with natural form – with what Owen Jones described as the 'law of the universal fitness of things in nature'. There were, however, many ways in which the 'law of universal fitness' could be interpreted, and Schools of Design certainties, with their evocations of science and methodology, could be, and were, considered both mechanistic and materialistic.

Here, for example, is John Ruskin (1819–1900), castigating the Schools in the 1870s:

The tap root of all this mischief is in the endeavour to produce some ability in the student to make money by designing for manufacture. No student who makes this his primary object will be able to design at all; and the very words 'School of Design' involve the profoundest of art fallacies.

By 1870 Ruskin had established himself as the conscience of the age, and the inspiration of the protagonists of the Arts and Crafts Movement. He had begun his long literary career by writing first about art, and then about architecture. As with Pugin, his judgements were based on personal ideals and values; unlike Pugin, however, he could never relate 'principles' of design to any academic convention. The first sentence of *The Seven Lamps of Architecture* (1849) proclaims his independence:

Architecture is the art which so disposes and adorns the edifices raised by man, for whatsoever uses, that the sight of them may contribute to his mental health, power and pleasure.

The 'Lamps' – such as Sacrifice, Truth, Obedience, represent moral virtues rather than aesthetic criteria, and although Ruskin later dismissed the book as naïve, certain passages indicate the nature of his future commitment. *The Lamp of Truth*, for example, is concerned with honesty of material and workmanship: 'architectural deceit' wrote Ruskin 'is as truly deserving of reprobation as any other moral delinquency; it is unworthy alike of architecture and nations'. Deceit, therefore, does not only relate to the use of false and fake materials, it also relates to the quality of labour:

> For it is not the material, but the absence of the human labour which makes the thing worthless, and a piece of terracotta, or plaster of Paris, which has been wrought by the human hand, is worth all the stone in Carrara cut by machinery.
>
> *(The Seven Lamps of Architecture*, 1849, p. 50)

Ruskin takes the rejection of 'mechanisation' a stage further than Carlyle; he uses it as a basis for the judgement of all the works of man, past and present. The judgement is, of course, moral as well as aesthetic; it is subjective rather than objective, and it rejects 'whatever can be measured and systematized' in favour of 'whatsoever is immeasurable, intangible, indivisible, and of the spirit'. Schools of Design philosophies, therefore, judged according to these criteria, were not only misguided, they were totally immoral.

Ruskin elaborated these theories in his next major publication – *The Stones of Venice* – which was published in three volumes between 1851 and 1853. 'On the nature of Gothic', a chapter in the second volume, was to form the basis of that very persuasive critical tradition in British nineteenth-century design theory – a tradition which survived into the twentieth century, when the 'craft' ideals proclaimed by Ruskin and his followers were applied to the products of industry. Published two years after the Great Exhibition, 'The nature of Gothic' ignored the euphoria which had inspired the event, and the lessons allegedly learned there. The division of labour, the principles of political economy, the attempts to establish systems or methods of design were all anathema to Ruskin, since they denied those vital qualities of 'experience and skill, and the authority and wealth which these must naturally and justly obtain'.

The book was reprinted throughout the nineteenth century, and 'On the nature of Gothic' was printed as a pamphlet in 1854 and distributed to students in the newly founded Working Men's College with the sub-title 'And herein of the true function of the workman in art'. William Morris produced a Kelmscott Press Edition in 1892, and wrote in the preface:

> To my mind, and I believe to some others, it is one of the most important things written by the author, and in future days will be considered as one of the very few necessary and inevitable utterances of the century. To some of us when we first read it, it seemed to point out a new road on which the world should travel.

'On the nature of Gothic' was a plea for humanism in design, a humanism that was to be reflected in the quality and art of workmanship. Ruskin's evaluation of architecture and designs, like that of Pugin, was judgemental. And like Pugin, Ruskin believed that Christian architecture was superior to that of the 'pagan'; he went further than Pugin, however, in his conviction that architecture and artefacts should proclaim their man-made origin, and demonstrate freedom rather than control – perfection, in any system, being suspect. The factory system, whatsoever its form, debased both workman and product – the qualities of order, reproducibility and perfection which Babbage so admired demonstrating constriction rather than creativity.

Individual as opposed to collective achievements, therefore, reflected the true nature of quality, and 'the great civilised invention of the division of labour' was destroying the traditional basis of society.

If Ruskin was not the first to condemn mechanisation as immoral, he was one of the first to judge the products of industry on moral rather than stylistic grounds. 'The spirit of improvement', in Ruskin's terms, therefore, could only be achieved through social change – convictions elaborated in a number of his later books which relate the current status of 'art' to social values and priorities. These include *The Political Economy of Art* (1857), reprinted as *A Joy Forever (and its Price in the Market)*, *The Two Paths* (1859), *Unto this Last* (1860), *Munera Pulveris* (1863) and *Fors Clavigera*, the series of letters addressed to the working men of England, which were published between 1871 and 1884. All his writing was concerned with moral and social issues, but these books in particular inspired a whole generation of designers to attempt to 'redesign the world'.

William Morris and colleagues

More has been written about William Morris (1834–96) than any other designer, living or dead; this persistent preoccupation with his achievements and his ideas is inspired as much by his social and political commitment as by the work he produced. For although, as F.R. Leavis has pointed out, 'Morris was a force that impinged decisively on the world of practice', his integrity was so challenged by the assumptions of that world that he was forced to question the validity of his own achievements, and to commit himself to the promotion of social revolution. His aim, when he became a Socialist, was 'to obtain for the whole people, duly organised, the possession and control of the means of production and exchange, destroying at the same time all national rivalries'. Morris's cause, therefore, was the Marxist cause; like Marx (and Ruskin), Morris recognised the alienation of the worker in the factory system, an alienation prompted by the implications of the division of labour.

The *devaluation* of the world of men is in direct proportion to the *increasing value* of the world of things. Labour produces not only commodities: it produces itself and the worker as a *commodity* . . . the worker is related to the *product of his labour* as to an *alien* object . . . the more the worker spends himself, the more powerful becomes the alien world of objects which he creates over and against himself, the poorer he himself – his inner world – becomes, the less belongs to him as his own.
(Karl Marx, *Economic and Philosophical Manuscripts of 1844, Collected Works*, vol. III, p. 272.)

Neither Ruskin nor Morris could have read the *Manuscripts* (although Morris was well aware of Marxist theory); their shared preoccupation with the implications of political economy and the division of labour, however, led all three thinkers to similar conclusions as far as the schism between the producer and product was concerned. But their proposed remedies were very different. In *Unto this Last*, for example, Ruskin suggested social reforms similar to those associated with British ideals for the post-war Welfare State.

Morris, on the other hand, could not, ultimately, envisage reform without revolution, and *News from Nowhere (1890)* locates his ideal society in a future when bitter and bloody struggles for reform have succeeded in establishing the Socialist millennium.

Before his 'conversion' to Socialism Morris was already well-established as a poet and designer. He had first read 'On the nature of Gothic' when he was at Oxford; his family intended him to become a clergyman, but he had other ideas. He wrote poetry, composed 'Romances' – stories about knightly conquests and despairs; he studied village churches, and travelled to France to see Gothic cathedrals at first hand. He tried and failed to be an architect. He found he could not paint (unlike his friend and contemporary at Oxford, Edward Burne-Jones), and it was only after his marriage to Jane Burden, and the move to Red House in Kent, that he discovered his vocation as a 'decorator'.

Red House ('more a poem than a house' as Rossetti was to describe it) was designed by Philip Webb (see colour pl. 10), the young architect Morris had met during his brief apprenticeship to G.E. Street in Oxford. Morris intended, with the help of his friends, to transform it into a 'small Palace of Art'. The furniture, like the house itself, was to be solid and durable, while the 'poetry' was to be in the decoration: murals and embroideries were planned and put in hand for the main rooms, the ceilings were to be stencilled and painted with simple 'medieval' patterns, painted glass was designed for some of the smaller windows, together with painted tiles for the fireplaces.

It was the decoration and furnishing of this house that determined Morris's career. Encouraged by the success of these efforts, he and his colleagues decided to set themselves up in business as 'Fine Art Workmen in Painting, Carving, Furniture and the Metals'. The founder members of what subsequently came to be known as the 'Firm' included, as well as Morris, Webb and Burne-Jones, the painters Dante Gabriel Rossetti and Ford Madox Brown. Their chief source of income in these early years was from work in stained glass, but their first major success came in 1862, when the Firm's designs (including furniture, glass, tiles and embroidery) were included in the second International Exhibition, and were awarded two Gold Medals. This was followed by two prestigious commissions – to redecorate the Armoury and Tapestry Rooms at St James's Palace, and to design and furnish the Green Dining Room in the South Kensington Museum (1866–7). By this time Morris had reluctantly sold Red House (it was too far from London to cope with commissions).

The move to London enabled Morris to set up workshops in Queen Square, and to concentrate on his personal interest and skill in pattern-making. He had designed his first wallpapers in the early 1860s; these, like the majority of his later designs for wallpapers, were hand-printed from wood blocks by Jeffrey & Co. They did not sell, however, and he did not produce any more until the 1870s, when he began his most prolific and creative period producing patterns that are still popular today. It was no doubt his growing confidence in this work in two-dimensional pattern-making which led him to his involvement with various forms of textile design, his struggles to achieve

'Peacock and design', wool tapestry by William Morris (1878).

the standards he required becoming a personal crusade against the compromises of commercialism. He began designing textiles in the late 1860s, but he was dissatisfied with the results – the chemical dyes then in use travestying the colours he aimed to achieve. In 1875, however (the year the original partnership was dissolved and Morris took over the control of the Firm), he began his long collaboration with Thomas Wardle, who had set himself up as a silk dyer and printer in Leek in Staffordshire.

Morris's letters to Thomas Wardle demonstrate his perfectionism and his refusal to compromise:

I am also, as you know, most deeply impressed with the importance of having our dyes the soundest and best that can be, and am prepared to give up all that part of my business which depends on textiles if I fail in getting them so.

Morris, of course, did not give up that part of his business, increasing the range of his expertise in 'the textile arts' when he set up workshops at Merton Abbey in Surrey in 1881. By this time he was producing woven as well as printed textiles, rugs, carpets (machine-made as well as hand-knotted), and tapestries. The names he gave to his fabrics – *Strawberry Thief, Eyebright, Avon* and *Windrush* – indicate that their inspiration lay in nature and the English countryside. But unlike the Design Schools practitioners, he rarely produced stylised abstractions from nature. He insisted on 'plenty of meaning' in pattern design: 'I must have unmistakable suggestions of gardens and fields, and strange trees, boughs and tendrils, or I can't do with your patterns.' He believed that patterns should express the vitality and growth of the plant forms that inspired them – 'even where a line ends it should look as though it had plenty of capacity for more growth if it so would'. These convictions, as well as his expertise, were based on his personal experience of pattern design, and his interpretation of its history. This understanding of past achievements was reinforced by his travels and by the growing collections at the South Kensington Museum (which he helped to select).

He was impressed by Persian and Indian textiles, particularly those produced before design had become 'no longer an art but a trade', and it was from textiles that he based his interpretation of the design process:

Never forget the material you are working with, and try always to use it for doing what it can do best; if you feel yourself hampered by the material in which you are working, instead of being helped by it, you have so far not learned your business, any more than a would be poet has, who complains of the hardship of working in measure and rhyme . . . a designer, therefore, should always fully understand the process of the special manufacture he is dealing with, or the result will be a mere *tour de force*.

(*Textiles, Arts and Crafts Essays*, 1893, p.38)

Morris assumed that the designer should have total control of the design process; there was to be no distinction between designing and making, and designing involved knowledge, skill and creativity. This did not necessarily imply that the designer should not work with industry – for example, he designed carpets for commercial firms. A direct and personal understanding of the processes involved, however, was essential if the design was to be successful.

Morris & Co. (which survived until the Second World War) continued to produce stained glass and furniture, as well as embroidery; Morris himself, however, concentrated on two-dimensional design and, after he had become involved in politics, increasingly delegated other aspects of the Firm's production. From the 1880s, for example, the design and production of the Firm's furniture were supervised by George Jack, an architect who had worked in Philip Webb's office. The 'Sussex' chairs which had been introduced when the Firm was establishing itself continued in production, while Jack himself designed superb furniture that was eighteenth-century rather than vernacular in style, more in keeping with the town and country house than the cottage. The Firm also designed interiors, including those for Standen (1891), designed by Philip Webb, and Wightwick (1887) built for the Mander paint family.

These and other commissions for aristocratic clients as well as the newly affluent upper middle classes sustained the Firm's income and its reputation. At the same time, however, Morris was increasingly irritated by the élitism of these activities. He personally enjoyed his work as a designer, but he was aware that he was spending his best years 'ministering to the swinish luxury of the rich', and that only a privileged few could afford to buy his work or share his own 'joy in labour'. His frustration with life in 'the age of shoddy' drove him to social and political commitment, and he pursued his Socialist

Rush-seated chairs based on a traditional Sussex design, by Morris, Marshall, Faulkner & Co. (left 1865; right 1870s); 'Pomegranate' wallpaper by William Morris (1864).

ideals with the energy and dedication he had applied to art and design. His Socialism, he explained, was 'Socialism seen through the eyes of an artist'. His ideal was an 'Art made by the people and for the people, a joy to the maker and the user', 'an art which could have no real life and growth under the present system of commercialism and profit-mongering'. His commitment was total; he left the day to day running of the Firm to his colleagues while he attended meetings and made speeches in dingy halls and on street corners, preaching the destruction of capitalism in the name of art and the people. Morris belonged to a long tradition of dissent against industrialisation and the commercial system. He was, however, only one of a few designers among his contemporaries to convert this dissent into overt political activity, and after he joined the Socialist League in 1884 he distanced himself from other designers' attempts to 'institutionalise' the Arts and Crafts. His 'swan-song' as a designer was the establishment in 1890 of the Kelmscott Press – an unashamedly self-indulgent experiment, which nevertheless drew attention to the inadequacies of contemporary commercial book-production. He designed type-faces for the Press, the inks and the paper were carefully selected, and several of the books were bound in vellum. Needless to say, this was not a commercial venture, and Morris gave several of the books away. When he died in 1896, more than fifty titles had been published, and several other private presses had been formed.

While Morris was politically a radical, his designs and his approach to design were essentially conservative (far more so, at least in theory, than those based on Schools of Design philosophies). Again, he did not, like other protagonists of craft revivals in Scandinavia, Hungary and Poland, attempt to draw from or recreate a vernacular or folk tradition; he was more interested in concept of workmanship than any ideal of 'Englishness' in design. At the same time Morris is unique among designers; his influence survives because of his integrity. As Lethaby was to point out, 'his work will necessarily remain supreme until as great a man as Morris again deals with that manner of expression with his *full force* as he did'.

Of the founder members of the Firm, only Burne-Jones and Philip Webb continued to work consistently for Morris when the original partnership was dissolved in 1875. Two of the younger designers associated with the Firm, however, who were originally involved in specialist commissions, were to become well known for their specific skills in ceramics and metalware: William De Morgan and W.A.S. Benson.

William De Morgan (1839–1917) was painting tiles and designing stained glass for the Firm as early as 1863. He set up his own pottery in Chelsea in the early 1870s, experimenting with colour and glazes, and was involved in various prestigious commissions, including the design of 'Persian' tiles for the Arabian Hall in Lord Leighton's extravagant studio house in Kensington (1879). In 1880 he moved to premises near Morris in Merton and continued the production of tiles, as well as the magnificent lustre ware which was displayed in exhibitions of British design both at home and abroad. His aim was to 'rediscover the art of pottery from the beginning', so that while the British ceramics industry was improving and extending its 'art manufacture', De Morgan was experimenting with medieval methods and kilns, as well as mastering the ancient skills of the Persians. Ill-health, however, and dwindling profits forced him to close his pottery in 1907. He could, of course, like Christopher Dresser, have worked for the many successful craft or semi-craft workshops that were established in the latter part of the nineteenth

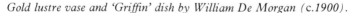

Gold lustre vase and 'Griffin' dish by William De Morgan (c.1900).

century, but William De Morgan always maintained that he 'could never work except by myself and in my own manner'. (See colour pl. 9).

W.A.S. Benson (1854–1924), so quiet and shy that his colleagues called him 'Was' Benson, specialised in metalwork. Like Morris, he was sent to public school and Oxford; like Morris he had no wish to enter an establishment profession; unlike Morris, however, he always intended to be an engineer which was not easy, in the wake of Babbage's predicted 'decline of science', for an upper-middle-class boy. Benson, therefore, did the next best thing, and began to train as an architect. He met Burne-Jones and he also met Morris, who encouraged him to set up a small workshop to produce metalwork. He wrote to his mother to justify his decision:

I must make something or be miserable. If one is working for anyone else, one's ideas are only in the way, they are no good to him and they are distracting . . . Here [in his projected workshops] are things wanting to be done and I long to do them, and I think there is every chance of profit as well as pleasure.

Benson's confidence was evidently not misplaced; two years later he moved to larger premises, building a factory in Hammersmith and opening his own showrooms in Bond Street in 1887. Benson produced simple metalware for domestic use – kettles, tea-pots, jugs, lamps and light-fittings for both gas and electricity – there was a growing demand for his work with the introduction of electricity in the domestic market. His work was not expensive, and the factory remained in production until 1920, when he retired.

Benson was unique among Arts and Crafts practitioners in that, as his obituary in *The Times* pointed out, 'he preferred to approach his subject as an engineer rather than a hand-worker; to produce his beautiful forms by machinery on a commercial scale rather than single works of art'. Benson's light fittings and metalwork were used in several of the interiors designed by Morris & Co.; he also designed furniture for the Firm, and became its

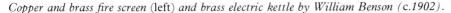

Copper and brass fire screen (left) *and brass electric kettle by William Benson* (c.1902).

chairman after the death of Morris in 1896. With allegiances both to Morris and machine production, Benson's priorities anticipated the changing nature of ideals for design at the turn of the century.

The consolidation of the crafts

Arts and Crafts ideals, or so it seemed, were consolidated in the 1880s: A.H. Mackmurdo set up his Century Guild in 1882; the Art Workers' Guild was established in 1884, and C.R. Ashbee launched his Guild of Handicraft in London's East End in 1888. Thirty years after the publication of 'On the nature of Gothic', therefore, some sort of bridgehead seemed to have been secured in the long fight against 'the modern practice of the unlimited manufacture of makeshifts for real wares', in Morris's words. Morris, as we have seen, tended to distance himself from these activities when he became committed to Socialism; at the same time, however, he welcomed 'even the feeble protest which is now being made against the vulgarization of all life' as a 'protest against intellectual tyranny', craftsmanship, for him, now becoming a demonstration of dissent.

To many designers, especially to the generation born in the 1850s, it seemed that craftsmanship might become a way of earning a living, as well as way of life. Arthur Heygate Mackmurdo (1851–1942) was one of the many craft protagonists who had trained as an architect, and who had decided that the only way to achieve 'unity in design' in that profession was through the crafts. Architecture, he believed, would once against become a 'vital' and 'organic' art if 'the decorator and furnisher' were 'craftsmen with souls awake to the inspiration and needs of the day'.

The Century Guild had high ideals, and was founded in order '. . . to render to all branches of art the sphere no longer of the tradesman, but of the artist,' and to 'restore building, decoration, glass painting, pottery and metal to their rightful place beside painting and sculpture'. Herbert Horne, who had joined Mackmurdo's office to train as an architect, was one of the founder members, and associates included Selwyn Image and Clement Heaton, whose family were stained glass manufacturers. The short-lived Guild was dissolved in 1888; its work (mainly furniture and fabrics) was interesting, however, because of its innovatory (and eccentric) stylisation. Mackmurdo produced essentially classical furniture incorporating a fretwork motif of undulating lines – leaf and plant forms that bear no relationship to School of Design abstraction or to the naturalism of Morris's work. Century Guild fabrics are equally unique, with their flowing, flaring and snakelike lines and acid colours. The seemingly avant-garde nature of these designs has ensured them a place in most histories of *art nouveau*, and they were probably inspired by Mackmurdo's admiration for the art of William Blake. At the same time Mackmurdo admired the architecture of the Renaissance, and these uneasy marriages of classical form with 'whiplash' decoration were, perhaps fortunately, unique. Mackmurdo was thirty-seven when The Century Guild was disbanded; he continued his architectural work, and was associated with the many craft and design reform organisations that were established in

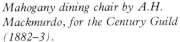

Mahogany dining chair by A.H. Mackmurdo, for the Century Guild (1882–3).

One of two brackets exhibited by W.G. Rogers in the Great Exhibition (1851). Carved wood and porcelain.

the 1880s and 1890s. During the latter part of his life, however, he was obsessed with theories of social reform, expounded in books such as *The Human Hive* (1926) and *A People's Charter* (1933).

The Guild of Handicraft, a far more ambitious venture, was set up by the young architect and idealist C.R. Ashbee (1863–1942) in 1888, the year that The Century Guild was disbanded. Ashbee was the son of a wealthy businessman; he read history at King's College, Cambridge, where he met Roger Fry, and where he also acquired a social conscience. When he left, he decided to become an architect, and while he was articled to G.F. Bodley (one of the Morris Firm's early patrons), he lived at Toynbee Hall, a pioneer university settlement for the education of the working classes which had recently been opened in the East End of London. His contribution to intellectual life there was to set up a Ruskin reading class, and to teach drawing and decoration. He found his students so enthusiastic that he decided to form a Guild and School of Handicraft. He launched the venture with four members, a working capital of £50, and without the blessing of William Morris. 'William Morris and a great deal of cold water', Ashbee wrote in his journal.

> I could not exchange a single argument with him till I granted his whole position as a Socialist and then said 'Look, I am going to forge a weapon for you; and I thus too work with you in the overthrow of Society.' To which he replied, 'The weapon is too small to be of any value.'
>
> (Quoted from Alan Crawford, *C.R. Ashbee Architect, Designer and Romantic Socialist*, 1985, p. 28)

Ashbee, however, was not deterred; membership grew (all the 'guildsmen' were from the East End), and so did the expertise. They worked mainly in wood and metal in the early years, acquiring their skills through trial and error:

It is in the learning of how to do things and do them well that many fresh design motives are evolved. So it comes about that when a little group of men learn to pull together in a workshop, to trust each other, to play into each other's hand, and understand each other's limitations, their combination becomes creative, and the character that they develop in themselves takes expression in the work of their fingers. Humanity and craftsmanship are essential.

(C.R. Ashbee, *Modern English Silverwork*, 1909, p. 6)

The Guild and the Guildsmen flourished until the end of the century (although Ashbee never had the finances to establish the school that he hoped to associate with the guild). In 1891 the group moved to Essex House, a Georgian house in the Mile End Road, and Ashbee opened a retail shop in London's West End. In 1894 he built a house for his mother on Cheyne Walk in Chelsea – Magpie and Stump – which was decorated and furnished by the Guild, and served as a 'showcase' for prospective clients. Designs by the Guild were regularly exhibited in Arts and Crafts Exhibition Society displays, they were featured in *Studio* and in continental magazines, and their work also began to be exhibited abroad (most notably in Munich and Vienna, towns with cults of sophisticated craftsmanship). Ashbee also set up a private press – the Essex House Press – in 1898, with some of the Kelmscott equipment.

The Guild was (and is) perhaps best known for its silverware and its jewellery (colour pl. 8), exquisite designs that have now found their way into most major museums of decorative design. Furniture was also designed, mostly to commission: superb and sophisticated work, with elaborate inlays and metalwork decoration.

In 1902, when the Guild seemed firmly established, Ashbee launched on his most Ruskinian and, as it proved, most quixotic adventure; he decided to move the Guild to Chipping Campden, an idyllic village in Gloucestershire. The immediate reason was the expiry of the lease on Essex House, and the difficulty of finding suitable alternative premises in London. Ashbee must also have felt, no doubt, that a life nearer the soil would be more appropriate to his enterprises, and he certainly believed that it would be interesting to extend his educational experiments among country people. The decision, nevertheless, was a democratic one. A poll was conducted, and about fifty guildsmen agreed to move, with their families.

There Ashbee made a valiant attempt to demonstrate the virtues and delights of the simple life to the villagers, as well as to the Guildsmen. He set up classes for 'swimming, gardening, cookery, carpentry, life and duties of the citizen'; he organised plays and performances, lectures and summer schools, outings, as well as laundry classes (for the girls) and physical drill (for the boys). He also attempted to sustain the Guild's production, and this proved harder than he had anticipated. He met, of course, with the antagonism of most of the local gentry, who resented this eccentric challenge

Silverware by C.R. Ashbee. l to r:
The Painter-Strainers' Cup, *silver,
enamel and precious stones (1900);
butter dish (1900); silver-mounted
jug (c.1900).*

to the status quo, and at the same time he had difficulty maintaining contact with clients and potential clients. The decline in the Guild's financial fortunes dates from the move to Campden, and in 1908, 'after three years of acute commercial depression and heavy losses', the Guild was dissolved.

Ashbee was a writer, as well as an entrepreneur, and he analysed the reasons for this failure in a number of books, including *Should We Stop Teaching Art?* (1911). He realised that Chipping Campden was too far from London to be a practical commercial proposition, and he believed that local indifference to his work was in part due to the growing fashion for antiques – 'turned out in their hundreds to the hum of the latest American machinery'. He also blamed amateur competition, and the growing number of retail stores marketing the 'new' jewellery and furniture, for undercutting the work of the genuine craftsman.

The failure of the Guild, however, gave him time to re-examine the premises on which it was based. He had been to America (where he had met Frank Lloyd Wright), and he had travelled in Europe, and these experiences had convinced him that 'the machine was here to stay'. At the same time, he came to believe that it was in the interests of industrialised economies to encourage the crafts, since they could provide 'the grammar of the Industrial Arts, Architecture and Industry'.

Institutionalising the crafts

By 1902, when Ashbee made the move to Campden, there had obviously been some consolidation of the craft ideal, if only because an increasingly affluent middle-class market demanded some sophistication in home decoration and furnishing. The wallpaper and textile industries regularly used 'designers'. The architect C.F.A. Voysey (1857–1941), for example, began designing wallpapers in the early 1880s when he was attempting to establish his architectural practice, and continued to produce wallpapers and textiles (most notably for Alexander Morton & Co.) until the 1920s. He also designed furniture and metalwork which was made for him by various specialist firms, and he was appointed one of the first Royal Designers for Industry in 1936, the ideals he represented (as well as his international reputation as an architect) still being acknowledged in spite of the challenges of Modern Movement ideology.

The institutionalising of the craft ideal in England was largely due to the persistent efforts of The Art Workers' Guild, an organisation which then, as now, refused to seek publicity. The initial impetus for the formation of the Guild (in 1884) came from a group of young architects who were working in Norman Shaw's thriving and prestigious office – the most significant among them, in this context, being W.R. Lethaby (1857–1931). Frustrated with the complacency of the Royal Academy and the commercialism of the Royal Institute of British Architects, they aimed to bring together 'craftsmen in architecture, painting, sculpture and the kindred arts', all those artists, in fact, 'who were neither oil painters . . . nor surveyors'. They were joined by a group of artists, architects and designers who called themselves the 'Fifteen', and who included Lewis Day (a successful designer of stained glass, wallpaper and textiles), and Walter Crane, a painter and illustrator, and Socialist admirer of William Morris. Members of both groups, therefore, had specific interests to pursue which, they felt, were not acknowledged by the powerful professional organisations. Their aim in the formation of the Guild was to provide a viable alternative association which would promote both their interests and their ideals, which meant, inevitably, that there was some initial conflict regarding the role and purpose of the Guild. Some of the early members were infuriated by the Guild's decision to avoid publicity and public recognition: the idea of an illustrated year book was rejected, the suggestion that the *Studio* might devote a whole issue to Guildsmen's work was considered 'absolutely repugnant', and exhibitions were out of the question.

The Arts and Crafts Exhibition Society, therefore, was founded to circumvent these difficulties, Walter Crane (the Society's first president) and W.A.S. Benson being among its most active initiators. The Society's early exhibitions were a great success, and they contributed to the growing reputation of British craftsmanship abroad. They were involved in the Turin Exhibition of 1902, the St Louis Exhibition of 1904, and were only prevented from exhibiting in Paris by the outbreak of the First World War. (This exhibition finally took place in 1925 with an exuberance which mocked the by then somewhat tarnished image of British craftsmanship.) In its early years the Society provided a platform for the display of a whole range of craft skills, demonstrating the versatility and the commitment of these latter-day art workers.

Both the Art Workers' Guild and the Arts and Crafts Exhibition Society considered themselves custodians of 'taste', or in their terms, of 'morality' in design, and towards the end of the century a new style (or 'strange decorative disease', as Walter Crane preferred to call it) appeared which offended all their ideals of truth and fitness – *art nouveau*. *Art nouveau* was associated with the wilder excesses of continental design, and a gift of seemingly contaminated furniture to the V&A in 1900 prompted angry letters to *The Times*:

This work is neither right in principle nor does it evince a proper regard for the materials employed. As cabinet-makers' work it is badly executed. It represents only a trick of design which developed from debased forms, and has prejudicially affected the design of furniture and buildings in neighbouring countries.

Earlier, in 1896, some work submitted to the Arts and Crafts Exhibition Society by a group of young Scottish designers had prompted a similar reaction, for it was obvious that the disease had already spread to British shores. The condemnation was instantaneous; like the judges in *Til Eulenspiegel*, the orthodox were determined to crush this frivolity. The 'spook style', as it was called, was both contagious and corrupting, and was never to appear in any Arts and Crafts approved context.

These alarming exhibits were by Charles Rennie Mackintosh (1868–1928) and his colleagues in Glasgow. Fortunately for the morale of the group Mackintosh had just won the competition for the design of new premises for the Glasgow School of Art and their genius was acknowledged, even in these early years, by Gleeson White, then editor of *Studio*. He published appreciative articles about their work, and this gained them acclaim on the continent, especially in Munich and Vienna, where Mackintosh and his wife were always acclaimed. Mackintosh is difficult to categorise within the context of the Arts and Crafts, although his work as an architect–designer achieves that total harmony that all Arts and Crafts architects aspired to. His architecture is always related to the Scottish tradition of building; at the same time, however, its spatial qualities make it unique, and his furniture was designed to complement the space, rather than to create a cosy or medievalising interior. To the British, however, this was not 'craft' furniture. The white paint, the stencilled flower motifs in pastel colours, and the strange exaggerated forms seemed to deny all the values they had fought for, and to some its success on the continent made it all the more suspect.

Mackintosh rarely wrote or spoke formally about his ideas and his work. He did give one lecture, however, in 1893, which attempted to define his architectural creed:

Architecture is the world of art and as it is everything visible and invisible that makes the world, so it is all the arts and crafts and industries that make architecture . . . architecture is the synthesis of the fine arts, the commune of all the crafts.

(Quoted from Robert Macleod, *Charles Rennie Mackintosh*, 1968, p. 33)

Furniture designed by Charles Rennie Mackintosh in the hall of Hill House, Helensburgh.

Now, as Robert Macleod discovered, it was W.R. Lethaby who was speaking here, not Mackintosh, and the substance (as well as the words) of this one lecture are plagiarised from Lethaby's book *Architecture, Mysticism and Myth* (1892).

Mackintosh and Lethaby both challenged nineteenth-century craft orthodoxies, Mackintosh with his work and Lethaby with his ideas. Lethaby, who was born in 1857, joined Norman Shaw's office in 1879; there he met Morris and Philip Webb, and as well as working on architectural

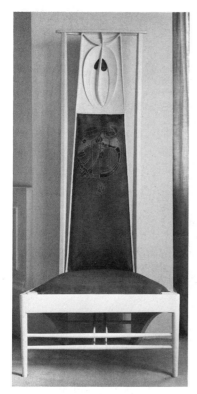

Chair by Charles Rennie Mackintosh (1902).

Burr-oak writing cabinet by Sidney Barnsley (early 1900s).

commissions, he also helped to initiate the Art Workers' Guild and the Arts and Crafts Exhibition Society. In 1890 (after he had set up an independent architectural practice) he founded a short-lived firm, Kenton & Co., together with a group of young architects, including Ernest Gimson (1864–1919) and Sidney Barnsley (1865–1926). Gimson and the Barnsley brothers were to become distinguished craft furniture makers and designers; working in the Cotswolds (and, unlike Ashbee, managing to remain financially solvent), they produced designs from English woods, deceptively simple 'cottage' furniture as well as prestige pieces with elaborate inlays. Describing Gimson's work, Lethaby wrote:

> every piece was thought definitely for particular woods and for clearly understood ways of workmanship, and the supervision was so thorough and so constant that the design was changed in the process of making as the materials and working might suggest.

We are now far removed from the 'paper designers' of the Schools of Design, and by this time most of the Art Schools were staffed by practising craftsmen, a development that could be credited to the Art Workers' Guild, that covert but powerful organisation. From the 1890s Guild members began to permeate the art schools, and design training was transformed by ideals of creativity, experiment, and workmanship. In 1896, what was then the

Oak gate-leg table by Sidney Barnsley (c.1894–5).

London County Council decided to establish a new school – the LCC
Central School of Arts and Crafts, and Lethaby was appointed joint principal.
Most of his staff were recruited from the Guild, and 'admission to the school
[was] only extended to those actually engaged in one or other of the crafts'.
Fine art, therefore, was not taught there, craft involved practical experience,
and Lethaby made valiant (but vain) efforts to abolish the examination
system. The School's most prestigious achievements in the years leading up
to the First World War were, interestingly enough, in typography and
printing. Edward Johnston, for example, went there to train as a calligrapher,
and then designed London Transport's (now familiar and threatened) type-
face; he also taught several distinguished typographers, including Eric Gill,
and so influenced the development of commercial typography.

   Just when it seemed that the craft ideal had been successfully consolidated,
some of its protagonists began to recant. Ashbee, lamenting the failure of his
own enterprise, declared that the craft movement had created a 'narrow and
tiresome little aristocracy working with great skill for the very rich'. These

thoughts were confined to his journal, but Lethaby's apostasy was more public. In a series of lectures in 1909 and 1910, and in his book on *Architecture* (1911) for the popular Home University Library series, he promoted the 'scientific method' as a practical basis for design in the twentieth century. Speaking to the Royal Institute of British Architects in 1910, for example, he declared:

What I do urge, in the simplest and plainest words, is concentration on practical, experimental and scientific education . . . the living stem of building design can only be found by following the scientific method.

In the chapter on 'The modern position in architecture' he maintained that 'architects should be trained as engineers are trained', and went on to describe his own education as 'wasteful':

It is absurd that the writer should have been allowed to study cathedrals from Quimper to Constantinople; it would have been far better to have an equivalent knowledge of concrete construction.

When he declared that houses should be designed to be as efficient as ships or bicycles he seems to be anticipating Le Corbusier. Lethaby's pre-war proto-modernism, however, drew directly on nineteenth-century definitions of functionalism, not the ideal of workmanship which inspired the craft revival, but the evolutionary theories that so preoccupied Semper. Lethaby came to believe that design inevitably reflects rather than imposes cultural values, and that his contemporaries were misguided in ignoring the advances of science and technology.

   The First World War destroyed any hopes he had for science and technology, however: 'Seeking isolated Truth has turned into Science', he wrote in one of his private note-books, 'which means bombing, vivisection and political economy – orthodox political economy is a creed – the theology of mammon.' This pessimism, however, like his promotion of science-based methodologies in design, was short-lived. In 1915 Lethaby had agreed to become one of the founder members of the Design and Industries Association, formed in order to 'promote a more intelligent demand amongst the public for what is best and soundest in design', as well as the Semperian idea that 'many machine processes tend to certain qualities of their own'. The problems of the Design and Industries Association and the fate of the crafts are discussed in the next volume. By 1920 mechanisation and consumerism were taking command as the whole basis of society was being transformed, but the spirit of reconstruction survived to motivate a new generation of idealists.

The bardic Gorsedd outside Caernarfon Castle, at the Eisteddfod of 1893.

9 The Eisteddfod

WILLIAM PRICE

One of the few Welsh words to have entered the vocabulary of international English is eisteddfod (pronounced ais-teth´-vod). Its root is 'eistedd', to sit, and literally it means a session. In the sixteenth century the word was used for law-courts – in William Salesbury's translation of the Gospels the Sanhedrin which tried Christ is termed an 'Eistedvot' – but by the eighteenth century its meaning had become restricted to gatherings of poets and musicians.

The concept of the Welsh eisteddfod includes competition, with prizes awarded for poetry, prose, drama, music, and arts and crafts. An eisteddfod may be held by a chapel or school, by a village or area, or nationally. The best-known is the peripatetic National Eisteddfod, established in its present form in the 1860s. A journalist once summed it up as

the most confused institution in a confused nation. Half circus and half concert, it has garnishings from chapel vestry, brains trust, school prize day, literary luncheon, sale of work and cocktail bar without cocktails.

The origins of the eisteddfod are lost in antiquity. Imaginative nineteenth-century minds dreamt of eisteddfodau (plural) millennia before Christ, perhaps from the time of Noah's grandson, Gomer, commonly believed to be the first Welshman. The first reliable record of a competitive festival on the lines of the eisteddfod, although not known by that name, is in *Brut y Tywysogion* (The Chronicle of the Princes) for 1176:

The Lord Rhys held a great festival at the castle of Cardigan, wherein he appointed two sorts of contention, one between the bards and poets, and the other between the harpers, fiddlers, pipers, and various performers of instrumental music, and he assigned two chairs for the victors in the contentions, and these he enriched with vast gifts . . . And that festival was proclaimed a year before it was held throughout Wales and England and Scotland and Ireland and many other countries.

In about 1450 an eisteddfod at Carmarthen was noteworthy for the acceptance of the Twenty-four Metres of poetry proposed by Dafydd ap Edmwnd, while the persistence of the old tradition of the bardic guild, in verse and music, was revealed at two eisteddfodau held at Caerwys in

Flintshire in 1523 and 1567. These were occasions for maintaining standards rather than meetings for entertaining the public. During the seventeenth and eighteenth centuries the eisteddfod declined in importance and dignity in new social conditions. Such eisteddfodau as were held tended to be impromptu contests between bards in taverns, the winning verses being printed, by the eighteenth century, in almanacs. Standards and attendances were low, and beer was the usual prize for the winning poet, but at least the tradition of making poetry was maintained, in the face of the scorn of the intelligentsia: 'our contemptible set of smatterers in *barddoniaeth* [poetry] that make a figure in our Welsh almanacs'.

In 1789 the Gwyneddigion, a society of London Welshmen, became involved in the organisation of eisteddfodau in Wales. Some order was imposed on the informality of the bardic contests, notably the requirement that a year's notice should be given of the subjects for competition. Several reformed eisteddfodau were held in the 1790s in North Wales. A few years later a group of Anglican clergymen in South and Mid Wales began to take an interest in the eisteddfod tradition. They were motivated primarily by genuine concern for Welsh literary customs, although perhaps they also saw the eisteddfod as a weapon for checking the rapid growth of Protestant Nonconformity.

In 1819 the first of ten provincial eisteddfodau, the 'Cambrian Olympics', took place at Carmarthen under the patronage of the scholarly English Bishop of St Davids, Thomas Burgess. Here the first link was formed between the ancient eisteddfod and the new 'Gorsedd [gor'-seth] of Bards of the Isle of Britain'. The gorsedd was the creation of a radical and romantic Glamorgan stonemason, Edward Williams, better known by his bardic title of Iolo Morganwg. Iolo's boundless imagination and genuine poetic gifts, fortified by a daily dose of laudanum, produced a new interpretation of Welsh history and a remarkable 'druidic' pageantry, first revealed on Primrose Hill (Bryn y Briallu) in London on 21 June 1792.

Iolo, who claimed to be one of the last in an arcane succession of Glamorgan druids, felt that it was high time for South Wales to reclaim leadership in Welsh cultural life and it seems that his first intention was to replace the eisteddfod with the gorsedd. This was not to be. At the Carmarthen Eisteddfod Iolo invested Bishop Burgess and others as members of the druidic order in the gorsedd, a cultural élite. Without Burgess the eisteddfod would not have developed as it did and the gorsedd might have disappeared, a transitory phenomenon of the age of 'druidomania'.

The events at Carmarthen in 1819 set the pattern for subsequent eisteddfodau, meetings of poets and musicians, especially harpists and *penillion* singers weaving contrapuntal harmonies to the harp. In 1832 Princess Victoria and her mother almost attended the eisteddfod at Beaumaris, Anglesey, until torrential rainfall kept them indoors in the nearby mansion. Local and regional eisteddfodau flourished in early-Victorian Wales, notably between 1834 and 1853 at Abergavenny in Gwent under the control of Lady Llanover, a formidable supporter of things Welsh, known by the title of Gwenynen Gwent, the Honey Bee of Gwent. As yet the support of the upper classes – 'nobility, rank and fashion' – was important, certainly until the Methodists changed attitudes and began to participate in eisteddfodau. As late as 1851, however, a leading Methodist could affirm that eisteddfodau were unquestionably 'an evil and hence it is that the Welsh Calvinistic Methodists as a body refuses to countenance and support them'.

Iolo Morganwg died in 1826, but his druidic fantasies lived on, with the gorsedd becoming a formal part of the 'Powys Provincial Eisteddfod' at Llangollen in Denbighshire in 1858. The provision of cheap excursion trains on the growing railway network helped to make it a national event. This chaotic gathering, significantly free of gentry patronage, was organised by an Anglican clergyman of Tractarian outlook, and an uncritical disciple of Iolo, the Revd John Williams, known as Ab Ithel, who had taken the trouble to travel to the Rocking Stone at Pontypridd in Glamorgan for initiation as a druid by Iolo's successor, Myfyr Morganwg. It was a curious additional ordination for one who was already a priest in the Established Church. Ab Ithel assumed druidic dress at the Eisteddfod, where the celebrated Dr William Price, a pioneer of cremation, appeared in fox-skin cap, a sort of Cambrian Davy Crockett, with a sword at his side, while Myfyr Morganwg felt it appropriate to wear an egg on a piece of string around his neck.

A prize for 'an Essay on the Discovery of America in the 12th century by Prince Madoc ap Owen' ought to have been awarded to the distinguished scholar Thomas Stephens of Merthyr, but it was felt that he should not be honoured on the grounds that he had shown too clearly that Madoc had *not* actually discovered America. Several awards found their way to Ab Ithel's relations, and the promoters seem to have made a large profit from the Eisteddfod. But the shambles, by some strange druidic providence, saved the gorsedd from extinction.

Sober men, unhappy at the condition of the eisteddfod before 1858, aghast at the events at Llangollen, and unwilling to read yet more condescending

The Eisteddfod at Rhuddlan Castle, 1850.

and flippant descriptions of eisteddfodau in the London press, especially *The Times* (then under the editorship of J.T. Delane, who was furiously anti-Welsh) and *The Daily Telegraph*, which saw the Llangollen Eisteddfod as 'a national debauch of sentiment', were moved to reform the eisteddfod. Their recommendations received a general welcome at the Denbigh Eisteddfod in 1860. Henceforward the 'National Eisteddfod' would alternate between North and South Wales. It would be governed by a Council, and the prize-winning entries would be published. It would also, although this was not an actual recommendation, come under the control of Nonconformist Liberals, rather than gentry or parsons. The Temperance Movement became involved too, so that G.K. Chesterton could much later stoop to write in *Wine and Water*:

> And you can't get wine at a P.S.A., or chapel, or Eisteddfod,
> For the Curse of Water has come again because of the wrath of God.

Annual meetings took place until that at Ruthin in 1868, when the Eisteddfod Council ran out of money. Eisteddfodau under local control did continue in North Wales, although by 1871 one distinguished supporter wrote of the eisteddfod as an institution of the past, which had not received the backing it deserved but of which future generations would speak well.

In 1880, however, the eisteddfod was placed on a surer foundation with the establishment of the National Eisteddfod Association. Hugh Owen and his collaborators saw the reformed eisteddfod as an educational venture, 'a wholesome recreation to the people', and 'the upholder of public virtue as well as the promoter of literature and the arts'. These respectable Victorians sought to exclude all that was 'low, vulgar, or in bad taste' from the eisteddfod and to promote 'propriety, decorum and even dignity'.

Thereafter the National Eisteddfod has been held annually, except in 1914 and 1940 (when the BBC put on a radio Eisteddfod). Occasionally the frontier was crossed for meetings, at Birkenhead and Liverpool (regarded as being in North Wales) and London ('according to ancient and recognised Bardic Statutes London forms part of Gwent and Morgannwg'). But following financial loss at Liverpool in 1929 the event has been held always in Wales, perhaps a telling indication of the gradual loss of distinctive Welsh identity among the diaspora. Possibly, too, the Welsh-speakers of, say, Liverpool would prefer to travel back to the homeland for the festival, after 1918 held always in the first week of August, than simply to cross the Mersey to Birkenhead. Who can blame them?

By 1899 the presence of representatives of other Celtic countries was a recognised part of the event. The visitors could witness dignified and elaborate ceremonial by the end of the nineteenth century. Sir Hubert von Herkomer, RA, designed robes for the gorsedd, and the rites became established for honouring the two chief bards of the week – the chaired bard and the crowned bard. A land of strong Protestant Nonconformity found in the gorsedd the ceremonial which it denied itself in its religious gatherings. The robes denoting different orders within the gorsedd – green for ovates, blue for bards, musicians, and literati, and white for druids, together with the insignia – the sword of peace, the drinking horn, the gift of flowers, the

A Breton delegate addresses the Gorsedd at Cardiff, c.1899.

gorsedd banner, and the Archdruid's crown, ring, breastplate, and sceptre, and the gorsedd stone circle may be 'pseudo-antique bric-à-brac' in the words of an Anglican Bishop in the 1950s, but they have by now acquired their own historical significance.

Throughout the nineteenth century the eisteddfod faced some criticism for an excessive use of the English language in its proceedings. The language of the Empire appealed to many of the Anglicised middle-class organisers of these events. English was the language of progress, and it was hoped that by means of education the Welsh would be able to 'take their proper part in the varied work of that great empire, to which, happily for them, they belong'. The Welsh language was often regarded as one which isolated its speakers from 'general civilisation' and which perpetuated prejudices which were 'the children of ignorance'. Eventually, as the proportion of the population able to speak Welsh became considerably smaller, the tide began to turn, the gorsedd resolving in 1908 that all its ceremonies would be conducted in Welsh.

To some extent the stress on music concealed the linguistic problems, and the high place given to singing spread from the National Eisteddfod to lesser eisteddfodau. The vogue for choral music was reflected in the bestowing of Handel and Haydn as first names. *Messiah* and *The Creation* were sung, to tonic sol-fa notation, at eisteddfodau all over the Principality and beyond. 'The Land of Song' was drowned in music, loud music, for it was calculated that the Welsh sang three times as loudly as the English.

Hugh Owen attempted to broaden the range of the National Eisteddfod by introducing a 'Social Science Section', for the discussion in English of issues of the day – housing, food, education, morals – but this sensible venture lasted only between 1862 and 1868. Utilitarianism did not have the appeal of druidism. Nonetheless one of the leading nineteenth-century poets, Talhaiarn, was not alone in his attitude to poetry:

Science is the favourite child of civilization. Poetry gives pleasure to dreamy indolence, but science for practical usefulness beats it hollow . . . I do not wish to depreciate the gentle art, but science should have the first place, and poetry may take the second if it chooses.

There were strong attacks on the eisteddfod and especially on the gorsedd throughout the second half of the nineteenth century and in due course by some academics in the new University of Wales, established in 1893. Sir John Morris-Jones, Professor of Welsh at Bangor, a fine poet and a popular adjudicator at the National Eisteddfod, considered that Iolo Morganwg had been duped into thinking that the gorsedd was ancient. It was later that the truth emerged that Iolo had been the creator of this bizarre farce, 'founded on fiction and deceit'. Gorsedd and eisteddfod survived, although it may be that standards were sometimes low, those of 'an amateur peasant festival', where mediocrity was often exalted.

H.V. Morton described the 1931 Eisteddfod at Bangor sympathetically in his *In Search of Wales*. He knew of no other country where a national competitive festival brought together academic and illiterate, cleric and miner:

This meeting of a nation on a purely mental and artistic occasion is surely an outstanding characteristic of life in Wales. Amateurism in sport is one of England's treasured characteristics; amateurism in art is that of Wales . . . The Eisteddfod is the Voice of Wales.

The Eisteddfod was held on the shores of the Menai Strait where 'an enormous wooden pavilion' had been erected. He was impressed by the enormous crowd:

Men boast that it holds ten thousand people, which is also said to be the capacity of the Albert Hall in London . . . I have seen crowds as big as this Welsh crowd whipped up into a dervish frenzy about sport; but never have I seen a crowd which represents all the lights and shades of an entire nation gathered together to sing, to play musical instruments and to recite verse.

The crowned bard at the Bangor Eisteddfod of 1931 was the Revd Albert Evans-Jones, a man of immense dignity universally known by his bardic name of Cynan, and later knighted. He led the movement for the reform of the eisteddfod in the dismal 1930s. A problem of long standing was the lack of a central authority over eisteddfod and gorsedd. The Eisteddfod Council controlled the eisteddfod, the gorsedd was a distinct and sometimes uncooperative body and local committees of varying degrees of competence oversaw much of the preparation for any eisteddfod. Cynan succeeded in establishing from 1937 a new Council of the National Eisteddfod, with Mr Lloyd George as its first President. In 1952 the Council evolved into a Court, which remains now the governing body of the National Eisteddfod. Since 1966 the eisteddfod has been under royal patronage, the Royal National Eisteddfod of Wales, including Elizabeth of Windsor and Philip Meirionydd as members of the gorsedd.

During the twentieth century the range of activities of the National Eisteddfod has broadened to include competitions in the visual arts, crafts, and theatre. Following protests by leading Welsh-speaking bards in 1937 an 'all-Welsh rule' had emerged by the early 1950s. This was to include the libretti of all choral works. Some complaints at the emergence of a 'linguistic fortress' from the eighty per cent of the population of Wales who do not speak Welsh have been inevitable, as has the withholding of financial assistance by a few local authorities in Anglicised areas.

By the 1980s the attendance at the National Eisteddfod during the week may reach 150,000, not all Welsh-speaking, and thousands more watch competitions and ceremonies on television. 'This nomadic metropolis' is for a week the capital of Welsh Wales, 'an amalgam made up of a competitive meeting, a national pageant and a great reunion'. The enormous pavilion, in which ceremonies and competitions take place, is surrounded by smaller pavilions for drama, verse-making, and like endeavours, while small booths are rented by all manner of organisations and commercial enterprises. A lively 'fringe', in part politically nationalist, grows larger year by year.

The gorsedd, from time to time still ridiculed as a fake and fraud, its bardic druids derided as old men in nightshirts, is now accounted by all to be Iolo's creation; but almost 200 years have made it a venerable and respectable institution in its own right, whose purpose is first and foremost to safeguard the Welsh language and to promote Welsh culture.

Regional, town, and village eisteddfodau flourish throughout Wales, using English as their language where Welsh is not commonly spoken. Exiles hold eisteddfodau throughout the world, from Wigan to Wilkes-Barre, from Paris to Patagonia. Another noted annual eisteddfod, which should not be confused with the National Eisteddfod, is the Llangollen International Musical Eisteddfod, founded in 1947 as a contribution towards reconciling the post-war nations.

Some years ago a Welsh historian likened the Welsh people to two goats who, according to a radio report, had eaten their labels while in transit on the railway between South and North Wales, so that they were stranded at Aberystwyth Station, no one knowing whence they had come or whither they should be going. The picture might be applied to the Welsh-speaking Welsh themselves, except during the National Eisteddfod, when for a week the universe speaks Welsh.

Dante Gabriel Rossetti, The Bower Meadow *(1871–2)*.

10 Music

MICHAEL KENNEDY

Introduction

The half-century from 1850 to 1900 was one of the richest periods in European musical history. It opened with the twilight of Schumann's career before he relapsed into madness. Berlioz was about to compose *L'Enfance du Christ* and *Les Troyens*, Liszt his *Faust Symphony* and several of his symphonic-poems. Between the years 1860 and 1890 the world's store of artistic masterpieces was enriched by Wagner's *Der Ring des Nibelungen, Die Meistersinger von Nürnberg* and *Parsifal*, the symphonies, concertos, chamber music and songs of Brahms, the symphonies of Bruckner, all the operas of Verdi from *Rigoletto* to *Falstaff*, the operas, symphonic-poems and chamber music of Smetana, the symphonies, ballets, concertos and operas of Tchaikovsky and the symphonies, operas, concertos and chamber music of Dvořák. The operas *Hérodiade* and *Manon* of Massenet appeared in the 1880s. Offenbach's operas and operettas spanned the years from 1860 to 1880. Between 1880 and 1900 Strauss wrote his series of tone-poems from *Macbeth* to *Ein Heldenleben*, Mahler composed his first four symphonies. In Russia there was not only Tchaikovsky but Rimsky-Korsakov; in France Saint-Saëns, Franck, D'Indy and Debussy, whose *Nocturnes* were written between 1897 and 1899. Vienna was not only the city of Brahms and Bruckner, but of Johann Strauss II. Wherever one looks, there was abundance; and today the names quoted above form the bedrock of the repertoire.

But the picture was very different in Britain. It still imported most of its music and musicians. Native talent among composers was thinly spread. From this half-century, only the operas of Sullivan and two works by Elgar composed as the nineteenth century was dying are heard at all regularly today. Why was this? The first obvious reason was the lack of a real musical background – few concert-halls, hardly any professional orchestras, no operatic tradition of any substance, poor educational facilities, and a general feeling among the populace that music was of little real importance. In such soil it is unlikely that an exotic bloom will grow, though there is no

accounting for maverick genius whenever and wherever it arises. Hence
Elgar. Hence, also, Purcell in the seventeenth century, although he was no
isolated figure.

If English music in the eighteenth century was dominated by Handel, the
flame of native composition was by no means extinguished if we consider
John Stanley and John Hebden (both of whom wrote excellent concertos),
Maurice Greene, William Croft, Thomas Arne and William Boyce. Yet if one
were asked to name the outstanding musical events in eighteenth-century
Britain, the answer would be the advent of Handel, the visits of Haydn, the
arrival of Clementi and J.C. Bach – and the composition of *The Beggar's
Opera*. In the early years of the nineteenth century, imported musicians were
all the rage – Rossini, Weber, and finally Mendelssohn. If the man in the
street believed that 'serious music' was something that came from across the
Channel, he could hardly be blamed. The British composer didn't stand a
chance unless he had genius to match his foreign rivals – and none of them
had, however worthy some of their efforts may have been.

But if the opera house and the symphony concert were regarded as exotica,
the enthusiasm for choral singing still provided the chief musical experience
for most of the populace. This developed in the Nonconformist chapels of
Wales and the north of England during the eighteenth century and was given
extra impetus by the astonishing popularity of Handel's *Messiah*. In Leeds in
1768 there were eighteen consecutive performances of this oratorio and
twenty years later Charles Dibdin remarked on 'the facility with which the
common people join together throughout the greatest part of Yorkshire and
Lancashire in every species of choral music'. From this 'facility' grew the
great choral festivals, usually held to aid a charity such as a hospital or, in
the case of the Three Choirs Festivals at Hereford, Worcester and
Gloucester, for the widows and orphans of the clergy. No one knows exactly
when the Three Choirs Festival started (about 1717). During the nineteenth
century, the Festival's favourite composer was Mendelssohn – *Elijah*, for
example, was performed in every year except two between 1847 and 1930.

The Manchester Festivals in the early years of the nineteenth century
attracted celebrities as illustrious as the mezzo-soprano Maria Malibran (who
died during one of them). Birmingham's triennial Festival dated from 1768
but its great period began in 1834 when it displaced the festival at York. It
was there, in 1846, that *Elijah* was first performed and thereafter every major
new choral work was performed at a Birmingham Festival. Leeds did not
begin its Festival until 1858, the year in which the Town Hall was opened.
Sixteen years elapsed before the next. Only after 1880 was the triennial
pattern established which lasted until 1970. Sheffield and Bristol also had big
choral festivals, as did North Staffordshire at Hanley. The Norwich Festival
was another major triennial affair. To feed these events there was what must
have seemed a limitless supply of oratorios and sacred and secular cantatas,
most of them now forgotten. If Handel, Mendelssohn, Spohr for a time, and
eventually, Bach were the mainstay of the repertoire, specially-composed
works came too from Gounod, Saint-Saëns and Dvořák and, of course,
Beethoven's Choral Symphony, Brahms's *Requiem* and Verdi's *Requiem* were
seized upon. Of the large contribution to the 'oratorio market' by British

composers, little now survives. At last, however, a really great work emerged, Elgar's *The Dream of Gerontius* – but that is to anticipate the end of this survey.

Walmisley and Wesley

In 1847, three years before the half-way mark in the nineteenth century and the thirteenth year of Queen Victoria's reign, Britain's musical hero died. He was not British. He was Felix Mendelssohn. He had been a favourite of Victoria and Prince Albert and he had found inspiration for his music in the British Isles – the *Hebrides* Overture and the *Scottish* Symphony, for example. The British public regarded *Messiah* and *Elijah* as British oratorios. What need had they for native composers, when they could 'adopt' German composers of such quality?

In 1848 another great composer visited Britain, during the last months of what remained to him of his short life. But Chopin was regarded as a pianist, and there were plenty in Britain who could not understand why so much fuss was made of him in Paris. We had our own composers, anyway. There was Michael Balfe (1808–70), from Ireland. His opera *The Bohemian Girl* was a big success in 1843. And, of course, there was Henry Bishop (1786–1855). He was not composing much by this time, but he had been knighted in 1842 and in 1848 was appointed Professor of Music at Oxford University, not at this point a post of any worthwhile significance. Balfe's new opera, *The Maid of Honour*, was produced at the Theatre Royal, Drury Lane, in December 1847, conducted, unlikely as it may seem, by Hector Berlioz, who had been engaged by the colourful conductor–impresario Louis Jullien (1812–60) to conduct a two-month season of opera. The season ended in bankruptcy and Berlioz was never paid, but two concerts of his own music in London won him a critical acclaim denied him in Paris.

In the audience for the Berlioz concerts was a British composer who, in 1836 at the age of twenty, had caused Mendelssohn to say of him: 'If he does not become a very great musician, it is not God's will but his own.' Were there many more like him, Schumann wrote in the *Neue Zeitschrift für Musik*, 'all fears for the future progress of our art would be silenced'. The object of this fulsome praise was William Sterndale Bennett (1816–75), whose teenage prowess as pianist and composer had set the London musical scene alight. His F minor Piano Concerto (No. 4), still played today, shows how much he had learned from his models and how well he could deploy it. Although it would be easy, and in some cases not inaccurate, to describe Sterndale Bennett's music as 'Schumann-and-water', his youthful orchestral works are still worth hearing. His concertos are in the classical spirit but are not rigid in structure, though the personality of the composer, shy and fastidious, emerges strongly. When he settled down in England after a spell in Leipzig, the need to earn his living caused him to rely mainly on teaching and playing. Gradually, conducting and administrative posts were added: conductor of the Philharmonic Society from 1856, professor of music at Cambridge University also from 1856, principal of the Royal Academy of

Music from 1866. A knighthood followed in 1871. But what happened to Schumann's saviour of the art of music? An overture and a symphony, two festival cantatas, *The May Queen* and *The Woman of Samaria*, and a few songs and anthems were all that he wrote after about 1850. Discouragement seems to have been the main reason for the snuffing out of this talent: he soon discovered that his fellow-countrymen preferred Mendelssohn and Schumann to Sterndale Bennett.

Another English *Wunderkind*, this time of the organ-loft, was in 1850 drinking himself to an early grave while holding the Cambridge Professorship to which Sterndale Bennett succeeded. Thomas Attwood Walmisley (1814–56) had been taught composition by his godfather, Thomas Attwood, who had been a pupil of Mozart. At the age of nineteen he took his Mus.B at Cambridge and also studied literature and mathematics. Three years later, still an undergraduate, he was appointed to the chair of music, which was virtually a sinecure and held to be of no account. Walmisley was the first occupant of the chair to have an MA degree and thus to be permitted into the Senate House to present candidates for music degrees. Without fee, he gave regular lectures illustrated by music examples, an innovation. In one lecture he forecast the supremacy of the music of J.S. Bach, still scarcely more than a name to most English musicians. Single-handed and overworked, he gave the faculty of music some standing in the University and, when he died, the chair was for the first time the object of an open election. In his church music, Walmisley began to give a new sense of purpose to the cathedral tradition (and reinforced his creative efforts by conducting performances of Bach). In his youth he wrote some chamber music, including three string quartets, and a symphony. Most of his organ compositions are lost, but his Evening Service in D minor survives as his abiding memorial.

Walmisley notwithstanding, the outstanding figure in English music in 1850 was Samuel Sebastian Wesley (1810–76), the illegitimate son of the composer and organist Samuel Wesley. From the age of sixteen, in 1826, he held a succession of posts as church or cathedral organist; his abrasive manner, outspoken criticisms of the clergy and of the organisation and standards of church music, and his paranoid attitude to rivals and to authority earned him a poor reputation. Yet so magnificent was his playing and so fine his compositions that the ecclesiastical authorities often ignored (for as long as they could) his eccentric behaviour, such as trying to bribe reviewers. In 1849 he resigned after seven fruitful years at Leeds Parish Church, where the choir was of an unusually high standard. Most cathedral choirs at this date were incompetent, largely as a result of the poor opinion of church music prevalent among the authorities.

After Leeds, Wesley spent fifteen years as organist of Winchester Cathedral. He was in effect dismissed in 1865 because he too frequently sent a deputy as organist while he travelled to conduct at festivals or edited a hymn-book or taught at the Royal Academy of Music. His last eleven years were spent at Gloucester Cathedral, where he found the dean and chapter no more co-operative than any other. He conducted the Three Choirs Festivals of 1865, 1868, 1871 and 1874, at the third of them introducing Bach's *St Matthew Passion* to the Festival. On several occasions he refused a knighthood, but two years before he died he was granted a Civil List pension. His anthems 'Blessed be the God and Father' and 'Let us Lift up our Heart' are among the glories of English church music. He was influenced by Spohr and Mendelssohn, but some of his work has a grandeur worthy of Bach and his Morning and Evening Service in E (composed 1841–4) will be sung for as long as the cathedrals stand for which it was composed.

The importance of Wesley's Service in E lay in its imaginative treatment of familiar texts. The setting was lengthy and fully worked out, but in shorter texts, such as the *Te Deum*, he was less successful. With anthems, however, he felt at liberty to vary the texts, or to mix Bible and Prayer Book, to suit the promptings of his invention. Thus some isolated passages of burning sincerity may be compared with the Tudor masters. His use of a small number of voices in full harmony, deriving from Mozart, led to some of his most memorable effects. It must still be said, however, that many passages in his works are conventional and uninspired, and these are nearly always those where the text has not prompted his imagination to wilder flights of fancy.

Not content with having suffocated Sterndale Bennett's talent on his return from Germany, the English musical establishment (for want of a better word) drove out another composer whose work had won acclaim in Germany. This was the shadowy figure of Henry Hugo Pierson (or Pearson, as he was born, 1815–73). After Cambridge, he spent five years abroad from 1839 to 1844 where he caught Schumann's attention, as Sterndale Bennett had done. In 1844 he was appointed Reid Professor of Music at Edinburgh, being chosen in preference to Bennett and S.S. Wesley, but eight months was enough and he returned to Germany where his opera *Leila* was a success and his incidental music to Part 2 of Goethe's *Faust* had a vogue. For some reason, he still hankered after success in his native country and wrote an oratorio, *Jerusalem*, for the 1852 Norwich Festival. This was savaged by the London critics, led by J.W. Davison of *The Times*, principally because it belonged to the 'aesthetic' Schumann movement. Pierson returned to Germany, where his standing as a composer of *Lieder* was high. He settled in Stuttgart, where Hubert Parry studied with him in 1867. Not, apparently, having learned his lesson, he wrote another Norwich oratorio in 1869, only to have it meet a similar fate to *Jerusalem*. His songs and part-songs, of which there are many, are worth exploration today, while his tone-poem *Macbeth* (1859) and the *Faust* music have been compared with Berlioz in their melodic and harmonic unexpectedness.

Operas and concerts

One can scarcely be surprised by the paucity of orchestral and chamber compositions by British composers at the mid-century, since opportunities for the performance of such works were almost non-existent. There will be no supply if there is neither demand nor outlet. Britain in 1850 had no regular professional orchestra. Today, when London supports more symphony orchestras than any other capital in the world, it is difficult to realise that less than 150 years ago it had an ad hoc assembly of players who performed for the opera at Covent Garden and other theatres and also probably made up the majority of the orchestra which played for the Philharmonic Society – and nothing else. Outside London, there was an orchestra in Manchester which played for the Gentlemen's Concerts but this had declined in standard and in 1850 the committee which ran the concerts had appointed a new conductor, the German pianist Charles Hallé (1819–95), who had settled in the city after fleeing from Paris in 1848. Not until 1858 did Hallé form his own orchestra and launch the series of concerts which bears his name to this day.

Matters began to improve generally from about 1850. The way was led by a showman with a touch of genius and several touches of the charlatan. He was Louis Jullien (to pick but one of his thirty-six Christian names) whose promenade concerts, performed throughout the country, attracted large audiences to listen to extracts from Beethoven – which he conducted with a jewelled baton handed to him on a silver salver – juxtaposed with quadrilles and items like 'a comic polka – Three Blind Mice'. He attracted the best players for his orchestra. It might have been thought that the Great Exhibition of 1851 would be a boost to artistic enterprise, but its aims were

Fire at the Royal Opera House, Covent Garden, 5 March 1856.

Louis Jullien's orchestra at Drury Lane Theatre (1850), augmented by military bands including the French National Guards with their tambour-major, performing The Great Exhibition Quadrille.

commercial and the nearest it came to the arts was a display of musical instruments, the quality of which was judged by an international jury including Berlioz. A sign of life was the launching in 1852, by a music publisher, of the New Philharmonic Society, designed as a rival to the conservative and inert Philharmonic Society. The cream of London's free-lance players was skimmed for the orchestra and Berlioz was invited to conduct Beethoven's Ninth Symphony and extracts from his own *Romeo and Juliet* Symphony. His verdict on the orchestra, conveyed in a letter dated 30 April 1852, was that it 'at times surpassed all that I have ever heard in verve, delicacy and power'.

Rivalry spurred the old Philharmonic. Michael Costa (1808–84), a Neapolitan who settled in England in 1829 at the age of twenty-one, was conductor and director of the Italian Opera at the King's (later Her Majesty's) Theatre from 1832 to 1846, when he was appointed conductor of the Philharmonic Society and, from 1847, conductor of the Royal Italian Opera at Covent Garden. He was a stern disciplinarian and undoubtedly the orchestra played well for him, even if he had little hesitation in 'improving' the orchestration of Beethoven symphonies and other works. Faced with replacing him for the 1855 season, the Society, with uncharacteristic boldness, took the advice of its orchestral leader, Prosper Sainton, and invited Richard Wagner – at a fee of £200 for eight concerts. Wagner felt that he had to accept, since the offer conferred respectability on one who was still a 'wanted man' in Germany. But, he told Liszt, 'it is not my line of country'. The appointment provoked howls of rage from Davison of *The Times* and the other most influential London critic, Henry F. Chorley of *The Athenaeum*.

Wagner liked the orchestra and it liked him, in spite of his thorough rehearsals to purge the playing of Mendelssohn's fast tempi and lack of variation in dynamics. He conducted works by Haydn, Mozart, Spohr, Weber, Mendelssohn and Beethoven – all the symphonies except the First and Second, and the Violin Concerto – and Chopin's E minor Piano Concerto with Hallé as soloist. He also conducted the G minor Symphony of Cipriani Potter (1792–1871), then principal of the Royal Academy of Music, who in 1818 had had advice on his scores from a friendly Beethoven. Wagner described him as 'an elderly amiable contrapuntist' and preferred the only other English work he conducted, the overture *Chevy Chase* by George Macfarren (1813–87).

Of his own music, he conducted some extracts from *Lohengrin*, and (twice) the overture to *Tannhäuser*. The second *Tannhäuser* performance was at a concert attended by Queen Victoria and Prince Albert. The Queen, who received him in her box, thought the overture 'a wonderful composition, quite overpowering, so grand & in parts wild, striking and descriptive'. Chorley, however, found it

one of the most curious pieces of patchwork ever passed off by self-delusion for a complete and significant creation. The instrumentation is ill-balanced, ineffective, thin and noisy.

Another critic described the *Lohengrin* extracts as 'an incoherent mass of rubbish'.

Not surprisingly, Wagner came to compare his time in London with the experiences of 'one of the damned in hell'. But he passed the mornings making the first draft of the scores of the first and second scenes of Act 2 of *Die Walküre* and in the afternoons read Dante, and Holtzmann's *Indische Sagen*. (He found the legend of Savitri 'divine', thereby anticipating Gustav Holst by half a century.) He spent some convivial evenings with Berlioz, who was conducting the 1855 season of the New Philharmonic. But he left London 'with a sense of bitterness such as I hope never to have to experience again'. The £200 was 'the *hardest* money I have ever earned in my life'. As for the Philharmonic Society, it turned in 1856 to the safer and less daemonic figure of Sterndale Bennett for its next conductor, a post he held for eleven years. He was elected professor of music at Cambridge University the same year, and there continued Walmisley's public lectures and also instituted examinations for music degrees (hitherto 'exercises' were all that was required). Is it any wonder, though, that as a composer he was virtually dormant?

Manns and Hallé

A more significant event for the future of English musical life and English composers had also occurred in 1855. In 1852, Paxton's huge glass-and-iron

Crystal Palace, erected in Hyde Park to house the 1851 Exhibition, was dismantled and rebuilt in the south-east London suburb of Sydenham. It was administered by a company of which the secretary was an engineer with a musical bent, George Grove (1820–1900). At first it provided military-band concerts conducted by two German *émigrés*, one of whom was August Manns (1825–1907). In 1855 Manns, then aged thirty, became sole conductor, enlarged the band to a symphony orchestra and launched the Saturday concerts, with low admission prices. Because most of its members played together continually, the orchestra became the best and best-rehearsed in London and Manns provided adventurous programmes which were rivalled in Britain after 1858 only by Hallé's Manchester concerts. He promoted the music of Schumann and Schubert; and works by Brahms, Liszt, Berlioz, Wagner, Smetana and, later, Elgar were heard at the Crystal Palace before they entered concert-programmes in Central London. The Crystal Palace also proved itself a natural venue for the huge Handel Festivals (over 2,000 performers) which began in 1857 under Costa's direction (Manns taking them over in 1883) and for the national competitions of the increasingly popular brass-band movement.

The suburbs could not, of course, be permitted to enjoy such success unchallenged and in 1858 the St James's Hall, built by two music publishers, opened between Piccadilly and Regent Street (the Piccadilly Hotel now occupies the site). Its main hall seated 2,100. A smaller hall, beneath the platform of the larger, was used by Christy's Minstrels. The acoustics were good and St James's immediately replaced the Exeter Hall in the Strand as London's premier concert-hall, a status it maintained until the opening of the Royal Albert Hall in 1871 and the Queen's Hall in 1893. Even so, it was far from satisfactory, since economic factors dictated that the orchestra had to be too small or the seat prices too high.

There was a happier situation outside London. In 1849 in Liverpool, the Philharmonic Hall was opened. Until its destruction by fire in 1933, this hall was regarded by many – Hans Richter specifically – as the best in Europe, with exceptional acoustics. Liverpool, with its prosperous business community and its large German population, was thus well placed to benefit from the musical revival which was under way thirty-five miles away in Manchester. Charles Hallé, who in his twelve years as a solo pianist and chamber-music player in Paris had become the friend of Chopin, Liszt, Wagner and particularly Berlioz, took over conductorship of the Gentlemen's Concerts on 20 February 1850, and began to attract a number of foreign musicians to work with him in the North West. Thus both Liverpool and Manchester had a pool of excellent musicians on whom to draw. The frequent and efficient railway services meant that international soloists could and would travel to these cities; and Manchester, like its neighbour, also had a culture-minded immigrant population in addition to local enthusiasts.

It was this 'explosion' of interest in the arts as well as the traditional desire to go one better than the capital that led Manchester in 1857 to stage its own 'Great Exhibition', this time of over 12,000 arts treasures assembled from private collections and elsewhere. It lasted six months and Hallé was invited to provide the music. He enlarged the Gentlemen's Concerts orchestra accordingly. Some concerts were given in the exhibition hall at Old Trafford, but most in the splendid new Free Trade Hall, opened in the city centre in 1856. Rather than disband the orchestra after the exhibition closed, Hallé initiated his own concerts, with a range of low-priced seats. The profit on his first season of thirty concerts was 2*s*. 6*d*. (12½p). Within ten years his profit was £2,000, and in 1860 the *Musical World* could write that

Mr Charles Hallé's Manchester concerts are becoming the vogue with all classes, from the rich merchant and manufacturer to the middle-class tradesman and bourgeois . . . to the respectable and thrifty, albeit humbler, artisans.

The advent of St James's Hall in London led in December 1858 to the foundation of the Monday Popular Concerts, designed to attract large audiences by programmes covering many genres of music. After 1864 the concentration was on classical chamber music. Thus string quartets, pianists and organists succeeded each other on the platform. Analytical notes were introduced, following George Grove's example at the Crystal Palace. In 1865 Saturday concerts were initiated and from 1876 until 1898, when the series ended, concerts were given on alternate Saturdays and Mondays. Browning, Tennyson, Swinburne, Leighton and D.G. Rossetti were among the regular attenders. In 1885, W.S. Gilbert put into the Mikado's mouth a reference to

. . . masses and fugues and 'ops'
By Bach interwoven
With Spohr and Beethoven
At classical Monday Pops.

So, in the decade after the death of Mendelssohn, a remarkable trans-formation had occurred in the provision of halls and concert series. Only at the opera had there been little change, Covent Garden keeping its policy of singing everything in Italian and engaging the leading international artists to sing it. In 1861 Adelina Patti made her début there, the same year that the previous reigning prima donna, Giulietta Grisi, retired. But when the Italian season ended, a company calling itself the Royal English Opera leased the theatre each winter from 1858 to 1864 to produce new operas by Balfe, Julius Benedict (*The Lily of Killarney*), Edward Loder and William Wallace. This gave more 'exposure' to native composers at this time than was occurring in the concert-hall. The Philharmonic Society's record from 1850 to 1870 where British composers were concerned makes depressing reading. Symphonies by Cipriani Potter were played in 1850, 1855 and 1869 and his Shakespearean overtures *Cymbeline* and *Antony and Cleopatra*. Sterndale Bennett bestirred himself to write a symphony for the 1865 season and his piano concertos were heard at regular intervals with Arabella Goddard as soloist. Wagner, as has already been stated, conducted a Macfarren overture; a symphony by Charles Lucas, one of the cellists, was conducted by its composer in 1855; and in 1867 the name Sullivan first appeared, with his *Marmion* overture.

Sullivan's supremacy

Arthur Sullivan (1842–1900) was the first composer to emerge from a new generation ready to inherit the advantages of the increasing scope for

performance in Britain. Son of an Irish military bandsman, Sullivan was
enrolled in the Chapel Royal in 1845, entered the Royal Academy of Music
in 1856 as a pupil of Sterndale Bennett (some early compositions were played
there) and went to Leipzig Conservatory in 1858. While there he composed,
and heard performed, his incidental music to Shakespeare's *The Tempest*. On
returning to London, he met and became friendly with Grove, who
recommended *The Tempest* music to Manns. The complete score of twelve
numbers was performed at the Crystal Palace on 5 April 1862 and was
described by Chorley as marking 'an epoch in English music'. Hallé
introduced this music to Manchester in January 1863, and repeated it three
weeks later with immense success. Within a year Sullivan was in Paris to
hear Pauline Viardot as Gluck's Orpheus and to meet Rossini, having in the
meantime composed a march for the wedding of the Prince of Wales to the
Danish Princess Alexandra. On holiday in Northern Ireland, he began to
compose a Symphony in E and in London became organist for Costa at
Covent Garden. This led to a commission for a cantata – *Kenilworth* – for the
Birmingham Festival, of which Costa was then conductor. The symphony
was played at the Crystal Palace conducted by Manns in 1866 (each
movement being applauded) and in Manchester at the end of the year. In
November 1866 came a cello concerto, with Piatti as soloist. In 1867 Sullivan
went with Grove to Vienna, where they unearthed two Schubert symphonies,
the Fourth and Sixth, an overture and the *Rosamunde* music.

It was not long before fault was being found with Sullivan's orchestral
works: it seemed he was to follow too closely for comfort in the steps of his
master Sterndale Bennett. But in 1867 he and the writer Francis Burnand,
later to edit *Punch*, collaborated in a one-act comic operetta, *Cox and Box*, to
be given in the same bill as Offenbach's *Les Deux Aveugles*. It was a popular
success; and, at the age of twenty-six, Sullivan was organist of a fashionable
Kensington church, elected to the Garrick Club and was developing a taste
for gambling and for the social delights of Ascot, Goodwood and Epsom.
Tennyson wrote the poems of a song-cycle for him and the 1869 Three
Choirs Festival at Worcester commissioned an oratorio, *The Prodigal Son*.
Yet far more significant were the melodic lilt and graceful orchestration of
the *Overture di Ballo* (to give it its published hybrid title) composed for the
1870 Birmingham Festival.

The Sullivan dichotomy is epitomised in the year 1871, in which he wrote
the most famous of his many hymn-tunes, 'Onward, Christian Soldiers', and
collaborated for the first time with the librettist W.S. Gilbert in a two-act
comic opera called *Thespis, or The Gods Grown Old*. Produced at the Gaiety,
Thespis was hissed on its first night and the score is now lost. Three years
were to pass before they collaborated again and in the meantime Sullivan
added another oratorio, *The Light of the World*, to Novello's catalogue,
composed a gigantic *Te Deum*, continued to spend country weekends with the
aristocracy and began his long and passionate liaison with an American
married woman. In 1875 Richard D'Oyly Carte, manager of a theatre
company presenting Offenbach's *La Périchole* at the Royalty, commissioned
Trial by Jury from Gilbert and Sullivan to fill out a short evening. It ran for
175 performances and D'Oyly Carte was quick to note the possibilities of this
partnership.

Even so, this aspect of his work was a mere sideline to Sullivan. In 1876 he accepted the post of director of a new music college, the National Training School for Music in South Kensington, while temporarily retaining the professorship of composition at the Royal Academy of Music which he had held since 1866. (In 1882 the School was absorbed into the new Royal College of Music.) One of the influential periodicals of the day, *The Orchestra*, was quick to deplore the appointment on the grounds that it would 'deprive the world of the services of the only English composer we have who has made his mark in what he has done'. Despite this timely warning, Sullivan held the post for five years, a period which covered the heyday of his stormy collaboration with Gilbert in what came to be known as the Savoy Operas (the first to be performed at the new Savoy Theatre in 1881 being *Patience*, transferred there in mid-run). *The Sorcerer* of 1877 began the series and was followed by *HMS Pinafore* (1878), *The Pirates of Penzance* (1879), *Patience* (1881), *Iolanthe* (1882), *Princess Ida* (1884), *The Mikado* (1885), *Ruddigore* (1887), *The Yeomen of the Guard* (1888) and *The Gondoliers* (1889).

These works, properly described as operettas, attained and have retained a popularity unique in English music. They became a cult. The topical jokes in Gilbert's libretti, far from fading and becoming incomprehensible, are understood and cherished today, though his misogyny is tolerated rather than approved. Sullivan's music is catchy, tuneful and instantly memorable – some of his melodies have virtually become part of folklore. His gift for parody was developed in these scores into an art-form – Handel, Donizetti, Verdi, madrigals, all are laid under contribution in brilliant fashion. His Mendelssohnian training stood him in good stead, for his craftsmanship was impeccable, as exemplified by his skill in combining different melodies in different time-measures. But there is a debit side to the popularity of the Savoy operas. It is difficult to avoid the suspicion that they pander to the latent philistinism of the British public where music is concerned. They provide a vicarious experience of opera. How often has one heard the remark: 'I don't like serious music, Gilbert and Sullivan is about my mark'?

Compared with the polish and sparkle of Offenbach and the melodic fecundity of Johann Strauss, the reach-me-down burlesques of Sullivan come a poor third. Is there one of the Savoy operas that can be mentioned in the same breath as *Die Fledermaus*? Yet the Viennese critic Eduard Hanslick, visiting London in 1886 and hearing *The Mikado*, boldly tackled the matter of Sullivan *vis-à-vis* Offenbach:

. . . To learn from Offenbach shows better judgment than to slander him. To be sure, Offenbach's luxuriant melody and scintillating *esprit* cannot be learned; but what can and should be learned from him is the concise form, the discreet moderation, the easy singability and the modest orchestra. In all these respects Sullivan took the composer of *Fortunio* as a model, without sacrificing his own self-sufficiency. It is not to be expected that the English should attain the effervescent vivacity and the piquant charm of the Frenchman – but Sullivan, in his multiple-voiced pieces, shows himself the more thoroughly schooled musician . . . Sullivan has accomplished something, if in a secondary genre, which no Englishman has ever accomplished before: to be melodious and amusing for an entire evening!
(*Music Criticisms 1846–99 by Eduard Hanslick*, tr. and ed. by Henry Pleasants, 1951).

Ironically, Sullivan himself and his admirers regarded the operettas as ephemera which took him away from his 'real' work. Only two large-scale choral works were composed during the Savoy period, *The Martyr of Antioch* (1880) and *The Golden Legend* (1886), both for the Leeds Festival, of which he became conductor in 1880. He was knighted in 1883 and from 1885 to 1887 added conductorship of the Philharmonic Society to his other work. Hanslick, in the 'Letter from London' quoted above, has left a devastating description of Sullivan at the Philharmonic:

He presides on the podium from the comfortable recesses of a commodious armchair, his left arm largely extended on the arm-rest, his right giving the beat in a mechanical way, his eyes fastened to the score. They played Mozart's Symphony in G minor [No. 40]. Sullivan never looked up from the notes; it was as though he were reading at sight. The heavenly piece plodded along, for better or worse, listlessly, insensibly. At the end the audience applauded long and loudly, but it apparently never occurred to Sullivan to turn around and face the audience. He sat stolid and immovable . . .

In 1891 Sullivan's one 'serious' opera, *Ivanhoe*, ran for 150 performances in London but was a failure in Germany. After the break in his partnership with Gilbert, resumed only in 1893 and 1896 in *Utopia (Limited)* and *The Grand Duke*, his attempts at comic opera with other librettists failed lamentably. For years he suffered from kidney trouble. After a life of working hard and playing hard, he died on St Cecilia's Day 1900 at the age of fifty-eight. Of his 'serious' works, only the overtures *Di Ballo* and *In Memoriam*, the song 'The Lost Chord' (of which half a million copies were sold in its first twenty-five years) and the hymn 'Onward, Christian Soldiers' are heard frequently today, with *The Golden Legend* maintaining a tenuous grip on survival and proving unexpectedly impressive when it is well performed. As far as one can predict immortality for works of art, the operettas with Gilbert are immortal.

The particular brilliance of Sullivan's operettas is that, while remaining musically witty and tasteful, they were the up-market apotheosis of the two musical forms with which the majority of the British people were familiar and to both of which Sullivan contributed – the hymn-tune and the drawing-room ballad. Most of the hymns sung in Victorian churches were feeble and flaccid, pandering to the worst sentimentality, but there were exceptions which, because of their inherent excellence, represent the Victorian period of English music more potently than any oratorio or cantata. Such fine tunes as 'Eternal Father, Strong to Save' and 'Lead, Kindly Light' by J.B. Dykes and 'Abide with Me' by W.H. Monk have passed into the national consciousness. The ballads were their secular equivalent and derived also from such operatic numbers as 'Home, Sweet Home'. They were highly marketable and appeared in the repertoire of the great singers at their solo recitals as well as being sung by every amateur with access to a captive domestic audience.

As significant a feature as any in the musical renaissance which began in Britain around 1880, was the gradual bridging of the gap between the meretricious ballad and the art-song. No inconsiderable part was played in this raising of standards by the women composers Maude Valérie White (1855–1937) and Liza Lehmann (1862–1918). The latter's *In a Persian Garden* (1896) has charm and atmosphere. Nor should the growing interest in

Joseph Jacques Tissot, Hush, *exhibited at the Royal Academy in 1875. The violinist may be either Madame Neruda, Mlle Diaz de Soria or Mlle Castellan. Others portrayed are Lord Leighton, Arthur Sullivan and Prince Dhuleep Singh.*

folk-song be underestimated in this respect. Although the practical collecting undertaken by Cecil Sharp, Vaughan Williams and others did not begin until 1903, it was preceded by the publications of such pioneers as Lucy Broadwood, the Revd Sabine Baring-Gould and Frank Kidson. In its influence on a new generation of composers, the folk-song revival was nothing but beneficial in its impact on the composition of English songs.

The Folk Song Society was founded in 1898 and was mainly devoted to English folk-song, since the Scottish, Irish and Welsh had woken up a bit earlier to their heritage. The Society brought all the apparatus of scholarship to the subject – a learned journal, cataloguing, and the preservation of phonographic recordings of the country singers. Elgar went to the inaugural meeting, but later declared: 'I write the folk songs of this country.' In no respect was he influenced by the songs, whereas Holst, Butterworth, Vaughan Williams and others were bowled over by their sheer beauty. Such melodies as 'Bushes and Briars', 'The Seeds of Love' and 'The Captain's Apprentice' they feared might die with the old singers in the villages, since the urbanisation of the countryside would mean that they would not be passed on to the next generation, who were supposed not to be interested in them. That was the theory on which Sharp worked. It has been hotly disputed since then, and he has been criticised for his belief that the folk-song was a rural phenomenon. But without his inspiration it is doubtful if the movement would have attained the influence it exerted on the generation of composers coming to maturity at the turn of the century.

Grove and the new College

The year 1880 is often cited as the start of the so-called renaissance of English music and musical life. The choice of any specific year is bound to be arbitrary, but there are more and better reasons for the selection of 1880 than the performance of Hubert Parry's *Scenes from Shelley's Prometheus Unbound* at the Gloucester Festival. The Corporation of the City of London founded the Guildhall School of Music in that year, George Grove's *Dictionary of Music and Musicians* was published in 1879–80 and a twenty-eight-year-old composer, Charles Villiers Stanford (1852–1924), wrote his Evening Service for the Festival of the Sons of the Clergy in St Paul's Cathedral. In their different ways, these unconnected events represented the coming to fruition of the gradual change in attitudes to music in Britain which we have traced from 1850.

Although London music-making was still dominated by foreign artists such as the violinist Joachim and the conductor Richter – who had come to London for the first time with Wagner in 1877 – these visitors now encountered additional features of British musical life that were to become permanencies. These included the formation of the Bach Choir in 1875 as a result of two complete performances of the Mass in B minor. The Royal Choral Society had grown from a choir formed and conducted by Gounod for the opening of the Royal Albert Hall in 1871. Its conductor from 1872 was Joseph Barnby (1838–96), the organist from 1863 to 1871 of St Anne's, Soho, where he had given annual performances of Bach's *St John Passion*.

Barnby is remembered today as the composer of the part-song 'Sweet and Low', but he conducted a concert performance of Wagner's *Parsifal* in 1884, two years after it was first staged in Bayreuth, and he conducted Bach's *St Matthew Passion* in Westminster Abbey, its first London revival since

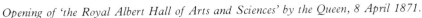

Opening of 'the Royal Albert Hall of Arts and Sciences' by the Queen, 8 April 1871.

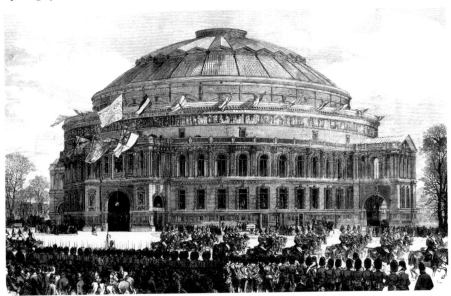

Sterndale Bennett had conducted the first complete English performance in 1854. Although Handel still reigned supreme in English hearts, the Bach revival was reflected in the programmes of the provincial choral festivals in Leeds, Birmingham, Bristol, Sheffield and, of course, the Three Choirs of Hereford, Gloucester and Worcester. Interest in music earlier than Bach's was stirring, too. The first English 'musicologist' to begin to explore music composed before Tallis and Byrd, was John Stainer (1840–1901), one of the founders in 1874 of the (Royal) Musical Association and author of books on Dufay and the early English music in the Bodleian Library at Oxford. Stainer was organist of St Paul's Cathedral from 1872 and wrote for it services and anthems which became widely popular although he later declared them to be 'rubbish'. His oratorio *The Crucifixion* (1887) has been cherished by church choirs for over a century, in spite of the scorn poured on it by successive generations of critics.

The foundation of the Royal College of Music in 1882 was the culmination of a long debate on the training of musicians in England, an area in which progress was deemed to lag far behind the continent. From its institution in 1822, the Royal Academy of Music had struggled for lack of sufficient funds. Its first professorial staff was ill-chosen and its first principal, William Crotch, was an incompetent administrator. His successor, Cipriani Potter, was not much better. Practice sessions were 'a communal bedlam', as described by Cyril Ehrlich in his *The Music Profession in Britain since the 18th Century*. The Academy's directors were aristocratic amateurs whose lack of knowledge did not deter them from interfering at every level. A voice raised against the way the place was run was that of George Macfarren, a professor there from 1837 and eventually to become principal in 1875. He urged that the management should be in the hands of practical musicians. His emphasis on professionalism, while admirable, was carried beyond the frontiers of prejudice. It is from Macfarren that we can trace the condescending attitude of college and university 'professionals' to those whom they regarded as amateurs. This incestuous attitude towards those musicians and administrators who did not pass formal examinations at college or university led to the bitter resentment felt by Elgar against the academic establishment and to the suspicion engendered in the young Britten at the Royal College of Music that any student who wished to stretch himself beyond what was academically thought fit and proper was damned.

A report by a committee of inquiry into the state of the Academy in 1865 exposed incompetence and inefficiency in every department. The critic Chorley, in his evidence, said that 'there has not been one commanding English artist, vocal or instrumental, turned out by the Academy during the last twenty-five years'. John Hullah, the leading exponent of the tonic sol-fa method and later to be a government inspector in music, noted that whereas across the Channel the aristocracy led musical taste, in Britain the upper classes were musically ignorant, something about which they were prepared to boast. The Committee was left in no doubt that the Military School of Music at Kneller Hall, Twickenham, founded in 1857, produced better musicians. The evidence given to the Committee makes better reading than its report. As usually happens, the authors of the report fudged the issues.

They recommended increased Government support, free scholarships, a new building and a new principal. Thus, in 1866, Sterndale Bennett added another administrative post to his tally.

One of those who gave evidence to the Committee had urged that the ideal principal should be a 'sound musician' but should not gain his living from the profession of music. This was not followed in 1876 when the National Training School was founded. Sullivan after five years handed over to Stainer, but when the School was absorbed into the Royal College of Music, the first director, the sixty-two-year-old George Grove, came near to this ideal. This extraordinary man was trained as a civil engineer and built railway stations in Britain and lighthouses in the West Indies. He part-edited a biblical dictionary and founded the Palestine Exploration Fund. As has already been described, his involvement with the Crystal Palace company led to his association with Manns, to his famous programme-notes and eventually to his great *Dictionary*.

When the college opened its door to students in 1883, the entrants found a better syllabus, better professors and a better attitude. They were encouraged to perform, even opera, although one of the professors, Stanford, complained from the start that opera was neglected. But the perspective was wrong. For what kind of musical career were these students being trained? To become teachers or to play in restaurants, musical comedy theatre pits, and small touring opera orchestras. For whatever else had changed since 1850, London still had no permanent professional symphony orchestra, merely a pool of freelance musicians who picked the best-paid job on any particular evening and paid a 'deputy' to take their place elsewhere. In spite of Sullivan and Sterndale Bennett, the average Englishman would still – might still today – have nodded agreement with the sage who in 1856 had argued against adequate pay for musicians by pointing out that the professions of law, medicine and the Church were necessary whereas that of music was not.

Stanford, Parry and Mackenzie

In singling out opera, Stanford was speaking from experience. It was still almost impossible for a British composer to have an opera staged in Britain. If there had been an opera tradition in England, as opposed (since Purcell's time) to a tradition of imported opera, Stanford might have developed into a different composer. In his youth in Dublin he was stagestruck, attending operas and plays whenever he could. He began his formal musical education in his native city, but went to Cambridge in 1870, becoming organist of Trinity College. In 1874 he went to Leipzig to study under Carl Reinecke and in 1877 to Berlin. He attended the first Bayreuth Festival (1876) – 'he that is not with me is against me', was the motto of the whole festival, he wrote – visited Salzburg and heard Johann Strauss conduct his waltzes in Vienna. At Cambridge he was the leading light of the University Musical Club and was largely instrumental in persuading Joachim to conduct the first English performance of Brahms's First Symphony at one of the Society's concerts in March 1877, four months after its Karlsruhe première.

Stanford's own music was by now being performed. His famous Service in B flat was composed in 1879, and the Poet Laureate, Tennyson, asked him for incidental music for his play *Queen Mary*. His first opera, *The Veiled Prophet of Khorassan* (1877), was considered for Frankfurt in 1878 but was produced in Hanover in 1881. This was followed in 1884 by *Savonarola*, a success in Hamburg but a flop a few months later under Richter in London. In the same year he began the vogue for setting Whitman to music and in 1886 his popular Tennyson ballad, *The Revenge*, was first performed at the Leeds Festival and was at once taken up by choral societies throughout the land. His *Irish Symphony* (his third) followed in 1887, conducted by Richter. The idea that no British orchestral music was played overseas until Elgar's advent is disproved by this symphony. The *Irish* was performed in Hanover, Berlin, Brussels, Rome, Bologne, New York, Boston and elsewhere. It was in the programme for the opening concert in the new Concertgebouw, Amsterdam, in 1888. When his Fourth Symphony had its first performance, this took place in Berlin.

The *Irish* is still the most frequently played of Stanford's symphonies (although all seven have now been recorded on compact discs). It has suffered because the first subject of its slow movement closely resembles its counterpart in Brahms's Fourth Symphony, composed at the same time. Stanford maintained he got there first and that the melody comes from an Irish folk-song. The facts are that Brahms's symphony was first performed in 1885 and the Stanford in 1887. Nevertheless, it need concern the listener no more than resemblances between melodies in Brahms's First Symphony and Beethoven's Ninth. Stanford was always at his best when the Irish element in his work was uppermost and it is its colourful scoring rather than symphonic structure that keeps this work alive.

Inexorably, the tentacles of the British musical establishment were coiling round Stanford. In 1883, at the age of thirty-one, he was appointed a professor of composition in the new Royal College of Music. In 1885 he became conductor of the Bach Choir – there can be little doubt he was an excellent conductor and not only of his own music – and in 1888 he was elected Professor of Music at Cambridge University. After the turn of the century he became conductor of the Leeds Festival. His music reflected these weighty preoccupations. His choral works increased in number – *The Three Holy Children* (1885), *Eden* (1891), *Requiem* (1897), *Te Deum* (1898), *Stabat Mater* (1907). He was on the festival treadmill. He met and came excessively to idolise Brahms.

Thenceforward Stanford wrote the music of an English Brahms, whereas his natural tendency lay towards being an English Dvořák or, better still, an Irish Stanford. Bernard Shaw was shrewd enough to suggest, after one of the splits between Gilbert and Sullivan, that Gilbert ought to persuade Stanford to be his collaborator. The vein of fantasy in Stanford's music, its delicate orchestration and its capability for wit, did not escape the ear of a critic who had poured vitriol over some of Stanford's oratorios. The best of him is in his songs, his *Irish Rhapsodies*, in the Fifth Symphony (1894) and in the late *Songs of the Fleet* (1910). As a teacher he was often irascible and discouraging, but most of his pupils adored him and a list of their names is a roll-call of fine British composers – Vaughan Williams, Holst, Ireland, Coleridge-Taylor and Gurney among them. He was also an entertaining writer with a journalists's eye for the unusual, as when he and his wife were in Venice and saw 'Charles Hallé in a frock-coat and a white top hat reading the *Daily Telegraph* while seated in a gondola and floating under the Bridge of Sighs'.

Stanford is indissolubly associated with Hubert Parry (1848–1918), although there is little similarity in their music. From the Gloucestershire squirearchy, Parry studied music under Sterndale Bennett and at Oxford under Macfarren and then entered business. But after three years he returned to music. In the 1870s he wrote several chamber works which were for years almost forgotten but have lately been resurrected and been found by many listeners to be of high quality. But it was with a Three Choirs Festival choral work, *Scenes From Shelley's Prometheus Unbound* in 1880, that his name moved to the forefront of English composers, even though it was regarded by most of the critics as too advanced. Unlike Stanford, Parry was a strong admirer of Wagner, although the Wagnerian influence in his music is only occasionally perceptible.

   Thereafter Parry, like Stanford, wrote a series of choral works, sacred and secular, for the various festivals. Of these, the oratorios *Judith* (1888) and *Job* (1892) attracted the scorn of Shaw, but *Job* also attracted the lifelong advocacy of Adrian Boult and has kept a precarious place on the fringe of English choral music. The secular and short Miltonic ode *Blest Pair of Sirens* (1887), for chorus and orchestra, was highly regarded by both Elgar ('one of the noblest works of man') and Vaughan Williams ('my favourite piece of music written by an Englishman') and is a fixture in the repertoire. His songs and part-songs contain some of his best music; the orchestral works have fared less well, although the *Symphonic Variation* (1897) may well have influenced Elgar's *Enigma Variations* (1899), and, of the symphonies, the Third (1889) and the Fifth (1912) deserve to be regularly performed. The *nobilmente* strain in Elgar's music is traceable to Parry.

   His career followed the prescribed pattern. In 1883 he joined the first professorial staff of the Royal College of Music and succeeded Grove as its director in 1894, holding the post until his death. He was knighted in 1898 and became Professor of Music at Oxford University from 1900 to 1908. Genial, generous and a keen yachtsman, he was venerated by his pupils and by his colleagues. Yet some of the songs and later choral works hint at a dark, melancholic strain in his nature. His tragedy was that he dissipated his creative talents amid his administrative work. Unlike Stanford, however, he restricted his activity as a conductor to his own works.

A year Parry's senior was Alexander Mackenzie (1847–1935). He went at the age of ten to Sondershausen Conservatory for five years, returned to spend three years at the Royal Academy of Music, and then worked as a violinist and conductor in Edinburgh from 1865 to 1879. While there he founded a series of chamber concerts. He then lived in Florence for ten years, seeing much of Liszt, and returned to Britain in 1888 to become principal of the

Royal Academy of Music in succession to Macfarren. Four years later he also became Conductor of the Philharmonic Society and conducted the first English performance of Tchaikovsky's *Pathétique* Symphony in 1894. Little of Mackenzie's music is played today, but its effect on one of the violinists in the orchestra at the Worcester Festival of 1881, when his cantata *The Bride* was first performed, remained vivid for fifty years. In 1931 Edward Elgar recalled that 'here was a man fully equipped in every department of musical knowledge, who had been a violinist in orchestras in Germany. It gave orchestral players a real lift'.

Even the Philharmonic Society was relatively quick to acknowledge the arrival on the scene of Parry, Stanford and Mackenzie. They were first represented in the Society's programmes in, respectively, 1881, 1882 and 1883. A fourth English composer of the time shared the limelight with them – Frederic Cowen (1852–1935). He steered clear of academic posts but earned his living as a conductor, working regularly with the Hallé, Liverpool Philharmonic and Scottish Orchestras and becoming the Philharmonic's conductor in succession to Sullivan in 1888, until he was summarily dismissed in 1892 because he informed the audience he had not had sufficient rehearsal time for Beethoven's *Pastoral* Symphony. He studied in Leipzig, became Costa's assistant at Covent Garden and established himself with a cantata and an opera, *Pauline*, before he was twenty-five. His *Scandinavian* Symphony (1880) earned him a European and American reputation. He was a prickly personality who felt – probably with some justification – that he had been cold-shouldered by his university-based colleagues and it is not surprising that he found favour in Elgar's sight.

Speaking in Manchester in 1886, Mackenzie mentioned Parry, Stanford, Sullivan and Cowen and said:

Excepting Verdi, Gounod and Brahms, of whom only the last may be said to be in full activity [Verdi's *Otello* was produced the following year!] the Englishmen named by me are the peers, if not more than the peers, of their musical contemporaries in other countries.

So much for Grieg, Tchaikovsky, Dvořák and Bruckner, with Richard Strauss and Mahler already writing their first masterpieces. Mackenzie might, had he known about her, have included the twenty-eight-year-old Ethel Smyth (1858–1944), who was at this date in Germany where she and Adolph Brodsky performed her violin sonata, with an admiring Tchaikovsky in the audience. With her dog Marco – Elgar was not the first composer to own a dog with that name – she was part of a musical circle in Leipzig which embraced Brahms, Busoni, Grieg, Mahler and Tchaikovsky.

Shaw, Dvořák and Wood

In January 1893, when Smyth's Mass in D was performed in London, it had a friendly if patronising welcome from Bernard Shaw (1856–1950), whose writings on music in *The World* from 1890 to 1894 and in *The Star* before that, had earned him a reputation as a scourge. He was the first of the great modern music critics. Like all critics, he had his 'blind spots', in his case a loathing of Brahms and an under-estimation of Schubert. But his fluent prose, his wit and his profound love of music shine through his writings so that after nearly a century they are as fresh on the page as when they were first written.

There would have been no 'Hear, hear' from Shaw to Mackenzie's remarks.

If you doubt that *Eden* is a masterpiece, ask Dr Parry and Dr Mackenzie, and they will applaud it to the skies. Surely Dr Mackenzie's opinion is conclusive; for is he not the composer of *Veni Creator*, guaranteed as excellent music by Professor Stanford and Dr Parry? You want to know who Dr Parry is? Why, the composer of *Blest Pair of Sirens*, as to the merits of which you have only to consult Dr Mackenzie and Professor Stanford.

Shaw was equally withering about Sullivan:

As to Sir Arthur's scores, they form an easy introduction to dramatic music and picturesque or topical orchestration for perfect novices; but as I . . . was pretty well tired of Offenbach before *Trial by Jury* was born, there was no musical novelty in the affair for me.

His victims could comfort themselves with his remark that Brahms's *Requiem* 'could only have come from the establishment of a first-class undertaker'. Splendid knockabout. But he was serious at heart, alone among music critics in daring to write – in 1893 – that 'a good orchestra is every whit as important to a town as a good hospital'.

When Hallé took his orchestra to London in 1890, Shaw described it as 'superior to the Crystal Palace orchestra in power and to the Richter in quality'. Since 1877 Richter had given a series of concerts in London which had raised standards of orchestral playing. He had been generous in his support of British composers and, like Hallé in Manchester and Manns at Sydenham, he quickly seized the opportunities of introducing into his programmes the symphonies and concertos of Brahms, Dvořák and Tchaikovsky. The timidity of the Philharmonic Society was, as a result, counterbalanced.

Dvořák (1841–1904) in particular became a favourite with British audiences after his first visit in 1884 to conduct his *Stabat Mater* and Symphony in D major [No. 6 by today's numbering, No. 1 then] at the Worcester Festival. Again Elgar was in the orchestra and again he was deeply impressed – 'the orchestration is wonderful; no matter how few instruments he uses it never sounds thin'. It was a lesson well learned. Dvořák paid eight more visits to Britain and several of his works were written for, or had their first performances in, England: the D minor Symphony [No. 7] in 1885, the cantata *The Spectre's Bride* (Birmingham, 1885), the oratorio *St Ludmila* (Leeds, 1886), the G major Symphony [No. 8] (London, 1888), and the *Requiem* (Birmingham, 1891). He even toyed with the idea of setting Newman's poem *The Dream of Gerontius*.

We come to another watershed in the year 1893, the date of two far-reaching and important events. A new concert hall, the Queen's Hall, was opened in Langham Place, 'a happy success acoustically', Shaw reported, a verdict with which everyone who played or listened there seems to have been in agreement (the hall was destroyed in an air raid in May 1941). In itself it was bound to be a welcome new feature of the London landscape, but its true significance did not emerge until 1895 when the Hall's lessees, Chappell's, appointed a new manager, Robert Newman. This remarkable impresario had noticed the talent of a young British conductor, Henry J. Wood (1869–1944), who had been working with the Carl Rosa and other touring opera companies. He engaged Wood as Conductor of Promenade Concerts to be given in the new Hall in the late summer and provided him with the Queen's Hall Orchestra of eighty players. So began one of the most fruitful chapters in the history of music-making in Britain. Wood's first programmes were a mixture of ballads, euphonium solos, operatic pot-pourris and movements from symphonies. They could not compete with the standard of programmes which Hallé – who died in 1895 – had for years been offering his Manchester audiences nor with those of Manns at Crystal Palace.

But gradually Wood won the public's confidence, dropped the miscellaneous items and used the 'Proms' as a platform for introducing as much new music and as much British music as he thought his audience could take. He also provided innumerable chances for young soloists to make their débuts in concertos. The laborious changes wrought in half a century were at last beginning to bring forth British instrumental soloists to add to the singers. The list of those who were to have Wood to thank for a start to their career is illustriously long.

The other major event of 1893 was the establishment of the Royal Manchester College of Music, with Sir Charles Hallé, as he had been since 1888, as the first principal. Willy Hess, who was the leader of Hallé's orchestra, was the first professor of violin; when he departed for Cologne in 1895, Adolph Brodsky replaced him in both posts. But hardly had Brodsky arrived than Hallé died. Brodsky succeeded him as principal, a factor which must have carried some weight with Hans Richter while he was coming to his decision to leave Vienna to become conductor of the Hallé Orchestra from 1899 to 1911. This expansion of provincial musical life was not confined to Manchester. Music schools had been founded in Birmingham in 1886 and in Glasgow in 1890. In Bournemouth in 1893, Dan Godfrey (1868–1939) took a post as bandmaster and became the corporation's musical director in the following year. As Wood was to do in London, he played popular programmes with his twenty-four-man municipal orchestra but gradually enlarged the repertoire and the orchestra until, by 1897, he was conducting the Fifth and Sixth Symphonies of Tchaikovsky. Soon he was hard on the heels of Wood and Manns to put new, and especially British, works into his programmes.

Wood and Godfrey – who was emulated from 1897 at New Brighton by Granville Bantock (1868–1946) – knew exactly how to gauge the taste of their audiences. They had faith in them. They knew that, although the vitality and splendid vulgarity of music hall songs and the lilting charm of the operettas by Sidney Jones, Leslie Stuart, Lionel Monckton and Edward German was the music most Britons preferred, it did not take much to persuade the same listeners that music had other charms. Their success for many years was testimony to their artistic and commercial acumen.

The popularity of the music halls developed from the growth of taverns in the ever-expanding suburbs of the major cities. Landlords engaged singers and comedians who travelled from one public house to another during an evening. The first 'official' music hall was the Surrey in Westminster Bridge Road, London, in 1848. Others followed, notably Collins's in Islington, and by the mid-1860s there were over thirty large halls in London. The audience sat at tables, where they were served with drinks, and a 'chairman', or compère, presided from a table near the stage, introducing the acts.

J.D. Linton, London Sketches: at a Music Hall.

Gradually the entertainment took priority over the drinking and new halls were built with proscenium arches.

The songs were catchy and derivative, with broad humour. The best of them are indestructible, such as 'Polly Perkins of Paddington Green', 'Two Lovely Black Eyes' and 'My Old Dutch'. From one of them, a new word entered the language – 'We Don't Want to Fight but by Jingo if We Do'. The great music hall artists flourished at the turn of the century – George Robey, Marie Lloyd, Vesta Tilley, Harry Champion, Gus Elen, Charles Coborn, Little Tich and Eugene Stratton. They are remembered still – Robey was eventually knighted – but few remember the names of the composers who wrote their songs, with the exception of Leslie Stuart ('Lily of Laguna' and 'Soldiers of The Queen').

The advent of Elgar

But what about the violinist in the Worcester Festival Orchestra of 1881 and 1884 who had been so enthusiastic about Mackenzie and Dvořák? Edward Elgar (1857–1934) was born in the village of Broadheath, a few miles outside Worcester. His father, a cheerful unbeliever, was organist at a Roman Catholic church in the city and was in partnership with his brother in a shop in the High Street which sold and repaired musical instruments and sold sheet-music. He also tuned the pianos in the large number of country houses in Worcestershire, often taking Edward along to demonstrate how well he had done his work by getting the boy to improvise on the newly-tuned instrument. Elgar's mother was the daughter of a farm-labourer and was a convert to Roman Catholicism. Her love of nature and of romantic and chivalric poetry was passed on to her second son (who was the fourth of her seven children).

Elgar thus grew up with two social disadvantages for which he never forgave 'providence', as he liked to call it: he was the son of a tradesman and he was a Roman Catholic in an Anglican cathedral city. The ills he suffered, both real and imagined, from this double handicap scarred him for life. Nevertheless, though moody, prone to depression and lonely as child and man, he also had a cheerful, practical-joking, friendly side. It was a case of light-Alberich and dark-Alberich and whether he took to you or not depended on which side happened to be dominant at the time. His gift for music was apparent in early childhood. He could play the piano, organ and, best of all, the violin.

On leaving school at fifteen, he worked briefly in a solicitor's office but abandoned it for a livelihood in music, helping in the shop, becoming assistant to his father, teaching the violin to schoolgirls and young ladies (which he hated) and playing in every kind of band or orchestra in the Worcester and Hereford districts. Apart from violin and piano lessons, he had no practical instruction in music. He taught himself theory from books in the shop and by studying scores – and by trial and error in his own work. One of the bands in which he played was at the county lunatic asylum at Powick, where dances were held for the staff. Quadrilles were much in demand and Elgar, whose abiding ambition since he was six was to be a composer, wrote or arranged them. From 1879 he conducted this band. Other Worcester organisations commissioned works from him for special festivities; and in 1878 he played in the second violins in the Worcester Festival Orchestra alongside his father. Three years later (the Mackenzie year) he was in the firsts.

He had cherished hopes of studying in Leipzig, but this was not financially possible. However, he went there on holiday in 1883 to visit the Worcester girl to whom he was engaged, for she was a violin student at the Conservatory. He went to the opera and heard the Gewandhaus Orchestra conducted by Carl Reinecke. He heard 'no end of stuff – Schumann principally (my ideal) and Wagner no end'. The previous year he had joined the violin section of W.C. Stockley's orchestra which gave popular concerts in Birmingham. Stockley included Elgar's *Sérénade Mauresque* in a programme in December 1883. 'Melodious, graceful and pleasing' was the local critic's verdict, an accurate summing-up of Elgar's lighter style.

Whenever he could, Elgar went by train to London to hear a new work or to try to interest publishers and conductors in his own music. On 12 May 1884 his *Sevillana* was conducted by Manns – who else? – at the Crystal Palace. But this was the end of his luck for a while. His engagement was broken off and his life reverted to the familiar round of playing and teaching. He was already twenty-seven. But he continued to compose. Stockley put on another Elgar work in Birmingham in 1888 and a few weeks later Elgar won £5 in a competition organised by a publisher. This was for a song, 'The Wind at Dawn', the words of which were by Caroline Alice Roberts. For two years Miss Roberts, daughter of an Indian Army general and eight years older than Elgar, had had piano lessons from him. Later in 1888, in spite of fierce opposition from her family, they became engaged and were married at the Brompton Oratory in May the following year.

With this remarkable woman, who had a blind faith in his ability, beside him, Elgar's creativity developed rapidly. The Worcester Festival of 1890 commissioned a concert-overture from him. *Froissart* was well received, but ten years would pass before it was played in London. Reluctantly, Novello's agreed to publish it. They also accepted some part-songs. In 1893 Breitkopf and Härtel published his *Serenade for Strings*, a wholly characteristic work, and in the same year his cantata *The Black Knight*, a setting of Longfellow's translation of the Uhland ballad, was performed in Worcester. This work was taken up by choral societies in the Midlands, who relished its bold writing and orchestral colour, far removed from the insipidity of other contemporary English works.

Three years later Elgar produced two more choral works, an oratorio *The Light of Life* for the Worcester Festival, and another Longfellow cantata, *Scenes from the Saga of King Olaf*, for the North Staffordshire Music Festival. *King Olaf* was an immediate and resounding success. Manns conducted it at the Crystal Palace, Cowen conducted it in Manchester and Liverpool. At last the name Elgar was being talked about, in spite of his lack of a university tag. There were those who found his music vulgar, but none found it dull. In an England used to *The Water Lily* and *Rose of Sharon*, it was all too easy to mistake uninhibited emotional fervour for vulgarity. The *Imperial March* Elgar wrote for the Diamond Jubilee of 1897 advanced his career several steps further and led to a commission from the Leeds Festival for a cantata for 1898. The outcome was *Caractacus*, the best of Elgar's early secular works in its combination of lyricism and extrovert display. The Queen accepted the dedication – but the composer was still teaching or serving behind his father's counter by day and writing his music at night, Alice having prepared his manuscript paper by ruling the bar-lines and writing in the names of the instruments.

On his return to their home in Malvern from Leeds, Elgar began to compose a set of orchestral variations on an original theme in which each variation was a musical portrait of a friend with whom he played chamber music or who had befriended him and Alice or who had encouraged him. The work is thus partly a social document of Victorian life in Malvern. The first variation was Alice herself, the ninth was 'Nimrod', an oblique reference to a German *émigré* August Jaeger (Jaeger = hunter = Nimrod, the 'mighty hunter' in the Bible). Jaeger was the manager of Novello's publishing office and saw Elgar's scores through the press. He recognised Elgar's quality before anybody else at Novello's and gave him the admiration and intelligent encouragement he needed. The original theme was superscribed 'Enigma' and almost certainly refers to Elgar himself.

But a second enigma caused more puzzlement. Elgar wrote that with each variation 'another and larger theme "goes", but is not played'. He implied that this hidden theme was a tune, but never disclosed its identity. Efforts to solve the mystery have continued ever since but are pointless, since no one can ever know the answer. It is, in any case, peripheral to the work itself, a masterpiece of fantasy and ingenuity scored with a clarity and aptness that never stale. He sent the manuscript to Hans Richter, who conducted the first performance in St James's Hall on 19 June 1899. Other performances soon followed, not merely in Britain but on the continent, where conductors were anxious to include it in their programmes. Elgar's international reputation was made.

His next major work was for the 1900 Birmingham Festival. He set Newman's poem *The Dream of Gerontius* for mezzo-soprano, tenor, bass, chorus and orchestra. Such a Roman Catholic subject encountered resistance – 'it stinks of incense', said Stanford – and the first performance was a near-disaster because the chorus had insufficient time to learn it, the chorus-master died during rehearsals and Richter under-estimated its difficulties. Elgar blamed 'providence', of course, but he knew that he had created a masterpiece and within a year or so he was vindicated. 'This is the best of me', he wrote at the end of the manuscript. This vision of a dead man's soul guided by a guardian angel on its way to judgement and purgatory was what Elgar needed to lift his art above the banalities of Longfellow to a higher plane. He succeeded utterly. The strength and beauty of the orchestration are no less striking than the incandescence of the choral writing.

It is, as we may hear now, music drawn from many sources. It is a curious mixture of plainsong, Verdian operatic arias, and Parsifalesque religiosity. The processional fervour of an imperial march accompanies the priest's envoi to the soul of Gerontius. The Angel's Farewell could almost be Delilah's. Distantly, in the Demons' Chorus, may be heard – dare one say it? – an echo of the music hall. All this is given unity and conviction by the white-hot creative energy surging through every bar of the music. Where Parry and Stanford could apply a conscientious and sincere talent to their works, Elgar was ablaze with genius. With the *Variations* and *Gerontius*, the real renaissance of English composition had begun, just in time for the twentieth century.

Mr Grimaldi at his farewell benefit, held five years after his last performance on stage.

11 Clowns and Augustes

ROLY BAIN

The easiest, most vivid, and certainly most common representation of a clown today is the red nose of the circus clown. That rather grotesque figure with a shock of red hair, ill-fitting gaudy clothes and enormous boots is literally larger than life – an absurd caricature of fashion, manners and social etiquette. He is the clumsy idiot, the original misfit, the eternal fall-guy, totally gullible but quite indefatigable. But this laughable buffoon is only a youngster when it comes to the history of the clown. There seem to have been clowns in all ages and cultures since time immemorial. Our image of the clown must be broadened to include jesters and tricksters, pierrots and harlequins, fools and freaks, whitefaces and tramps. The red-nosed zany only dates back to 1864, or so the story goes. Tom Belling was with Ernest Renz's circus in Berlin but was under suspension for falling during his act. Although banned from the ring, he wanted to go and watch, so put his wig on back to front and his coat inside out in a ludicrous disguise, and crept in, hoping not to be recognised. Perhaps inevitably he came across Renz himself and in the confusion of escape backed away and fell head over heels into the circus ring. The audience screamed with delight, shouted 'August! August!' at him (the traditional German nickname for a clumsy idiot), and a new clown was born and christened – he remains the auguste. It is somehow appropriate that it all happened by accident!

And yet in hindsight there was a certain inevitability about it. The clown had been going through something of a decline in England at least. The harlequinade had reached its peak in the first quarter of the nineteenth century. The Commedia dell'Arte had been popular throughout Europe for two centuries and Harlequin, Pierrot, Columbine and Pantaloon had been the leading characters with Clown very much in the background, but a clown called Grimaldi changed all that. Grimaldi came to be known as the King of Clowns as pantomime enjoyed its heyday. He made his name in *Mother Goose* in 1806 and thereafter people flocked to Sadlers Wells and Drury Lane to enjoy high comedy and practical satire at its sharpest. Dubbed 'the Garrick of clowns' and 'Hogarth in action', Grimaldi ruled the roost, and while the critics may have denounced his vulgarity to begin with, they changed their

Harlequin, Pantaloon, Columbine and Clown in John Brandard's King of the Castle, or
Harlequin Prince Diamond and Princess Brighteyes *(1858)*.

tune in the light of comic genius. There were other more practical reasons
too, as Richard Findlater points out:

Pantomime had been a staple ingredient of the British theatrical diet for some seventy
years by the time that Joe Grimaldi established himself as clown of Sadlers Wells at
the turn of the century. At first despised by actors, authors and critics for its
'disgraceful mummeries', it kept its place in the bills of the patent theatres because of
its role in the budget. The profit on a successful production helped substantially to
meet the frequent losses on literature, Shakespeare often included . . . In a chancy
trade they were the most consistently predictable hits.
        (Charles Dickens, *Memoirs of Joseph Grimaldi*, ed. Richard Findlater, 1968)

   After Grimaldi's premature retirement in 1823, pantomime gave way to the
extravaganza. The harlequinade had changed a great deal with Grimaldi as

its focus, and songs and stunts had become popular features. That
progression continued and hard as clowns like Grimaldi's own son and Tom
Matthews tried, the clowns and the harlequinade were lucky to be tacked on
to the end of the pantomime, and by the end of the century the harlequinade
had vanished. David Mayer III suggests that

as the English tired of George IV's absurdities, so they wearied of the ingredients of
the harlequinade. As Englishmen developed a sense of what they believed to be
humane, decent and sensible, they dismissed the harlequinade as the antithesis of
these virtues. The pantomime could flourish in the Regency, but the chill of
Victorianism, a cold wind that began to blow some years before the Queen came to
the throne, was inhospitable. Only through mutations could the pantomime survive.
(*Harlequin in his Element*, Cambridge, Mass., 1969)

But that had always been the case in the clown's long history. The middle of
the seventeenth century had seen the Church in the person of Archbishop
Laud ensure the demise of the court jester, and the puritans' closure of the
theatres had seen the clown disappear from the stage. But the clown
reappeared on the streets, and as the post-Restoration Commedia dell 'Arte
grew in popularity so the clown trod the boards again. And of course
Shakespeare's fools, true to type, could never be kept out of action for long.
Clowns are irrepressible, and their resilience keeps them bouncing back.
Their chameleon nature gives them a different and appropriate appearance
each time, but they remain recognisably the original creature. Shakespearean
clowns were the vogue for a while, the most popular and the most remarkable
being the self-styled 'Queen's Jester', William Wallett. His career lasted from
1828 to 1868 and the basis of the art was to parody speeches and plays from
Shakespeare. When the critics complained that this very verbal performance
had little to do with clowning, Wallett took to giving great lectures on the
fool's history. He remained pompous and high-handed and impossible to
work with, but he had his audiences. Yet the arrogance and pretentiousness
of the Shakespearean jester of this period were unfaithful to the clown's
characteristic humility and love. Tom Belling's dramatic appearance in the
circus ring was extremely timely, as it turned out. The auguste was to prove
a very vulnerable clown, always on the receiving end of everything. He wins
his audience over so that he can hold up a mirror to show them themselves in
their ridiculousness, and then in laughing at him they laugh at themselves. It
is the clown's art and calling to reflect and demonstrate humanity's folly and
then in the laughter to seek reconciliation and healing.

   The English circus had begun almost 100 years previously when Philip
Astley retired from the army, bought a site in London, and began displays of
trick-riding. Very soon the comic element was introduced and these
burlesques proved so popular that they were advertising clowns on horseback
by 1780. Circus clowns, like the pantomime ones, had to be acrobats and
some clowns managed to be successful in the ring and on the stage; but they
were few. By the 1850s the standard of clowning had again declined and the
clown, or Mr Merryman as he was often called, had been reduced to a tired
selection of traditional jokes and was usually only used to fill the time while
the next act was getting ready or the last act was getting their breath back.

Although this is a necessary function it was hardly conducive to either innovative or inspiring clowning.

Strangely enough this was not the case abroad, where British clowns enjoyed the highest reputation. The most unusual and the most popular were the Hanlon-Lees troupe who were hugely successful both in London and in Paris in the seventies and eighties. Together with a juggler called Henri Agoust they devised and performed a series of acrobatic pantomimes.

Edmond de Goncourt wrote of the kind of working class poetry and fantasy which English clowns use a great deal in their performances . . . England is the only country in Europe which has succeeded in introducing true imagination into its feats of bodily strength . . . Great Britain has developed an entirely new form of satirical comedy, largely created by unknown performers . . . It was as if the Italian comedies had been rediscovered . . . In recent years the art of the English clown has developed a sinister quality . . . the clown's art is now rather terrifying and full of anxiety and apprehension, their suicidal feats, their monstrous gesticulations and frenzied mimicry reminding one of the courtyard of a lunatic asylum.

(George Speaight, *A History of the Circus*, 1980)

Clowns have always been terrifying to some and disturbing to others, and little children especially find the auguste clown in all his outrageousness a frightening figure.

The clown remains a mystery, suspected by some to be a messenger from the gods and by others to be the very devil himself. People are never quite sure where to place him, because he is at heart an outsider, an observer, neither male nor female, magical and wise. While we can sympathise with the clown and laugh with and at him, while we can see and know him to be human beneath the mask, we also know him to be more than that, more than human, tapped into a different sphere. It is also a world that the arts take us into, a world of wild and wonderful imaginings, but it is sometimes a dangerous world, certainly an unknown and often uncharted world, and therefore frightening.

Part of either the fright or the mirth induced by clowns is their make-up. In the second half of the nineteenth century there were two distinct styles to choose from. There was the old tradition of the pierrot with a white face and delicate features; and there was the tradition begun by Baptiste Dubois, the first great circus clown at the end of the previous century, and continued by Grimaldi in rather more stylised form, of red nose and cheeks and grotesque features. Some clowns compromised with a combination of the two, others chose one or the other, and even today the two influences are marked. But clown make-up today has become an art in itself and a professional clown's make-up is his copyright. There are as many possible different make-up designs as there are individual faces, for each clown face must follow the lines and features of that person's face. It should also be noted that the clown's make-up or mask identifies him – it isn't something he can hide behind. The clown is instantly recognisable as a clown, but each clown is also instantly recognisable as himself.

One of the most instantly recognisable clowns of the 1880s was Little Sandy (Alexander Coleman) and he reigned supreme, whether as acrobat, rider, mime or talking clown. The circus clowns gave the lie to the later film

William Frederick Wallett as 'Queen's Jester' at the Alhambra Theatre, London, in the 1870s.

Tom Matthews, the clown commonly regarded as Grimaldi's heir.

adage that you never work with children or animals, for many of the clowns did their own particular animal acts. Little Sandy trained anything from dogs and horses to geese and bantams, and clowns without animals in a circus was almost as impossible as a circus with neither. But the clowns had many skills. They might be tumblers or jugglers or acrobats, or great wits or musicians; but the clown had to be extremely proficient in any of those skills or abundantly gifted and much rehearsed for it to 'work'. To be able to parody well one must first be thoroughly versed in the skill one is parodying. Many of the circus clowns through the years have been past horse-riders or acrobats or tight-rope walkers who have taken to clowning in later life when their best days are perhaps over; but the great clowns as a rule are born to it – skills, tricks and traditions aren't nearly enough if they are learnt second-hand without either passion or desire.

Clowns are by no means comedians even if they are generally comic. Nevertheless one of the reasons given for the decline of clowning towards the end of the last century was the increasing influence of music hall and its great popularity. Some comedians but few clowns followed the procession back to the stage, and again, as the clowns had discovered earlier in the century, they needed different techniques in the ring to what was required on stage. Whimsical Walker, who has been described as 'the wittiest Joey who ever trod the sawdust ring', considered the circus to be far harder than pantomime:

a circus clown has to knock about, tumble, crack wheezes, and do without properties . . . You must, in addition, be apprenticed to the circus fun, whereas to be a pantomime clown an apprenticeship isn't necessary.
(Ruth Manning-Sanders, *The English Circus*, 1952)

Grock, who became the greatest of all music hall clowns, found the transition a difficult one, but once he had achieved it there he stayed. Whimsical Walker had been of the school of talking clowns, but clowns were becoming silent again. This was either because of practical necessity or because of style and clown personality. The practical necessity arose in America where the size and scope of the three ring circus necessitated spectacle and great numbers of clowns clowning together – not that quality of clowning was necessarily sacrificed for quantity. But together with that phenomenon arose the practice of clowns going and mingling with the audience, often silently, so that a new type of individual clowning was introduced that thrived on the building of relationships, albeit brief.

Emmett Kelly's tramp clown 'Wearie Willie' caught the imagination earlier this century. This scruffy hobo or sad-sack clown was a ragged trousered philanthropist who shuffled gently around the edges of the ring, apparently oblivious to all that was going on in it. He described himself as

a sad and ragged little guy who is very serious about everything he attempts – no matter how futile or how foolish it appears to be. I am the hobo who found out the hard way that the deck is stacked, the dice frozen, the race fixed and the wheel crooked, but there is always present that one tiny, forlorn spark of hope still glimmering in his soul which makes him keep on trying.
(*Clown*, 1956)

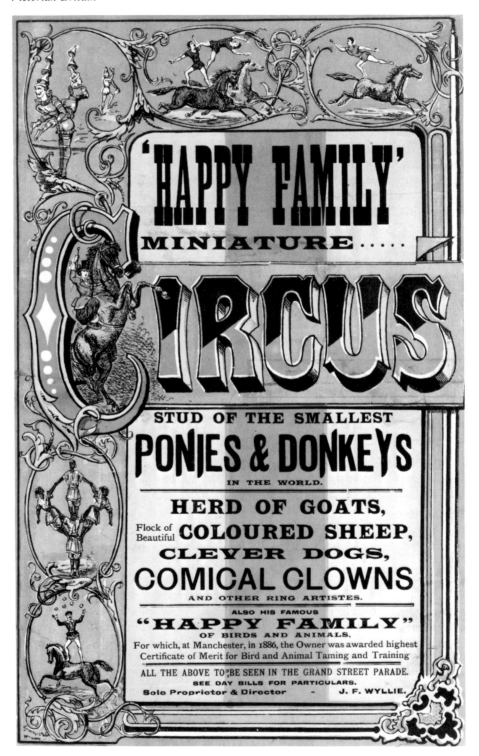

A circus poster from the late 1880s.

Another clown for the times had arisen, perhaps reflecting the experiences of the Depression and the confusion of war, and again he found kindred spirits who identified with him. But it was Chaplin who really established the tramp clown, even if Charlie was an altogether much more dapper character than Wearie Willie. Again his costume spoke of what he was and what he was trying to be:

> that costume helps me to express my conception of the average man, of myself. The derby, too small, is a striving for dignity. The moustache is vanity. The tightly-buttoned coat and the stick and his whole manner are a gesture towards gallantry and dash and 'front'. He is chasing folly and he knows it. He is trying to meet the world bravely, to put up a bluff, and he knows that too. He knows it so well that he can laugh at himself and pity himself a little.
>
> (M. Willson Disher, *Clowns and Pantomimes*, 1925)

The clown has an amazing resilience that makes him quite irrepressible. Society seems to need his insane voice of sanity for its continued survival, as a kind of conscience. And yet society is threatened by the clown to the extent that it always tries to dispose of him. But the clown is a dynamic, changing creature who remains abreast of the times and in touch with reality. So he constantly reappears in different places, in different guises, that are always fitting and eloquent. Neither the Puritans nor the Victorians were quite sure about clowns because they spoke of different worlds, of life and colour, humour and adventure, and because they somehow weren't respectable. But the clown is the great debunker and truth-teller who won't let people get away with trying to be respectable. The clown also knows that truth cannot be told outright, it can only be conveyed, and that it can most successfully and consistently be conveyed by humour and by art.

Somerset Maugham suggested that

> art, if it is to be reckoned with as one of the great values of life, must teach man humility, tolerance, wisdom, and magnanimity. The value of art is not beauty, but right action.

The clown certainly teaches all those virtues with the vulnerability of love, but neither the value of art nor the value of the clown can be measured in terms of right action. The clown celebrates and personifies the value of uselessness and the wisdom of folly. In an increasingly concrete and unimaginative world, the clown turns it upside down, suggesting that nothing is impossible or final or finite, and that there are a whole host of worlds and possibilities waiting to be explored. Life is for living and exploring and adventuring, and the world of the arts is the best place to start. The clown introduces a new dimension and a different perspective, like every good artist and artiste.

Part III
Appendix: Further Reading and Artists' Biographies

NORMAN VANCE

Contents

Abbreviations

b.	born
d.	daughter
educ.	educated
PRB	Pre-Raphaelite Brotherhood
qv/qqv	which see, denoting an individual entry on this person/these persons elsewhere in the Appendix
RA	Royal Academy (of Arts); Royal Academician
RAM	Royal Academy of Music
RCM	Royal College of Music
RIBA	Royal Institute of British Architects
s.	son
ser.	series
V&A	Victoria and Albert Museum

Introduction

This Appendix consists of brief lists of books relating to each chapter and short biographical and bibliographical notes on the leading figures in the arts. The lists, necessarily selective, favour fairly recent titles where available as most of these incorporate the findings of earlier work and have extensive bibliographies. For this period the best original sources are contemporary professional or general periodicals and the often copious writings of the artists themselves, usually available in the larger libraries. The *Dictionary of National Biography* (original edition 66 vols., 1885–1900; 22-vol. edition 1908–9, Compact edition 2 vols., Oxford, 1975) has detailed entries on most of the leading spirits.

More comprehensive reading lists and artists' biographies can be found in the hardback edition of this volume, published as *The Cambridge Guide to the Arts in Britain: The Later Victorian Age*. The place of publication, unless otherwise indicated, is London.

1 Cultural and Social Setting

The most helpful guide to recent developments and new work in all aspects of Victorian studies is the quarterly journal *Victorian Studies*, published in Bloomington, Indiana. Each year the journal publishes an invaluable sectionalised bibliography of recent publications. Other general guides to further reading are:

Annual Bulletin of Historical Literature, published by the Historical Association
Hanham, H.J., *Bibliography of British History 1851–1914*, 1976) [wide-ranging, and helpful on the arts]
Madden, L., *How to Find out about the Victorian Period* (Oxford, 1970)

General and political history

Appleman, P., Madden, W.A. and Wolff, M. (eds.), *1859: Entering an Age of Crisis* (Bloomington, Indiana, 1959)
Best, G.F.A., *Mid Victorian Britain, 1851–75* (1971; new edn 1979)
Briggs, A., *The Age of Improvement 1783–1867* (1961; new edn 1979)
Harrison, J.F.C., *Late Victorian Britain, 1875–1901* (1990)
McCord, N., *British History, 1815–1906* (Oxford, 1991)
Pelling, H., *Popular Politics and Society in Late Victorian Britain* (1968; rev. edn 1979)
Shannon, R., *The Crisis of Imperialism 1865–1915* (1974) [lively general history]

Social and economic background

Briggs, A., *Victorian Cities* (1963; new edn 1968)
Victorian People (1954; new edn 1965)
Victorian Things (1988, new edn 1990)
Dyos, H.J. and Wolff, M. (eds.), *The Victorian City: Images and Realities* 2 vols. (1973) [wide-ranging, multi-disciplinary essays]
Hobsbawm, E.J., *Industry and Empire* (1968)
MacKenzie, N. and J., *The First Fabians* (1978)
Marsh, J., *Back to the Land: the Pastoral Impulse in England from 1880 to 1914* (1982)

Mayhew, H., *London Labour and the London Poor* (1862; repr. 4 vols., 1968) [influential pioneer social surveys; selections ed. V. Neuburg (1985); S. Rubinstein (1947); E.P. Thompson and E. Yeo (1971; repr. 1973)]
Mingay, G.E. (ed.), *The Victorian Countryside*, 2 vols. (1981)
Royle, E., *Modern Britain: a Social History 1750–1985* (1987) [arranged by theme; full treatment of Scotland and Wales; good bibliography]
Shonfield, Z., *The Precariously Privileged: a Professional Family in Victorian London* (Oxford, 1987) [illuminating about medical profession, fashion, arts and crafts]
Smout, T.C., *A Century of the Scottish People, 1830–1950* (1986)
Thompson, F.M.L., *The Rise of Respectable Society: a Social History of Victorian Britain 1830–1900* (1988)
Vicinus, M. (ed.), *Suffer and be Still: Women in the Victorian Age* (Bloomington, Indiana, 1972; repr. 1980)
A Widening Sphere (1977) [wide-ranging collections of essays on the social history of women]

Cultural history

Harvie, C., Martin, G. and Scharf, A. (eds.), *Industrialisation and Culture 1830–1914* (1970) [extracts from contemporary sources]
Reitlinger, G., *The Economics of Taste*, 3 vols. (1960–70) [vols. I and II relevant to the period]
Wiener, M.J., *English Culture and the Decline of the Industrial Spirit 1850–1950* (Cambridge, 1981) [controversial explanation of British economic decline]

Periodicals

Houghton, W.E. (ed.), *The Wellesley Index to Victorian Periodicals 1824–1900*, 5 vols. (Toronto, Buffalo and London, 1966–89) [complete contents-lists of leading periodicals; identifies contributors; usefully indexed]
Madden, L. and Dixon, D., *The Nineteenth-century Periodical Press in Britain: a Bibliography of Modern Studies, 1901–1971* (New York and London, 1976)
Vann, J.D. and Van Arsdel, R.T. (eds.), *Victorian Periodicals: a Guide to Research* (New York, 1978) [includes newspapers]

Bevington, M.M., *The Saturday Review 1855–1868* (New York, 1941; repr. 1966)

De Vries, L. (ed.), *History as Hot News 1865–1897: the Late Nineteenth Century World as Seen Through the Eyes of 'The Illustrated London News' and 'The Graphic'* (1973)

Everett, E.M., *The Party of Humanity: the 'Fortnightly review' and its Contributors 1865–74* (Chapel Hill, N. Carolina, 1939)

Koss, S., *The Rise and Fall of the Political Press in Britain: the Nineteenth Century* (1981)

Price, R.G.G., *A History of 'Punch'* (1957)

Shattock, J. and Wolff, M. (eds.), *The Victorian Periodical Press: Samplings and Soundings* (Leicester, 1982)

Photography

Bartram, M., *The Pre-Raphaelite Camera* (1985)

Hopkinson, A., *Julia Margaret Cameron* (1986)

Jay, B. (ed.), *Victorian Cameraman: Francis Frith's Views of Rural England 1850–1898* (Newton Abbot, 1973)

Sansom, W. (introd.), *Victorian Life in Photographs* (1974, repr. 1988) [181 photographs; essays on both life and photography]

Stamp, G., *Changing Metropolis: the Earliest Photographs of London, 1839–79* (1984)

The Real Thing: an Anthology of British Photographs 1840–1950, Arts Council (1975–6)

Religious and intellectual background

Burrow, J.W., *Evolution and Society* (Cambridge, 1966)

A Liberal Descent: Victorian Historians and the English Past (Cambridge, 1981)

Chadwick, W.O., *The Victorian Church*, 2 vols. (1966–70; new edn 1971–2)

Culler, A.D., *The Victorian Mirror of History* (New Haven, 1985)

Himmelfarb, G., *Victorian Minds* (New York, 1968)

Houghton, W., *The Victorian Frame of Mind 1830–1870* (New Haven, 1957)

Jay, E., *Faith and Doubt in Victorian Britain* (1986)

Vance, N., *The Sinews of the Spirit: the Ideal of Christian Manliness in Victorian Literature and Religious Thought* (Cambridge, 1985)

Wright T.R., *The Religion of Humanity: the Impact of Comtean Positivism on Victorian Britain* (Cambridge, 1986)

Science and technology

Burchfield, J.D., *Lord Kelvin and the Age of the Earth* (1975)

Chapple, J.A.V., *Science and Literature in the Nineteenth Century* (1986) [useful, wide-ranging introduction; good bibliography]

De Vries, L., *Victorian Inventions*, tr. B. Suermondt (1973) [gleanings from nineteenth-century scientific press including many illustrations]

Himmelfarb, G., *Darwin and the Darwinian Revolution* (New York, 1959; new edn, 1968)

Rolt, L.T.C., *Victorian Engineering* (1970)

Wallace, A.R., *The Wonderful Century: its Successes and Failures* (1898; repr. 1970) [idiosyncratic, ecologically concerned scientific review]

2 Architecture

The most important sources for the subject are the professional periodicals of the time, especially *The Builder* and *The Building News*, published weekly and containing illustrations and descriptions of all buildings of importance. Useful reference-guides are:

Pevsner, N., Fleming, H. and Honour, H., *A Dictionary of Architecture* (originally the Penguin Dictionary of Architecture (1966); rev. edn 1975)

Richards, J.M. (ed.), *Who's Who in Architecture from 1400 to the Present Day* (1977)

CATALOGUES

The English House 1860–1914, Building Centre, London, Exhibition Catalogue, by G. Stamp (1980)

'Marble Halls'. Drawings and Models for Victorian Secular Buildings, V and A Exhibition Catalogue, by J. Physick and M. Darby (1973)

GENERAL WORKS

Bayley, S., *The Albert Memorial: the Monument in its Social and Architectural Context* (1981)

Blau, E., *Ruskinian Gothic: the Architecture of Deane and Woodward* (1982)

Brooks, M.W., *John Ruskin and Victorian Architecture* (1989)

Crook, J.M. (ed.), *Victorian Architecture: a Visual Anthology.* (New York and London, 1971) [large-format reproductions from leading architectural journals]

Cunningham, C., *Victorian and Edwardian Town Halls* (1981)

Dixon, R. and Muthesius, S., *Victorian Architecture* (1978) [includes useful bibliography and short dictionary of architects]

Fawcett, J. (ed.), *Seven Victorian Architects* (1976) [Burn, Hardwick, Smirke, Pearson, Bodley, Waterhouse, Lutyens: includes lists of chief works]

Ferriday, P. (ed.), *Victorian Architecture* (1963) [useful, often pioneering, essays]

Girouard, M., *Sweetness and Light: the 'Queen Anne' Movement, 1860–1900* (Oxford, 1977)
  The Victorian Country House (1971; rev. edn, New Haven and London, 1979)

Greater London Council, *The Survey of London*, vol. XXXVIII: *The Museum Area of South Kensington and Westminster* (1975)

Harper, R.H., *Victorian Architectural Competitions* (1983)

Howell, P. and Sutton, S., *The Faber Guide to Victorian Churches* (1989)

Jones, E., *Industrial Architecture in Britain 1750–1939* (1985)

Muthesius, H., *The English House*, tr. J. Seligman (1979) [influential study originally published, in German, in 1904–5]

Muthesius, S., *The English Terraced House* (New Haven and London, 1982)
  The High Victorian Movement in Architecture 1850–1870 (1972)

Pevsner, N., *Some Architectural Writers of the Nineteenth Century* (1972)
  The Sources of Modern Architecture and Design (1968; new edn 1986)
  Studies in Art, Architecture and Design: Victorian and After (1968; new edn 1982)

Service, A. (ed.), *Edwardian Architecture and its Origins* (1975)

Stamp, G. and Amery, C., *Victorian Buildings of London, 1837–1887: an Illustrated Guide* (1980)

Stamp, G. and Goulancourt, A., *The English House 1860–1914* (1986)

Summerson, J., *The Architecture of Victorian London* (Charlottesville, Virginia, 1976)
  Victorian Architecture: Four Studies in Evaluation (New York and London, 1970)

Architects

Bently, John Francis (1839–1902)
b. Doncaster; a pupil of Henry Clutton; followed Clutton's example in becoming Roman Catholic 1861; independent practice 1862–, designing church furnishings, additions, alterations. Major works include Westminster Cathedral, 1895, his Byzantine design for which avoided the use of iron.

Butler, A.S.G., *John Francis Bentley, the Architect of Westminster Cathedral* (1961)

Ricardo, Halsey, 'John Francis Bentley' [obituary] repr. in P. Ferriday (ed.), *Victorian Architecture* (1961)

Scott-Moncrieff, W., *John Francis Bentley* (1924)

Bodley, George Frederick (1827–1907)
b. Hull but family soon moved to Brighton where as a boy he met G.G. Scott (qv) and became his first pupil. Partnership with Thomas Garner 1869–98. Friend of William Morris, Burne-Jones, Ford Madox Brown, D.G. Rossetti (qqv); by 1870s leading authority on interior church decoration.

Clarke, B.F.L., *Church Builders of the Nineteenth Century* (1938)

Verey, D., 'George Frederick Bodley: climax of the Gothic Revival' in J. Fawcett (ed.), *Seven Victorian Architects* (1976) [contains check-list of chief works]

Burges, William (1827–81)
Son of a civil engineer; briefly studied engineering at King's College, London, before being articled to Edward Blore 1844; entered office of Digby Wyatt 1849; increased knowledge of medieval building by travelling and making careful drawings in Normandy and, later, in Belgium, Germany, France and Italy. Began to collect illuminated manuscripts and antiquities, especially armour; favoured French Gothic style. Designed jewellery, silverware and furniture as well as buildings. Noted as original architect with great antiquarian knowledge.

Catalogue:
The Strange Genius of William Burges, exhibition catalogue by J. Mordaunt Crook (Cardiff, 1981) [includes furniture, etc.; well-illustrated]

Crook, J.M., *William Burges and the High Victorian Dream* (1981)

Summerson, J., in *Victorian Architecture: Four Studies in Evaluation* (New York and London, 1970)

Butterfield, William (1814–1900)
b. London; early interest in English medieval building developed by study and drawing of Worcester Cathedral; associated

with Cambridge Camden society for which he designed and supervised execution of improved church plate and wrote on church furnishings and building in *Ecclesiologist*. His first important work was the adaptation of the remains of St Augustine's, Canterbury, as a missionary college (1845). His important buildings, chiefly churches, include All Saints', Margaret Street (1859) and Keble College, Oxford, begun 1875, which demonstrates his bold, controversial use of colour.

Thompson, P., *William Butterfield* (1971)

Lethaby, William Richard (1857–1931) Architect, designer and author; b. Barnstaple, Devon, son of a Bible Christian carver and gilder; local architect's office then 1879 won Sloane Medallion and joined office of Richard Norman Shaw (qv). A founder of Art Workers' Guild (1884) and Arts and Crafts Exhibition Society (1887). With Ernest Gimson (qv) set up Kenton & Co. to supply furniture of good design and workmanship. Independent architectural practice from 1891, mainly designing houses. One of the first inspectors of London County Council Technical Education board and a director of the new Central School of Arts and Crafts. For later work and writings see Appendix to vol. 8.

Backemeyer, S. and Gronberg, T. (eds.), *W.R. Lethaby, 1857–1931: Architecture, Design and Education* (1984) [companion volume to exhibition of same name at Central School of Arts and Crafts]
Rubens, G., *William Richard Lethaby* (1986)

Mackintosh, Charles Rennie (1868–1928) Architect, designer and painter; b. Glasgow; apprenticed to Glasgow architect John Hutchinson 1884 and attended Glasgow School of Art in evenings; travelling scholarship to France and Italy 1891; won competition for new building of Glasgow School of Art (built 1897–1909); decorated and furnished four Glasgow Tea-Rooms for Miss Cranston (1897–1904). Married Margaret Macdonald (1900), decorative designer and metalworker like her younger sister Frances. Exhibitor with Arts and Crafts Society, London. For his later, increasingly international, career as designer, especially in textiles, and as painter, see Appendix to vol. 8.
Bibliography:
Dixon, E., *Charles Rennie Mackintosh: a Selective Bibliography* (1981)

Catalogues:
Charles Rennie Mackintosh (1868–1928): Architecture, Design and Painting, Scottish Arts Council exhibition catalogue by A.McL. Young (1968)
Charles Rennie Mackintosh: Some Designs, Architectural Association Exhibition (1981)

Billcliffe, R., *Charles Rennie Mackintosh* (1979, rev. edn 1980)
Charles Rennie Mackintosh Furniture (1985)
Brett, D., *C.R. Mackintosh: the Poetics of Workmanship* (1991)
Cooper, J. (ed.), *Charles Rennie Mackintosh: the Complete Buildings and Selected Projects* (1978; rev. edn 1980)
Macleod, R., *Charles Rennie Mackintosh* (1968; rev. edn 1983)
Pevsner, N., *Charles Rennie Mackintosh* (Milan, 1950) [in Italian; English version in vol.II of *Studies in Art, Architecture and Design* (1968; new edn 1982)]

Paxton, Joseph (1801–65) Gardener and architect; b. Milton-Bryant, Bedfordshire and trained as a gardener. Became superintendent of gardens and woods of Duke of Devonshire at Chatsworth where built Great Conservatory (1836–40) and laid out village of Edensor (1839–41); submitted successful design for Great Exhibition building, on model of Chatsworth Conservatory, 1850, and knighted on completion, 1851. Supervised rebuilding of this Crystal Palace at Sydenham 1853–4. Wrote or edited numerous works on gardening; MP for Coventry 1854–65.
Catalogue:
Joseph Paxton, Arts Council and Victorian Society Centenary exhibition catalogue (1965)

Anthony, J., *Joseph Paxton: an Illustrated Life 1803–65* (Aylesbury, 1973)
Chadwick, G.F., *The Works of Sir Joseph Paxton, 1803–1865* (1961)

Pearson, John Loughborough (1817–97) b. Brussels; trained in Durham and London where a pupil of Philip Hardwick under whom he worked on the Hall and Library at Lincoln's Inn. Independent practice 1843, chiefly building or restoring churches though also built country and town houses. From 1870 much involved with cathedral restoration including substantial restoration of N. transept of Westminster Abbey. His increasingly simple designs often favour early French Gothic models and are sparing of decorative detail.

Clarke, B.F.L., *Church Builders of the Nineteenth Century* (1938)
Quiney, A., *John Loughborough Pearson* (1979)

Pugin, Augustus Welby Northmore (1812–52)
b. London, son of architectural draughtsman, archaeologist and illustrator. Assisted his father; designed furniture for Windsor Castle 1827; designed silver for Rundell and scenery and stage-machinery for Drury Lane (1830). Employed by Sir Charles Barry on decorative detailing at King Edward VI Grammar School, Birmingham (1833–7) and Houses of Parliament (1837–). Became Roman Catholic 1835 and insisted on intimate connection between his religion and gothic architecture. He designed the medieval court at the Great Exhibition (1851) and was an energetic, polemical, influential advocate of the Gothic style. His many publications include *An Apology for the Revival of Christian Architecture in England* (1843, repr. Oxford, 1969) and *Contrasts, or a Parallel between the Noble Edifices of the Fourteenth and Fifteenth Centuries and Similar Buildings of the Present Day* (1836, repr. Leicester, 1969). His designs for furniture, iron, brass, gold and silver work have been republished under the title *Designs* (Westmead, Hants, 1972).

Clark, A.G., 'A.W.N. Pugin' in P. Ferriday (ed.), *Victorian Architecture* (1963)
Gwynn, D., *Lord Shrewsbury, Pugin and the Catholic Revival* (1946)
Stanton, P.B., *Pugin* (1971)

Scott, George Gilbert (1811–78)
b. Gawcott, Buckinghamshire, son of Evangelical clergyman. Despite discouragement from James Edmeston and Robert Smirke, under whom he studied, developed predilection for Gothic architecture and ecclesiological concerns of Cambridge Camden Society and became most prolific architect of Gothic Revival. Restoration work at Ely, Hereford, Salisbury and Gloucester Cathedrals; controversial because of alleged disregard of original plan of building he restored. Architect to Westminster Abbey from 1849; knighted 1872. His writings include *Lectures on the Rise and Development of Medieval Architecture*, 2 vols. (1879).

Clarke, B.F.L., in *Church Builders of the Nineteenth Century* (1938)

Cole, D., *The Work of Sir Gilbert Scott* (1980)

Shaw, Richard Norman (1831–1912)
b. Edinburgh; came to London aged fifteen and entered William Burn's office; studied at RA schools where won gold medal and travelling scholarship 1854; admired work of William Butterfield (qv) and became chief assistant to G.E. Street (qv) 1859. Independent practice from 1862; with his partner W.E. Nesfield evolved style based on English vernacular buildings; designed many country and town houses. His most famous work was New Scotland Yard, London (1887–90).

Blomfield, R., *Richard Norman Shaw R.A.* (1940)
Pevsner, N., 'Richard Norman Shaw' in P. Ferriday (ed.), *Victorian Architects* (1963)
Saint, A., *Richard Norman Shaw* (New Haven and London, 1976)

Street, George Edmund (1824–81)
b. Woodford, Essex; 1841 pupil of Winchester architect O.B. Carter where developed interest in ecclesiology; 1844 assistant in office of G.G. Scott (qv); independent practice 1849; diocesan architect for Oxford (later also York, Winchester and Ripon). Travelled in France, Italy, Germany and Spain to study buildings. Won competition for design for Law Courts in Strand (1866) (built 1874–82).

Brownlee, D.B., *The Law Courts: the Architecture of George Edmund Street* (1984)
Kinnard, J., 'G.E. Street, the Law Courts and the Seventies' in P. Ferriday (ed.), *Victorian Architecture* (1963)
Street, A.E., *Memoir of G.E. Street* (1888)

Thomson, Alexander (1817–75)
b. Balfour, Stirlingshire; entered office of Robert Foote and John Baird in Glasgow; partner with John Baird the younger 1849–57 then with his own brother 1857–71. Known as 'Greek' Thomson for his buildings in this style.

Crook, J. Mordaunt, *The Greek Revival* (1972)
McFadzean, R., *The Life and Work of Alexander Thomson* (1979)

Voysey, Charles Frances Annesley (1857–1941)
b. near Hull, son of clergyman and grandson of architect; pupil of J.P. Seddon 1874–9; established independent practice in

1880s designing town and country houses and, under influence of William Morris (qv), designed furniture, tapestries, wallpaper, stained glass.

Brandon-Jones, J., *C.F.A. Voysey, Architect and Designer* (1978)
Gebhard, D., *Charles F.A. Voysey, Architect* (Los Angeles, 1975)
Simpson, D., *C.F.A. Voysey: an Architect of Individuality* (1979)

Waterhouse, Alfred (1830–1905)
b. Liverpool; articled to Manchester architect; travelled in France, Italy, Germany, then began independent practice in Manchester 1853; moved to London 1865; President of RIBA 1888–91. His main work was designing public or quasi-public buildings including Natural History Museum, S. Kensington (1868).

Hitchcock, L.R., in *Architecture: Nineteenth and Twentieth Centuries* (1969)
Smith, S.A., 'Alfred Waterhouse: civic grandeur' in J. Fawcett (ed.), *Seven Victorian Architects* (1976)

Webb, Philip Speakman (1831–1915)
b. Oxford, articled to a Reading architect, then entered office of G.E. Street (qv) in Oxford where met William Morris for whose firm he produced designs for tableware, furniture, embroideries, stained glass, metal fittings. Shared Morris's socialism and founder with him of Society for Protection of Ancient Buildings (1877). Architectural practice 1856–1900 mainly building or tactfully altering houses.

Brandon-Jones, J., 'Philip Webb' in P. ·Ferriday (ed.), *Victorian Architecture* (1963)
Lethaby, W.R., *Philip Webb and his Work* (1935)

3 Clowns

The subject is often discussed in the course of general works on circus, theatre or early film. There seems to be no recent bibliographical source devoted to the clown but see:

Toole-Stott, R., *Circus and Allied Arts: a World Bibliography*, 4 vols. (Derby, 1958–71)

Booth, M. (ed.), *English Plays of the Nineteenth Century vol. V: Pantomimes, Extravaganzas and Burlesques* (Oxford, 1976)
Findlater, R., *Grimaldi, King of Clowns* (1955)

Hugill, B., *Bring on the Clowns* (Newton Abbot and London, 1980)
Madden, D., *Harlequin's Stick, Charlie's Cane* (Bowling Green, Ohio, 1975) [comparative study of *commedia dell' arte* and slapstick comedy; numerous photographs]
Manchel, F., *Yesterday's Clowns: the Rise of Film Comedy* (New York, 1973)
Speaight, G., *A History of the Circus* (1980)
Towsen, J.H., *Clowns* (New York, 1976)
Welsford, E., *The Fool: his Social and Literary History* (1935; repr. Garden City, New York, 1961) [a standard work]

4 Design, Craft and Industry

REFERENCE

Fleming, J. and Honour, H., *The Penguin Dictionary of Decorative Arts* (1977)
Jervis, S., *The Penguin Dictionary of Design and Designers* (1984)
Lewis, P. and Darley, G., *Dictionary of Ornament* (1986)
Osborne, H. (ed.), *The Oxford Companion to the Decorative Arts* (1975)

EXHIBITION CATALOGUES

The Arts and Crafts Movement: Artists, Craftsmen and Designers 1890–1930, Fine Art Society (1973)
British Sources of Art Nouveau: an Exhibition of Nineteenth and Twentieth Century British Textiles and Wallpapers, Whitworth Art Gallery, Manchester (1969)
Victorian and Edwardian Decorative Art. The Handley-Read Collection, RA and V&A (1972)
Victorian Church Art, V&A (1971)

GENERAL WORKS

Anscombe, I., *A Woman's Touch: Women in Design from 1860 to the Present Day* (1984)
Anscombe, I. and Gere, C., *Arts and Crafts in Britain and America* (1978)
Arts and Crafts Essays, by members of Arts and Crafts Exhibition Society with Preface by William Morris (1893; repr. New York and London, 1977)
Bell, Q., *The Schools of Design* (1963)
Callen, A., *Angel in the Studio: Women in the Arts and Crafts Movement 1870–1914* (1979) [includes biographical notes on eighty craftswomen]

Cooper, J., *Victorian and Edwardian Furniture and Interiors, from the Gothic Revival to Art Nouveau* (1987) [lavishly illustrated]

Cooper, N., *The Opulent Eye: Late Victorian and Edwardian Taste in Interior Design* (1976) [200 photographs of domestic interiors]

Davey, P., *Arts and Crafts Architecture; the Search for Earthly Paradise* (1981)

Gere, C., *Victorian Jewellery Design* (1972)

Haslam, M., *English Art Pottery 1865–1915* (1975)

Lloyd, T.E., *Victorian Art Pottery* (1974)

Klingender, F.D., *Art and the Industrial Revolution* (1947; rev. edn 1968)

MacCarthy, F., *A History of British Design 1830–1970* (1979) [earlier version entitled *All Things Bright and Beautiful* (1972)]

Muir, P.H., *Victorian Illustrated Books* (1971)

Naylor, G., *The Arts and Crafts Movement* (1971)

Nicholson, S., *A Victorian Household: Based on the Diaries of Marion Sambourne* (1988) [colour photographs by Snowdon]

Pevsner, N. *The Sources of Modern Architecture and Design* (1968; new edn 1986)
Studies in Art, Architecture and Design, vol. II (1968; new edn, 1982)

Physick, J., *The Victoria and Albert Museum: the History of its Building* (1982) [well-illustrated; detailed treatment of decoration]

Richardson, M., *Architecture of the Arts and Crafts Movement* (1983) [fully illustrated; published in association with RIBA Drawings Collection]

Riley, N., *Victorian Design Source Book. A Visual Reference to Decorative Style 1837–1901* (1989)

Selz, P. and Constantine, M. (eds.), *Art Nouveau: Art and Design at the Turn of the Century* (1959; rev. edn 1975)

Stansky, P., *Redesigning the World: William Morris, the 1880s and the Arts and Crafts* (Princeton, 1985)

Taylor, J.R., *The Art Nouveau Book in Britain* (Cambridge, Mass., 1968)

Watkinson, R., *Pre-Raphaelite Art and Design* (1970)

Artists and designers

Ashbee, Charles Robert (1863–1942)
Architect, craftsman, designer; read history at Cambridge; articled to G.F. Bodley, architect; designed silverware and cutlery while working at Toynbee Hall in London's East End; founded Guild of Handicraft (1888) under influence of Ruskin and Morris (qqv) training men in furniture-making, silversmithing, printing, etc. Member Art Workers' Guild 1897; founded Essex House Press 1898. For later career and writings see vol. 8 Appendix.

Crawford, A., *C.R. Ashbee: Architect, Designer and Romantic Socialist* (1985)

Benson, W.A.S. (1854–1924)
Designer; b. London; after Winchester and Oxford trained as architect with Basil Champneys; set up metalwork workshop in Hammersmith, designing teapots, light fittings, etc. Instrumental in founding Art Workers' Guild (1884) and Arts and Crafts Exhibition Society (1886); chairman of Morris & Co. after Morris's death 1896. Designed grates and fireplaces for Coalbrookdale and Falkirk Iron Companies. Took artistic advantage of mechanical processes of manufacture of which he had sound technical knowledge. See his *Drawing: its History and its Uses* (Oxford, 1925) incorporating 'A brief memoir of W.A.S. Benson' by W.H. Bruce.

Burne-Jones, Sir Edward Coley (1833–98)
Designer and painter: see section 6.

Crane, Walter (1845–1915)
Designer, illustrator, writer; b. Liverpool, son of an artist; apprenticed to London wood engraver 1859; book-illustrator for Routledge and others, particularly children's books. Prominent in Art Workers' Guild and Arts and Crafts Exhibition Society. Designed textiles, wallpapers, carpets and ceramics. Principal of Royal College of Art 1898–9 when introduced Art Workers' Guild methods.
Bibliography:
Massé, G.C.E., *A Bibliography of the First Editions of Books Illustrated by Walter Crane* (1923)

Spencer, I., *Walter Crane* (1975)

De Morgan, William Frend (1839–1917)
Designer, inventor, novelist. Son of mathematician; attended RA Schools and encountered Burne-Jones, Rossetti and William Morris (qqv). Experimented with new processes for stained glass and tile design. In partnership with Halsey Ricardo 1888–98. Growing reputation as potter but little financial success; commission for decorative panels on six P&O liners; new career as novelist inaugurated with *Joseph Vance* (1906); six more novels.

Catalogue:
William De Morgan (1839–1917), Friends of Leighton House exhibition catalogue (1972)

Gaunt, W. and Clayton-Stamm, M.D.E., *William De Morgan* (1971)

Dresser, Christopher (1834–1904)
Botanist, designer, writer; b. Glasgow; studied at Somerset House Government School of Design 1847; lectured there on botany 1854 and interested in relations between botany and applied arts; PhD Jena 1860 for botanical work; successful commercial designer, employing ten assistants in his Barnes studio from 1889: designed silver, ceramics, textiles, glass, carpets and wallpapers for leading firms.
Catalogues:
Christopher Dresser, 1834–1904, Arkwright Arts Trust, Camden Arts Centre, exhibition catalogue (1979)
Christopher Dresser, Fine Art Society exhibition catalogue by R. Dennis and J. Jesse (1972)

Gimson, Ernest (1864–1919)
Architect, craftsman, designer; b. Leicester; apprenticed to local architect and attended Leicester School of Art; met Morris 1884 and at his recommendation moved to London and entered office of J.P. Sedding. Joined Society for Protection of Ancient Buildings 1889 and inspected buildings; studied and practised plasterwork and chairmaking to traditional designs; established his own Daneway House workshops at Sapperton in Cotswolds 1902.
Catalogue:
Ernest Gimson, Leicester Museums and Art Gallery exhibition catalogue (1969)

Lethaby, W.R., Powell, A.H. and Griggs, F.L., *Ernest Gimson: his Life and Work* (Oxford, 1924)

Jones, Owen (1809–74)
Pioneer designer and writer; b. London; articled to an architect and attended RA Schools. Toured Middle East and Spain studying Islamic and Hispanic-Moresque arts (1832–4) described in his influential *Grammar of Ornament* (1856). Superintendent of works at Great Exhibition 1851 and active in decorating and arranging building. Pioneered chromolithographic printing technique, initially to illustrate architectural polychromy in his own works. Designed furniture, metalwork, carpets, textiles, wallpapers demonstrating possibilities of non-European designs.

Bøe, A. in *From Gothic Revival to Functional Form* (Oslo and Oxford, 1957)

Pevsner, N., in *Academics of Art, Past and Present* (1940)

Lethaby, William Richard (1857–1931)
Architect, designer, author: see section 2

Mackintosh, Charles Rennie (1868–1928)
Architect, designer, painter: see section 2.

Mackmurdo, Arthur Heygate (1851–1942)
Architect, craftsman, designer; studied drawing in Oxford with Ruskin (qv) and travelled to Italy with him 1872; trained as architect; founded Century Guild with Selwyn Image and others (1882) to enhance status of applied arts; from 1883 designed furniture, metalwork, stained glass, textiles, wallpaper; revolutionary title page for his book *Wren's City Churches* (1883) the first *art nouveau* design. Edited Century Guild magazine *The Hobby Horse* and contributed 'Nature in ornament' to it (1892). Later career devoted to social and economic reform.
Catalogue:
A.H. Mackmurdo and the Century Guild Collection, William Morris Gallery, Walthamstow (1967)

Pevsner, N., in *Studies in Art, Architecture and Design*, vol. II (1968; new edn 1982)

Morris, William (1834–96)
Designer, poet, socialist, translator, typographer; b. Walthamstow; went up to Oxford 1852 already fascinated with and knowledgeable about natural world and Middle Ages. Articulated to architect G.E. Street (qv); with Burne-Jones, Rossetti (qqv) and other worked on Oxford Union frescoes (1858) and founded firm of Morris, Marshall, Faulkner & Co. to produce well-designed, well-made furniture, textiles, stained glass and wallpaper (1859). Established society for Protection of Ancient Buildings (1877), Socialist League (1884), Kelmscott Press (1890). Writings include translation and prose romance, notably the utopian *News from Nowhere* (1891), as well as socialist verse and prose. Varied artistic work available in *Collected Works*, 24 vols. (1910–15; repr. 1966) and in the following:
Briggs, A. (ed.), *William Morris: Selected Writings and Designs* (1962; new edn entitled *'News from Nowhere' and Selected Writings and Designs*, 1984)
Catalogue of the Morris Collection, William Morris Gallery, Walthamstow (1969)

Clark, F., *William Morris: Wallpapers and Chintzes* (1973)

Collected Letters, ed. N. Kelvin (1984 – in progress)

Johnson, F. (introd.), *William Morris: Ornamentation and Illustrations from the Kelmscott Chaucer* (New York, 1973)

Melvin, A. (ed.), *William Morris Wallpapers and Designs* (1971)

Sewter, A.C., *The Stained Glass of William Morris and his Circle*, 2 vols. (New Haven and London, 1974–5) [vol. II a catalogue]

Bradley, I., *William Morris and his World* (1978) [readable introduction]

Faulkner, P., *Against the Age: an Introduction to William Morris* (1980)

Hodgson, A., *The Romances of William Morris* (Cambridge, 1987)

Stansky, P., *Redesigning the World: William Morris, the 1880s and the Arts and Crafts* (Princeton, 1985)

Thompson, E.P., *Morris, Romantic to Revolutionary* (1955; rev. edn 1977)

Thompson, P., *The Work of William Morris* (1967)

Pugin, A.W.N. (1812–52)

Architect, designer and writer: see section 2.

Ruskin, John (1819–1900), critic: see section 9.

Scott, Mackay Hugh Baillie (1865–1945)

Architect and designer; b. nr Ramsgate; articled to City Architect of Bath; settled in Douglas, Isle of Man, studying at School of Art and designing glass and ironwork with his teacher Archibald Knox. Exhibited furniture, metalwork, wallpaper at Arts and Crafts Exhibition 1896. Indebted to Voysey and Mackmurdo (qqv) for his 'Manxman' design for cottage piano (1896). Designed furniture made by Guild of Handicraft for Palace of Darmstadt (1898) and acquired international recognition as designer and architect.

Kornwulf, J.D., *M.H. Baillie Scott and the Arts and Crafts Movement* (Baltimore and London, 1972)

Semper, Gottfried (1803–79)

Architect and aesthetic theorist; b. Hamburg; studied Göttingen, Munich and Paris; travelled in Italy and Greece. Settled in Dresden where designed Dresden Synagogue (1834); political refugee after May Insurrection; lived in Paris and London where took keen interest in Great Exhibition, contributing 'On the origin of polychromy in architecture' to Owen Jones (qv)'s *An Apology for the Colouring of the Greek Court in the Crystal Palace* (1854). Exhibition prompted writing of *Wissenschaft, Industrie und Kunst* (Braunschweig, 1852). Settled in Zurich. Later writing on aesthetics of applied art.

Pevsner, N., in *Academies of Art, Past and Present* (Cambridge, 1940)

Voysey, C.F.A. (1857–1941)

Architect and designer: see section 2.

Webb, Philip (1831–1915)

Architect and designer: see section 2.

5   Eisteddfod

There are surprisingly few books specifically concerned with the eisteddfod, and fewer still in English, but more general books on Welsh literature and culture incorporate discussion of the subject. Some of the main figures in the history of the revived esiteddfodau have entries in the *Dictionary of National Biography*: Thomas Burgess (1756–1837), John Jones [Talhaiarn] (1810–69), Sir John Morris-Jones (1864–1929), Sir Hugh Owen (1804–81), Edward Williams [Iolo Morganwg] (1746–1826), John Williams [Ab Ithel] (1811–62).

Miles, D., *The Royal National Eisteddfod of Wales* (Swansea, 1978)

Morgan, P., *Iolo Morganwg* (Cardiff, 1975)

Parry, T., *A History of Welsh Literature*, tr. [from Welsh] H.I. Bell (Oxford, 1955) [last three chapters devoted to nineteenth century]

Stephens, M. (ed.), *The Oxford Companion to the Literature of Wales* (Oxford, 1986)

6   Fine Arts

REFERENCE

Roberts, H.E., 'British art periodicals of the eighteenth and nineteenth centuries', *Victorian Periodicals Newsletter* **9** (1970) [useful exhaustive tabulated list of titles]. An enormous amount of information about the later Victorian art world can be unearthed from contemporary journals, often magnificently illustrated. Perhaps the most important were the *Art Journal (1849–1912)* and the *Magazine of Art* (1878–1904).

Wood, C., *A Dictionary of Victorian Painters* (1971) [illustrated: comprehensive and very useful, including (now dated) detailed bibliographies and sale-price information]

CATALOGUES

The Aesthetic Movement 1869–1890, Camden Arts Centre exhibition catalogue, ed. C. Spencer (1973)

The Art and Mind of Victorian England: Paintings from the Forbes Magazine Collection, University of Minnesota, Minneapolis (1974) [includes useful artist-biographies and bibliographies]

Artists of the Newlyn School, 1880–1900, Newlyn Art Gallery exhibition catalogue by C. Fox and F. Greenacre (1979)

The Early Years of the New English Art Club, Fine Arts Society exhibiiton catalogue, intro. B. Hillier (1968)

Great Victorian Pictures: their Paths to Fame, Arts Council exhibition catalogue, intro. R. Treble (1978)

Landscape in Britain, 1850–1950, Hayward Gallery exhibition catalogue (1983)

The Pre-Raphaelites, Tate Gallery Exhibition Catalogue by A. Bowness (1986)

Victorian High Renaissance, Minneapolis Institute of Arts and Manchester City Art Gallery exhibition catalogue by A. Staley *et al.* (1978) [painting and sculpture]

GENERAL WORKS

Bayley, S., *The Albert Memorial: the Monument in its Social and Architectural Context* (1981)

Beattie, S., *The New Sculpture* (New Haven and London, 1983) [approximately 1875–1910; detailed study with useful notes on forty-four significant sculptors]

Bell, Q., *A New and Noble School: the Pre-Raphaelites* (1982)
Victorian Artists (1967; rev. edn 1975)

Bendiner, K., *An Introduction to Victorian Painting* (New Haven and London, 1985) [sophisticated study of seven artists with background; valuable bibliography and notes]

Boase, T.S.R., *English Art, 1800–1870* (Oxford, 1959) [deals with architecture, decorative arts and sculpture as well as painting]

Conrad, P., *A Victorian Treasure House* (1973) [connections between paintings and literature]

Farr, D., *English Art, 1870–1940* (Oxford, 1978) [like Boase (1959) above, part of the *Oxford History of English Art*; similar range]

Gaunt, W., *The Aesthetic Adventure* (1945; rev. edn, 1975)
The Restless Century: Painting in Britain 1800–1900 (1972) [plates with introduction and useful bibliography]
Victorian Olympus (1952; rev. edn 1975)

Hardie, W., *Scottish Painting 1837–1939* (1976)

Hutchison, S.C., *The History of the Royal Academy 1768–1986* (1986) [revised and updated version of bicentennial history (1968)]

Klingender, F.D., *Art and the Industrial Revolution* (1947; rev. edn 1968)

Lambourne, L., *An Introduction to 'Victorian' Genre Painting from Wilkie to Frith* (1982)

Lister, R., *Victorian Narrative Paintings* (New York, 1966)

Maas, J., *Victorian Painters* (1969) [good illustrations]

Newall, C., *Victorian Watercolours* (Oxford, 1987)

Parris, L. (ed.), *Pre-Raphaelite Papers* (1984) [wide-ranging essays by some of the leading scholars of the period, to accompany 1984 Tate Gallery Exhibition]

Pointon, M. (ed.), *Pre-Raphaelites Re-viewed* (Manchester, 1989)

Read, B., *Victorian Sculpture* (New Haven and London, 1982) [approximately 1830–1914; useful introduction]

Robertson, D., *Sir Charles Eastlake and the Victorian Art World* (Princeton, 1978) [very informative, useful, detailed appendices]

Rosenblum, R. and Janson, H.W., *Art of the Nineteenth Century: Painting and Sculpture* (1984)

Rossetti, W.M., *The P.R.B. Journal*, ed. W.E. Fredeman (Oxford, 1975) [diary of the Pre-Raphaelite Brotherhood 1849–53]

Strong, R., *And when Did You Last See Your Father? The Victorian Painter and British History* (1978)

Wolff, J. and Seed, J. (eds.), *The Culture of Capital: Art, Power and the Nineteenth-Century Middle Class* (Manchester, 1987)

Wood, C., *Olympian Dreamers: Victorian Classical Painters 1860–1914* (1983)
The Pre-Raphaelites (1981)
Victorian Panorama: Paintings of Victorian Life (1976)

Artists and sculptors

Alma-Tadema, Sir Lawrence, O.M.
(1836–1912)
b. Dronryp, Holland; studied Antwerp
Academy where much influenced by Louis
de Taye, Professor of Archaeology. Settled
London 1870. More than 400 paintings,
chiefly Greek and Roman subjects, noted
for archaeological and architectural accuracy
and renderings of marble, silver, gold, silks,
etc.; concentrated on everyday, often
domestic scenes. Immensely popular.
Catalogue:
Sir Lawrence Alma-Tadema, Mappin Art
    Gallery, Sheffield and Laing Art
    Gallery, Newcastle, exhibition
    catalogue (1976)

Swanson, V.G., *Alma-Tadema: the Painter
    of the Victorian Vision of the Ancient
    World* (1977)

Beardsley, Aubrey Vincent (1872–98)
b. Brighton; self-taught as an artist,
resolving on artistic career after visiting
studio of Burne-Jones (qv). Morris (qv) and
Pre-Raphaelite influence in his illustrations
for Malory's *Morte d'Arthur* (1892) but
fully developed independent style in
illustrations for *Salome* (1893) by Wilde
(qv). Art editor and illustrator for *Yellow
Book* and then *Savoy*.

Brophy, B., *Beardsley and his World* (1976)
Reade, B., *Aubrey Beardsley* (1966)
Weintraub, S., *Beardsley: a Biography*
    (1967)

Brown, Ford Madox (1821–93)
b. Calais; studied in Belgium, Paris, Rome
where met Overbeck and other 'Nazarene'
painters: influenced by their clear colour
and medieval subject-matter. Came to
England 1846; his *Wycliffe* (1847–8)
impressed Rossetti (qv) who became his
pupil.
Catalogue:
Ford Madox Brown, 1821–1893, Walker Art
    Gallery, Liverpool, exhibition catalogue
    by Mary Bennett (1964)

Hueffer, F.M., *Ford Madox Brown: a
    Record of his Life and Work* (1896)
Rabin, L., *Ford Madox Brown and the
    Pre-Raphaelite History Picture* (New
    Haven and London, 1981)

Burne-Jones, Sir Edward Coley
(1833–98)
b. Birmingham; befriended William Morris
(qv) at Oxford; worked on Oxford Union
murals (1857). Travelled in Italy 1859;
visited Milan and Venice (1862) with
Ruskin (qv); designed tapestries and stained
glass for Morris & Co.; exhibited at opening
of Grosvenor Gallery (1877) and often
thereafter, favouring Arthurian subjects.
Much admired in France and USA.
Catalogue:
*Burne-Jones: the Paintings, Graphic and
    Decorative Work*, Arts Council
    exhibition catalogue by J. Christian
    (1975)

Fitzgerald, P., *Edward Burne-Jones: a
    Biography* (1975)
Spalding, F., *Magnificent Dreams:
    Burne-Jones and the Late Victorians*
    (Oxford, 1978)

**Du Maurier, George Louis Palmella
Busson** (1834–96)
Artist and cartoonist; b. Paris; studied art in
Paris 1856–7 and Antwerp 1857–60. Joined
Punch 1864 as successor to Leech (qv); also
illustrated stories in *Cornhill* 1863–83. His
novels include *Trilby* (1894) which reflects
artistic life of period and incorporates
sketch of Poynter (qv).

Ormond, L., *George Du Maurier* (1969)

Dyce, William (1806–64)
b. Aberdeen; on visits to Italy came under
influence of Overbeck, Cornelius and the
'Nazarenes' and of the Italian Renaissance.
His works included portraits, religous
paintings and fresco cycles in the House of
Lords, Lambeth Palace and Buckingham
Palace. Taught at the government Schools
and reported to Commons on schools of
design on continent in connection with
plans to remodel School of Design of which
he was director (1840). Professor of Fine
Art, King's College, London (1844).
Catalogue:
*Centenary Exhibition of the Work of William
    Dyce, R.A. (1806–1864)*, Aberdeen Art
    Gallery (1964)

Pointon, M., *William Dyce 1801–1864*
    (Oxford, 1970)

Fildes, Sir Samuel Luke (1844–1927)
b. Liverpool; studied at Warrington School
of Art, then (1863) S. Kensington. Worked
as illustrator on *Once a Week* and *The
Graphic* and, on recommendation of Millais
(qv), commissioned to illustrate *Edwin
Drood*. Best known for his social
'documentary' pictures.

Fildes, L.V., *Luke Fildes, R.A., a Victorian
    Painter* (1968)

Forbes, Stanhope Alexander
(1857–1947)
b. Dublin; studied Lambeth School of Art
and RA schools (1874–8) and in Paris where

influenced by Bastien-Lepage. Painted in Brittany 1880; settled at Newlyn, Cornwall, 1884, where founded Newlyn school with Walter Langley, Frank Bramley, etc. Founded a school of art in Newlyn 1899 with his wife Elizabeth Adela, also a successful painter.
Catalogue:
Artists of the Newlyn School, 1880–1900, Newlyn Art Gallery (1979)

Bendiner, K., in *An Introduction to Victorian Painting* (New Haven and London, 1985)
Birch, Mrs L., *Stanhope A. Forbes and Elizabeth Stanhope Forbes* (1906)

Frith, William (1819–1909)
b. Ripon and trained at RA schools. Early subjects derived from Shakespeare, Goldsmith, Sterne, Scott, Dickens. Fame and commercial success came from his panoramas of contemporary life including *Derby Day* (1858). Other work includes moralistic series such as *The Road to Ruin* (1878).
Catalogue:
W.P. Frith, Whitechapel Art gallery exhibiiton catalogue intro. J. Mayne (1951)

Noakes, A., *William Frith: Extraordinary Victorian painter* (1978)

Gilbert, Sir Alfred (1854–1934)
Sculptor; b. London; entered RA schools 1873; studied and worked in Paris (1876), Italy (1878–84). The most influential sculptor of his generation, his work includes the statue of Eros in Piccadilly Circus, London. He was Professor of Sculpture at the RA 1900.
Catalogue:
Commemorative catalogue of an Exhibition of Models and Designs by the Late Sir Alfred Gilbert, ed. E.M. Cox, V&A (1936)

Bury, A., *Shadow of Eros* (1954)
Dorment, R., *Alfred Gilbert* (New Haven and London, 1985)

Guthrie, Sir James (1859–1930)
b. Greenock; abandoned study of law for painting 1877; largely self-taught though briefly in John Pettie's London studio. Visited Paris 1882 and came under influence of Bastien-Lepage. Painted landscapes and subject-pictures in early 1880s but turned to portraiture after successful portrait of his father 1885–6. Became President of Scottish Academy.
Catalogue:
The Glasgow Boys 1880–1900, Scottish Arts Council exhibition catalogue (1968)

Billcliffe, R., *Guthrie and the Scottish Realists* (1982)
Caw, J.E., *Sir James Guthrie, P.R.S.A., LL.D.* (1932)

Von Herkomer, Sir Hubert (1849–1914)
b. Waal, Bavaria; came to England 1857; entered S. Kensington schools where taught by Fildes (qv); illustrator on *The Graphic*. Social documentary painting, then 1880 turned to portraits. Slade Professor at Oxford, 1885. Much respected at home (knighted 1907) and abroad (French legion of Honour 1889; ennobled by Kaiser 1899).

Baldry, A., *Hubert von Herkomer, C.V.O., R.A.: a Study and Biography* (1901)
Saxon, M., *Life and Letters of Sir Hubert Herkomer* (1923)

Hunt, William Henry (1790–1864)
('Bird's Nest' Hunt)
b. London; apprenticed early to John Varley and exhibited at RA 1807 before entering RA schools 1808. About 1827 began to paint fruit, flowers and rustic landcapes, developing special technique of hatching broken colours together over a white ground. His enamel-like watercolours greatly admired by Ruskin (qv); immensely popular and much imitated. Among his most celebrated work was *Bird's Nest with Briar Rose* (1850).
Catalogue:
William Henry Hunt, Wolverhampton, Preston and Hastings exhibition catalogue (1972, 1981)

Witt, J., *William Henry Hunt (1790–1864): Life and Work with a Catalogue* (1982)

Hunt, William Holman (1827–1910)
b. London; RA schools 1844 where met Millais, then Rossetti and F.M. Brown (qqv). With first two a leader of Pre-Raphaelite Brotherhood, founded 1848, and adhered to its principles throughout his career. Travelled to Egypt and Holy Land for biblical setting for *The Scapegoat* (1856). Other work includes a share in the Moxon illustrated Tennyson (1857). Wrote *Pre-Raphaelitism and the Pre-Raphaelite Brotherhood* 2 vols. (1905).
Catalogue:
William Holman Hunt, Walker Art Gallery, Liverpool, exhibition catalogue by M. Bennett (1969)

Landow, G.P., *William Holman Hunt and Typological Symbolism* (New Haven, 1979)
Maas, J., *Holman Hunt and The Light of the World* (1984)

Landseer, Sir Edwin (1802–73)
b. London, son of an artist; animal
drawings as very young child and first
Royal Academy exhibition aged twelve; his
paintings of animals, often with
quasi-human expressions, were immensely
popular in the engravings made by his
eldest brother and he was the favourite
painter of Queen Victoria.
Catalogues:
Landseer and his World, Mappin Art
    Gallery, Sheffield, exhibiiton catalogue
    by J. Hague (1972)
Sir Edwin Landseer, Philadelphia Museum
    of Art exhibition catalogue by R.
    Ormond *et al.* (1981)

Lennie, C., *Landseer: the Victorian Paragon*
    (1976)

Lavery, Sir John (1856–1941)
b. Belfast; studied Glasgow School of Art,
London and Paris. With James Guthrie (qv)
a leading member of the 'Glasgow School'.
Success with controversial and important
The Tennis Party (1885); painted official
record of Queen Victoria's visit to
international exhibition in Glasgow, 1888.
Moved to London and became international
society portrait-painter with house and
studio in Tangiers and clientele including
1930s Hollywood stars.
Catalogue
Sir John Lavery, Ulster Museum and Fine
    Art Society exhibition catalogue (1984)

McConkey, K., *Sir John Lavery* (1984)

Leech, John (1817–64)
b. London; attended Charterhouse where
friendship with Thackeray (qv) probably
began. Abandoned proposed medical career
for work as illustrator and caricaturist. First
Punch cartoon 1841 and soon regarded as
the most important contributor. Illustrated
many works including Dickens's *Christmas
Stories* (1843–8).

Bodkin, T., *The Noble Science: John Leech
    in the Hunting Field* (1948)
Houfe, S., *John Leech and the Victorian
    scene* (1954)

Leighton, Frederic (1830—96)
b. Scarborough; travelled abroad with
family and then studied in Florence, Rome
and Frankfurt. Many of his paintings on
classical themes, incorporating nude studies.
Illustrated *Romola* by George Eliot (qv).
President of the RA and knighted 1878; a
pillar of Victorian art establishment
rewarded with a peerage shortly before his
death.

Barrington, R., *The Life, Letters and Work
    of Frederic Leighton*, 2 vols. (1906)
Ormond, L. and R., *Lord Leighton* (New
    Haven and London, 1975)

Millais, Sir John Everett (1829—96)
b. Southampton but spent some of
childhood at family home on Jersey; infant
prodigy winning prizes in RA schools,
1840, and exhibiting at RA 1846. Founder
with Hunt and Rossetti (qqv) of
Pre-Raphaelite Brotherhood (1848). Became
fashionable and technically brilliant
academic painter of portraits,
costume-history and genre pieces. He
illustrated five of Trollope's novels and
contributed to the Moxon illustrated
Tennyson.
Catalogue:
P.R.B.: Millais: P.R.A., Walker Art
    Gallery, Liverpool, etc., exhibition
    catalogue by M. Bennett (1967)

Lutyens, M., *Millais and the Ruskins* (1967)
Millais, G., *Sir John Millais* (1979) [largely
    illustrations]
Millais, J.G., *Life and Letters of Sir John
    Everett Millais*, 2 vols (1899)

Moore, Albert Joseph (1841–93)
b. York, s. of a portrait-painter, one of five
painter brothers including the marine
painter Henry Moore, RA (1831–95).
Precocious detailed nature-painting under
Pre-Raphaelite influence; began to exhibit
classical subjects in the 1860s. His
Japanese-influenced interest in
colour-relationships impressed Whistler
(qv) and anticipates late-Victorian
aestheticism.
Catalogue:
Albert Moore and his Contemporaries, Laing
    Art Gallery, Newcastle, exhibiiton
    catalogue (1972)

Baldry, A.L., *Albert Moore: his Life and
    Works* (1894)

Poynter, Sir Edward John (1836–1919)
b. Paris, s. of distinguished architect;
resolved on artistic career after meeting
Leighton (qv) in Rome 1853; trained in
Gleyr's Paris studio. Biblical and classical
paintings and from late 1860s involved with
decorative schemes for Houses of
Parliament, S. Kensington Museum, etc.
Recognised as greatest academic
draughtsman of his day. President of RA
(1896–1918).

Bell, M., *The Drawings of Sir E.J. Poynter,
    P.R.A.* (1906)
Monkhouse, W. Cosmo in *British
    Contemporary Artists* (1899)

Rossetti, Dante Gabriel (1828–82)
Poet and painter; b. London, s. of Italian
scholar-poet and political refugee; studied
art with F.M. Brown (qv) and a founder of
Pre-Raphaelite Brotherhood (1848). Took
part in Oxford Union murals scheme
(1857), paintings (on which often wrote
poems) include *The Girlhood of Mary
Virgin* (1849), *Astarte Syriaca* (1877). Also
designed stained glass under influence of
Morris (qv) and wrote *The Early Italian
Poets* (1861).
Catalogues:
Surtees, V., *The Paintings and Drawings of
    Dante Gabriel Rossetti, 1828–1882: a
    Catalogue Raisonné*, 2 vols. (Oxford,
    1971)
Dante Gabriel Rossetti: Painter and Poet,
    Royal Academy exhibition catalogue
    (1973)

Doughty, O., *A Victorian Romantic*
    (Oxford, 1949) [biography]
Fleming, G.H., *Rossetti and the
    Pre-Raphaelite Brotherhood* (1967)
Nicoll, J., *Dante Gabriel Rossetti* (1975)

Ruskin, John (1819–1900), critic: see
section 9.

Sickert, Walter (1860–1942)
b. Munich of Danish, English and Irish
ancestry; briefly attended Slade School,
1881 and worked in studio of Whistler (qv).
Influenced by French Impressionists, esp.
his friend Degas. Associated with P. Wilson
Street (qv) and others in New English Art
Club. Lived abroad, mainly in Dieppe,
1898–1905. See vol. 8 Appendix for later
career.
Catalogue:
*Sickert: an Exhibition of Paintings and
    Drawings*, Arts Council catalogue intro.
    R. Pickvance (1964)

Lilly, M., *Sickert: the Painter and his Circle*
    (1971)
Sutton, D., *Walter Sickert* (1976)
    [biography with bibliography]

Steer, Philip Wilson (1860–1942)
b. Birkenhead; abandoned professional
numismatics for painting but remained a
collector; studied Gloucester School of Art
and Paris (1882) where saw work of
Whistler (qv) and Manet. Member of New
English Art Club; began to teach at Slade at
1894; developed interest in watercolour
1900; Order of Merit 1931.

Laughton, B., *Philip Wilson Steer,
    1860–1942* (Oxford, 1971) [full and
    well-illustrated]

Stevens, Alfred (1817–75)
Sculptor, painter, decorator, designer; b.
Dorset; studied Italy 1833–42; 1841
assistant in Thorwaldsen's studio in Rome;
in London designed schemes of painted
decoration, panels in relief, etc.; at School
of Design, Somerset House, 1845–7; 1850
moved to Sheffield as designer to
ironfounder.
Catalogue:
Alfred Stevens, 1817–75, V&A exhibition
    catalogue by S. Beattie (1975)

Towndrow, K.R., *Alfred Stevens* (1939)
    [biography]
    *The Works of Alfred Stevens in the Tate
    Gallery* (1950)

Thorneycroft, William Hamo
(1850–1925)
Sculptor; b. London, s. of Mary and
Thomas Thorneycroft, sculptors; RA
schools 1869 and assisted in parents' studio.
Visited Italy 1871; executed series of
classical-realist figures in marble, then
bronze. Active in Arts and Crafts
Exhibition Society. Knighted 1917.

Manning, E., *Marble and Bronze: the Art
    and Life of Hamo Thorneycroft* (1982)

Watts, George Frederic (1817–1904)
Painter and sculptor; b. London;
apprenticed to William Behnes the sculptor
and attended RA schools 1835; prizes for
pictures *Caractacus* (1843) and *Alfred*
(1847) but only became popular painter
after 1881–2 Grosvenor Gallery Watts
Exhibition introducing general public to his
allegorical works. His portraits of
contemporaries including Manning, Mill
and Tennyson much admired. Presented
twenty-two of his large allegorical works to
new Tate Gallery for moral instruction of
the people (1897–1902).
Catalogue:
*G.F. Watts: a Nineteenth Century
    Phenomenon*, Whitchapel Art Gallery
    exhibition catalogue by J. Gage (1974)

Blunt, W., *'England's Michelangelo'* (1975)
    [biography]
Shrewsbury, H.M., *The Vision of an Artist:
    studies in G.F. Watts, R.A., O.M.*
    (1918)

Whistler, James Abbott McNeill
(1834–1903)
b. Lowell, Mass., and lived as boy in Russia
and England; entered West Point 1851 but
left to be naval cartographer which taught
him etching. Went to Paris 1855. Moved to
London 1859. His *Nocturne in Black and*

Gold: the Falling Rocket (1878) was derided by Ruskin (qv) and ensuing legal action left Whistler bankrupt. His conscious aestheticism led him to rejection of conventional Victorian ideas of subject in painting. President of Royal Society of British Artists 1888; settled Paris 1892.
Catalogue:
From Realism to Symbolism: Whistler and his World, Columbia University and Philadelphia Museum of Art exhibition catalogue (1971)
James McNeill Whistler, Arts Council, etc., exhibition catalogue by A.McL. Young (1960)

McMullen, R., *Victorian Outsider* (1973) [biography]
Young, A.McL. and others, *The Paintings of James McNeill Whistler*, 2 vols. (New Haven and London, 1980) [whole volume of plates]

Woolner, Thomas (1825–92)
Sculptor and Pre-Raphaelite Brother; b. Suffolk; apprenticed to sculptor William Behnes and attended RA schools; literary and historical subjects in early work such as *Boadicea* (1844). Later work includes portrait medallions of distinguished contemporaries and busts of Dickens, Newman, Tennyson.

Read, B., 'Was there Pre-Raphaelite sculpture?' in L. Parris (ed.), *Pre-Raphaelite Papers* (1984)
Woolner, A., *Thomas Woolner, R.A., Sculptor and Poet* (1894; new edn 1917, repr. 1971)

7 Glasgow

For general books about the architecture, design, painting and sculpture of the period in which Glasgow significantly participates see sections 2, 4 and 6 respectively. There are individual entries for Charles Rennie Mackintosh and Alexander 'Grecian' Thomson in section 2 and for Sir James Guthrie and Sir John Lavery in section 6. Specialist studies of aspects of the arts in Glasgow during this period can be found in *Scottish Arts Review*.

Catalogue

The Glasgow Boys 1880–1900, Glasgow Art Gallery and Museum exhibition catalogue, 2 vols. (Glasgow, 1968/71) [vol. I has notes on exhibits and on 23 painters as well as a bibliography]

Billcliffe, R., *The Glasgow Boys: the Glasgow School of Painting, 1875–1895* (1984)
Guthrie and the Scottish Realists (1982)
Donelly, M., *Glasgow Stained Glass* (1981)
Gibb, A., *Glasgow: the Making of a City* (1983)
Gomme, A. and Walker, D., *The Architecture of Glasgow* (1968; new edn 1987) [illustrated; full bibliography]
Larner, G. and C., *The Glasgow Style* (1980) [beautifully illustrated with good descriptive bibliography]
Worsdall, F., *Victorian City* (Glasgow, 1982)
Young, A.M. and Doak, A., *Glasgow at a Glance* (1965; new edn, 1983)

8 House and Home

Books on the general architectural background are listed in section 2, which includes individual entries on William Butterfield, A.W.N. Pugin, Richard Norman Shaw, C.F.A. Voysey and Philip Webb. For William Morris and later Victorian interior decoration, see section 4. For Ebenezer Howard, Raymond Unwin, the garden city and housing developments in the twentieth century inspired by the late Victorians see vol. 8 Appendix section 2. see also:
Creese, W.L., *The Search for Environment* (New Haven and London, 1966)
Franklin, J., *The Gentleman's Country House and its Plan 1835–1914* (1981) [well-illustrated, with examples from all over England]
Girouard, M., *The Victorian Country House* (1971; new edn New Haven and London, 1979)
Tarn, J.N., *Five Per Cent Philanthropy* (1973)

9 Literature and Drama

BIBLIOGRAPHIES
Annual Bibliography of English Language and Literature, Modern Humanities Research Association (from 1920)
New Cambridge Bibliography of English Literature, vol. III, ed. G. Watson (Cambridge, 1969)
New Pelican Guide to English Literature ed. B. Ford, vol. VI: *From Dickens to Hardy* (1982, repr. 1986) [bibliographical Appendix updated for each reprint]

Victorian Studies [journal] incorporates
  annual bibliography with generous
  tretment of literature
Year's Work in English Studies, published
  annually (since 1921) by English
  Association

GENERAL WORKS

Chandler,A., *A Dream of Order: the
  Medieval Ideal in Nineteenth-Century
  English Literature* (1971)
Fletcher, I. (ed.), *Decadence and the 1890s*
  (1979)
Ford, B. (ed.), *New Pelican Guide to English
  Literature,* vol. VI: *From Dickens to
  Hardy* (1982, repr. 1986)
Fraser, H., *Beauty and Belief: Aesthetics
  and Religion in Victorian Literature*
  (Cambridge, 1986)
Houghton, W.E., *The Victorian Frame of
  Mind 1830–1870* (New Haven, 1957)
Lerner, L. (ed.), *The Victorians* (1978)
  [literature treated in relation to
  socio-economic, cultural and
  intellectual context]
Moers, E., *Literary Women* (New York,
  1976, repr. 1980)
Orel, H., *Victorian Literary Critics* (1984)
Prickett, S., *Victorian Fantasy* (Hassocks,
  1979)
Tillotson, G., *A View of Victorian
  Literature* (Oxford, 1978)

Drama

ANTHOLOGIES

Booth, M.R. (ed.), *English Plays of the
  Nineteenth Century*, vol. II: *Dramas
  1850–1900* (Oxford, 1969); vol. III
  Comedies (Oxford, 1973); vol. IV *Farces*
  (Oxford, 1973)
  *The Magistrate and other Nineteenth
  Century Plays* (Oxford, 1974)
Rowell, G. (ed.), *Late Victorian Plays,
  1890–1914* (1968; 2nd edn, Oxford, 1972)
  Nineteenth Century Plays (1953; 2nd edn,
  Oxford, 1972)

BIBLIOGRAPHICAL

Conolly, L.W. and Wearing, J.P., *English
  Drama and Theatre 1800–1900: a Guide
  to Information Sources* (Detroit, 1978)

GENERAL

Booth, M.R., *Prefaces to English
  Nineteenth-Century Theatre*
  (Manchester, 1979)
  Theatre in the Victorian Age (Cambridge,
  1991)

Donaldson, F., *The Actor-Managers* (1970)
Gielgud, K.T., *A Victorian Playgoer*, ed.
  M. St C. Byrne (1980) [informal
  comment on theatre, mainly
  1892–1903, from John Gielgud's
  mother (a niece of Ellen Terry)]
Jenkins, A., *The Making of Victorian
  Drama* (Cambridge, 1991)
Nicoll, A., *Late Nineteenth Century Drama
  1850–1900* (1946; new edn Cambridge,
  1959)
Rowell, G., *Theatre in the Age of Irving*
  (Oxford, 1981)
  Victorian Dramatic Criticism (1971)
  The Victorian Theatre 1792–1914 (1956;
  2nd edn, Cambridge, 1978) [full
  bibliography]
Shaw, G.B., *Our Theatres in the Nineties*, 3
  vols. (1932)
Stokes, J., *Resistible Theatres: Enterprise
  and Experiment in the Late Nineteenth
  Century* (1972)

Novel

Beer, G., *Darwin's Plots: Evolutionary
  Narrative in Darwin, George Eliot and
  Nineteenth Century Fiction* (1983)
Eigner, E.M. and Worth G.J. (eds.),
  Victorian Critics of the Novel
  (Cambridge, 1985)
Foster, S., *Victorian Women's Fiction* (1985)
Gilmour, R., *The Novel in the Victorian
  Age: a Modern Introduction* (1986)
Hardy, B., *Forms of Feeling in Victorian
  Fiction* (1986)
Harvey, J.R., *Victorian Novelists and their
  Illustrators* (1970)
Hawthorn, J. (ed.), *The Nineteenth Century
  British Novel* (1986)
Horsman, A., *The Victorian Novel* (Oxford,
  1990)
Jay, E., *The Religion of the Heart: Anglican
  Evangelicalism and the Nineteenth
  Century Novel* (Oxford, 1979)
Levine, G., *The Realistic Imagination*
  (Chicago, 1981)
*The Longman Companion to Victorian
  Fiction* (1990)
Wheeler, M., *English Fiction of the
  Victorian period 1830–1890* (1985)

Poetry

ANTHOLOGIES

Messenger, N.P. and Watson, J.R.,
  *Victorian Poetry: The City of Dreadful
  Night and Other Poems* (1974)
Quiller-Couch, A.T. (ed.), *The Oxford Book
  of Victorian Verse* (Oxford, 1912)
Richards, B., (ed.), *English Verse 1830–1890*
  (1979)

Ricks, C. (ed.), *The New Oxford Book of Victorian Verse* (Oxford, 1987) [interestingly different selection from Quiller-Couch (above)]

CRITICISM

Armstrong, I., *Language and Living Form in Nineteenth Century Poetry* (1982)
Hough, G, *The Last Romantics* (1949; repr. 1961)
Richards, B., *English Poetry of the Victorian Period 1830–1890* (London, 1988)
Shaw, W.D., *The Lucid Veil: Poetic Truth in the Victoria Age* (Madison, Wisconsin, 1987)

Authors

Arnold, Matthew (1822–88)
Poet and critic; son of Dr Thomas Arnold of Rugby; fellow of Oriel College, Oxford; private secretary to Lord Lansdowne 1847–51; Inspector of Schools 1851; Oxford Professor of Poetry 1857–67; travelled to study European education systems. *Complete Prose Works*, ed. R.H. Super, 11 vols. (Ann Arbor, Michigan, 1960–77); *Poems*, ed. K. Allott (1965; rev. edn ed. M. Allott, 1979). Life by P. Honan (1981)

Allott, K. (ed.), *Matthew Arnold. Writers and their Background* (1975)
Collini, S., *Matthew Arnold* (Oxford, 1988)
De Laura, D.J. in *Hebrew and Hellene* (1969)

Browning, Elizabeth Barrett (1806–61)
Poet; b. Durham; grew up in Herefordshire; moved to London 1833; became invalid 1838; corresponded with Robert Browning (qv) from 1844 and married him against father's wishes (1846). Lived mostly in Italy. *Complete Works*, ed. C. Porter and H.A. Clarke, 6 vols. (1900; repr. 1973); *Poetical Works* (Oxford complete edn) (Oxford, 1904). Life by M. Forster (1988).

Leighton, A., *Elizabeth Barrett Browning* (Brighton, 1986)
Mermin, D., *Elizabeth Barrett Browning: the Origins of a New Poetry* (Chicago, Ill., 1989)

Browning, Robert (1812–89)
Poet; b. London; educ. at home and locally. Early reputation for obscurity but popular success with *Bells and Pomegranates* (1841–6). Married Elizabeth Barrett (qv above) 1846 and lived in Italy. Returned to London after wife's death. Browning Society founded 1881. *Poems*, ed. J. Pettigrew and T.J. Collins, 2 vols. (1981); *Poetical Works*, ed. I. Jack and M. Smith

(Oxford, 1983– in progress); *Works*, ed. R.A. King *et al* (Athens, Ohio, 1969– in progress). Life by W. Irvine and P. Honan (1975); by J. Maynard (1977).

Armstrong, I. (ed.), *Robert Browning. Writers and their Background* (1974)
Jack, I., *Browning's Major Poetry* (Oxford, 1973)

Butler, Samuel (1835–1902)
Satirist, theorist, painter; educ. Shrewsbury and Cambridge; emigrated to New Zealand 1859; became interested in Darwinian evolution; returned to England 1864; exhibited at RA. Developed eccentrically original views on evolution and Homeric authorship and increasingly critical of Victorian convention especially on religious matters. *Works*, ed. H.F. Jones and A.T. Bartholomew, 20 vols. (the Shrewsbury Edition) (1923–6). Life by P. Raby (1991).

Willey, B., *Darwin and Butler: Two Versions of Evolution* (1960)

Dickens, Charles John Huffam (1812–70)
Novelist; b. Portsea; early career as clerk and parliamentary reporter; by 1850 an established and successful novelist. Became editor of *Household Words* (1850); separated from his wife (1858); ed. *All the Year Round* from 1859; gave public readings from his works, originally for charity, in England and USA. *Collected Works*, Oxford Illustrated edn, 21 vols. (1947–58); *The Clarendon Dickens*, ed. K. Tillotson (Oxford, 1966– in progress). Life by E. Johnson, 2 vols. (1953; rev. edn 1965)

Carey, J., *The Violent Effigy* (1973)
Collins, P. (ed.), *Dickens. The Public Readings* (1975)
Grant, A., *A Preface to Dickens* (1984)
Leavis, F.R. and Q.D., *Dickens the Novelist* (1970)
Lucas, J., *The Melancholy Man* (1970, rev. edn Brighton, 1980)
McMaster, J., *Dickens the Designer* (1986)

Du Maurier, George (1834–96)
novelist and illustrator: see section 6.

Eliot, George (Mary Ann Evans) (1819–80)
Novelist, b. Arbury, Warwickshire; reacted against strict religious upbringing when family moved to Coventry and she met rationalists Charles Bray and Charles Hennell (1841); moved to London 1849. Assistant editor, *Westminster Review*, from 1851; lived with G.H. Lewes, critic, biographer and philosopher, who encouraged her to write fiction. *Collected Works*, 21 vols. (1908–11); Clarendon edn

of novels (Oxford, 1980– in progress);
Essays, ed. T.C. Pinney (1963); Life by
G.S. Haight (Oxford, 1968); by R.V.
Redinger (New York, 1975).

Beer, G., *George Eliot* (Brighton, 1986)
Knoepflmacher, U.C., *George Eliot's Early Novels* (Berkeley, 1968)
Shuttleworth, S., *George Eliot and Nineteenth Century Science* (Cambridge, 1984; new edn, 1987)
Smith, A. (ed.), *George Eliot: Centenary Essays and an Unpublished Fragment* (1980)

Gaskell, Elizabeth Cleghorn (1810–65)
Novelist; b. London; brought up in
Knutsford, Cheshire; m. Rev. Wm Gaskell
(1832) and settled in Manchester. *Mary Barton* (1848) brought invitation of Dickens
(qv) to contribute to *Household Words*
where *Cranford* (1853) and *North and South*
(1855) originally appeared as serials.
Collected Works, ed. C.K. Shorter, 11 vols.
(1906–19); Life by W. Gérin (Oxford, 1976).

Easson, A., *Elizabeth Gaskell* (1979)
Pollard, A., *Mrs Gaskell* (Manchester, 1965)

Gissing, George Robert (1857–1903)
Novelist; b. Wakefield; attended Owens
College, Manchester; passed early life in
great poverty, supporting himself through
private teaching, in England and America.
Demos (1886) attracted attention but the
unremitting realism of his novels did not
make them popular. *New Grub Street* (1891)
is an unromantic account of late-Victorian
literary life. *Collected Works* (Hassocks,
1977– in progress); Life by J. Korg (1965;
repr. Brighton, 1980)

Goode, J., *George Gissing: Ideology and Fiction* (1978)
Grylls, D., *The Paradoxes of Gissing* (1986)

Hardy, Thomas (1840–1928)
Novelist and poet; b. Dorset; articled to
architect 1859; assistant to Sir Arthur
Blomfield 1862; RIBA medal 1863;
encouraged to write by Meredith (qv). *Far
from the Madding Crowd* (1874), his first
popular success, introduced a series of
regional or 'Wessex' novels set in and
around his native county culminating in
Tess of the D'Urbervilles (1891) and *Jude the
Obscure* (1896), both of which caused public
controversy because of unconventional
treatment of sexual problems. For his later
career as verse-dramatist and poet see vol. 8
Appendix. *Works*, 37 vols. (1919–20); Life
by F.E. Hardy [formally, though largely by
Hardy himself], 2 vols. (1928–30); by R.

Gittings, 2 vols. (1975–8); by M. Millgate
(Oxford, 1982; new edn, 1987).

Bayley, J., *An Essay on Hardy* (Cambridge, 1978)
Bullen, J.B., *The Expressive Eye. Fiction and Perception in the Work of Thomas Hardy* (Oxford, 1986)
Gregor, I., *The Great Web* (1974; repr. 1982)
Jackson, A.M., *Illustration and the Novels of Thomas Hardy* (1982)

Hopkins, Gerard Manley (1844–89)
Poet; b. London; pupil of Jowett and Pater
(qv) at Oxford and a friend of Robert
Bridges; became Roman Catholic 1866 and
entered Jesuit novitiate; ordained priest
1877; worked in London, Oxford,
Liverpool, Glasgow; Professor of Greek,
University College, Dublin (1884). Work
unpublished in his lifetime so not known
until Bridges' edition of 1918. *Sermons and
Devotional Writings*, ed. C. Devlin (Oxford,
1959); *Poems*, ed. Norman H. Mackenzie
(Oxford, 1990). Life by R.B. Martin (1990).

MacKenzie, N.H., *A Reader's Guide to Gerard Manley Hopkins* (1981)
Milward, P. and Schoder, P., *Landscape and Inscape* (Grand Rapids, Michigan, 1975)
Robinson, J., *In Extremity: a Study of Gerard Manley Hopkins* (Cambridge, 1977)
Story, G., *A Preface Hopkins* (1981)

James Henry (1843–1916)
Novelist and critic; b. New York, s. of
Swedenborgian theologian and a younger
brother of William James and philosopher.
After desultory education in US and
Europe he published reviews and short
stories in US from 1864; settled in England
1876. In addition to his novels he wrote
(unsuccessful) plays, travel-sketches and
short stories of which the most famous is
The Turn of the Screw (1898). For his
career after 1900 see vol. 8 Appendix.
Novels and Stories ed. P. Lubbock, 35 vols.
(1921–3); *Complete Tales* ed. L. Edel, 12
vols. *Selected Literary Criticism*, ed. M.
Shapira (1963; repr. 1968); Life by L. Edel,
4 vols. (1953–72; 2 vols. edn, 1977).
Bibliography:
Edelson, L. and Laurence, D.H., *A Bibliography of Henry James* (Oxford 1957; rev. edn 1982)

Anesko, M., *Friction with the Market: Henry James and the Profession of Authorship* (Oxford, 1986)
Bewley, M. in *The Complex Fate* (1952) and *The Eccentric Design* (1959)

Krook, D., *The Ordeal of Consciousness in Henry James* (Cambridge, 1962)

Mathiessen, F.O., *Henry James: the Major Phase* (Oxford, 1964)

Kipling, Rudyard (1865–1936)
Novelist and poet; b. Bombay, s. of artist John Lockwood Kipling who later illustrated his earlier works; his mother was a sister-in-law of Burne-Jones (qv); educ. United Services College, Westward Ho, the basis for his school stories *Stalky & Co.* (1895); returned to India 1882 as journalist. Already famous for short stories on return to England 1889. Nobel Prize for Literature 1907. For later work see vol. 8 Appendix. *Complete works in Prose and Verse*, 25 vols. (1937–9); Life by C. Carrington (1955; repr. 1986); by A. Wilson (1977; new edn 1979).
Bibliography:
Stewart, J.M., *Rudyard Kipling: a Bibliographical Catalogue* (1959)

Gross, J. (ed.), *Rudyard Kipling, the Man, his Work and his World* (1972)
Kemp, S., *Kipling's Hidden Narratives* (Oxford, 1988)
Stewart, J.I.M., *Rudyard Kipling* (1966, repr. 1976)

Meredith, George 1828–1909)
Novelist and poet; b. Portsmouth; educ. in Germany; worked as freelance journalist, war-correspondent, editor, literary adviser to Chapman and Hall (where encouraged Hardy and Gissing, qqv). *The Ordeal of Richard Feveral* (1859) established him as important if controversial novelist; his poetic sequence *Modern Love* and *Poems of the Roadside* appeared 1862. Though many of his novels commanded respect, popular success not achieved until *Diana of the Crossways* (1885). *Collected Works*, 29 vols. (1909–12; repr. 1965); *Poems*, ed. P.B. Bartlett, 2 vols. (New Haven, 1978), Life by D. Williams (1977).

Beer, G., *Meredith: a Change of Masks* (1970)
Shaheen, M., *George Meredith: a Reappraisal of his Novels* (1981)
White, A., in *The Uses of Obscurity* (1981)

Mill, John Stuart (1806–73)
Philosopher, economist, social thinker; b. London, s. of utilitarian theorist and historian James Mill; extraordinary intensive education from his father; lived in France 1820–1; official in India House 1822–56. A founder of Women's Suffrage Society; MP for Westminster 1865; spent last years in France. His important *Autobiography* published 1873 though written earlier. *Collected Works*, 20 vols. (Toronto 1963– in progress); Life by M. St J. Packe (1954).

Himmelfarb, G., *On Liberty and Liberalism: the Case of John Stuart Mill* (New York, 1974)
Ryan, A., *John Stuart Mill* (1975)
Thomas, W., *Mill* (Oxford, 1985) [brief general introduction]

Morris, William (1834–96), poet, translator, designer, etc.: see section 4.

Newman, John Henry (1801–90)
Theologian, educationalist, poet, novelist; b. London; fellow of Oriel College, Oxford; ordained in the Church of England and a founder of the Oxford or Tractarian movement within that church; after becoming Roman Catholic (1845) ordained priest; established Edgbaston Oratory, Birmingham; Rector of Dublin University 1854–8; Cardinal 1879. Writings after 1850 include *Apologia pro Vita Sua* (1864) (autobiographical account of his Anglican years) and *The Dream of Gerontius* (1866). *Collected Works*, 40 vols. (1874–1921). Life by I. Ker (Oxford, 1990).

Culler, A.D., *The Imperial Intellect: a Study of Newman's Educational Ideal* (New Haven, 1955)
De Laura, D.J. in *Hebrew and Hellene* (1969)
Levine, G. in *The Boundaries of Fiction* (Princeton, 1968)

Pater, Walter Horatio (1839–92)
Essayist and novelist; b. Stepney; educ. Oxford and a fellow of Brasenose from 1864; first noted for his *Studies in the History of the Renaissance* (1873). His aesthetic and philosophical concerns reflected in his historical novel *Marius the Epicurean* (1885). As author and teacher exercised considerable influence on late-Victorian taste in art and letters. *Collected Works*, 10 vols. (1910, repr. 1967); Life by M. Levey (New York and London, 1978).

De Laura, D.J., in *Hebrew and Hellene* (1969)
Iser, W., *Walter Pater: the Aesthetic Moment* (1960) tr. D.H. Wilson (1987)
Monsman, G., *Walter Pater* (Boston, 1977)

Pinero, Arthur Wing (1855–1934)
Dramatist; b. London; started acting at Theatre Royal, Edinburgh, 1874; joined Lyceum Company in London 1876–81. Success with *The Money Spinner* (1881) and wrote popular farces such as *The Magistrate* (1885) and *The Schoolmistress* (1886).

Recognised also as a serious dramatist after *The Second Mrs Tanqueray* (1893). Knighted 1909. *Social Plays*, ed. C. Hamilton, 4 vols. (New York, 1917–22, repr. 1967); *Plays*, intro. and ed. G. Rowell (Cambridge, 1986); *Three Plays* intro. S. Wyatt (1985). Life by W.D. Dunkel (Chicago, 1941, repr. Port Washington, New York, 1967).

Lazenby, W., *Arthur Wing Pinero* (New York, 1972)
Rowell, G., in *Theatre in the Age of Irving* (Oxford, 1981) and in *The Victorian Theatre 1791–1914* (Cambridge, 1978)

Rossetti, Dante Gabriel (1828–82), poet and painter: see section 6.

Ruskin, John (1819–1900)
Critic; b. London; educated privately by aesthetically-minded parents and travelled widely before entering Christ Church, Oxford; with first volume of *Modern Painters* (1843) emerged as controversial critic of painting; work completed in 5 vols., 1860. Championed Pre-Raphaelitism; public lectures on art and architecture; taught at Working Men's College; increasing hostility to materialist and competitive social attitudes and their effect on art and the experience of work. Popular but controversial Slade Professor of Art at Oxford 1870. Hostility to Whistler (qv) led to legal action 1877. *Complete Works*, ed. E.T. Cook and A.D.O. Wedderburn, 39 vols. (1903–12); Life by M. Lutyens (1967); by J.D. Hunt (1981).

Fellows, J., *The Failing Distance: the Autobiographical Impulse in John Ruskin* (Baltimore, 1975)
Fuller, P., *Theoria* (1989)
Helsinger, E., *Ruskin and the Art of the Beholder* (Cambridge, Mass., 1982)
Hewison, R., *John Ruskin: the Argument of the Eye* (Princeton and London, 1976)
Wihl, G., *Ruskin and the Rhetoric of Infallibility* (New Haven, 1985)

Shaw, George Bernard (1856–1950)
Critic and dramatist; b. Dublin; moved to London 1876; worked as music critic and wrote five unsuccessful novels; literary and art critic and drama critic of *The Saturday Review* (1895–8). Joined Fabian Society and served on executive committee 1885–1911: edited *Fabian Essays in Socialism* (1889); wrote *The Quintessence of Ibsenism* (1891; rev. 1913). Already known as controversial journalist and public speaker when attacked social issues in plays such as *Widowers' Houses* (1893). For later work see vol. 8

Appendix. *Works*, Standard edn, 37 vols. (1931–51); *Complete Musical Criticism*, ed. D.H. Laurence 3 vols. (1981); *Collected Plays with Prefaces*, ed. D.H. Laurence, 7 vols. (1970–4); Life by M. Holroyd, 3 vols. (1988–91).
Bibliography:
Laurence, D.H., *Bernard Shaw: A Bibliography*, 2 vols. (Oxford, 1983)

Gibbs, A.M., *The Art and Mind of Shaw: Essays in Criticism* (1983)
Holroyd, M. (ed.), *The Genius of Shaw* (1979)
Whitman, R.F., *Shaw and the Play of Ideas* (1977)

Swinburne, Algernon Charles (1837–1909)
Poet and critic; b. London; educ. Eton and Balliol where got to know Jowett and Rossetti (qv); his influential critical interest in Elizabethan dramatists apparent in *The Queen Mother* and *Rosamund* (1860); recognition with his pseudo-classical verse-drama *Atalanta in Calydon* (1865) and notoriety because of anti-Christian and sado-masochistic strain in *Poems and Ballads* (1st ser.) (1866). Libertarian *Songs before Sunrise* (1871) widely popular. Health broke down 1879; spent rest of his life quietly in Putney. *Collected Works*, 20 vols. (1925–7; repr. 1968); *Swinburne as Critic*, ed. C.K. Hyder (1972); Life by P. Henderson (1974); by D. Thomas (1979).

Hyder, C.K., *Swinburne: the Critical Heritage* (1970)
McGann, J., *Swinburne: an Experiment in Criticism* (Chicago, 1972)

Tennyson, Alfred (1809–92)
Poet; b. Lincolnshire; attended Trinity College, Cambridge, with his brothers and with A.H. Hallam, who died young. Work from 1850 includes *In Memoriam*, an extended elegy for Hallam. In 1850 Tennyson also married after long engagement and became Poet Laureate. Enormous popularity of *Maud* (1855) and *Idylls of the King* (1859–72) provoked disrespect of some younger poets in 1870s. Raised to peerage by Gladstone. *Poems*, ed. C. Ricks (1968; 2nd edn, 3 vols., 1986); Life by R.B. Martin (Oxford, 1980).

Albright, D., *Tennyson: the Muses' Tug-of-war* (Charlottesville, Va, 1986)
Ricks, C., *Tennyson* (1972)
Sinfield, A., *Alfred Tennyson* (Oxford, 1985)
Turner, P., *Tennyson* (1976)

Thackeray, William Makepeace (1811–63)
Novelist and journalist; b. Calcutta; after Charterhouse and Trinity College,

Cambridge, travelled in Germany and studied art in Paris; worked as journalist, contributing to *Punch* from 1845. *Collected Works*, 26 vols. (1910–11, repr. 1968); Life by A. Trollope (1879); by G.N. Ray, 2 vols. (Oxford, 1955–8); by C. Peters (1987).

Carey, J., *Thackeray: Prodigal Genius* (1977)
Hardy, B., *The Exposure of Luxury: Radical Themes in Thackeray* (1972)
McMaster, J., *Thackeray: the Major Novels* (Manchester, 1971)

Trollope, Anthony (1815–82)
Novelist; b. London; mother, father and older brother all writers; day-boy at Winchester and Harrow; clerk in GPO in London 1834, transferring to Ireland 1841. Popularity and financial reward with his Barchester novels (1855–67). A later, more political series, the Palliser novels, appeared 1864–80. Other novels include the pessimistic *The Way We Live Now* (1875). His posthumous *Autobiography* (1883) records his business-like approach to writing. There is no complete edition of his numerous novels but many are now available in the Oxford World Classics series. Life by R. Mullen (1990); N.J. Hall (Oxford, 1991).

Edwards, P.D., *Anthony Trollope: his Art and Scope* (Hassocks, 1978)
Hamer, M., *Writing by Numbers: Trollope's Serial Fiction* (Cambridge, 1986)
McMaster, J., *Trollope's Palliser Novels* 1978)
Wall, S., *Trollope and Character* (1988)

Ward, Mary Augusta (Mrs Humphry Ward) (1851–1920)
Novelist and activist; b. Hobart Town, Tasmania, d. of Thomas Arnold the younger and niece of Matthew Arnold (qv); family returned to England 1856 and lived in Oxford where she became authority on early Spanish literature and history and married T.H. Ward, an Oxford don, 1872. Her best-known novel was *Robert Elsmere* (1888), which challenged religion orthodoxy and highlighted the social problems of London's East End. All her work reflects her interest in social questions; she was an active philanthropist and campaigner for higher education for women. *A Writer's Recollections* (autobiography) (1918); *Writings*, 16 vols. (1911–12); Life by J. Sutherland (Oxford, 1990)

Peterson, W.S., *Victorian Heretic; Mrs Humphry Ward's 'Robert Elsmere'* (Leicester, 1976)

Smith, E.M.G., *Mrs Humphry Ward* (Boston, Mass., 1980)

Wilde, Oscar Fingal O'Flahertie Wills (1854–1900)
Dramatist and novelist; b. Dublin, s. of literary surgeon and nationalist poetess; educ. Trinity College, Dublin and Magdalen College, Oxford; journalist and self-advertising aesthete particularly while lecturing in America 1882; success as a dramatist with *Lady Windermere's Fan* (1892) and other plays including *The Importance of Being Earnest* (1895); play *Salome* banned in England but published in France (1893); illustrated by Beardsley (qv) (1894 edn). Unsuccessfully used Marquis of Queensbury for libel 1895, which led to two-year prison sentence for sodomy and to bankruptcy. Last years in Paris. *The Importance of Being Earnest* ed. R. Jackson (1980); *Lady Windermere's Fan*, ed. I. Small (1980); *Two Society Comedies*, ed. I. Small and R. Jackson (1983); Life by H. Montgomery Hyde (1976); by R. Ellmann (1987).

Bird, A., *The Plays of Oscar Wilde* (1977)
Raby, P., *Oscar Wilde* (Cambridge, 1988)
Tydeman, W. (ed.), *Wilde's Comedies: a Casebook* (1982)
Worth, K., *Oscar Wilde* (1983)

10 Music

The music and musicians of the period are well served by Sadie, S. (ed.), *The New Grove Dictionary of Music*, 20 vols. (1980) (includes full lists of works and bibliographies) and by Arnold, D. (ed.), *The New Oxford Companion to Music* 2 vols. (Oxford, 1983). For recordings see the catalogues normally published quarterly by *The Gramophone* and consult Greenfield, E. *et al.*, *The Complete Penguin Stereo Record and Cassette Guide* (1984), Greenfield, E. *et al.*, *The Penguin Guide to Compact Discs, Cassettes and LPs* (1986) and Greenhalgh, M.J., *English Music before 1900: a Guide to Recently Issued Recordings* (1985).

Abraham, G. (ed.), *Romanticism (1830–1890)* (*New Oxford History of Music IX*) (Oxford, 1990) [substantial bibliography]
Ehrlich, C., *The Music Profession in Britain since the Eighteenth Century* (Oxford, 1985)
The Piano: a History (1976)

Fuller-Maitland, J.A., *English Music in the Nineteenth Century* (1902, repr. Portland, Maine, 1976)

Gatens, W.J., *Victorian Cathedral Music in Theory and Practice* (Cambridge, 1986)

Howes, F., *The English Musical Renaissance* (1966) [very useful study]
Folk Music of Britain and Beyond (1969)

Hyde, D., *New Found Voices: Women in Nineteenth-century English Music* (1984)

Kennedy, M., *Hallé, 1858–1983: a History of the Orchestra* (Manchester, 1983)

Pearsall, R., *Victorian Popular Music* (Newton Abbot, 1973)

Rainbow, B., *The Choral Revival in the Anglican Church 1839–1872* (1970)
The Land without Music: Musical Education in England (1967)

Russell, D., *Popular Music in England 1840–1914* (Manchester, 1987)

Shaw, G.B., *Shaw's Music: the complete Musical criticism*, ed. D.H.Laurence, 3 vols. (1981)

Smyth, E., *Impressions that Remained* (1919, repr. 1981)

Temperley, N., *The Music of the English Parish Church*, 2 vols. (Cambridge, 1979) [vol. II is musical examples]

Temperley, N. (ed.), *The Romantic Age 1800–1914*, vol. V of *The Athlone History of Music in Britain* (1981)
The Lost Chord: Essays on Victorian Music (Bloomington, Ind., 1989)

Turner, M.R. (ed), *The Parlour Song Book* (1972; new edn 1974) [generous selection of popular songs with music and notes]

Musicians

Balfe, Michael William (1808–70)
Operatic composer; b. Dublin; violinist and baritone; studied in Italy; sang in Paris where met Rossini who furthered his singing career. Greatest success with *The Bohemian Girl* (1843). Famous settings of Tennyson ('Come into the Garden, Maud' (1857)) and Longfellow (including 'Excelsior' (1855)). The only English opera composer of nineteenth century with European renown.

Kenney, C.L., *Memoir of Michael William Balfe* (1875; repr. 1978)

White, E.W. in *The Rise of English Opera* (1951)

Bennett, William Sterndale (1816–75)
Composer and teacher; b. Sheffield into musical family; boy chorister King's College, Cambridge; RAM 1826; studied violin and, under Crotch, composition;

brilliant pianist. Mendelssohn invited him to Germany 1832 where much celebrated; Schumann admired his concertos, symphonies and songs. Later career chiefly as teacher: Professor of Music, Cambridge, 1856; Principal of RA 1866.

Bennett, J.R. Sterndale, *The Life of William Sterndale Bennett* (Cambridge, 1907)

Stanford, C.V. in *Interludes, Records and Reflections* (1922)

Broadwood, Lucy (1858–1929)
Folk-song collector; d. of H.F. Broadwood of piano firm and niece of Rev. John Broadwood (1798–1864), folk-song collector. She collected folk-songs, esp. in Surrey, Sussex, Scottish Highlands and S. Ireland; a founder of Folk Song Society (1898): Secretary (1904) and President (1927–9); editor of *Folk Song Society Journal* 1904–9, 1916–26. Published *English Country Songs* (1893) with J.A. Fuller Maitland and *English Traditional Songs and Carols* (1909). Many of tunes she collected were harmonised or adapted by R. Vaughan Williams as hymn tunes.

Howes, F. in *Folk-Music of Britain – and Beyond* (1969)

Cowen, Sir Frederick Hymen (1852–1935)
Composer and conductor; b. Jamaica; child prodigy; studied Leipzig conservatory and Germany; returned to England 1868 working as concert pianist and accompanist and assisting Costa at Her Majesty's Theatre. Succeeded Sullivan (qv) at Philharmonic Society (1884); conducted in Melbourne for Exhibition (1888–9); conducted Hallé Orchestra (1896–9) and Scottish Orchestra. Composed more than 300 songs, secular and sacred, oratorios and orchestral music such as his *'Scandinavian' Symphony* (1880) and his suite *The Language of Flowers* (1880).

Hughes, G., in *Sidelights on a Century of Music 1825–1924* (1969)

Elgar, Edward (1857–1934)
Composer; b. Worcester; brought up as Roman Catholic; worked in solicitor's office and freelance musician from 1873; assistant then successor to father as organist of St George's, Worcester; play bassoon; taught violin and played it in Worcester Festivals 1878, 1881, 1884. Moved to London after marriage 1889. First major work *Froissart* (1890); moved to Malvern. Early work includes oratorio *The Light of Life* (1896), *Imperial March* for 1897 Jubilee and *Caractacus* for Leeds Festival (1898).

Conducted Worcestershire Philharmonic Society 1898–1904 where showed wide knowledge of contemporary European music including Weber, Wagner and Gounod. National fame with *Enigma Variations* (1899) and *Dream of Gerontius* (Birmingham Triennial Festival, 1900). For later career see vol. 8 Appendix.

Recordings:

Knowles, J., *Elgar's Interpreters on Record: an Elgar Discography* (1977; rev. edn 1986)

Moore, J.N., *Elgar on Record: the Composer and the Gramophone* (1974) [composer-conductor recordings 1913–33]

Kennedy, M., *Portrait of Elgar* (1968; 3rd edn Oxford, 1987) [good introduction]
Elgar Orchestral Music (1970)

Moore, J.N., *Edward Elgar: a Creative Life* (1984; new edn Oxford, 1987) [substantial and comprehensive study]

Redwood, C. (ed.), *An Elgar Companion* (1982)

Lehmann, Elizabeth Nina Mary Frederika ('Liza') (1862–1918)
d. of German painter and of Amelia Lehmann, composer of popular songs. Studied singing with Alberto Randegger and Jenny Lind in London and composition in Rome, Wiesbaden and London. Successful career as soprano recitalist 1885–94. Composed popular song-cycles including *In a Persian Garden* (1896) based on Fitzgerald's translation of *Rubáiyát*; also settings of Tennyson (*In Memoriam*, 1899) and Lewis Carroll (*Nonsense Songs*, 1908). Became Professor of singing at Guildhall.

Hyde, D., *New Found Voices: Women in Nineteenth-century English Music* (1984)

Macfarren, Sir George (1813–87)
Composer; b. London; RAM 1829 where studied composition with Cipriani Potter (qv). Made his name with *Chevy Chase* (overture) (1836) which Mendelssohn put on in Leipzig. Composed instrumental music and operas including successful *Robin Hood* (1860) but most noted for oratorios such as *King David* (Leeds Festival 1883). In 1875 he succeeded Sterndale Bennett as Professor of Music at Cambridge and became Principal of RAM. Wrote textbooks on harmony and musical history and several hundred songs as well as *Shakespeare's Songs for Four Voices* (1860–4).

Bannister, H.C., *George Alexander Macfarren* (1891)

Mackenzie, Sir Alexander Campbell (1847–1935)
Composer; from a musical family; studied music in Germany and at RAM; violinist and conductor in Edinburgh 1865–79; lived in Florence and befriended Liszt. His cantata *The Bride* (Worcester Festival 1881) influenced the young Elgar (qv). Other work includes, *The Rose of Sharon* (1884) (oratorio – his best large-scale work), *Britannia* (1894) (overture based on 'Rule Britannia!') and incidental music for the stage. Principal, Royal Academy of Music 1887–1924. Wrote *A Musician's Narrative* (1927)

Howes, F., in *The English Musical Renaissance* (1966)

Klein, H., *Thirty Years of Musical Life in London 1870–1900* (1907)

Parry, Sir Charles Hubert Hastings (1848–1918)
Composer and author; BMus while still at Eton; then Oxford. Made his name with Piano Concerto performed at Crystal Palace (1880) and *Prometheus Unbound* at Gloucester Festival (1880). Composed five symphonies, orchestral *Variations* (1897) and oratorios, but best known for shorter choral works such as setting of Milton's ode 'Blest Pair of Sirens' (1887), the coronation anthem, 'I was Glad' (1902) and motets including the famous unison setting of Blake's lyric 'Jerusalem' (1916). Professor of Music at Oxford 1900–8. His song-settings include *Songs of Farewell* (1916).

Fuller-Maitland, J.A., *The Music of Parry and Stanford* (Cambridge, 1934)

Graves, C.L., *Hubert Parry* (1926)

Howes, F., in *The English Musical Renaissance* (1966)

Pierson (b. Pearson), Henry Hugo (1815–73)
Composer; son of Dean of Salisbury; educ. Harrow and Cambridge; got to know Mendelssohn and Schumann while in Germany. Briefly Reid Professor of Music at Edinburgh (1844) but made his career chiefly in Germany where more popular than in Britain. Composed incidental music for Goethe's *Faust II* and an adaptation of his part-song 'Ye Mariners of England' for Ludwig Bauer's 'O Deutschland Hoch in Ehren' (1854) which became very popular in Germany 1914–18. Composed many songs and hymn-tunes.

Scholes, P., in *The Mirror of Music* (1947)

Temperley, N., 'Henry Hugo Pierson, 1815–73', *Musical Times* **114** (1973) and **115** (1974) [with musical examples]

Shaw, George, Bernard (1856–1950)
Music critic and dramatist: see section 9.

Smyth, Dame Ethel Mary (1858–1944)
Composer, suffragist and writer; d. of Colonel of Artillery; despite strenuous paternal opposition studied at Leipzig Conservatorium 1877 where encountered Brahms circle; began by composing chamber music but 1890 *Serenade in D* for orchestra performed Crystal Palace, *Mass in D* conducted by Barnby at Albert Hall (1893) and operas included *Fantasio* (Weimar, 1898) and *The Forest* (Dresden, 1901). Militant feminist who demonstrated women could successfully handle largest musical forms on highest themes. Her writings include *Impressions that Remained* (1919, repr. 1981) and other autobiographical works abridged as *Memoirs*, ed. R. Crichton (New York, 1987).

Bowers, J. and Tick, J. (eds.), *Women Making Music* (Urbana and Chicago, 1986)
Howes, F., in *The English Musical Renaissance* (1966)
Hyde, D., in *New Found Voices: Women in Nineteenth Century English Music* (1984)
St John, C., *Ethel Smyth* (1959) [includes list of works]

Somervel, Sir Arthur (1863–1937)
Composer; b. Windermere and studied composition under Stanford at Cambridge and then in Berlin (1883–5) and with Parry (qv). Joined RCM staff 1894. Remembered for cantata *The Forsaken Merman* (Leeds Festival, 1895) and for his masterpiece, a song-cycle from Tennyson's *Maud* (1898), as well as a setting of Housman's *Shropshire Lad* (1904). Inspector of Music to Board of Education 1901–28.

Howes, F., in *The English Musical Renaissance* (1966)
Stevens, D. (ed.), in *A History of Song* (1960)

Stainer, John (1840–1901)
Composer, editor and teacher; choirboy at St Paul's Cathedral to which he returned as organist after Oxford. Served as Inspector of Schools until 1888; knighted and Oxford Professor of Music 1889. He wrote musical textbooks, composed hymn tunes and other church music, notably his oratorio *The Crucifixion* (1887),and edited (with J.F.R. and E.C. Stainer) the invaluable *Early Bodleian Music* (1901, repr. 1967).

Charlton, P., *John Stainer and the Musical Life of Victorian Britain* (Newton Abbot, 1984)

Stanford, Charles Villiers (1852–1924)
Composer; b. Dublin; choral scholar Queens' College, Cambridge 1870 and organist Trinity College 1873–92; studied Leipzig and Berlin; taught composition at RCM 1883; conducted London Bach Choir 1885; Professor of Music at Cambridge 1887. Composed operas, church music and songs including a setting of A.P. Graves's 'Father O'Flynn' and Tennysons's 'The Revenge'. He edited *Songs of Old Ireland* (1882) and (with A.P. Graves) *Irish Songs and Ballads* (1893).

Fuller-Maitland, J.A., *The Music of Parry and Stanford* (Cambridge, 1934)
Norris, G., *Stanford, the Cambridge Jubilee and Tchaikovsky* (New Abbot, 1980)
Plunkett-Greene, H., *Charles Villiers Stanford* (1935)

Sullivan, Sir Arthur (1842–1900)
Composer; son of Irish military band master; chorister at Chapel Royal; studied RAM and Leipzig Conservatory (1858–61); first success was his incidental music to Shakespeare's *The Tempest* (Leipzig 1861). Worked as organist and teacher. In 1866 with F.C. Burnand of *Punch* produced musical adaptation of popular comedy *Box and Cox*. Met famous collaborator William Schwenck Gilbert 1869; their many successful operettas include *Trial by Jury* (1875) and *Patience* (1881)which transferred to new Savoy Theatre – hence 'Savoy Operas'. Other work includes a romantic opera *Ivanhoe* with Julian Sturgis (1891), the ballad 'The Lost Chord' (1877) and many hymn-tunes.

Ayre, L., *The Gilbert and Sullivan Companion* (1986)
Bradley, I., *The Annotated Gilbert and Sullivan*, 2 vols. (1982–4)
Jacobs, A., *Arthur Sullivan: a Victorian Musician* (Oxford, 1984)
Wolfson, J., *Sir Arthur Sullivan* (New York, 1976)

Walmisley, Thomas Attwood (1814–56)
Composer and teacher; son of organist and glee-composer; Mus.B Cambridge 1833 and Professor of Music there aged twenty-two before proceeding BA. Introduced enlivening programme of lectures. A pioneer enthusiast for Bach and a friend of Mendelssohn. Church music includes Walmisley in D (Full service) (1843) and Evening Service in D minor (1855). With

S.S. Wesley (qv) revived the tradition of English Cathedral music.

Gatens, W.J., in *Victorian Cathedral Music in Theory and Practice* (Cambridge, 1986)

Wesley, Samuel Sebastian (1810–76) Organist and composer; illegitimate son of Samuel Wesley (1766–1837), musician, and great-nephew of the great John Wesley; chorister at Chapel Royal and St Paul's Cathedral; organist in London and then at Hereford Cathedral (1832–5), Exeter Cathedral, Leeds Parish Church, Winchester Cathedral (1849–5), Exeter Cathedral, Leeds Parish Church, Winchester Cathedral (1849–65) and Gloucester Cathedral (1865–76). Professor of organ, Royal Academy of Music, 1850. Eccentric and quarrelsome but courageously innovative in church music. His compositions include a Service in E (1845), many hymn-tunes and celebrated anthems sucha as 'Blessed be the God and Father' (1833–5).

Chappell, P., *Dr S.S. Wesley, 1810–1876* (Great Wakering, 1977)
Gatens, W.J., in *Victorian Cathedral Music in Theory and Practice* (Cambridge, 1986)
Matthew, B., *Samuel Sebastian Wesley*

1810–1876: a Centenary Memoir (Bournemouth, 1976)

Wood, Sir Henry Joseph (1869–1944) Conductor; b. London; studied piano, violin and organ; began as theatre and opera conductor; engaged to conduct Queen's Hall summer promenade concerts 1895 and used these annual concerts to combine important new work with deliberately popular programmes. Early compositions were quite successful but best known for arrangements such as *Fantasia on Briitsh Sea Songs* (1905). Writings include *My Life of Music* (1937, repr. 1971).

Cox, D., *The Henry Wood Proms* (1980)
Pound, R., *Sir Henry Wood* (1969)

9   Parks

Amherst, A., *London Parks and Gardens* (1907)
Carter, T., *The Victorian Garden* (1984)
Chadwick, G.F., *The Park and the Town: Public Landscape in the Nineteenth and Twentieth Centuries* (1966)
Conway, H., *People's Parks* (Cambridge, 1991)
Howard, E., *Garden Cities of Tomorrow* (1902; new edn 1985)
Koppelkamm, S., *Glasshouses and Wintergardens of the 19th century* (1981)

Sources of Illustrations

The publishers gratefully acknowledge the help of the many individuals and organisations who cannot be named in collecting the illustrations for this volume. In particular, they would like to thank Callie Crees for the picture research. Every effort has been made to obtain permission to use copyright materials; the publishers apologise for any errors and omissions and would welcome these being brought to their attention.

2, 42, 44, 51, 54, 56, 57, 58, 60, 62, 63, 65, 71, 73, 74 Royal Commission on the Historical Monuments of England
46 Oxfordshire County Council Library Services
68, 231 The British Architectural Library, RIBA, London
69 The Architectural Press Ltd
70, 199 A.F. Kersting
76 From G. Doré & B. Jerrold, *London, a Pilgrimage* (1872). By permission of the Syndics of Cambridge University Library
78 From A. Mangin, *Histoire des Jardins* (1877)
80, 82t, 83, 85 Jacques Carré
82b From JCA Alphand, *Les Promenades de Paris*, vol. III (1867–72)
86, 108 The Dickens House
114, 140, 148 By permission of the Syndics of Cambridge University Library
145, 304 By courtesy of the Trustees of the Theatre Museum, Victoria and Albert Museum
50, 240, 245, 247, 253 By courtesy of the Board of Trustees of the Victoria and Albert Museum
150 From V. Holland, *Oscar Wilde and His World* (1966)
151 Garrick Club; Eileen Tweedy, photographer
152, 155, 157, 158, 160 J.N. Tarn
162 City of Manchester Art Galleries
167, 185 The Tate Gallery, London
169 By kind permission of Guinness plc
171 Private Collection, on loan to Perth Museum and Art Gallery
172 By courtesy of E.W. Huddart, photograph by R.J. Williams, County Studio, Plymouth
175 Cliché des Musées Nationaux, Paris
176 Plymouth City Museums and Art Gallery Collection
178 Courtesy of the Trustees of the British Library
188 Reproduced by Permission of the Syndics of the Fitzwilliam Museum, Cambridge
192 By courtesy of the National Gallery, London
195, 196 Reproduced by permission of the Trustees of the Watts Gallery

198 Conway Library, Courtauld Institute of Art; The Salters' Company
202 National Museum of Wales
204 Crown copyright: Courtauld Institute Library
208 Conway Library, Courtauld Institute of Art
210 T. & R. Annan
211, 215br A.H. Gomme
212, 215bl, 216, 218, 220, 256 Royal Commission on Ancient Monuments, Scotland
214–215t From A.H. Gomme & D. Walker, *The Architecture of Glasgow* (1968)
223 By permission of the Company of Cutlers in Hallamshire
224 Sheffield City Museum
233, 235, 251r, 263, 275, 283 Illustrated London News Picture Library
248 Reproduced courtesy of The Royal Borough of Kensington and Chelsea, Leighton House Museum
249 By courtesy of The Fine Art Society
251l William Morris Gallery, London
257l Hunterian Art Gallery, University of Glasgow, Mackintosh Collection
257r Edward Barnsley Educational Trust
258 Leicestershire County Council
261, 265 National Museum of Wales (Welsh Folk Museum)
269, 282 Manchester City Art Galleries
274 Royal Opera House Archives
291 Guildhall Library, City of London; D.F. Cheshire
296 Hulton-Deutsch Collection
298, 301 Raymond Mander & Joe Mitchenson Theatre Collection
302 Courtesy of the Trustees of the British Museum

Colour Plates

1. The Tate Gallery, London
2. Windsor Castle, Royal Library. © Her Majesty the Queen
3. The Tate Gallery, London
4. Reproduced by permission of the Trustees of the Watts Gallery
5. © The Detroit Institute of Arts, Gift of Dexter M. Ferry, Jr.
6. The Tate Gallery, London
7. National Museums and Galleries on Merseyside, Lady Lever Art Gallery
8. In the possession of the Ashbee family
9. By courtesy of the Board of Trustees of the Victoria and Albert Museum
10. By courtesy of The Fine Art Society
11. National Museums and Galleries on Merseyside, Walker Art Gallery

Index